ACC

Paper 2.1

INFORMATION SYSTEMS

For exams in December 2005 and June 2006

Study Text

In this June 2005 new edition

- A new **user-friendly format** for easy navigation
- **Exam-centred topic coverage**, directly linked to ACCA's syllabus and study guide
- **Exam focus points** showing you what the examiner will want you to do
- Regular **fast forward** summaries emphasising the key points in each chapter
- **Questions** and **quick quizzes** to test your understanding
- **Exam question bank** containing exam standard questions with answers
- A full index

BPP's **i-Learn** and **i-Pass** products also support this paper.

FOR EXAMS IN DECEMBER 2005 AND JUNE 2006

BPP PROFESSIONAL EDUCATION

First edition 2001
Fifth edition June 2005

ISBN 0 7517 2316 9 (Previous edition 0 7517 1663 4)

British Library Cataloguing-in-Publication Data
A catalogue record for this book
is available from the British Library

Published by

BPP Professional Education
Aldine House, Aldine Place
London W12 8AW

www.bpp.com

Printed in Great Britain by Ashford Colour Press

We are grateful to the Association of Chartered Certified Accountants for permission to reproduce past examination questions. The suggested solutions in the exam answer bank have been prepared by BPP Professional Education.

Contents

Page

Computer-based learning products from BPP

If you want to reinforce your studies by **interactive** learning, try BPP's **i-Learn** product, covering major syllabus areas in an interactive format. For **self-testing**, try **i-Pass,** which offers a large number of **objective test questions**, particularly useful where objective test questions form part of the exam.

See the order form at the back of this text for details of these innovative learning tools.

Learn Online

Learn Online uses BPP's wealth of teaching experience to produce a fully **interactive** e-learning resource **delivered via the Internet**. The site offers comprehensive **tutor support** and features areas such as **study**, **practice**, **email service**, **revision** and **useful resources**.

Visit our website www.bpp.com/acca/learnonline to sample aspects of Learn Online free of charge.

Learning to Learn Accountancy

BPP's ground-breaking **Learning to Learn Accountancy** book is designed to be used both at the outset of your ACCA studies and throughout the process of learning accountancy. It challenges you to consider how you study and gives you helpful hints about how to approach the various types of paper which you will encounter. It can help you **focus your studies on the subject and exam**, enabling you to **acquire knowledge**, **practise and revise efficiently and effectively**.

The BPP Study Text

Aims of this Study Text

To provide you with the knowledge and understanding, skills and application techniques that you need if you are to be successful in your exams

This Study Text has been written around the **Information Systems** syllabus.

- It is **comprehensive**. It covers the syllabus content. No more, no less.
- It is written at the **right level**. Each chapter is written with ACCA's syllabus and study guide in mind
- It is targeted to the **exam**. We have taken account of the pilot paper, guidance the examiner has given and the assessment methodology.

To allow you to study in the way that best suits your learning style and the time you have available, by following your personal Study Plan (see page (viii))

You may be studying at home on your own until the date of the exam, or you may be attending a full-time course. You may like to (and have time to) read every word, or you may prefer to (or only have time to) skim-read and devote the remainder of your time to question practice. Wherever you fall in the spectrum, you will find the BPP Study Text meets your needs in designing and following your personal Study Plan.

To tie in with the other components of the BPP Effective Study Package to ensure you have the best possible chance of passing the exam (see page (vi))

The BPP Effective Study Package

Recommended period of use	The BPP Effective Study Package
From the outset and throughout	**Learning to Learn Accountancy** Read this invaluable book as you begin your studies and refer to it as you work through the various elements of the BPP Effective Study Package. It will help you to acquire knowledge, practice and revise, efficiently and effectively.
Three to twelve months before the exam	**Study Text and i-Learn** Use the Study Text to acquire knowledge, understanding, skills and the ability to apply techniques. Use BPP's **i-Learn** product to reinforce your learning.
Throughout	**Learn Online** Study, practise, revise and take advantage of other useful resources with BPP's fully interactive e-learning site with comprehensive tutor support.
Throughout	**i-Pass** **i-Pass**, our computer-based testing package, provides objective test questions in a variety of formats and is ideal for self-assessment.
One to six months before the exam	**Practice & Revision Kit** Try the numerous examination-format questions, for which there are realistic suggested solutions prepared by BPP's own authors. Then attempt the two mock exams.
From three months before the exam until the last minute	**Passcards** Work through these short, memorable notes which are focused on what is most likely to come up in the exam you will be sitting.
One to six months before the exam	**Success CDs** The CDs cover the vital elements of your syllabus in less than 90 minutes per subject. They also contain exam hints to help you fine tune your strategy.

Help yourself study for your ACCA exams

Exams for professional bodies such as ACCA are very different from those you have taken at college or university. You will be under **greater time pressure before** the exam – as you may be combining your study with work. There are many different ways of learning and so the BPP Study Text offers you a number of different tools to help you through. Here are some hints and tips: they are not plucked out of the air, but **based on research and experience**.

The right approach

1 **The right attitude**

Believe in yourself	Yes, there is a lot to learn. Yes, it is a challenge. But thousands have succeeded before and you can too.
Remember why you're doing it	Studying might seem a grind at times, but you are doing it for a reason: to advance your career.

2 **The right focus**

Read through the Syllabus and learning outcomes	These tell you what you are expected to know and are supplemented by Exam focus points in the text.
Study the Exam Paper section	Past papers are likely to be good guides to what you should expect in the exam.

3 **The right method**

The whole picture	You need to grasp the detail - but keeping in mind how everything fits into the whole picture will help you understand better. • The **Introduction** of each chapter puts the material in context. • The **Syllabus content, Study guide** and **Exam focus points** show you what you need to **grasp**.
In your own words	To absorb the information (and to practise your written communication skills), it helps to **put it into your own words**. • **Take notes.** • Answer the **questions** in each chapter. You will practise your written communication skills, which become increasingly important as you progress through your ACCA exams. • Draw **mindmaps**. We have an example for the whole syllabus. • Try **'teaching' a subject** to a colleague or friend.
Give yourself cues to jog your memory	The BPP Study Text uses **bold** to **highlight key points**. • Try **colour coding** with a highlighter pen. • Write **key points** on cards.

4 **The right review**

Review, review, review	It is a **fact** that regularly reviewing a topic in summary form can **fix it in your memory**. Because **review** is so important, the BPP Study Text helps you to do so in many ways. • **Chapter roundups** summarise the 'Fast forward' key points in each chapter. Use them to recap each study session. • The **Quick quiz** is another review technique you can use to ensure that you have grasped the essentials. • Go through the **Examples** in each chapter a second or third time.

Developing your personal Study Plan

BPP's **Learning to Learn Accountancy** book emphasises the need to prepare (and use) a study plan. Planning and sticking to the plan are key elements of learning success.
There are four steps you should work through.

Step 1 **How do you learn?**

First you need to be aware of your style of learning. The BPP **Learning to Learn Accountancy** book commits a chapter to this **self-discovery**. What types of intelligence do you display when learning? You might be advised to brush up on certain study skills before launching into this Study Text.

BPP's **Learning to Learn Accountancy** book helps you to identify what intelligences you show more strongly and then details how you can tailor your study process to your preferences. It also includes handy hints on how to develop intelligences you exhibit less strongly, but which might be needed as you study accountancy.

Are you a **theorist** or are you more **practical**? If you would rather get to grips with a theory before trying to apply it in practice, you should follow the study sequence on page (ix). If the reverse is true (you like to know why you are learning theory before you do so), you might be advised to flick through Study Text chapters and look at examples, case studies and questions (Steps 8, 9 and 10 in the **suggested study sequence**) before reading through the detailed theory.

Step 2 **How much time do you have?**

Work out the time you have available per week, given the following.

- The standard you have set yourself
- The time you need to set aside later for work on the Practice & Revision Kit and Passcards
- The other exam(s) you are sitting
- Very importantly, practical matters such as work, travel, exercise, sleep and social life

		Hours
Note your time available in box A.	A	

Step 3 **Allocate your time**

- Take the time you have available per week for this Study Text shown in box A, multiply it by the number of weeks available and insert the result in box B. B ☐
- Divide the figure in box B by the number of chapters in this text and insert the result in box C. C ☐

Remember that this is only a rough guide. Some of the chapters in this book are longer and more complicated than others, and you will find some subjects easier to understand than others.

Step 4 **Implement**

Set about studying each chapter in the time shown in box C, following the key study steps in the order suggested by your particular learning style.

This is your personal **Study Plan**. You should try and combine it with the study sequence outlined below. You may want to modify the sequence a little (as has been suggested above) to adapt it to your **personal style**.

BPP's **Learning to Learn Accountancy** gives further guidance on developing a study plan, and deciding where and when to study.

Suggested study sequence

It is likely that the best way to approach this Study Text is to tackle the chapters in the order in which you find them. Taking into account your individual learning style, you could follow this sequence.

Key study steps	Activity
Step 1 **Topic list**	Each numbered topic is a numbered section in the chapter.
Step 2 **Introduction**	This gives you the big picture in terms of the context of the chapter. The content is referenced to the Study Guide, and Exam Guidance shows how the topic is likely to be examined. In other words, it sets your objectives for study.
Step 3 **Knowledge brought forward boxes**	In these we highlight information and techniques that it is assumed you have 'brought forward' with you from your earlier studies. If there are topics which have changed recently due to legislation for example, these topics are explained in more detail.
Step 4 **Fast forward**	Fast forward boxes give you a quick summary of the content of each of the main chapter sections. They are listed together in the roundup at the end of each chapter to provide you with an overview of the contents of the whole chapter.
Step 5 **Explanations**	Proceed methodically through the chapter, reading each section thoroughly and making sure you understand.
Step 6 **Key terms and Exam focus points**	• Key terms can often earn you *easy marks* if you state them clearly and correctly in an appropriate exam answer (and they are highlighted in the index at the back of the text). • Exam focus points state how we think the examiner intends to examine certain topics.
Step 7 **Note taking**	Take brief notes, if you wish. Avoid the temptation to copy out too much. Remember that being able to put something into your own words is a sign of being able to understand it. If you find you cannot explain something you have read, read it again before you make the notes.

Key study steps	Activity
Step 8 **Examples**	Follow each through to its solution very carefully.
Step 9 **Case studies**	Study each one, and try to add flesh to them from your own experience. They are designed to show how the topics you are studying come alive (and often come unstuck) in the real world.
Step 10 **Questions**	Make a very good attempt at each one.
Step 11 **Answers**	Check yours against ours, and make sure you understand any discrepancies.
Step 12 **Chapter roundup**	Work through it carefully, to make sure you have grasped the significance of all the fast forward points.
Step 13 **Quick quiz**	When you are happy that you have covered the chapter, use the Quick quiz to check how much you have remembered of the topics covered and to practise questions in a variety of formats.
Step 14 **Question practice**	Either at this point, or later when you are thinking about revising, make a full attempt at the Question(s) suggested at the very end of the chapter. You can find these in the Exam Question Bank at the end of the Study Text, along with the answers so you can see how you did. We highlight those that are introductory, and those which are of the standard you would expect to find in an exam. If you have bought i-Pass, use this too.

Short of time: Skim study technique?

You may find you simply do not have the time available to follow all the key study steps for each chapter, however you adapt them for your particular learning style. If this is the case, follow the **skim study** technique below.

- Study the chapters in the order you find them in the Study Text.
- For each chapter:
  - Follow the key study steps 1-3
  - Skim-read through step 5, looking out for the points highlighted in the fast forward boxes (step 4)
  - Jump to step 12
  - Go back to step 6
  - Follow through steps 8 and 9
  - Prepare outline answers to questions (steps 10/11)
  - Try the Quick quiz (step 13), following up any items you can't answer
  - Do a plan for the Question (step 14), comparing it against our answers
  - You should probably still follow step 7 (note-taking), although you may decide simply to rely on the BPP Passcards for this.

Moving on...

However you study, when you are ready to embark on the practice and revision phase of the BPP Effective Study Package, you should still refer back to this Study Text, both as a source of **reference** (you should find the index particularly helpful for this) and as a way to **review** (the Fast forwards, Exam focus points, Chapter roundups and Quick quizzes help you here).

And remember to keep careful hold of this Study Text – you will find it invaluable in your work.

More advice on Study Skills can be found in BPP's **Learning to Learn Accountancy** book.

Syllabus

Aim

To develop knowledge and understanding of the audit process and its application in the context of the external regulatory framework and for business control and development.

Objectives

On completion of this paper, candidates should be able to:

- understand the nature, purpose and scope of auditing and internal review, including the role of external audit and its regulatory framework, and the role of internal audit in providing assurance on risk management and on the control framework of an organisation
- identify risks, describe the procedures undertaken in the planning process, plan work to meet the objectives of the audit or review assignment and draft the content of plans
- describe and evaluate accounting and internal control systems and identify and communicate control risks, potential consequences and recommendations
- explain and evaluate sources of evidence, describe the nature, timing and extent of tests on transactions and account balances (including sampling and analytical procedures) and design programs for audit and review assignments
- evaluate findings, investigate inconsistencies, modify the work program as necessary, review subsequent events, and justify and prepare appropriate reports for users within and external to the organisation, including recommendations to enhance business performance
- discuss and apply the requirements of relevant Statements of Auditing Standards
- demonstrate the skills expected in Part 2.

Position of the paper in the overall syllabus

The paper assumes a familiarity with the basic applications of information technology.

The paper provides the knowledge and understanding of information systems required to enable the candidate to progress to the more strategic perspectives considered in Paper 3.4 Business Information Management.

The ideas introduced in this paper are also drawn upon in Paper 2.6 Audit and Internal Review, Paper 3.1 Audit and Assurance Services and Paper 3.5 Strategic Planning and Development.

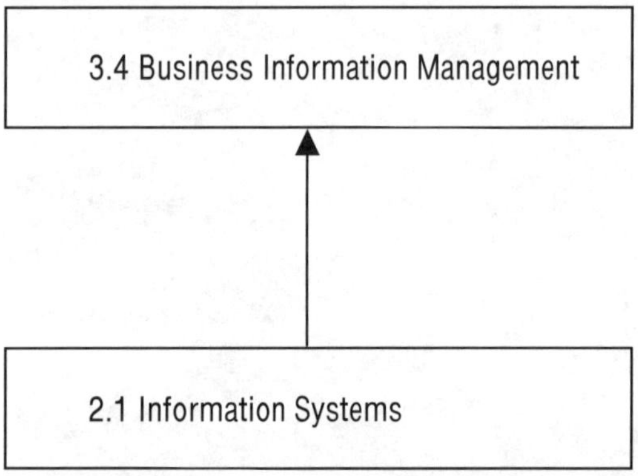

1 **Managing information systems (IS)**

(a) Business strategy and IS/IT alignment.
(b) Delivering information systems – organisational arrangements.
(c) Delivering information systems – accounting issues.
(d) Organising information systems – structural issues.
(e) Feasibility study.
(f) Project initiation.
(g) Project planning.
(h) Project monitoring and control.
(i) Software support for project management.

2 **Designing information systems**

(a) The information systems development process.
(b) Investigating and recording user requirements.
(c) Documenting and modelling user requirements – processes.
(d) Documenting and modelling user requirements – static structures.
(e) Documenting and modelling user requirements – events.
(f) External design.
(g) Developing a solution to fulfil requirements.
(h) Software package selection.
(i) Software support for the systems development process.

3 **Evaluating information systems**

(a) Technical information systems requirements.
(b) Legal compliance in information systems.
(c) Implementing security and legal requirements.
(d) Quality assurance in the management and development process.
(e) Systems and user acceptance testing.
(f) Implementation issues and implementation methods.
(g) Post-implementation issues.
(h) Change control in systems development and maintenance.
(i) Relationship of management, development process and quality.

Excluded topics

Detailed systems design – file/database design and program design is an excluded topic. Computer hardware will not be explicitly examined.

Key areas of the syllabus

The three key areas are:

- Managing information systems
- Designing information systems
- Evaluating information systems

Paper 2.1

Information Systems

Study Guide

1 BUSINESS STRATEGY AND IS/IT ALIGNMENT

- Explain an approach that an organisation may follow to formulate its strategic business objectives.
- Discuss how information systems may be used to assist in achieving these objectives.
- Identify current trends in information technology (IT) and the opportunities they offer to organisations.
- Distinguish between a business strategy and an information systems strategy.
- Identify responsibility for the ownership of the IS strategy.

2 DELIVERING INFORMATION SYSTEMS – ORGANISATIONAL ARRANGEMENTS

- Describe the traditional structure of a centralised Information Systems department and the roles and responsibilities of each function.
- Explain the principles of a decentralised Information Systems function.
- Discuss the advantages and disadvantages of centralising or decentralising the Information Systems function.
- Explain the principles of outsourcing the Information Systems function.
- Describe the advantages and disadvantages of outsourcing the Information Systems function.

3 DELIVERING INFORMATION SYSTEMS – ACCOUNTING ISSUES

- Briefly describe the types of cost incurred in delivering information systems.
- Describe how the costs of the Information Systems function may be distributed between customer departments.
- Explain the principles, benefits and drawbacks of cross-charging costs.
- Discuss the issues raised by establishing the Information Systems function as a cost or profit centre.
- Describe the advantages and disadvantages of establishing the Information Systems function as a separate company.
- Explain the problems of accounting for shared infrastructure costs.

4 ORGANISING INFORMATION SYSTEMS – STRUCTURAL ISSUES

- Describe the typical hardware, software, data and communications infrastructures found within Information Systems functions.
- Discuss the meaning and need for a disaster recovery plan.
- Discuss the meaning and need for a risk management process.
- Describe the meaning and implications of legacy systems.
- Discuss the relationship of Information Systems with end-users and the implications of the expectations and skills of end-users.

5 FEASIBILITY STUDY

- Explain the purpose and objectives of a feasibility study.
- Evaluate the technical, operational, social and economic feasibility of the proposed project.
- Describe and categorise the benefits and costs of the proposed project.
- Apply appropriate investment appraisal techniques to determine the economic feasibility of a project.

- Define the typical content and structure of a feasibility study report.

6 PROJECT INITIATION

- Define the content and structure of terms of reference.
- Describe the typical contents of a Project Quality Plan and explain the need for such a plan.
- Identify the roles and responsibilities of staff who will manage and participate in the project.
- Define in detail the role and responsibilities of the project manager.
- Explain the concept of a flat management structure and its application to project-based systems development.

7 PROJECT PLANNING

- Assist in splitting the project into its main phases.
- Participate in the breakdown of work into lower-level tasks.
- Assist in the estimation of the time taken to complete these lower-level tasks.
- Define dependencies between lower-level tasks.
- Construct and interpret a project network.
- Construct and interpret a Gantt Chart.

8 PROJECT MONITORING AND CONTROL

- Describe methods of monitoring and reporting progress.
- Define the reasons for slippage and how to deal with slippage when it occurs.
- Discuss the reasons for changes during the project and the need for a project change procedure.
- Reflect the effects of progress, slippage and change requests on the project plan.
- Discuss the particular problems of planning and controlling Information Systems projects.

9 SOFTWARE SUPPORT FOR PROJECT MANAGEMENT

- Define the meaning of a project management software package and give a brief list of representative products.
- Describe a range of features and functions that a project management software package may provide.
- Explain the advantages of using a project management software package in the project management process.

10 THE INFORMATION SYSTEMS DEVELOPMENT PROCESS

- Define the participants in the systems development process – managers, analysts, designers, programmers and testers.
- Describe the waterfall approach to systems development and identify its application in a representative systems development methodology.
- Describe the spiral approach to systems development and identify its application in a representative systems development methodology.
- Discuss the relative merits of the waterfall and spiral approaches, including an understanding of hybrid methodologies that include elements of both.

11 INVESTIGATING AND RECORDING USER REQUIREMENTS

- Define the tasks of planning, undertaking and documenting a user interview.
- Identify the potential role of background research, questionnaires and special purpose surveys in the definition of requirements.
- Describe the purpose, conduct and recording of a facilitated user workshop.
- Explain the potential use of prototyping in requirement's definition.
- Explain how requirements can be collected from current computerised information systems.
- Discuss the problems users have in defining, agreeing and prioritising requirements.

12 DOCUMENTING AND MODELLING USER REQUIREMENTS – PROCESSES

- Describe the need for building a business process model of user requirements.

- Briefly describe different approaches to modelling the business process.
- Describe in detail the notation of one of these business process models.
- Construct a business process model of narrative user requirements using this notation.
- Explain the role of process models in the systems development process.

13 DOCUMENTING AND MODELLING USER REQUIREMENTS – STATIC STRUCTURES

- Describe the need for building a business structure model of user requirements.
- Briefly describe different approaches to modelling the business structure.
- Describe in detail the notation of one of these business structure models.
- Construct a business structure model of narrative user requirements using this notation.
- Explain the role of structure models in the systems development process.

14 DOCUMENTING AND MODELLING USER REQUIREMENTS – EVENTS

- Describe the need for building a business event model of user requirements.
- Briefly describe different approaches to modelling business events.
- Describe in detail the notation of one of these business event models.
- Construct a business event model of narrative user requirements using the notation.
- Explain the role of event models in the systems development process.

15 EXTERNAL DESIGN

- Define the characteristics of a 'user-friendly' system.
- Describe the task of external design and distinguish it from internal design.
- Design effective output documents and reports.
- Select appropriate technology to support the output design.
- Design effective inputs.
- Select appropriate technology to support input design.
- Describe how the user interface may be structured for ease of use.
- Explain how prototyping may be used in defining an external design.

16 DEVELOPING A SOLUTION TO FULFIL REQUIREMENTS

- Define the bespoke software approach to fulfilling the user's information systems requirements.
- Briefly describe the tasks of design, programming and testing required in developing a bespoke systems solution.
- Define the application software package approach to fulfilling the user's information systems requirements.
- Briefly describe the tasks of package selection, evaluation and testing required in selecting an appropriate application software package.
- Describe the relative merits of the bespoke systems development and application software package approaches to fulfilling an information systems requirement.

17 SOFTWARE PACKAGE SELECTION

- Describe the structure and contents of an Invitation to Tender (ITT).
- Describe how to identify software packages and how their suppliers may potentially fulfil the information systems requirements.
- Develop suitable procedures for distributing an ITT and dealing with subsequent enquiries and bids.
- Describe a process for evaluating the application software package, the supplier of that package and the bid received from the supplier.
- Describe risks of the application software package and how these might be reduced or removed.

18 SOFTWARE SUPPORT FOR THE SYSTEMS DEVELOPMENT PROCESS

- Define a Computer Aided Software Engineering (CASE) tool and give a brief list of representative products.
- Describe a range of features and functions that a CASE tool may provide. Explain the advantages of using a CASE tool in the systems development process.
- Explain the advantages of using a CASE tool in the systems development process.
- Define a Fourth Generation Language and give a brief list of representative products.
- Describe a range of features and functions that a Fourth Generation Language may provide.
- Explain how a Fourth Generation Language contributes to the prototyping process.

19 TECHNICAL INFORMATION SYSTEMS REQUIREMENTS

- Define and record performance and volume requirements of information systems.
- Discuss the need for archiving, backup and restore, and other 'house-keeping' functions.
- Explain the need for a software audit trail and define the content of such a trail.
- Examine the need to provide interfaces with other systems and discuss the implications of developing these interfaces.
- Establish requirements for data conversion and data creation.

20 LEGAL COMPLIANCE IN INFORMATION SYSTEMS

- Describe the principles, terms and coverage typified by the UK Data Protection Act.
- Describe the principles, terms and coverage typified by the UK Computer Misuse Act.
- Explain the implications of software licences and copyright law in computer systems development.
- Discuss the legal implications of software supply with particular reference to ownership, liability and damages.

21 IMPLEMENTING SECURITY & LEGAL REQUIREMENTS

- Describe methods to ensure the physical security of IT systems.
- Discuss the role, implementation and maintenance of a password system.
- Explain representative clerical and software controls that should assist in maintaining the integrity of a system.
- Describe the principles and application of encryption techniques.
- Discuss the implications of software viruses and malpractice.
- Discuss how the requirements of the UK Data Protection and UK Computer Misuse legislation may be implemented.

22 QUALITY ASSURANCE IN THE MANAGEMENT AND DEVELOPMENT PROCESS

- Define the characteristics of a quality software product.
- Define the terms, quality management, quality assurance and quality control.
- Describe the V model and its application to quality assurance and testing.
- Explain the limitations of software testing.
- Participate in the quality assurance of deliverables in requirement specification using formal static testing methods.
- Explain the role of standards and, in particular, their application in quality assurance.
- Briefly describe the task of unit testing in bespoke systems development.

23 SYSTEMS AND USER ACCEPTANCE TESTING

- Define the scope of systems testing.
- Distinguish between dynamic and static testing.
- Use a cause-effect chart (decision table) to develop an appropriate test script for a representative systems test.

- Explain the scope and importance of performance testing and usability testing.
- Define the scope and procedures of user acceptance testing.
- Describe the potential use of automated tools to support systems and user acceptance testing.

24 IMPLEMENTATION ISSUES AND IMPLEMENTATION METHODS

- Plan for data conversion and creation.
- Discuss the need for training and suggest different methods of delivering such training.
- Describe the type of documentation needed to support implementation and comment on ways of effectively organising and presenting this documentation.
- Distinguish between parallel running and direct changeover and comment on the advantages and disadvantages of each.

25 POST-IMPLEMENTATION ISSUES

- Describe the metrics required to measure the success of the system.
- Discuss the procedures that have to be implemented to effectively collect the agreed metrics.
- Identify what procedures and personnel should be put in place to support the users of the system.
- Explain the possible role of software monitors in measuring the success of the system.
- Describe the purpose and conduct of an end-project review and a post-implementation review.
- Describe the structure and content of a report from an end-project review and a post-implementation review.

26 CHANGE CONTROL IN SYSTEMS DEVELOPMENT AND MAINTENANCE

- Describe the different types of maintenance that a system may require.
- Explain the need for a change control process for dealing with these changes.
- Describe a maintenance lifecycle.
- Explain the meaning and problems of regression testing.
- Discuss the role of user groups and their influence on system requirements.

27 RELATIONSHIP OF MANAGEMENT, DEVELOPMENT PROCESS AND QUALITY

- Describe the relationship between project management and the systems development process.
- Describe the relationship between the systems development process and quality assurance.
- Explain the time/cost/quality triangle and its implications for information systems projects.
- Discuss the need for automation to improve the efficiency and effectiveness of information systems management, delivery and quality assurance.
- Explain the role of the accountant in information systems management, delivery and quality assurance.

The exam paper

The examination is a three hour paper constructed in two sections. The bulk of the questions will be discursive but some questions involving computational elements will be set from time to time.

Section A is compulsory. The questions will cover the key elements of the syllabus relevant to both internal and external audit assignments. Section B requires candidates to answer two out of three questions. The questions will cover all areas of the syllabus.

		Number of Marks
Section A:	3 compulsory scenario-based questions (no single question will exceed 25 marks)	60
Section B:	Choice of 2 from 3 questions (20 marks each)	40
		100

Additional information

The examination does not assume any use of any systems development methodology. Practical questions will be set in such a way that they can be answered by any methodology. The following examples of models may be useful:

Syllabus heading	Example models
Documenting and modelling user requirements – processes	Data Flow Diagram Flowchart
Documenting and modelling user requirements – static structures	Entity-relationship model Object Class model
Documenting and modelling user requirements – events	Entity Life History State Transition Diagram

Analysis of past papers

The analysis below shows the topics which have been examined in all sittings of the current syllabus so far and in the Pilot Paper.

June 2005

Section A scenario (three compulsory questions – 20 marks each)

1 Risk management; Disaster recovery plan

2 Project precedences; Process model; Data and data conversion

3 Data protection and computer misuse legislation; Viruses

Section B (two from three questions – 20 marks each)

4 Project management software; Cost-benefit analysis

5 Business structure model; Requirements gathering interview

6 Software testing; system change process

December 2004

Section A scenario (three compulsory questions – 20 marks each)

1 Usability requirements
2 Training delivery options; Software support and maintenance; User groups
3 Information presentation; Audit trail; Archiving; Maintenance

Section B (two from three questions – 20 marks each)

4 Centralisation v decentralisation; Analysts; Flat structure
5 User interview; Process model; Questionnaire
6 Decision table; User acceptance testing

June 2004

Section A scenario (three compulsory questions – 20 marks each)

1 One from either a Class model, Entity relationship model or Logical data structure model; and one from either a Data flow diagram, Flowchart or Activity diagram
2 Critical path analysis; Textual and diagrammatic models; Time/Cost/Quality triangle
3 Requirements specification; Project Terms of Reference

Section B (two from three questions – 20 marks each)

4 Accounting for information systems projects
5 Invitation to Tender
6 Data conversion issues; Unit testing and system testing

December 2003

Section A scenario (three compulsory questions – 20 marks each)

1 Feasibility study and issues
2 Software package approach; Performance (load) testing
3 System changeover; Project manager and sponsor

Section B (two from three questions – 20 marks each)

4 Outsourcing
5 Fact gathering techniques for user and system requirements
6 Software quality; System maintenance

June 2003

Section A scenario (three compulsory questions – 20 marks each)

1 Standardising systems; System costs and benefits
2 Software package selection
3 System security; Documentation and training

Section B (two from three questions – 20 marks each)

4 Project plan; Critical path; Project management software
5 External design; User-friendliness; Prototyping; User workshop
6 Quality assurance, testing and the V model

December 2002

Section A scenario (three compulsory questions – 20 marks each)

1 Terms of Reference; Project Quality Plan
2 Data capture; User-friendly interface
3 Feasibility issues; Audit trial; Data conversion; Data protection; Implementation

Section B (two from three questions – 20 marks each)

4 Business strategy and information systems strategy; Risk management; Disaster recovery
5 Viruses, malicious damage and associated legislation
6 Process model construction

June 2002

Section A scenario (three compulsory questions – 20 marks each)

1 Principles of cross-charging system for IS/IT costs; Problems of cost allocation
2 Changing user requirements; Change control; Graphical techniques to define user requirements
3 Sections of an Invitation to Tender; Using IS/IT to improve competitiveness

Section B (two from three questions – 20 marks each)

4 Decision table; load (performance testing); Usability testing
5 Technical, economic, social and operational feasibility
6 Waterfall and spiral approach; Event model

December 2001

Section A scenario (three compulsory questions – 20 marks each)

1 Roles of the project manager, systems analyst, programmer and data analyst; Department structure

2 Systems development methodologies; Modelling and CASE tools

3 Formal specification, quality assurance and change control; Outsourcing

Section B (two from three questions – 20 marks each)

4 Network analysis/critical path; Risk management process

5 User-friendly software features; Prototyping

6 Maintenance; User groups; Testing

Pilot paper

Section A scenario (three compulsory questions – 20 marks each

1 Project risk assessment

2 Solving and preventing system problems

3 Quality assurance and testing in systems development

Section B (two from three questions – 20 marks each)

4 Outsourcing; Legacy systems; Project management software

5 Systems analysis interviews; Event model construction

6 Post-implementation review; Measuring software effectiveness; Controlling change

Oxford Brookes BSc (Hons) in Applied Accounting

The standard required of candidates completing Part 2 is that required in the final year of a UK degree. Students completing Parts 1 and 2 will have satisfied the examination requirement for an honours degree in Applied Accounting, awarded by Oxford Brookes University.

To achieve the degree, you must also submit two pieces of work based on a **Research and Analysis Project.**

- A 5,000 word **Report** on your chosen topic, which demonstrates that you have acquired the necessary research, analytical and IT skills.
- A 1,500 word **Key Skills Statement**, indicating how you have developed your interpersonal and communication skills.

BPP was selected by the ACCA and Oxford Brookes University to produce the official text *Success in your Research and Analysis Project* to support students in this task. The book pays particular attention to key skills not covered in the professional examinations.

BPP also offers courses and mentoring services.

The Oxford Brookes project text can be ordered using the form at the end of this study text.

Oxford Institute of International Finance MBA

The Oxford Institute of International Finance (OXIIF), a joint venture between the ACCA and Oxford Brookes University, offers an MBA for finance professionals.

For this MBA, credits are awarded for your ACCA studies, and entry to the MBA course is available to those who have completed their ACCA professional stage studies. The MBA was launched in 2002 and has attracted participants from all over the world.

The qualification features an introductory module (*Foundations of Management*). Other modules include *Global Business Strategy, Managing Self Development,* and *Organisational Change & Transformation.*

Research Methods are also taught, as they underpin the **research dissertation**.

The MBA programme is delivered through the use of targeted paper study materials, developed by BPP, and taught over the Internet by OXIIF personnel using BPP's virtual campus software.

For further information, please see the Oxford Institute's website: www.oxfordinstitute.org.

Continuing Professional Development

ACCA introduced a new continuing professional development requirement for members from 1 January 2005. Members will be required to complete and record 40 units of CPD annually, of which 21 units must be verifiable learning or training activity.

BPP has an established professional development department which offers a range of relevant, professional courses to reflect the needs of professionals working in both industry and practice. To find out more, visit the website: www.bpp.com/pd or call the client care team on 0845 226 2422.

Syllabus mindmap

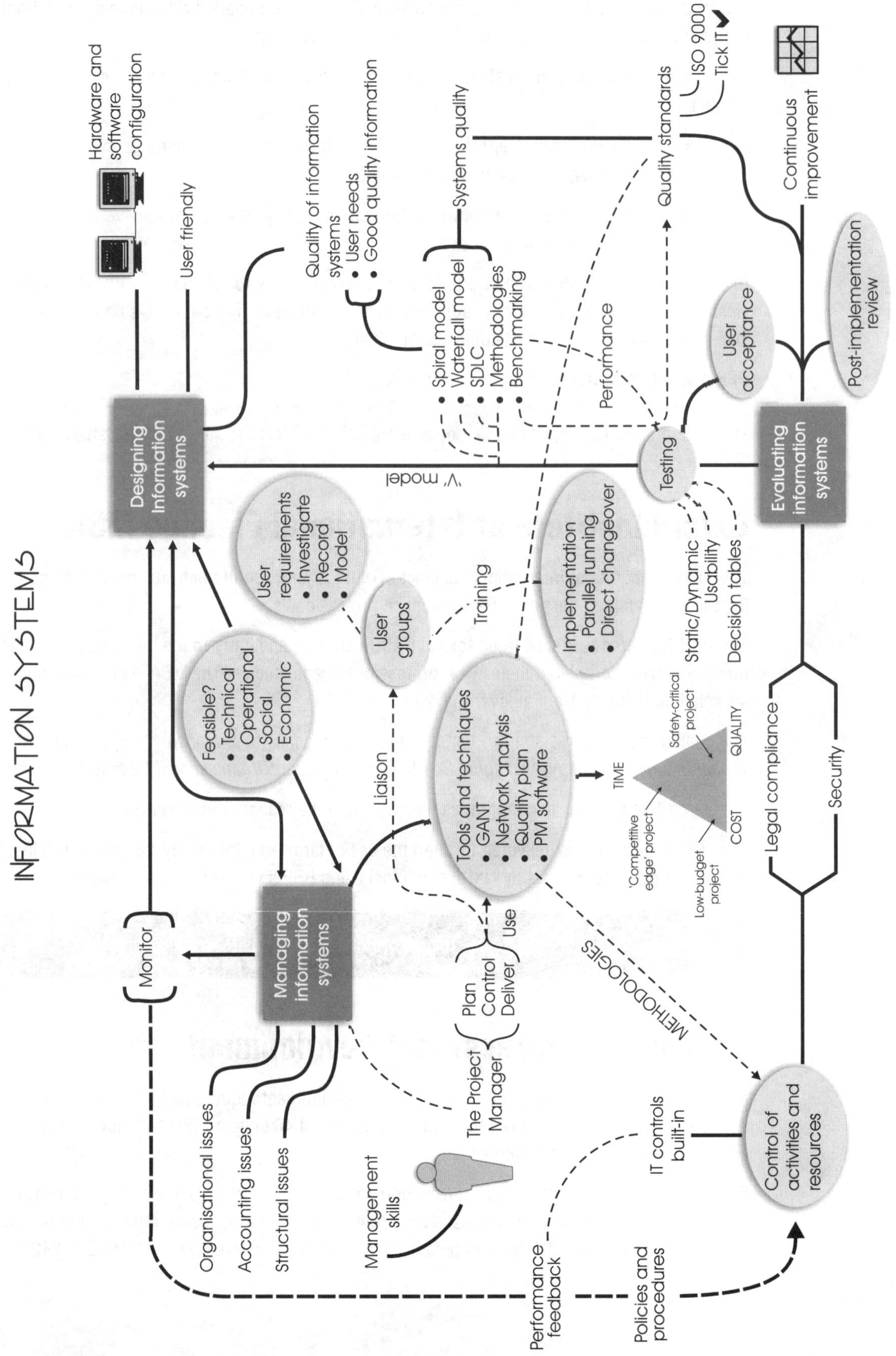

Part A
Managing information systems

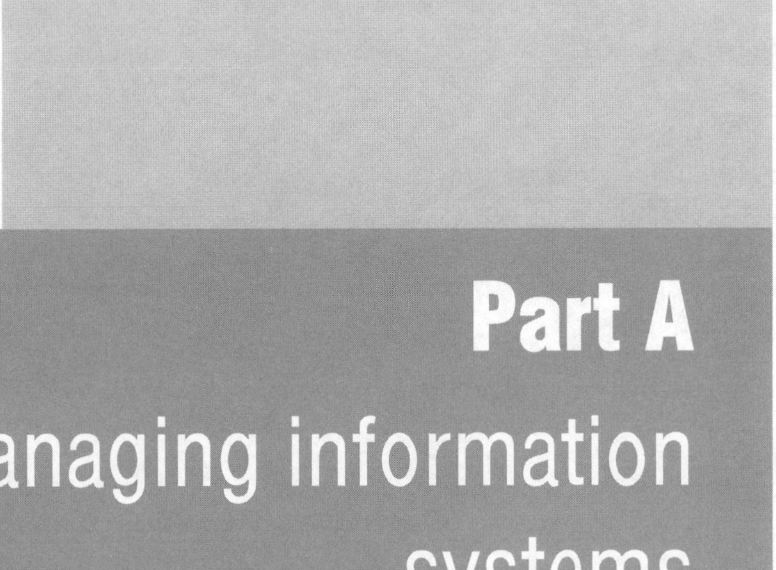

1

Information systems and business strategy

Topic list	Syllabus reference
1 Organisational information requirements	1(a)
2 Business strategy and information systems strategy	1(a)
3 Developing a strategy for information systems and information technology	1(a)
4 Critical success factors	1(a)

Introduction

Welcome to Paper 2.1 Information Systems. This Study Text follows the structure of the official ACCA syllabus and study guide.

The first two pages of each chapter provide syllabus and study guide references showing the areas covered within the chapter.

We start Chapter 1 with a look at the concept of **business strategy** and **strategic planning**.

Later in this chapter we examine the relationships between **business strategy**, **information systems** (IS) and **information technology** (IT).

Study guide

Part 1.1 – Business strategy and IS/IT alignment

- Explain an approach that an organisation may follow to formulate its strategic business objectives
- Discuss how information systems may be used to assist in achieving these objectives (this issue is relevant throughout this text)
- Distinguish between a business strategy and an information systems strategy
- Identify responsibility for the ownership of the IS strategy

Exam guide

The scenario that will appear in Section A of the examination provides the examiner with an ideal opportunity to test your understanding of the importance of an organisation's IS/IT strategy complimenting the overall business strategy.

1 Organisational information requirements

FAST FORWARD

All organisations require information for a range of **purposes** including:

- **Planning**
- **Controlling**
- **Recording transactions**
- **Performance measurement**
- **Decision making**

1.1 Planning

Planning requires a knowledge of the available resources, possible time-scales and the likely outcome under alternative scenarios. Information is required that helps **decision making**, and how to implement decisions taken.

1.2 Controlling

Once a plan is implemented, its actual performance must be controlled. Information is required to assess **whether it is proceeding as planned** or whether there is some unexpected deviation from plan. It may consequently be necessary to take some form of corrective action.

1.3 Recording transactions

Information about **each transaction or event** is required. Reasons include:

(a) Documentation of transactions can be used as **evidence** in a case of dispute.

(b) There may be a **legal requirement** to record transactions, for example for accounting and audit purposes.

(c) **Operational information** can be built up, allowing control action to be taken.

1.4 Performance measurement

Just as individual operations need to be controlled, so overall performance must be measured. **Comparisons against budget or plan** are able to be made. This may involve the collection of information on, for example, costs, revenues, volumes, time-scale and profitability.

1.5 Decision making

Strategic planning, management control and operational control may be seen as a hierarchy of planning and control decisions. (This is sometimes called the Anthony hierarchy, after the writer *Robert Anthony*.)

FAST FORWARD

A **strategy** is a general statement of long-term objectives and goals and the ways by which these will be achieved. **Strategic planning** is the formulation, evaluation and selection of strategies for the purpose of preparing a long-term plan of action to attain objectives.

Strategic planning is a complex process which involves taking a view of the **organisation** and the **future** that it is likely to encounter, and then attempting to organise the structure and resources of the organisation accordingly.

Key terms

Strategy can be defined as 'a course of action, including the specification of resources required, to achieve a specific outcome'.

Strategic planning is the formulation, evaluation and selection of strategies for the purpose of preparing a long-term plan of action to attain objectives.

Planning and control hierarchy

1.5.1 Strategic information

Strategic information is used to **plan** the **objectives** of the organisation, and to **assess** whether the objectives are being met in practice. Such information includes overall profitability, the profitability of different segments of the business, future market prospects, the availability and cost of raising new funds, total cash needs, total manning levels and capital equipment needs.

Strategic information is:

- Derived from both **internal and external** sources
- **Summarised** at a high level
- Relevant to the **long term**
- Concerned with the **whole organisation**
- Often prepared on an **'ad hoc'** basis
- Both **quantitative** and **qualitative**
- **Uncertain**, requiring assumptions to be made regarding the future

1.5.2 Tactical information

Tactical information is used to decide **how the resources of the business should be employed**, and to **monitor** how they are being and have been employed. Such information includes productivity measurements (output per hour) budgetary control or variance analysis reports, and cash flow forecasts, staffing levels and profit results within a particular department of the organisation, labour turnover statistics within a department and short-term purchasing requirements.

Tactical information is:

- Primarily generated internally (but may have a limited external component)
- **Summarised** at a relatively low level
- Relevant to the **short**– and **medium**-terms
- Concerned with **activities** or **departments**
- Prepared **routinely** and regularly
- Based on **quantitative** measures

1.5.3 Operational information

Operational information is used to ensure that **specific operational tasks** are planned and carried out as intended.

In a payroll office, for example, operational information would include the hours worked by each employee and the rate of pay per hour.

Operational information is:

- Derived from **internal** sources
- **Detailed**, being the processing of raw data
- Relevant to the **immediate term**
- **Task-specific**
- Prepared very **frequently**
- Largely **quantitative**

1.6 The qualities of good information

'Good' information is information that adds to the understanding of a situation. The qualities of good information are outlined in the following table.

Quality	Example
A ccurate	Figures should add up, the degree of rounding should be appropriate, there should be no typos, items should be allocated to the correct category, assumptions should be stated for uncertain information.
C omplete	Information should include everything that it needs to include, for example external data if relevant, or comparative information.
C ost-benificial	It should not cost more to obtain the information than the benefit derived from having it. Providers or information should be given efficient means of collecting and analysing it. Presentation should be such that users do not waste time working out what it means.
U ser-targeted	The needs of the user should be borne in mind, for instance senior managers need summaries, junior ones need detail.
R elevant	Information that is not needed for a decision should be omitted, no matter how 'interesting' it may be.
A uthoritative	The source of the information should be a reliable one (**not**, for instance, 'Joe Bloggs Predictions Page' on the Internet unless Joe Bloggs is known to be a reliable source for that type of information).
T imely	The information should be available when it is needed.
E asy to use	Information should be clearly presented, not excessively long, and sent using the right medium and communication channel (e-mail, telephone, hard-copy report etc).

Exam focus point

You will **not be asked simply to produce a list** of the qualities of good information in the exam. Exam questions will expect you to be able to **recognise information deficiencies** and **suggest improvements**.

1.7 Improvements to information

The table below contains suggestions as to how poor information can be **improved**.

Feature	Example of possible improvements
Accurate	Use computerised systems with automatic input checks rather than manual systems. Allow sufficient time for collation and analysis of data if pinpoint accuracy is crucial. Incorporate elements of probability within projections so that the required response to different future scenarios can be assessed.
Complete	Include past data as a reference point for future projections. Include any planned developments, such as new products. Information about future demand would be more useful than information about past demand. Include external data.
Cost-beneficial	Always bear in mind whether the benefit of having the information is greater than the cost of obtaining it.
User-targeted	Information should be summarised and presented together with relevant ratios or percentages.
Relevant	The purpose of the report should be defined. It may be trying to fulfil too many purposes at once. Perhaps several shorter reports would be more effective. Information should include exception reporting, where only those items that are worthy of note – and the control actions taken by more junior managers to deal with them – are reported.
Authoritative	Use reliable sources and experienced personnel. If some figures are derived from other figures the method of derivation should be explained.
Timely	Information collection and analysis by production managers needs to be speeded up considerably, probably by the introduction of better information systems.
Easy-to-use	Graphical presentation, allowing trends to be quickly assimilated and relevant action decided upon. Alternative methods of presentation should be considered, such as graphs or charts, to make it easier to review the information at a glance. Numerical information is sometimes best summarised in narrative form or vice versa. A 'house style' for reports should be devised and adhered to by all. This would cover such matters as number of decimal places to use, table headings and labels, paragraph numbering and so on.

2 Business strategy and information systems strategy

The relationship between corporate, business and operational strategies is shown in the following diagram.

Levels of strategy

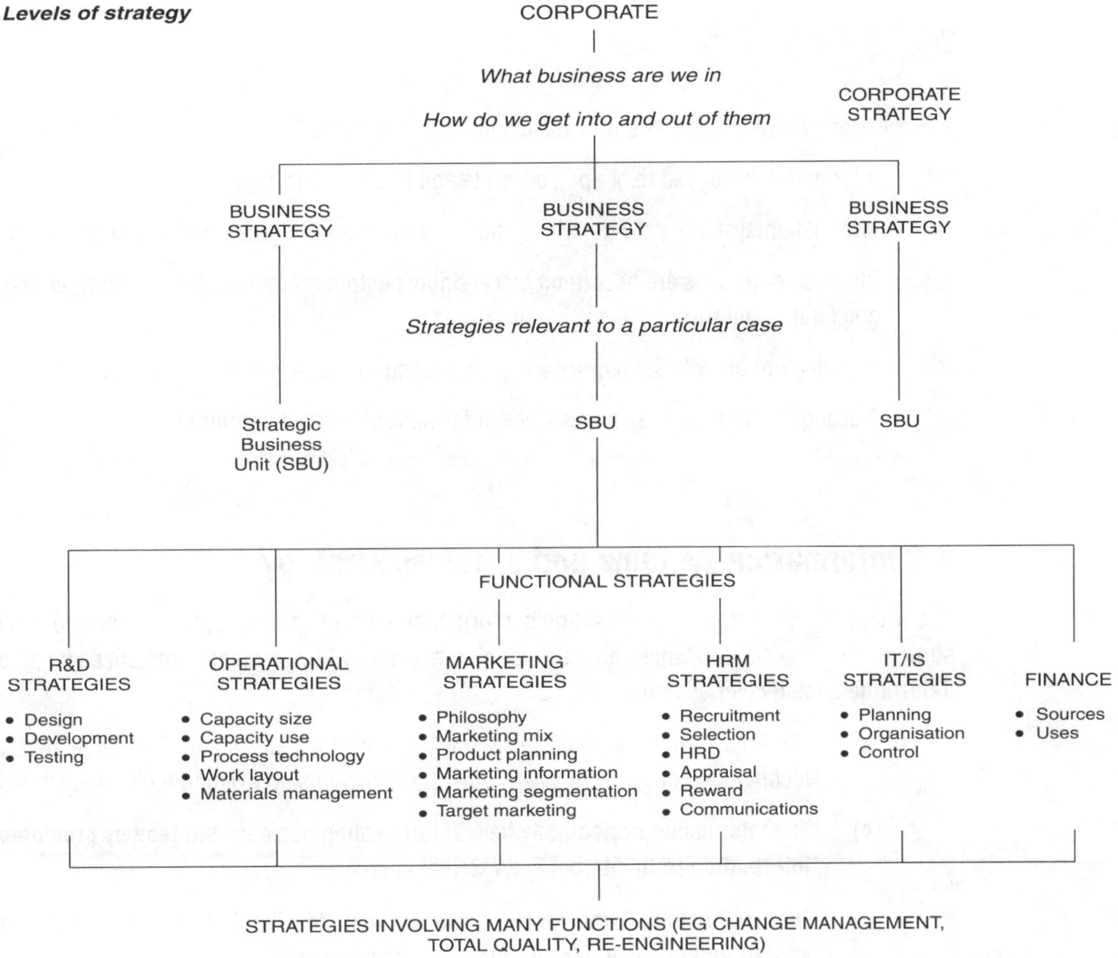

2.1 Functional/operational strategies; information systems strategy

FAST FORWARD

IS/IT strategy is an example of a functional/operational strategy, but may have **strategic implications**.

Information systems strategy is an example of a **functional/operational strategy** (although in some cases it may have strategic implications). Functional/operational strategies deal with specialised areas of activity.

Functional area	Comment
Information systems	A firm's information systems are becoming increasingly important, as an item of expenditure, as administrative support and as a tool for competitive strength.
Marketing	Devising products and services, pricing, promoting and distributing them, in order to satisfy customer needs at a profit.
Production	Factory location, manufacturing techniques, outsourcing etc.
Finance	Ensuring that the firm has enough financial resources to fund its other strategies.
Human resources	Secure personnel of the right skills in the right quantity at the right time.
R&D	New products and techniques.

Question

Strategy and information systems

List five ways in which corporate and business strategy are relevant to the types of information system required in an organisation?

Answer

Five ways are shown below. You may have come up with others.

(a) Information is needed to shape corporate and business strategy.

(b) Information systems provide information that monitors progress towards strategic objectives.

(c) Business objectives are becoming increasingly customer focused. Good customer service requires good quality information available on demand.

(d) A strategy of growth will require a corresponding increase in the information system.

(e) A change of strategy may mean a new information system is required.

2.2 Information systems and business strategy

It is widely accepted that an organisation's information system should **support** corporate and business strategy. In some circumstances an information system may have a greater influence and actually help **determine** strategy. For example:

(a) IS/IT may provide a possible source of competitive advantage. This could involve new technology not yet available to others or simply using existing technology in a different way.

(b) The information system may help in formulating business strategy by **providing information** from internal and external sources.

(c) Developments in IT may provide **new channels** for distributing and collecting information, and /or for conducting transactions eg the Internet.

An important role of both the finance and information technology functions is to help ensure the agreed business strategy is proceeding according to plan. The table below (devised by the US Institute of Management Accountants) outlines the rationale behind this view.

	Traditional view	Strategic implications
Cost	The finance and information technology functions can be relatively expensive	Shared services and outsourcing could be used to capture cost savings
IT	IT has traditionally been transaction based	IT/IS should be integrated with business strategy
Value	The finance and IT functions do not add value	Redesign the functions
Strategy	Accountants and IT managers are seen as scorekeepers and administrators rather than as a business partner during the strategic planning process	Change from cost-orientated to market-orientated ie development of more effective strategic planning systems

3 Developing a strategy for information systems and information technology

Key terms

Information systems (IS) include all systems and procedures involved in the collection, storage, production and distribution of information.

Information technology (IT) describes the equipment used to capture, store, transmit or present information. IT provides a large part of the information systems infrastructure.

Information management refers to the approach an organisation takes towards the management of its information systems, including:

- Planning IS/IT developments
- Organisational environment of IS
- Control
- Technology

FAST FORWARD

The term **information systems (IS) strategy** refers to the long-term plan concerned with exploiting IS and IT either to support business strategies or create new strategic options.

3.1 Vision and reality

A company that has a **vision** of its own future, and some idea of how information technology can be used to turn that vision into **reality**, may be able to use new technologies for strategic advantage.

One approach to creating a vision is to adopt a familiar three step approach, involving answering three questions about the organisation.

- Where are we now?
- Where do we want to be?
- How will we get there?

The first question can be answered using standard techniques such as a strengths, weaknesses, opportunities, threats **(SWOT) analysis**. This approach ensures that both internal and external factors are considered. We cover SWOT analysis in the context of information systems development in Chapter 6.

Answering the second question requires vision. This does not have to be a continuation in the organisation's current direction. It must be challenging, attainable and communicated to those who will implement it.

Once this has been done, the strategy (in answer to the third question) can be defined.

A second approach takes the view that insiders are too tied to 'the way we do things now', and recommends the involvement of **outsiders**. An outsider may be able to more readily anticipate dramatic shifts which might occur in the future. Additionally, an outsider does not have the insider's investment in **maintaining the status quo**.

3.2 Information systems, strategy and competitive advantage

It is now recognised that information can be used as a source of competitive advantage. The realisation that information (and therefore information systems and information technology) may be a source of competitive advantage and be key to achieving organisational goals, has led to increased emphasis on the importance of formal management strategies and plans for information and information systems.

A strategy is needed for areas in which decisions have the potential to have a major impact on an organisation. Many organisations have recognised the importance of information and developed an **information strategy**, covering both IS and IT.

In commercial organisations it could be argued that one of the main aims of any strategy is competitive advantage – as success ultimately depends upon doing something better than competitors do. Business objectives, if achieved, should result in competitive advantage in one or more areas. This process is contributed to by ensuring the organisation's strategy for information and information systems is **tied to business objectives**.

(a) The **corporate strategy** is used to plan functional **business plans** which provide guidelines for information-based activities.

(b) On a year by year basis, the **annual plan** would try to tie in business plans with **information systems projects**, perhaps through a **steering committee**.

3.3 Information systems strategy

An IS strategy therefore deals with the integration of an organisation's information requirements and information systems planning with its **long-term overall goals** (customer service etc). IS strategy is formulated at the level of business where specific customer needs etc can be delineated. It deals with what applications should be developed, and where resources should be deployed.

The **information technology (IT) strategy** leads on from the IS strategy above. It deals with the **technologies** of:

- Computing
- Communications
- Data
- Application systems

This provides a framework for the analysis and design of the **technological infrastructure** of an organisation. This strategy indicates how the information systems strategies that rely on technology will be **implemented**.

3.4 Why have an IS/IT strategy?

FAST FORWARD

A strategy is needed for IS/IT because these areas involve **high costs**, are **critical to the success** of many organisations, can be used as a **strategic weapon** and affects internal and external **stakeholders**. IS/IT are sufficiently important and widespread to require proper **planning** and management attention.

A strategy for information systems and information technology is **justified** on the grounds that IS/IT:

- Involves **high costs**
- Is **critical to the success** of many organisations
- May be utilised as part of the commercial strategy in the battle for **competitive advantage**
- Can significantly change the business environment
- Affects **all levels of management**
- Affects the way **management information** is created and presented
- **Requires effective management** to obtain the maximum benefit
- Involves many **stakeholders** inside and outside the organisation

3.4.1 IS/IT is a high cost activity

Many organisations invest large amounts of money in IS, but not always wisely.

The unmanaged proliferation of IT is likely to lead to expensive mistakes. Two key benefits of IT – the ability to **share** information and the avoidance of duplication – are likely to be lost.

All IT expenditure should therefore require approval to ensure that it enhances rather than detracts from the overall information management strategy.

3.4.2 IS/IT is critical to the success of many organisations

When developing an IS/IT strategy a firm should assess **how important IT is** in the provision of products and services. The role that IT fills in an organisation will vary depending on the type of organisations. IS/IT could be:

- A **support** activity
- A **key** operational activity
- **Potentially** very important
- A **strategic** activity (without IT the firm could not function at all)
- A source of **competitive advantage**

3.4.3 IT can significantly change the business environment

IT is an **enabling** technology, and can produce dramatic changes in individual businesses and whole industries. For example, the deregulation of US airline system encouraged the growth of computerised seat-reservation systems (eg SABRE, as used by American Airlines which always displayed American Airlines flights preferentially). IT can be both a **cause** of major changes in doing business and a **response** to them.

3.4.4 IT affects all levels of management

IT has become a routine a feature of office life, **a facility for everyone to use**. IT is no longer used solely by specialist staff.

3.4.5 IT and its effect on management information

FAST FORWARD

IT developments have increased the **amount of information available** to organisations. It is important to ensure information is useful – that it is of **good quality**.

The use of IT has permitted the design of a range of **Management Information Systems (MIS)**. Executive Information Systems (EIS), Decision Support Systems (DSS), and expert systems can be used to enhance the flexibility and depth of MIS. (We look at different types of information system in Chapter 2.)

IT has also had an effect on **production processes**. For example, Computer Integrated Manufacturing (CIM) changed the methods and cost profiles of many manufacturing processes. The techniques used to **measure and record costs** have also adapted to the use of IT.

3.4.6 IT and stakeholders

Parties interested in an organisation's use of IT are as follows.

(a) **Other business users** – for example to facilitate Electronic Data Interchange (EDI).

(b) **Governments** – eg telecommunications regulation, regulation of electronic commerce.

(c) **IT manufacturers** looking for new markets and product development. User-groups may be able to influence software producers.

(d) **Consumers** – for example as reassurance that product quality is high, consumers may also be interested if information is provided via the Internet.

(e) **Employees** – as IT affects work practices.

3.5 Developing an IS/IT strategy

FAST FORWARD

Developing strategy involves taking a number of steps, from setting strategic objectives right through to evaluating actual performance. Three basic issues are the organisation's **overall business objectives** and in consequence its **IS/IT needs**, the organisation's **current IT usage** and the potential **opportunities** that IT can bring.

An IS/IT strategy should be developed with the aim of ensuring IS/IT is utilised as efficiently and effectively as possible in the pursuit of organisational goals and objectives.

The inputs and outputs of the IS/IT strategic planning process are summarised on the following diagram. (We explain SWOT analysis in the context of information systems in Chapter 6.)

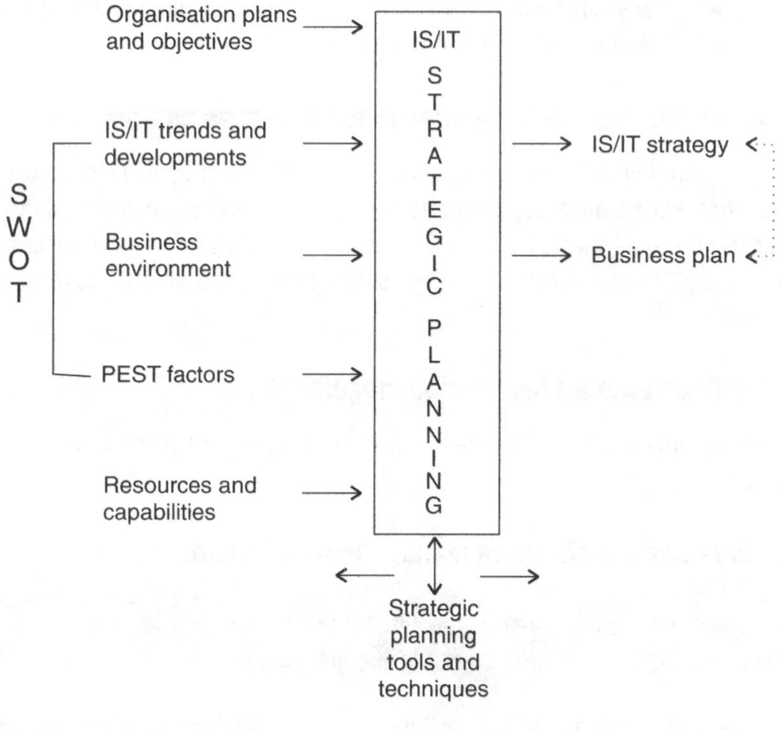

An IS strategy therefore deals with the integration of an organisation's information requirements and information systems planning with its **long-term overall goals** (customer service etc). IS strategy deals with what applications should be developed and where resources should be deployed.

The **information technology (IT) strategy** leads on from the IS strategy above. It deals with the **technologies** of:

- Computing
- Communications
- Data
- Application systems

This provides a framework for the analysis and design of the **technological infrastructure** of an organisation. This strategy indicates how the information systems strategies that rely on technology will be **implemented**.

3.6 Establishing organisational information requirements

The identification of organisational information needs and the information systems framework to satisfy them is at the heart of a strategy for information systems and information technology.

The IS and IT strategies should complement the overall strategy for the organisation. It follows therefore that the IS/IT strategy should be considered whenever the organisation prepares other long-term strategies such as marketing or production.

3.7 Earl's three leg analysis

The writer Earl identified **three legs of IS strategy development**:

- Business led (top down emphasis, focuses on **business plans and goals**)
- Infrastructure led (bottom up emphasis, focuses on **current systems**)
- Mixed (inside out emphasis, focuses on **IT/IS opportunities**)

A diagrammatic representation of the three legs follows:

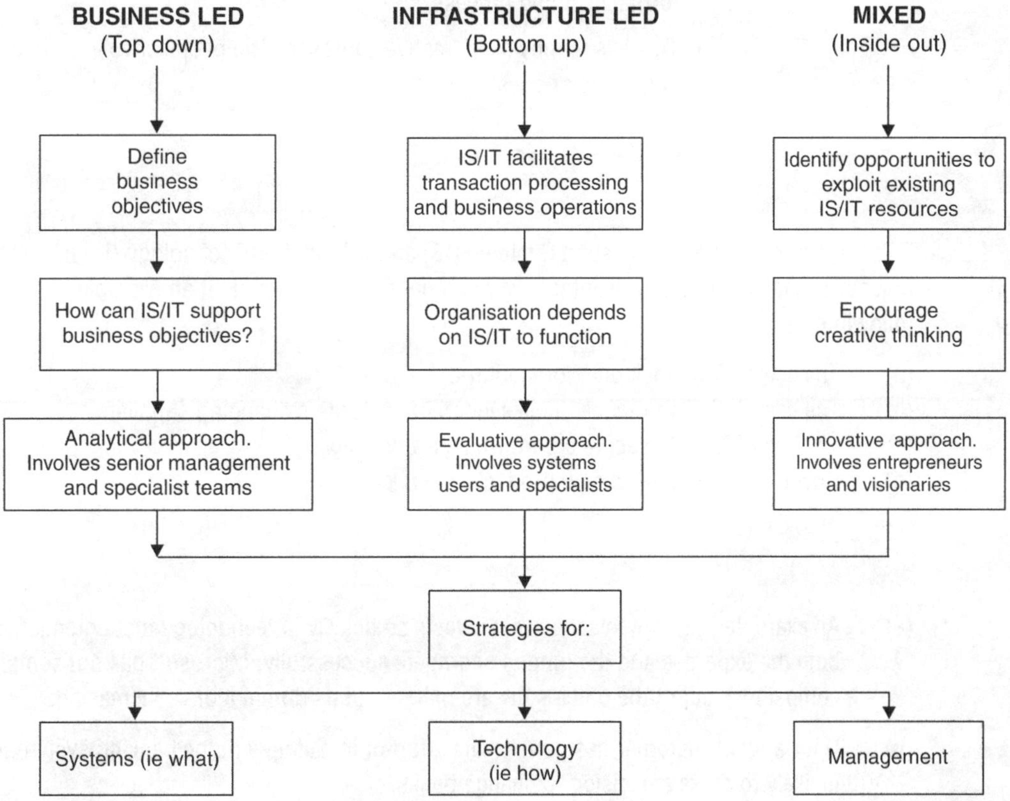

Earl's three leg analysis is explained in the following table.

Leg or approach	Comment
Business led (top down)	The overall objectives of an organisation are identified and then IS/IT systems are implemented to enable these objectives to be met. This approach relies on the ability to break down the organisation and its objectives to a series of business objectives and processes and to be able to identify the information needs of these. This is an analytical approach. The people usually involved are senior management and specialist teams.
Infrastructure led (bottom up)	Computer based transaction systems are critical to business operations. The organisation focuses on systems that facilitate transactions and other basic operations. This is an evaluative approach. The people usually involved are system users and specialists.
Mixed (inside out)	The organisation encourages ideas that will exploit existing IT and IS resources. Innovations may come from entrepreneurial managers or individuals outside the formal planning process. This is an innovative/creative approach. The people involved are entrepreneurs and/or visionaries.

Question

IS/IT and competitive advantage

Think about the role of Information Systems (IS) and Information Technology (IT) in achieving business objectives and securing an advantage over competitors. Try to think of an example of each of the following.

(a) The use of IT to 'lock out' competitors.
(b) The use of IS/IT to reduce the likelihood of customers changing suppliers.
(c) The use of IS/IT to secure a performance advantage.
(d) How IT may generate a new product or service.

Answer

(a) An example is an organisation that invests so heavily in technology that potential competitors lack both the expertise and the funds to compete successfully. Microsoft has not completely locked competitors out of the office software market but its domination is increasing.

(b) Once a bank customer has gone to the effort of installing a home banking system, he or she is unlikely to make a decision to change banks.

(c) Accurate stock systems that facilitate Just-In-Time stock management, and organisations participating in Electronic Data Interchange (EDI) are two examples of how IT can increase efficiency and facilitate better service – providing an advantage over competitors. (They may also make an organisation more dependent on existing suppliers therefore discouraging the changing of suppliers.)

(d) Internet Service Providers (ISPs) did not exist before the advent of the Internet.

4 Critical success factors

FAST FORWARD

Critical success factors are a small number of key operational goods vital to the success of an organisation CSFs may be used to establish organisational information requirements.

The use of **critical success factors (CSFs)** can help to determine the information requirements of an organisation. CSFs are operational goals. If operational goals are achieved the organisation should be successful.

Key term

Critical success factors are a small number of key operational goals vital to the success of an organisation. CSFs may be used to establish organisational information requirements.

The CSF approach is sometimes referred to as the **strategic analysis** approach. The philosophy behind this approach is that managers should focus on a small number of objectives, and information systems should be focussed on providing information to enable managers to monitor these objectives.

4.1 Types of CSF

Two separate types of critical success factor can be identified. A **monitoring** CSF is used to keep abreast of existing activities and operations. A **building** CSF helps to measure the progress of new initiatives and is more likely to be relevant at senior executive level.

- **Monitoring** CSFs are important for **maintaining** business
- **Building** CSFs are important for **expanding** business

4.2 Revising CSFs

One approach to **determining the factors** which are critical to success in performing a function or making a decision is as follows.

- List the organisation's **objectives** and **goals**
- Determine which factors are **critical** for accomplishing the objectives
- Determine a small number of **key performance indicators** for each factor

4.3 Key Performance Indicators (KPIs)

The determination of measures or **key performance indicators** to monitor CSFs is not necessarily straightforward. Some measures might use **factual**, verifiable data, while others might make use of 'softer' concepts, such as opinions, perceptions and hunches.

For example, the reliability of stock records can be measured by means of physical stock counts, either at discrete intervals or on a rolling basis. Forecasting of demand variations will be much harder to measure.

Where measures use quantitative data, performance can be measured in a number of ways.

- In **physical quantities**, for example units produced or units sold
- In **money terms**, for example profit, revenues, costs or variances
- In **ratios** and **percentages**

4.4 Sources of CSFs

In general terms Rockart identifies four **sources** of CSFs.

(a) The **industry** that the business is in.

(b) The **company** itself and its situation within the industry.

(c) The **environment**, for example consumer trends, the economy, and political factors of the country in which the company operates.

(d) Temporal organisational factors, which are areas of corporate activity which are causing **concern**, for example, high stock levels.

4.5 Possible specific sources of CSFs and KPis

More specifically, possible internal and external data sources for CSFs include the following.

(a) The **existing system**. The existing system can be used to generate reports showing failures to meet CSFs.

(b) **Customer service department**. This department will maintain details of **complaints, refunds** and **queries**.

(c) **Customers**. A survey of customers, provided that it is properly designed and introduced, would reveal (or confirm) those areas where **satisfaction** is high or low.

(d) **Competitors**. Competitors' operations, pricing structures and publicity should be closely monitored.

(e) **Accounting system**. The **profitability** of various aspects of the operation would be a key factor in any review of CSFs.

(f) **Consultants**. A specialist consultancy might be able to perform a detailed review of the organisation to identify CSFs.

4.6 The CSF approach

The CSF approach to IS/IT planning is illustrated in the following diagram.

The critical success factor approach to IS/IT planning

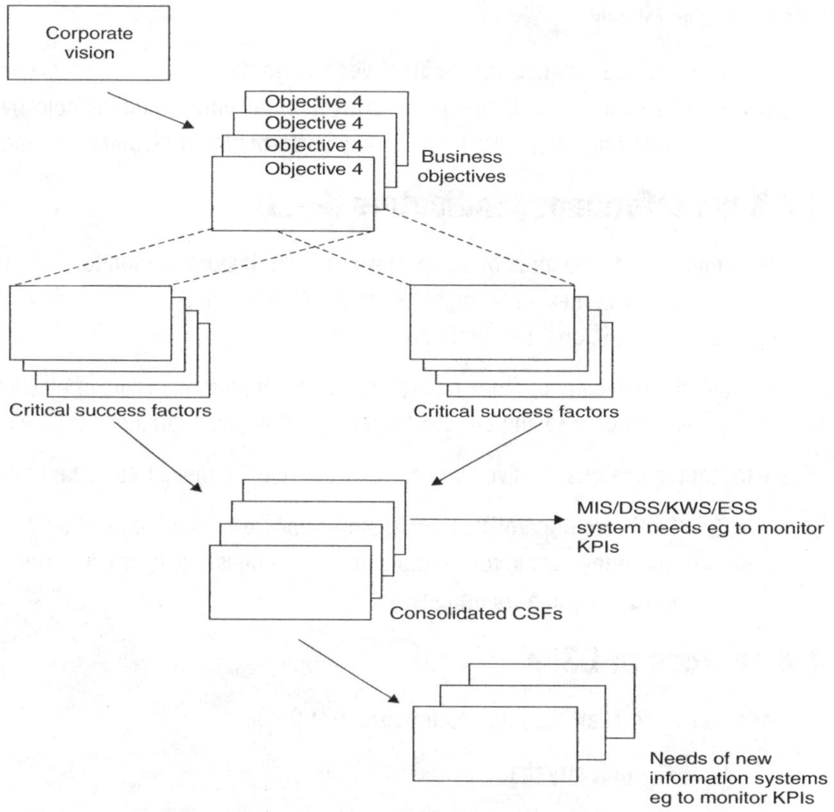

Source: *IT Strategy for Business*, Joe Peppard Chapter 4, Garret Hickey

4.7 Example

An organisation has an objective to maintain a high level of service direct from stock without holding uneconomic stock levels. This is quantified in the form of a **goal**, which might be to ensure that 95% of orders for goods can be satisfied directly from stock, while minimising total stockholding costs and stock levels. **CSFs** and KPIs might then be identified as the following.

CSF	KPI
Supplier performance	Average order lead time
Stock records reliability	Number of discrepancies found
Accurate demand forecasting	Difference between forecast and actual demand

4.8 CSF approach: strengths and weaknesses

CSF approach – strengths	Comment
Takes into account environmental changes	The CSF approach requires managers to examine the environment and consider how it influences their information requirements.
Focuses on information	The approach doesn't just aim to establish organisational objectives. It also looks at the information and information systems required to establish and monitor progress towards these objectives.
Facilitates top management participation in system development	The clear link between information requirements and individual and organisational objectives encourages top management involvement in system (DSS, EIS) design.

CSF approach – weaknesses	Comment
Aggregation of individual CSFs	Wide-ranging individual CSFs need to be aggregated into a clear organisational plan. This process relies heavily on judgement. Managers who feel their input has been neglected may be alienated.
Bias towards top management	When gathering information to establish CSFs it is usually top management who are interviewed. These managers may lack knowledge of operational activities.
CSFs change often	The business environment, managers and information systems technology are subject to constant change. CSFs and systems must be updated to account for change.

Chapter Roundup

- Organisations **require information for a variety of purposes** including
  - Planning
  - Controlling
  - Recording transactions
  - Measuring performance
  - Decision making
- A **strategy** is a general statement of long-term objectives and goals and the ways by which these will be achieved. **Strategic planning** is the formulation, evaluation and selection of strategies for the purpose of preparing a long-term plan of action to attain objectives.
- **Information systems** and **Information Technology (IS/IT) strategy** refers to the long-term plan concerned with exploiting IS and IT either to support business strategies or create new strategic options. IS/IT strategy is an example of a functional/operational strategy, but may have **strategic implications.**
- A strategy is needed for IS/IT because these areas involve **high costs**, are **critical to the success** of many organisations, can be used as a **strategic weapon** and affects internal and external **stakeholders**. IS/IT are sufficiently important and widespread to require proper **planning** and management attention.
- IT developments have increased the **amount of information available** to organisations. It is important to ensure information is useful – that it is of **good quality**.
- Developing strategy involves taking a number of steps, from setting strategic objectives right through to evaluating actual performance. Three basic issues are the organisation's **overall business objectives** and in consequence its **IS/IT needs**, the organisation's **current IT usage** and the potential **opportunities** that IT can bring.
- **Critical success factors** are a small number of key operational goods vital to the success of an organisation. CSFs may be used to establish organisational information requirements.

Quick Quiz

1 List five general purposes an organisation may use information for.

2 'Operational information is derived mainly from external sources.' TRUE or FALSE?

3 List four features of strategic information.

4 List five reasons why an organisation should have a strategy for IS/IT.

5 What three issues must an IS/IT strategy deal with?

6 Identify three general sources of CSFs.

7 'A well thought out CSF will always be valid for at least two years'. TRUE or FALSE?

Answers to Quick Quiz

1 Planning, controlling, recording transactions, measuring performance, making decisions.

2 FALSE.

3 [Four of]

Derived from both internal and external sources

Summarised at a high level.

Relevant to the long term.

Concerned with the whole organisation.

Often prepared on an 'ad hoc' basis.

Both quantitative and qualitative.

Uncertain, as the future cannot be accurately predicted.

4 [Five of]

IT involves high costs.

IT is critical to the success of many organisations.

IT is now used as part of the commercial strategy in the battle for competitive advantage.

IT is required by customers.

IT affects all levels of management.

IT affects the way management information is created and presented.

IT requires effective management to obtain the maximum benefit.

IT involves many stakeholders inside and outside the organisation.

5 The organisation's overall business needs.

The organisation's current use of IT.

The potential opportunities and threats that IT can bring.

6 The industry that the organisation is in.

The environment that the organisation operates in.

Factors within the organisation itself.

7 FALSE. There is no guarantee that any CSF will be valid for a particular period of time. Changes in the environment that invalidate the CSF may occur at any time.

Now try the question below from the Exam Question Bank

Number	Level	Marks	Time
Q1	Introductory	8	14 mins

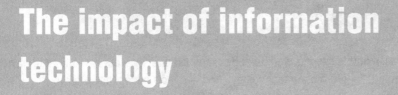

The impact of information technology

2

Topic list	Syllabus reference
1 Manual systems	1(a)
2 The computer	1(a)
3 Software	1(a)
4 Data processing in a computerised environment	1(a)
5 Developments in communications	1(a)
6 Deciding upon a communication tool	1(a)
7 System architectures	1(a)
8 The effect of office automation on business	1(a)
9 The Internet	1(a)

Introduction

We will now look at some of the ways that organisations are **utilising information technology**. We include technologies such as the Internet and established tools of office automation (eg word-processing and spreadsheet software).

While working through this chapter remember that the examiner does **not** expect you to be an expert on the technical aspects of information technology (IT).

What is required in Paper 2.1 is an awareness of how **IT** may be used in the development of information systems that **help an organisation achieve its goals.**

Study guide

Part 1.1 – Business strategy and IS/IT alignment

- Identify current trends in information technology (IT) and the opportunities they offer to organisations

Part 1.4 – Organising information systems; structural issues

- Describe the typical hardware, software, data and communications infrastructures found within information systems functions (also see Chapter 3)

Exam guide

Much of the information provided in this chapter would not be examined directly – but is required to gain an understanding of current trends in information technology and the opportunities they offer to organisations. Exam questions are likely to focus on how organisations could use technology, rather than directly testing your knowledge of a particular technology.

1 Manual systems

Many tasks (and people) are still better suited to manual methods of working, for example a single quick calculation may best be done mentally or by using a pocket calculator.

Many people also prefer **communicating face to face** with their colleagues, rather than using tools such as e-mail. People may prefer to interact both to fulfil social needs and because they find this form of communication more effective eg use of body language, tone of voice etc.

The use of poorly designed computer systems, or using 'good systems' with inadequately trained users, will result in inefficiencies that negate the benefits computerised processing should bring.

1.1 Manual systems v computerised systems

FAST FORWARD

In many circumstances, **manual** systems are **less productive** than computerised systems.

However, in many situations manual systems are inferior to computerised systems. Some **disadvantages of manual systems** are outlined in the following table.

Disadvantage	Comment
Productivity	Productivity is usually lower, particularly in routine or operational situations such as transaction processing.
Slower	Processing is slower where large volumes of data need to be dealt with. Slower processing means that some information that could be provided if computerised systems were used, will not be provided at all, because there is not time.
Risk of errors	The risk of errors is greater, especially in repetitive work like payroll calculations.
Less accessible	Information is generally less accessible. Access to information is often restricted to one user at a time. Paper files can easily be mislaid or buried in in-trays, in which case the information they contain is not available at all.

Disadvantage	Comment
Alterations	It is difficult to make corrections. If a manual document contains errors or needs updating it is often necessary to recreate the whole document from scratch, rather than just a new version with the relevant details changed.
Quality of output	Quality of output is less consistent and often not well-designed. At worst, hand-written records may be illegible and so completely useless. Poorly presented information may fail to communicate key points.
Bulk	Paper based systems are generally very bulky both to handle and to store, and office space is expensive.

2 The computer

A computer is a device which accepts input data, processes it according to programmed rules, calculates results and then stores and/or outputs these results.

2.1 Types of computer

FAST FORWARD

Computers can be classified as supercomputers, mainframes, minicomputers and microcomputers or PCs.

Computers can be classified as follows.

- Supercomputers
- Mainframe computers
- Minicomputers
- Microcomputers, now commonly called PCs

A **supercomputer** is used to process **very large amounts of data very quickly**. They are particularly useful for occasions where high volumes of calculations need to be performed, for example in meteorological or astronomical applications.

A **mainframe** computer system uses a powerful central computer, linked by cable or telecommunications to terminals. A mainframe has many times more **processing power** than a PC and offers **extensive data storage** facilities.

Mainframes are used by organisations such as banks that have very large volumes of processing to perform and have special security needs. Many organisations have now replaced their old mainframes with networked 'client-server' systems of mid-range computers and PCs because this approach is thought to be cheaper and offer more flexibility.

A **minicomputer** is a computer whose size, speed and capabilities lie somewhere between those of a mainframe and a PC. The term was originally used before PCs were developed, to describe computers which were cheaper but less well-equipped than mainframe computers.

With the advent of PCs and of mainframes that are much smaller than in the past, the definition of a minicomputer has become rather vague. There is really no definition which distinguishes adequately between a PC and a minicomputer.

Microcomputers (or PCs) are now the norm for small to medium-sized business computing and for home computing, and most larger businesses now use them for day-to-day needs such as word-processing. Often they are linked together in a **network** to enable sharing of information between users.

2.2 Portables

The original portable computers were heavy, weighing around five kilograms, and could only be run from the mains electricity supply. Subsequent developments allow true portability.

(a) The **laptop** or **notebook** is powered either from the electricity supply or using a rechargeable battery and can include all the features and functionality of desktop PCs.

(b) The **palmtop** or handheld is increasingly compatible with true PCs. Devices range from basic models which are little more than electronic organisers to relatively powerful processors running 'cut-down' versions of Windows and Microsoft Office, and including communications features.

FAST FORWARD

The amount of **RAM** and the **processor speed** are key determinants of computer performance. Hard drive size is another important factor.

2.3 The processor or Central Processing Unit (CPU)

The processor is the **'brain'** of the computer. The processor may be defined as follows. The processor (sometimes referred to as the central processing unit or CPU) is divided into three areas:

- Arithmetic and logic unit
- Control unit
- Main store or memory

The processing unit may have all its elements – arithmetic and logic unit, control unit, and the input/output interface on a single **'chip'**. A chip is a small piece of silicon upon which is etched an integrated circuit, on an extremely small scale.

The most common chips are those made by the Intel company. Each generation of Intel CPU chip has been able to perform operations in fewer clock cycles than the previous generation, and therefore works more quickly.

2.3.1 MHz and clock speed

The processor receives program instructions and sends signals to peripheral devices. The signals are co-ordinated by a **clock** which sends out a 'pulse' – a sort of tick-tock sequence called a **cycle** – at regular intervals.

The **number of cycles** produced per second is usually measured in **MegaHertz** (MHz) or **GigaHertz** (GHz).

- 1 MHz = one **million** cycles per **second**
- 1 GHz = one **billion** cycles per **second**

2.4 Memory

The computer's memory is also known as main store or internal store. The memory will hold the following.

- Program instructions
- The input data that will be processed next
- The data that is ready for output to an output device

The processing capacity of a computer is in part dictated by the capacity of its memory. Capacity is calculated in kilobytes (1 kilobyte = 2^{10} (1,024) bytes) and megabytes (1 megabyte = 2^{20} bytes) and gigabytes (2^{30}). These are abbreviated to Kb, Mb and Gb.

2.4.1 Bits and bytes

Each individual storage element in the computer's memory consists of a simple circuit which can be switched **on** or **off**. These two states can be conveniently expressed by the numbers 1 and 0 respectively.

Each 1 or 0 is a **bit**. Bits are grouped together in groups of eight to form **bytes**. A byte may be used to represent a **character**, for example a letter, a number or another symbol.

2.4.2 RAM

RAM (Random Access Memory) is memory that is directly available to the processing unit. It holds the data and programs in current use. RAM in microcomputers is 'volatile' which means that the contents of the memory are erased when the computer's power is switched off.

2.4.3 Cache

The **cache** is a small capacity but **extremely fast** part of the memory which saves a second copy of the pieces of data most recently read from or written to main memory. When the cache is full, older entries are 'flushed out' to make room for new ones.

2.4.4 ROM

ROM **(Read-Only Memory)** is **a memory chip into which fixed data is written permanently** at the time of its manufacture. When you turn on a PC you may see a reference to **BIOS** (basic input/output system). This is part of the ROM chip containing all the programs needed to control the keyboard, screen, disk drives and so on.

2.5 Hard disks

Disks offer **direct access** to data. Almost all PCs have an **internal hard disk** to store software and data. At the time of writing the average new **PC** has a hard disk size of around **40 Gigabytes**, a massive increase from just a couple of years ago.

2.6 Floppy disks

The floppy disk provides a **cost-effective** means of on-line storage for **small** amounts of information. A 3½" disk can hold up to **1.44 Mb** of data.

2.7 Zip disks

A **Zip disk** is a different type of **removable** disk, with much larger capacity (100 Mb) that requires a special Zip drive. A Zip disk is suitable for back-up, general storage or for moving files between computers.

2.8 Tape storage

Tape cartridges have a **much larger capacity** than floppy disks and they are still widely used as a **backing storage** medium. Fast tapes which can be used to create a back-up file very quickly are known as **tape streamers**.

Like an audio or video cassette, data has to be recorded **along the length** of a computer tape and so it is **more difficult to access** than data on disk (ie direct access is not possible with tape). Reading and writing are separate operations.

2.9 CD-ROM (Compact Disc – Read Only Memory)

A CD-ROM can store 650 megabytes of data.

The **speed** of a CD-ROM drive is relevant to how fast data can be retrieved: an **eight speed** drive is quicker than a **four speed** drive.

CD recorders are now available for general business use with blank CDs (CD-R) and **rewritable disks** (CD-RW) are now available.

2.10 DVD (Digital Versatile Disc)

DVD development was encouraged by the advent of multimedia files with video graphics and sound – requiring greater disk capacity.

Digital Versatile Disc (DVD) technology can store almost 5 gigabytes of data on one disk. Access speeds are improved as is sound and video quality

2.11 Memory stick or 'Pen drive'

A pen drive or memory stick is a physically small external storage device usually connected via a USB port. Capacity ranges from 16Mb to 512Mb.

Question — Storage devices

Briefly outline two features and one common use of magnetic disks, magnetic tapes and optical disks.

Answer

(a) *Magnetic disks* offer fast access times, direct access to data and offer suitability for multi-user environments. Magnetic disk storage is therefore the predominant storage medium in most commercial applications currently. Direct access is essential for many commercial applications (eg databases) and in addition speed is necessary for real-time applications.

(b) *Magnetic tapes* offer cheap data storage, portability and serial or sequential access only. Magnetic tape is most valuable as a backup medium.

(c) *Optical disks* (eg CD and DVDs)pacity to store vast amounts of data but offer slower access speeds than magnetic disks. They are most suitable for backup and archiving, or keeping old copies of files which might need to be retrieved. However, the technology behind optical drives is still in development, and it may not be too long before they are a viable alternative to magnetic disk drives for most applications.

3 Software

FAST FORWARD

Four types of software are:

- The **operating system**
- **Utilities**
- **Off-the-shelf applications**
- **Bespoke applications**

The different types of computer software can be classified into five types, as shown in the following table.

Type	Comment
Operating systems	The operating system provides the interface between the computer hardware and both the user and the other software. An operating system will typically perform the following tasks. • Initial set-up of the computer, when it is switched on • Communication between the user and hardware • Calling up of files from storage into memory • File management The most widely-used operating system is Microsoft Windows. Other operating systems include UNIX, the Apple Macintosh O/S system and Linux.
Utilities	Software utilities are relatively small software packages, usually designed to perform a task related to the general operation of a computer system. An example of a utility is software designed to perform back-ups.
Programming tools	Some software is designed specifically to help programmers produce computer programs. Examples include program compilers and assemblers, and Computer Assisted Software Engineering (CASE) tools (which are covered in Chapter 7).
Off-the-shelf applications	This term is used to describe software produced by a software manufacturer and released in a form that is ready to use. 'Office' type software (spreadsheet, word-processing, database etc) and integrated accounting systems such as Sage Line 50 are examples.
Bespoke applications	Bespoke software is tailor-made to meet the needs of an organisation. Bespoke software is relatively expensive, but may be the only feasible solution in unusual situations. We cover the factors to consider when deciding upon off-the-shelf or bespoke software in Chapter 10.

4 Data processing in a computerised environment

In data processing a data **file** is a collection of **records** with similar characteristics. Examples of data files include the sales ledger, the purchase ledger and the nominal ledger.

A **record** in a file consists of data relating to one logically definable unit of business information. A collection of similar records makes up a file. For example, the records for a sales ledger file consist of customer records (or 'customer accounts').

Records in files consist of **fields** of information. For example, a customer record on the sales ledger file will include name, address, customer reference number, balance owing, and credit limit.

Records on a file should contain one **key field**. This is an item of data within the record by which it can be uniquely identified.

Files are conventionally classified into **transaction** files, and **master** files. These distinctions are particularly relevant in batch processing applications.

A **transaction file** is a file containing records that relate to individual transactions. The sales day book entries are examples of transaction records in a transaction file.

A **master file** contains reference data and also cumulative transaction data. For example, in a purchase ledger system, the master file is the purchase ledger itself. This is a file consisting of:

(a) **Reference data** for each supplier (supplier name and address, reference number, amount currently owed etc) and

(b) **Cumulative transaction data** for each supplier – periodic totals for purchases, purchase returns and payments.

FAST FORWARD

Both manual and computer data processing can be divided into two broad types: **batch processing** and **real-time processing**. Batch processing systems are becoming less common, particularly if the process concerned impacts on customer service.

4.1 Batch processing

Batch processing involves transactions being **grouped** and **stored** before being processed at regular intervals, such as daily, weekly or monthly. Because data is not input as soon as it is received the system will not always be up-to-date.

Transactions will be collected up over a period of time, and will then be dealt with together in a batch. Some **delay** in processing the transactions must therefore be acceptable.

The lack of up-to-date information means batch processing is usually not suitable for systems involving customer contact. Batch processing is suitable for internal, regular tasks such as payroll.

4.2 Example: batch processing of sales ledger application

A company operates a computerised sales ledger using batch processing based on paper records. The main stages of processing are as follows.

Step 1 Sales invoices are hand-written in a numbered invoice book (in triplicate ie three copies per invoice). At the end of the day all invoices are clipped together and a batch control slip is attached. The sales clerk allocates the next unused batch number from the batch control book. He or she enters the batch number on the control slip, together with the total number of documents and the total value of the invoices. These details are also entered in the control book.

Step 2 The batch of invoices is then passed to the accounts department for processing. An accounts clerk records the batch as having been received.

Step 3 The relevant account codes are written on the invoices and control slip. Codes are checked, and the batch is keyed into the computerised sales ledger system

Step 4 The clerk reconciles the totals on the batch control slip with the totals for valid and rejected data.

Step 5 The ledger update program is run to post data to the relevant accounts.

Step 6 A report is printed showing the total of invoices posted to the ledger and the clerk reconciles this to the batch totals.

Step 7 All rejected transaction records are carefully investigated and followed up, usually to be amended and then re-input with the next processing run.

4.3 On-line processing

On-line processing involves transactions being input and processed immediately, in 'real time'. On-line refers to a machine which is under the **direct control** of the main **processor** for that system. (The term 'on-line' is also used to describe an active Internet connection.)

On-line, real time processing is appropriate when immediate processing is required, and the delay implicit in batch processing would not be acceptable.

On-line systems are practically the **norm** in modern business. **Examples** include the following.

(a) As a sale is made in a department store or a supermarket, the item barcode is scanned on the **point of sale terminal** and the stock records are updated immediately.

(b) In **banking and credit card** systems whereby customer details are often maintained in a real-time environment. There can be immediate access to customer balances, credit position etc and authorisation for withdrawals (or use of a credit card).

(c) **Travel agents**, **airlines** and **theatre ticket** agencies all use real-time systems. Once a hotel room, plane seat or theatre seat is booked up everybody on the system must know about it immediately so that they do not sell the same holiday or seat to two (or more) different customers.

The workings of both batch and on-line processing methods are shown in the following diagram.

Batch processing and on-line processing

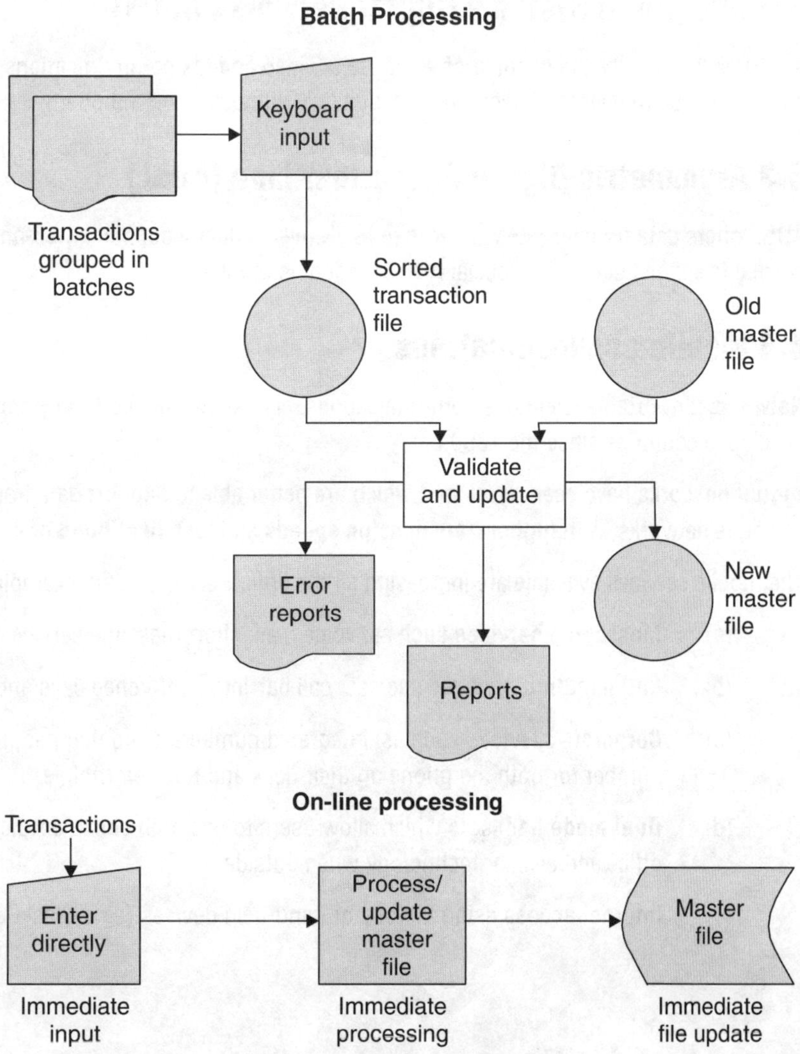

5 Developments in communications

In this section we discuss some of the most significant developments in communications, and the impact these developments have had on the way organisations operate.

Key terms

Digital means 'of digits or numbers'. Digital information is information in a coded (binary) form.

Information in **analogue** form uses continuously variable signals.

5.1 Modems and digital transmission

New technologies require **transmission systems** capable of delivering substantial quantities of data at great speed.

For data transmission through the existing 'analogue' telephone network to be possible, there has to be a device at each end of the telephone line that can convert (MOdulate) the data from digital form to analogue form, and (DEModulate) from analogue form to digital form, depending on whether the data is being sent out or received along the telephone line. This conversion of data is done by devices called **modems**.

More recent communication technologies such as ISDN and ADSL (see below) provide data transmission speeds for superior than possible using standard modems and telephone lines. These faster communication technologies are often collectively referred to as **broadband**.

5.2 Integrated Systems Digital Networks (ISDN)

An ISDN line enables the sending of voice, data, video and fax communications from a single desktop computer system over the telecommunication link, without using a modem.

5.3 Asymmetric Digital Subscriber Line (ADSL)

ADSL offers data transfer rates faster than ISDN over ordinary copper wires-and simultaneous of the normal telephone service. A special ADSL modem is required.

5.4 Mobile communications

Networks for portable telephone communications, also known as '**cellular phones**', have boomed in developed countries since the 1990s.

Digital networks have been developed which are better able to support data transmission than the older analogue networks, with **higher transmission speeds** and **less likelihood of data corruption**.

The mobile services available are increasing all the time. Here are some examples.

(a) **Messaging services** such as: voice mail; short message service (SMS) or 'text messaging'

(b) **Call handling services** such as: call barring, conference calls and call divert

(c) **Corporate services** such as: integrated numbering, so that people have a single contact number for both the phone on their desk and for their mobile.

(d) **Dual mode handsets** which allow users to use both cheap cordless technology when in the office and cellular technology when outside.

(e) **Internet access** using laptops or hand-held devices (eg a BlackBerry for wireless e-mail).

5.5 Voice messaging systems

Voice messaging systems answer and route telephone calls. Typically, when a call is answered a **recorded message** tells the caller to dial the extension required, or to hold if they want to speak to the operator. Sometimes other options are offered, such as 'press 2 if you want to know about X service and 3 if you want to know about Y'.

Such systems **work well** if callers often have **similar needs** and these can be accurately anticipated. They can be **frustrating** for callers with **non-standard enquiries**. There should be an option that allows callers to speak to somebody to explain non-standard queries eg 'Press 0 to speak to an operator /customer service representative.

5.6 Computer Telephony Integration (CTI)

Computer Telephony Integration (CTI) systems **gather information about callers** such as their telephone number and customer account number or demographic information (age, income, interests etc). This is stored on a customer database and can be **called up and sent to the screen** of the person dealing with the call, perhaps before the call has even been put through.

5.7 Computer bulletin boards

A computer bulletin board consists of a central mailbox or area on a computer server where people can **deposit messages** for everyone to see, and, in turn, **read what other people have left** in the system.

Bulletin boards can be appropriate for a team of individuals at different locations to compare notes. It becomes a way of keeping track of progress on a **project** between routine team meetings.

5.8 Videoconferencing

Videoconferencing is the use of computer and communications technology to **conduct meetings**.

Videoconferencing has become increasingly common as the Internet and webcams have brought the service to desktop PCs at reasonable cost. More expensive systems feature a **separate room with several video screens**, which show the images of those participating in a meeting.

5.9 Electronic Data Interchange (EDI)

EDI is a form of computer-to-computer **data** interchange. Instead of sending each other reams of paper in the form of invoices, statements and so on, details of inter-company transactions are sent via telecoms links, **avoiding the need for output** and paper at the sending end, and **for re-keying of data** at the receiving end.

5.10 Electronic Funds Transfer (EFT)

EFT describes a system whereby organisations are able to use their computer system to **transfer funds** – for example make payments to a **supplier**, or pay salaries into **employees'** bank accounts.

6 Deciding on a communication tool

FAST FORWARD

The **channel of communication** will impact on the effectiveness of the communication process. The characteristics of the message will determine what communication tool is best for a given situation.

Technological advances have increased the number of communication tools available. The features and limitations of ten common tools are outlined in the following table.

Tool	Features / Advantages	Limitations
Conversation	Usually unstructured so can discuss a wide range of topics Requires little or no planning Gives a real impression of feelings	Temptation to lose focus May be easily forgotten
Meeting	Allows multiple opinions to be expressed Can discuss and resolve a wide range of issues	Can highlight differences and become time-wasting confrontations 'Louder' personalities may dominate Costly in terms of personnel time A focused agenda and an effective Chair should minimise the impact of these limitations
Presentation	Complex ideas can be communicated Visual aids such as slides can help the communication process The best presentations will leave a lasting impression	Requires planning and skill Poorly researched or presented material can lead to audience resentment
Telephone	Good for communications that do not require (or you would prefer not to have) a permanent written record Can provide some of the 'personal touch' to people in geographically remote locations Conference calls allow multiple participants	Receiver may not be available; 'phone-tag' is a frustrating pass-time! (Voice-mail may help) Can be disruptive to receiver if in the middle of another task No written record gives greater opportunity for misunderstandings
Facsimile	Enables reports and messages to reach remote locations quickly	Easily seen by others Fax machine may not be checked for messages Complex images do not transmit well
Memorandum	Provides a permanent record Adds formality to internal communications	If used too often or the message is too general people may ignore it Can come across as impersonal

Tool	Features / Advantages	Limitations
Letter	Provides a permanent record of an external message Adds formality to external communications Use a clear, simple structure, eg... • Letterhead • Reference or heading • Date • Recipient name and address • Greeting/salutation • Subject • Substance • Close • Signature • Author name and position • Enclosure/copy reference	If inaccurate or poorly presented provides a permanent record of incompetence May be slow to arrive depending on distance and the postal service
Report	Provides a permanent, often comprehensive written record Use a clear, simple structure. There is no one correct format. An example that could be adapted to suit the report requirements is... • Meaningful Title • Author name and position • Purpose/Terms of Reference • Procedure followed • Findings • Conclusion / Recommendations Where necessary use a hierarchy of headings to aid clarity, eg... • 1 Section heading • 1.1 Related paragraph • 1.1(a) Related sub-paragraph	Complex messages may be misunderstood in the absence of immediate feedback Reports that reach (necessarily) negative conclusions can lead to negative impressions of the author
Electronic mail	Provides a written record Attachments (eg Reports or other documents) can be included Quick – regardless of location Automated 'Read receipts' or a simple request to acknowledge receipt by return message mean you know if the message has been received Can be sent to multiple recipients easily, can be forwarded on to others	Requires some computer literacy to use effectively People may not check their e-mail regularly Lack of privacy – can be forwarded on without your knowledge Long messages (more than one 'screen') may best be dealt with via other means, or as attached documents

Tool	Features / Advantages	Limitations
Video-conference	This is in effect a meeting conducted using a computer and video system Provides more of a personal touch than the telephone, but less than a 'physical' meeting Some non-verbal messages (eg gestures) will be received	The hardware is expensive compared to telephone May be dominated by the most confident participant(s) Cross-border cultural differences may be unintentionally ignored as participants feel 'at home' Image quality is often poor – resulting in not much more than an expensive telephone conference call!

7 System architectures

The term **system architecture** refers to the way in which the various components of an information system are linked together, and the way they relate to each other.

(a) At one extreme an organisation may have just a **single** 'stand-alone' computer.

(b) At the other extreme, an organisation may have **hundreds** of computers, all able to be used simultaneously and to communicate with each other.

7.1 Networks

Key term

The term **network** is general term used to describe any computing architecture that includes connected **autonomous** processors.

There are two main network architectures – client-server and peer-to-peer.

FAST FORWARD

The main network architectures are **client-server** and **peer-to-peer**. Client-server systems aim to ensure best utilisation of computing resources.

7.2 Client-server architecture

The term 'client-server' is a way of describing the relationship between the devices in a network. 'Client-server' describes a network architecture in which each computer or process on the network is either a client or a server.

Servers are powerful computers or processes dedicated to managing disk drives (file servers), printers (print servers), or network traffic (network servers).

Clients are PCs or workstations on which users run applications. Clients rely on servers for resources, such as files, devices, and sometimes processing power.

Key terms

A **client** is a machine which requests a service, for example a PC running a spreadsheet application which the user wishes to print out.

A **server** is a machine which is dedicated to providing a particular function or service requested by a client. Servers include file servers (see below), print servers, e-mail servers and fax servers.

7.2.1 Client-server hardware

A typical client-server system includes three **hardware** elements.

- A central server (sometimes called the corporate server)
- Local servers (sometimes called departmental servers)
- Client workstations

A server computer (such as a file server) may be a powerful PC or a minicomputer. As its name implies, it **serves** the rest of the network offering a generally-accessible hard disk and sometimes offering other resources, such as a **shared printer**.

A client-server architecture is shown below.

Client-server architecture

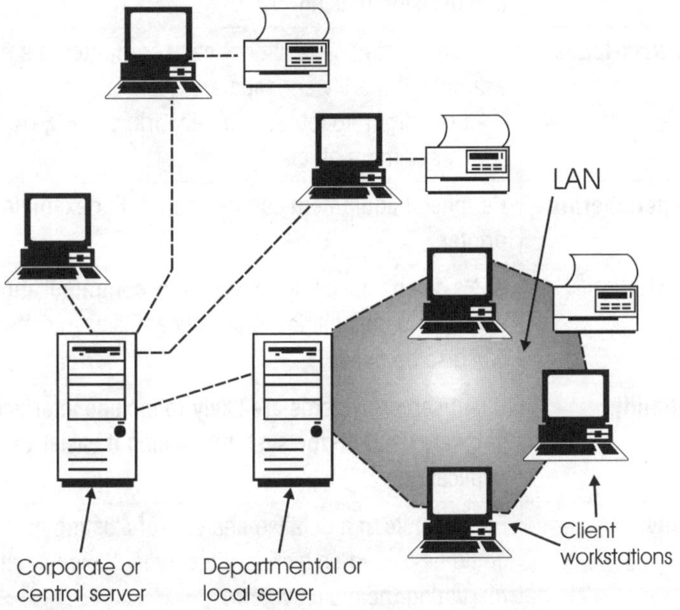

7.2.2 Client-server software

Client-server systems aim to locate software where it is most efficient – based on the number and location of users requiring access and the processing power required. There are three main types of software applications.

(a) **Corporate applications** are run on the central (or corporate) server. These applications are accessed by people spread throughout the organisation, and often require significant processor power (eg a centralised Management Information System).

(b) **Local applications** are used by users within a particular section or department, and therefore are run on the relevant local or departmental server (eg a credit-scoring expert system may be held on the server servicing the loans department of a bank).

(c) **Client applications** may be unique to an individual user, eg a specialised Executive Support System (ESS). Other software that may be run on client hardware could include 'office' type software, such as spreadsheet and word processing programs. Even though many people may use these applications, individual copies of programs are often held on client hardware – to utilise the processor power held on client machines.

7.3 The advantages of a client-server architecture

Advantage	Comment
Greater resilience	Processing is spread over several computers. If one server breaks down, other locations can carry on processing.
Scalability	They are highly scalable. Instead of having to buy computing power in large quantities you can buy just the amount of power you need to do the job.
Shared programs and data	Program and data files held on a file server can be shared by all the PCs in the network. With stand-alone PCs, each computer would have its own data files, and there might be unnecessary duplication of data. A system where everyone uses the same data will help to improve data processing and decision making.
Shared work-loads	The processing capability of each computer in a network can be utilised. For example, if there were separate stand-alone PCs, A might do job 1, B might do job 2 and C might do job 3. In a network, any PC, (A, B or C) could do any job (1, 2 or 3). This is more efficient.
Shared peripherals	Peripheral equipment can be shared. For example, five PCs might share a single printer.
Communication	LANs can be linked up to the office communications network, thus adding to the processing capabilities in an office. Electronic mail, calendar and diary facilities can also be used.
Compatibility	Client/server systems are likely to include interfaces between different types of software used on the system, making it easier to move information between applications.
Flexibility	For example, if a detailed analysis of existing data is required, a copy of this data could be placed on a separate server, allowing data to be manipulated without disrupting the main system.

7.4 The disadvantages of a client/server architecture

The client/server approach has some drawbacks.

(a) A single **mainframe** may be more efficient performing some tasks, in certain circumstances. For example, where the process involves routine processing of a very large number (eg millions) of transactions.

(b) It is easier to **control** and **maintain** a centralised system. In particular it is easier to keep data **secure**.

(c) It may be **cheaper** to 'tweak' an existing mainframe system rather than throwing it away and starting from scratch: for example it may be possible to give it a graphical user interface and to make data exchangeable between Windows and non-Windows based applications.

(d) Each location may need its own **network administrator** to keep things running smoothly – there may be unnecessary duplication of **skills** and staff.

(e) Duplication of information may be a problem if individual users do not follow a disciplined approach.

7.5 Network topology

Key term

Topology means how a computer network is physically arranged.

FAST FORWARD

Three popular **network topologies** are **star**, **ring** and **tree**.

7.5.1 Star networks

Star networks have one central computer that acts as a service provider (server) to other computers. All communication on the network passes through the central computer.

A start network

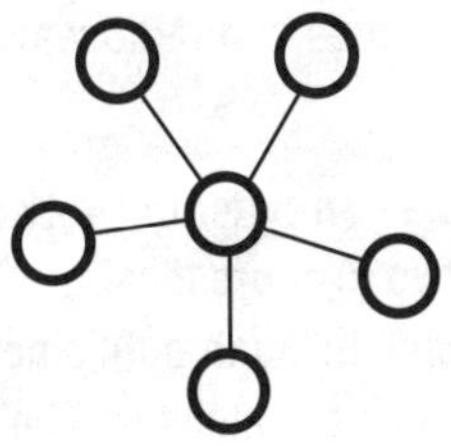

7.5.2 Ring networks

A ring network consists of a number of computers each linked to two others in the network. As with the Star topology, any computer is able to communicate with any other in the network – although to achieve this it may require data passing via other computers.

A ring network

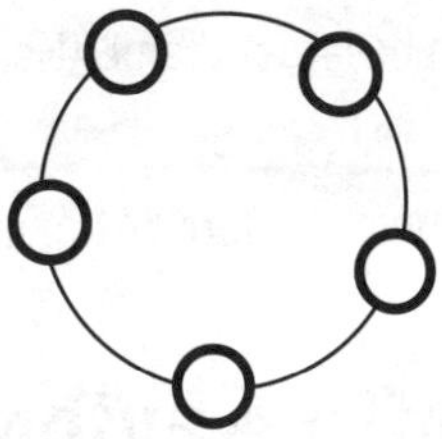

7.5.3 Tree networks

A tree network comprises a hierarchy of computers (or processors). The processor at the top of the tree is the most powerful – often a mainframe. Computers at lower levels are less powerful, for example microcomputers (PCs). Communication and data transfer must follow an existing path (eg processors on the second level in the diagram below are able to transfer data between the top computer and lower level processors).

A tree network

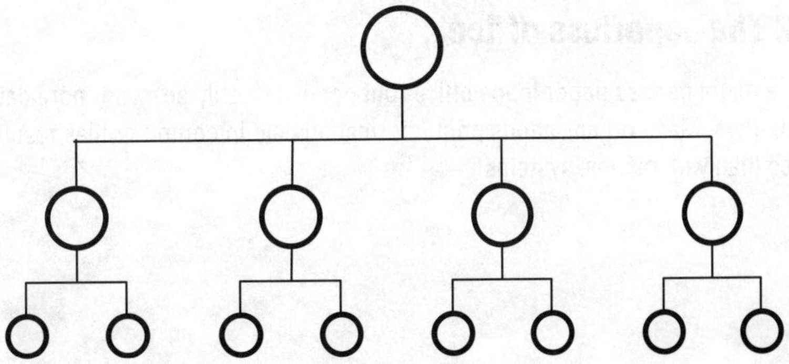

7.6 Peer-to-peer architecture

'Peer-to-peer' refers to a type of network in which each workstation has equivalent capabilities and responsibilities. This differs from client/server architectures, in which some computers are dedicated to serving the others. Peer-to-peer networks are generally simpler, but they usually do not offer the same performance under heavy workloads.

7.7 Local Area Networks (LANs) and Wide Area Networks (WANs)

Client-server and peer-to-peer describe the relationship between devices within a network. Another way of classifying networks is the geographical area that they cover.

A local area network (LAN) is a computer network that spans a relatively small area. Most LANs are confined to a single building or group of buildings. However, one LAN can be connected to other LANs over any distance via telephone lines and radio waves. A system of LANs connected in this way is called a wide-area network (WAN).

A wide-area network (WAN) is a computer network that spans a relatively large geographical area. Typically, a WAN consists of two or more local-area networks (LANs). Computers connected to a wide-area network are often connected through public networks, such as the telephone system. They can also be connected through leased lines or satellites. The largest WAN in existence is the Internet.

The **main differences** between a LAN and a WAN are as follows.

(a) The **geographical area** covered by a WAN is greater, not being limited to a single building or site.

(b) WANs will send data over **telecommunications links.**

(c) WANs will often use a **larger computer** as a file server.

(d) WANs will often be larger than LANs, with **more terminals or computers** linked to the network.

(e) A WAN can link two or more LANs, using **gateways**.

8 The effect of office automation on business

Office automation has an enormous effect on business. We discuss some of the most significant effects in this section.

8.1 Routine processing

The processing of routine data can be done in **bigger volumes**, at **greater speed** and with **greater accuracy** than with non-automated, manual systems.

8.2 The paperless office

There might be **less paper** in the office (but not necessarily so) with more data-processing done using computers. Many organisations print information held in computer files resulting in more paper in the office than with manual systems!

8.3 Management information

The nature and **quality of management information** has changed.

(a) Managers are likely to have **access to more information** – for example from a database. Information is also likely to be **more accurate, reliable and up to date**. The range of **management reports** is likely to be wider and their content more comprehensive.

(b) **Planning activities** should be more thorough, with the use of **models** (eg spreadsheets for budgeting) and **sensitivity analysis**.

(c) Information for **control** should be more readily available. For example, a computerised sales ledger system should provide prompt reminder letters for late payers, and might incorporate other credit control routines. Stock systems, especially for companies with stocks distributed around several different warehouses, should provide better stock control.

(d) **Decision making** by managers can be helped by **decision support systems**.

8.4 Organisation structure

The **organisation structure** might change. PC networks give local office managers a means of setting up a good **local management information system**, and **localised data processing** while retaining access to **centrally-held databases** and programs. Office automation can therefore encourage a tendency towards **decentralisation** of authority within an organisation.

On the other hand, such systems help **head office** to **keep in touch** with what is going on in local offices. Head office can therefore readily monitor and control the activities of individual departments, and retain a co-ordinating influence.

8.5 Customer service

Office automation, in some organisations, results in **better customer service**. When an organisation receives large numbers of telephone enquiries from customers, the staff who take the calls should be able to provide a prompt and helpful service if they have **on-line access** to the organisation's data files.

8.6 Homeworking or remote working

Advances in communications technology have, for some tasks, **reduced the need for the actual presence of an individual in the office**.

8.6.1 Advantages for the organisation

The **advantages to the organisation** of homeworking are as follows.

(a) **Cost savings on space**. Office rental costs and other charges can be very expensive. If firms can move some of their employees on to a homeworking basis, money can be saved.

(b) A **larger pool of labour**. The possibility of working at home might attract more applicants for clerical positions, especially from people who have other demands on their time (eg going to and from school) which cannot be fitted round standard office hours.

(c) If the homeworkers are **freelance**, then the organisation **avoids the need to pay them** when there is insufficient work, when they are sick, on holiday etc.

8.6.2 Advantages for the individual

The **advantages to the individual** of homeworking are as follows.

(a) No time and money is wasted commuting.
(b) Work can be organised around domestic commitments.

8.6.3 Possible disadvantages for the organisation

Problems for the organisation might be as follows.

(a) **Co-ordination** of the work of different homeworkers. The job design should ensure that homeworkers perform to the required standard.

(b) **Training**. If a homeworker needs a lot of help on a task, this implies that the task has not been properly explained.

(c) **Culture**. A homeworker is relatively isolated from the office and therefore, it might be assumed, from the firm. However, questions of loyalty and commitment do not apply for an organisation's sales force, whose members are rarely in the office.

(d) A loss of direct **control**.

8.6.4 Possible disadvantages for the individual

Problems for homeworkers may include:

- Isolation
- Interruptions
- Adequate space
- Possibly fewer employment rights (if employed on a 'casual' basis)

8.7 Technological change

Technological change can affect the activities of organisations as follows.

(a) **The type of products or services that are made and sold**. For example, consumer markets have seen the emergence of home computers, compact discs and satellite dishes for receiving satellite TV; industrial markets have seen the emergence of custom-built microchips, robots and local area networks for office information systems.

(b) **The way in which products are made**. There is a continuing trend towards the use of modern labour-saving production equipment, such as robots. The manufacturing environment is undergoing rapid changes with the growth of advanced manufacturing technology. These are changes in both apparatus and technique.

(c) **The way in which services are provided**. High-street banks encourage customers to use 'hole-in-the-wall' cash dispensers, or telephone or PC banking. Most larger shops now use computerised **Point of Sale terminals** at cash desks. Many organisations are starting to use **e-commerce**: selling products and services over the Internet.

(d) **The way in which markets are identified**. Database systems make it much easier to analyse the market place.

(e) **The way in which employees are mobilised**. Computerisation encourages delayering of organisational hierarchies, and greater workforce empowerment and skills. Using technology frequently requires changes in working methods. This is a change in organisation.

8.7.1 Possible benefits from utilising technology

The **benefits of technological change** might therefore be as follows.

- To cut production costs
- To develop better quality products and services
- To develop new products and services
- To provide products or services to customers more quickly or effectively
- To free staff from repetitive work and to tap their creativity

8.7.2 Flexibility

Organisations that operate in an environment where the pace of technological change is very fast **must be flexible enough to adapt to change quickly** and must **plan** for change and innovation. Technological change can be planned for by **developing strategies** for improved productivity and for innovation.

8.8 The importance of management

It is argued that **success or failure** in implementing IT is a result not so much of the systems themselves but the **management effort** behind them. Information systems implementations may not bring the benefits expected for a variety of reasons. Some examples are:

(a) The system does not address the real **problem** (eg the use of IT has not been thought through in the context of the wider organisational context).

(b) **Senior management** do not provide sufficient backing or involvement.

(c) **User needs are ignored** in design and development.

If an organisation develops and follows a realistic **strategy** for information systems and technology then there is less chance that these problems will arise.

8.9 Types of information system

Exam focus point

The types of information system are not referred to in the syllabus or teaching guide for this paper (they are referred to specifically in Paper 3.4), so are unlikely to be specifically examined. However, the Paper 2.1 teaching guide does refer to 'current trends in IT' and also how IT may be used to assist in achieving business objectives – the information in this section may be useful in that context.

FAST FORWARD

Different **types of information systems** exist with different characteristics – reflecting the different **roles** they perform.

Although opinions differ and not all categories are agreed, we can identify seven **types of information system**.

- Executive Support Systems (ESS)
- Management Information Systems (MIS)
- Decision-Support Systems (DSS)
- Expert systems
- Knowledge Work Systems (KWS)
- Office Automation Systems (OAS)
- Transaction Processing Systems (TPS)

8.10 Executive Support Systems (ESS)

Key term

> An **Executive Support System (ESS)** pools data from internal and external sources and makes information available to senior managers in an easy-to-use form. ESS help senior managers make strategic, unstructured decisions.

An ESS should provide senior managers with easy access to key **internal and external** information. The system summarises and tracks strategically critical information, possibly drawn from internal MIS and DSS, but also including data from external sources eg competitors, legislation, external databases such as Reuters.

An ESS usually includes flexible but sophisticated data analysis and modelling tools. A model of a typical ESS is shown below.

An Executive Support System (ESS)

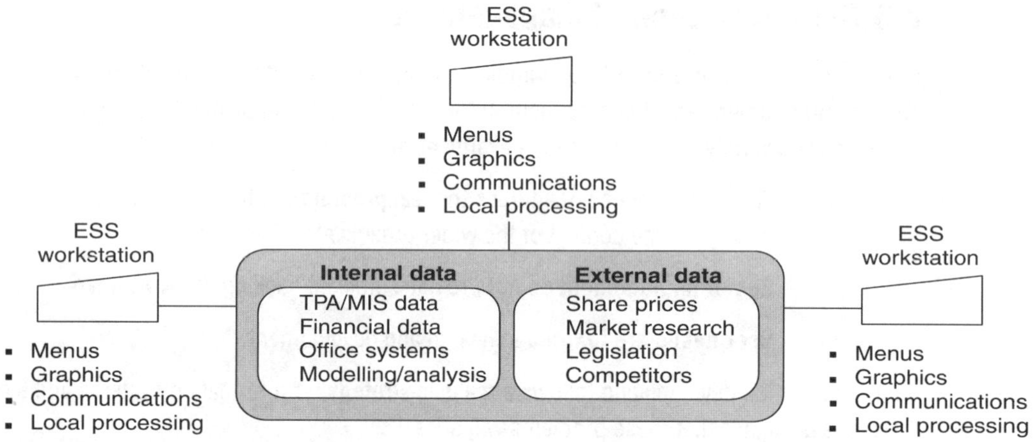

8.11 Management Information Systems (MIS)

Key term

> **Management Information Systems (MIS)** convert data from mainly internal sources into information (eg summary reports, exception reports). This information enables managers to make timely and effective decisions for planning, directing and controlling the activities for which they are responsible.

An MIS provides regular reports and (usually) on-line access to the organisation's current and historical performance.

MIS usually transform data from underlying transaction processing systems into summarised files that are used as the basis for management reports.

MIS have the following characteristics:

- Support **structured** decisions at operational and management control levels
- Designed to report on **existing** operations
- Have little analytical capability
- Relatively **inflexible**
- Have an **internal** focus

8.12 Decision Support Systems (DSS)

Key term

Decision Support Systems (DSS) combine data and analytical models or data analysis tools to support semi-structured and unstructured decision making.

DSS are used by management to assist in making decisions on issues which are subject to high levels of uncertainty about the problem, the various **responses** which management could undertake or the likely **impact** of those actions.

Decision support systems are intended to provide a wide range of alternative information gathering and analytical tools with a major emphasis upon **flexibility** and **user-friendliness**.

DSS have more analytical power than other systems enabling them to analyse and condense large volumes of data into a form that aids managers make decisions. The objective is to allow the manager to consider a number of **alternatives** and evaluate them under a variety of potential conditions.

8.13 Expert systems

Key term

An **expert system** is a computer program that captures human expertise in a limited domain of knowledge.

Expert system software uses a **knowledge base** that consists of **facts, concepts** and the **relationships** between them on a particular domain of knowledge and uses pattern-matching techniques to 'solve' problems.

For example, many financial institutions now use expert systems to process straightforward **loan applications**. The user enters certain key facts into the system such as the loan applicant's name and most recent addresses, their income and monthly outgoings, and details of other loans. The system will then:

(a) **Check the facts** given against its database to see whether the applicant has a good previous credit record.

(b) **Perform calculations** to see whether the applicant can afford to repay the loan.

(c) **Make a judgement** as to what extent the loan applicant fits the lender's profile of a good risk (based on the lender's previous experience).

(d) Suggest a decision.

An organisation can **use an expert system** when a number of **conditions** are met.

(a) The problem is **well defined**.
(b) The expert can define **rules** by which the problem can be solved.
(c) The **investment** in an expert system is cost-justified.

8.14 Knowledge Work Systems (KWS)

Key terms

Knowledge Work Systems (KWS) are information systems that facilitate the creation and integration of new knowledge into an organisation.

Knowledge Workers are people whose jobs consist of primarily creating new information and knowledge. They are often members of a profession such as doctors, engineers, lawyers and scientists.

KWS help knowledge workers create new knowledge and expertise. Examples include:

- Computer Aided Design (CAD)
- Computer Aided Manufacturing (CAM)
- Specialised financial software that analyses trading situations

8.15 Office Automation Systems (OAS)

Key term

Office Automation Systems (OAS) are computer systems designed to increase the productivity of data and information workers.

OAS support the major activities performed in a typical office such as document management, facilitating communication and managing data. Examples include:

- Word processing, desktop publishing, and digital filing systems
- E-mail, voice mail, videoconferencing, groupware, intranets, schedulers
- Spreadsheets, desktop databases

8.16 Transaction Processing Systems (TPS)

Key term

A **Transaction Processing System (TPS)** performs and records routine transactions.

TPS are used for **routine tasks** in which data items or transactions must be processed so that operations can continue. TPS support most business functions in most types of organisations. The following table shows a range of TPS applications.

Transaction processing systems					
	Sales/ marketing systems	**Manufacturing /production systems**	**Finance/ accounting systems**	**Human resources systems**	**Other types (eg university)**
Major functions of system	• Sales management • Market research • Promotion Pricing • New products	• Scheduling • Purchasing Shipping/ receiving • Engineering • Operations	• Budgeting • General ledger • Billing • Management accounting	• Personnel records • Benefits • Salaries • Labour relations • Training	• Admissions • Student academic records • Course records • Graduates
Major application systems	• Sales order information system • Market research system • Pricing system	• Materials resource planning • Purchase order control • Engineering • Quality control	• General ledger • Accounts receivable /payable • Budgeting • Funds management	• Payroll • Employee records • Employee benefits • Career path systems	• Registration • Student record • Curriculum/ class control systems • Benefactor information system

BPP PROFESSIONAL EDUCATION

8.17 Intranets and extranets

Organisations are increasingly using **intranets** and **extranets** to **disseminate information**.

(a) An **intranet** is like a mini version of the Internet (covered in the following section). Organisation members use networked computers to access information held on a server. The user interface is a browser – similar to those used on the Internet. The intranet offers access to information on a wide variety of topics, and often includes access to the Internet.

(a) An **extranet** is an intranet that is accessible to **authorised outsiders**, using a valid username and password. The user name will have access rights attached – determining which parts of the extranet can be viewed. Extranets are becoming a very popular means for business partners to exchange information.

9 The Internet

Key term

The **Internet** is a global network connecting millions of computers.

The Internet is the name given to the technology that allows any computer with a telecommunications link to **send and receive information** from any other suitably equipped computer.

The **World Wide Web** is the multimedia element which provides facilities such as full-colour, graphics, sound and video. Web-sites are points within the network created by members who wish to provide an information point for searchers to visit and benefit by the provision of information and/or by entering into a transaction.

Almost all companies have a **Website** on the Internet. A site is a collection of screens providing **information in text and graphic form**, any of which can be viewed simply by clicking the appropriate button, word or image on the screen.

FAST FORWARD

Many organisations are now utilising **the Internet** as a means of gathering and disseminating information, and conducting transactions.

9.1 Current uses of the Internet

The scope and potential of the Internet are still developing. Its uses already embrace the following:

(a) **Dissemination** of information.

(b) **Product/service development** – through almost instantaneous test marketing.

(c) **Transaction processing** (electronic commerce or e-commerce) – both business-to-business and business-to-consumer.

(d) **Relationship enhancement** – between various groups of stakeholders.

(e) **Recruitment** and job search – involving organisations worldwide.

(f) **Entertainment** – including music, humour, art, games and some less wholesome pursuits!

It is estimated that approximately 50% of households in the UK currently have Internet access.

The Internet provides opportunities to organise for and to automate tasks which would previously have required more costly interaction with the organisation. These have often been called low-touch or zero-touch approaches.

9.1.1 Websites

Tasks which a **website may automate** include:

(a) **Frequently-Asked Questions (FAQs)**: carefully-structured sets of answers can deal with many customer interactions.

(b) **Status checking**: major service enquiries (Where is my order? When will the engineer arrive? What is my bank balance?) can also be automated, replacing high-cost human service processes, and also providing the opportunity to proactively offer better service and new services.

(c) **Keyword search**: the ability to search provides web users with opportunities to find information in large and complex websites.

(d) **Wizards** (interview style interface) and **intelligent algorithms**: these can help diagnosis, which is one of the major elements of service support.

(e) **E-mail and systems to route and track inbound e-mail**: the ability to route and/or to provide automatic responses will enable organisations to deal with high volumes of e-mail from actual and potential customers.

(f) **Bulletin boards**: these enable customers to interact with each other, thus facilitating self-activated customer service and also the opportunity for product/service referral. Cisco in particular has created communities of Cisco users who help each other – thus reducing the service costs for Cisco itself.

(g) **Call-back buttons**: these enable customers to speak to someone in order to deal with and resolve a problem; the more sophisticated systems allow the call-centre operator to know which web pages the users were consulting at the time.

9.2 Problems with the Internet

To a large extent the Internet has grown organically **without any formal organisation**. There are specific communication rules, but it is not **owned** by any one body and there are no clear guidelines on how it should develop.

The **quality** of much of the information on the Internet leaves much to be desired.

Speed is a major issue. Data only downloads onto the user's PC at the speed of the slowest telecommunications link – downloading data can be a painfully **slow** procedure.

So much information and entertainment is available that employers worry that their **staff will spend too much time** browsing through non-work-related sites.

Connecting an information system to the Internet exposes the system to numerous **security issues**. We will explore these issues in Chapter 13.

Chapter Roundup

- In many circumstances, **manual** systems are **less productive** than computerised systems.
- **Computers** can be classified as supercomputers, mainframes, minicomputers and microcomputers or PCs.
- The amount of **RAM** and the **processor speed** are key determinants of computer performance. Hard drive size is another important factor.
- Four types of software are:
  - The **operating system**
  - **Utilities**
  - **Off-the-shelf applications**
  - **Bespoke applications**
- Both manual and computer data processing can be divided into two broad types: **batch processing** and **real-time processing**. Batch processing systems are becoming less common, particularly if the process concerned impacts on customer service.
- The **channel of communication** will impact on the effectiveness of the communication process. The characteristics of the message will determine what communication tool is best for a given situation.
- The main network architectures are **client-server** and **peer-to-peer**. Client-server systems aim to ensure best utilisation of computing resources.
- Three popular **network topologies** are **star**, **ring** and **tree**.
- Different **types of information systems** exist with different characteristics – reflecting the different **roles** they perform.
- Many organisations are now utilising **the Internet** as a means of gathering and disseminating information, and conducting transactions.

Quick Quiz

1. List four reasons why manual office systems maybe less beneficial than computerised systems.
2. What is RAM?
3. List four types of software.
4. Distinguish between batch and real-time processing.
5. What is EDI and how could it encourage a closer relationship between organisations?
6. Distinguish between an intranet and an extranet.
7. List four general business uses of the Internet.
8. List five tasks a website may automate.
9. Do you agree with the statement 'information derived from the Internet is unreliable'? Justify your answer.

Answers to Quick Quiz

1 Manual systems may be slower, more prone to error, require more labour and may be unable to handle large volumes of data. (This assumes the computerised system is operating correctly, is reliable and that staff know how to utilise it fully.)

2 RAM stands for Random Access Memory. It holds the data and programs in current use. RAM and processor speed are important indicators of processing power.

3 Operating systems, utilities, off-the-shelf packages, bespoke packages.

4 Batch processing is the processing as a group of a number of transactions of a similar kind in a batch. Real-time processing is the continual receiving and processing of data. Real-time processing uses an 'on-line' computer system to interrogate or update files as requested, rather than batching for subsequent processing.

5 Electronic Data Interchange (EDI) is a form of computer-to-computer data interchange. Instead of sending reams of paper in the form of invoices, statements and so on, details of transactions are sent via telecoms links. An efficient EDI link encourages a closer relationship between organisations as it encourages organisations to do business with those organisations it has EDI links with. Faster document transmission should reduce order lead times.

6 An intranet is available to those inside an organisation – members use networked computers to access information held on a server. The user interface is a browser – similar to those used on the Internet. An extranet is an intranet that is accessible to authorised outsiders. Extranets are becoming a very popular means for business partners to exchange information.

7 [Four of]

External e-mail.
Dissemination of information.
Product/service development – through almost instantaneous test marketing.
Transaction processing (electronic commerce or e-commerce).
Relationship en enhancement – between various groups of stakeholders.

Recruitment and job search – involving organisations worldwide.

8 [Five of]

Frequently-Asked Questions (FAQs).
Status checking service enquiries.
Keyword search.
Recruitment and job search – involving organisations worldwide.
Bulletin boards that enable customers to interact with each other.
Call-back buttons that enable customers to request a customer services representative contacts them.

9 The Internet provides a means of accessing information from a wide range of organisations. Some of these organisations will provide good quality information (eg ACCA, BBC etc), others may provide information that proves to be unreliable. Who is behind the information is a more significant indicator of reliability than the fact that the information was transmitted over the Internet.

Now try the questions below from the Exam Question Bank

Number	Level	Marks	Time
Q7	Examination	20	36 mins
Q10	Examination	20	36 mins

The information systems function: Organisational issues

3

Topic list	Syllabus reference
1 Information systems department	1(b)
2 Centralisation and decentralisation	1(b)
3 Accounting issues	1(c)
4 Other organisational issues	1 (d), 2(a)
5 Outsourcing	1(b)

Introduction

We begin this chapter by looking at the different ways of **structuring or organising the information systems function.**

Later, we explore wider organisational issues including **accounting for the costs** associated with information systems.

The chapter concludes with the advantages and disadvantages of **outsourcing**.

Study guide

Part 1.2 – Delivering information systems; organisational arrangements

- Describe the traditional structure of a centralised information systems department and the roles and responsibilities of each function
- Explain the principles of a decentralised information systems function
- Discuss the advantages and disadvantages of centralising or decentralising the information systems function
- Explain the principles of outsourcing the information systems function
- Describe the advantages and disadvantages of outsourcing the information systems function

Part 1.3 – Delivering information systems; accounting issues

- Briefly describe the types of cost incurred delivering information systems (also see Chapter 14)
- Describe how the costs of the information systems function may be distributed between customer departments
- Explain the principles, benefits and drawbacks of cross-charging costs
- Discuss the issues raised by establishing the information systems function as a cost or profit centre
- Describe the advantages and disadvantages of establishing the information systems function as a separate company
- Explain the problems of accounting for shared infrastructure costs

Exam guide

The material covered in this chapter lends itself to both longer scenario type questions (eg a miss-match between organisation information requirements and the IS structure) and shorter Section B questions (eg charging out information system costs).

1 Information systems department

Most organisations choose to have an information systems department, or team responsible for the tasks and responsibilities associated with information systems. Information systems increasingly utilise information technology.

FAST FORWARD

At the head of the information systems/information technology function will be either the IS/IT manager, or the **IS/IT director**. This person will be responsible for:

- IS/IT strategy development
- IS/IT risk management
- Overseeing the steering committee
- The IS/IT infrastructure

At the head of the information systems/information technology function will be either the IS/IT manager, or the IS/IT director.

The IS/IT director would have responsibility for the following areas.

IS/IT director responsibility	Comment
IS/IT strategy development	The IS/IT strategy must compliment the overall strategy of the organisation. The strategy must also be achievable given budgetary constraints. Returns on investments in IS/IT should be monitored.
IS/IT risk management	This is a wide ranging area including legal risks, such as ensuring compliance with relevant data protection legislation, ensuring adequate IS/IT security measures and disaster recovery arrangements.
Steering committee	The IS/IT director should play a key role in a steering committee set up to oversee the role of IS/IT within the organisation. There is more on steering committees later in this chapter.
IS/IT infrastructure	Standards should be set for the purchase and use of hardware and software within the organisation.
Ensuring employees have the IS/IT support and tools they require	Efficient links are required between IS/IT staff and the rest of the organisation. Technical assistance should be easily obtainable.

An IS/IT director therefore requires a wide range of skills. The ideal person would possess technical know-how, excellent general management ability, a keen sense of business awareness and a good understanding of the organisations' operations.

1.1 IS/IT steering committee

FAST FORWARD

The general purpose of an IS/IT **steering committee** is to make decisions relating to the future use and development of IS/IT by the organisation.

The general purpose of an IS/IT steering committee would be to make decisions relating to the future use and development of IS/IT by the organisation. The steering committee should contain representatives from all departments of the organisation.

Common tasks of such a committee could include:

- Ensuring IS/IT activities comply with IS/IT strategy
- Ensuring IS/IT activities compliment the overall organisation strategy
- Ensuring resources committed to IS/IT are used effectively
- Monitoring IS/IT projects
- Providing leadership and guidance on IS/IT

Committee members should be chosen with the aim of ensuring the committee contains the wide range of technical and business knowledge required. The committee should liase closely with those affected by the decisions it will make.

1.2 Database administrator

FAST FORWARD

A key information systems role is that of **database administrator**. A database administrator is responsible for all data and information held within an organisation.

A key information systems role is that of database administrator. A database administrator is responsible for all data and information held within an organisation.

Key tasks of the database administrator include:

- Preparing and maintaining a record of all data held (the data dictionary)
- Co-ordinating data and information use to avoid duplication and maximise efficiency
- Analysing the data requirements of new applications
- Implementing and controlling procedures to protect data integrity
- Recording data ownership

1.3 Operations control

Operations control is concerned with ensuring IS/IT systems are working and available to users. Key tasks include:

- Maintaining the IS/IT infrastructure
- Monitoring network usage and managing network resources
- Keeping employees informed, eg advance warning of service interruptions
- Virus protection measures eg ensuring anti-virus software updates are loaded
- Fault fixing

1.4 Systems development staff

In medium to large organisations in is likely that the IS department will include staff with programming and systems analysis skills. Key tasks for staff involved in systems development include:

- Systems analysis
- Systems design and specification
- Systems testing
- Systems evaluation and review

1.5 Data processing staff

Over the past two decades the traditional centralised data processing department has become less common. Most departments now process their own data using on-line systems, rather than batching up transactions and forwarding paper copies of them to a centralised department for processing.

Staff involved in data processing today are spread throughout the organisation, for example a call centre employee may input an order, an accounts clerk may process journal entries etc. Accurate data entry skills and an understanding of the task they are performing are key skills.

1.6 Information centre staff

Key term

An **Information Centre (IC)** is a small unit of staff with a good technical awareness of computer systems, whose task is to provide a support function to computer users within the organisation.

FAST FORWARD

Information centres, sometimes referred to as **support centres**, are particularly useful in organisations which use distributed systems and so are likely to have hardware, data and software scattered throughout the organisation. The IC provides a centralised source of support and co-ordination.

1.6.1 Help

An IC usually offers a **Help Desk** to solve IT problems. Help may be via the telephone, e-mail, through a searchable knowledge base or in person.

Remote diagnostic software may be used which enables staff in the IC to take control of a computer and sort out the problem without leaving their desk.

The help desk needs sufficient staff and technical expertise to respond quickly and effectively to requests for help. IC staff should also maintain good relationships with hardware and software suppliers to ensure their maintenance staff are quickly on site when needed.

1.6.2 Problem solving

The IC will maintain a record of problems and identify those that occur most often. If the problem is that users do not know how to use the system, training is provided.

Training applications often contain analysis software, drawing attention to trainee progress and common problems. This information enables the IC to identify and address specific training needs more closely.

If the problem is with the system itself, a solution is found, either by modifying the system or by investment in new hardware or software.

1.6.3 Improvements

The IC may also be required to consider the viability of suggestions for improving the system, and to bring these improvements into effect.

1.6.4 Standards

The IC is also likely to be responsible for setting, and encouraging users to conform to, common **standards**.

(a) Hardware standards ensure that all of the equipment used in the organisation is compatible and can be put into use in different departments as needed.

(b) Software standards ensure that information generated by one department can easily be shared with and worked upon by other departments.

(c) Programming standards ensure that applications developed by individual end-users (for example complex spreadsheet macros) follow best practice and are easy to modify.

(d) Data processing standards ensure that certain conventions such as the format of file names are followed throughout the organisation. This facilitates sharing, storage and retrieval of information.

1.6.5 Security

The IC may help to preserve the security of data in various ways.

(a) It may develop utility programs and procedures to ensure that back-ups are made at regular intervals.

(b) The IC may help to preserve the company's systems from attack by computer viruses, for instance by ensuring that the latest versions of anti-virus software are available to all users, by reminding users regularly about the dangers of viruses, and by setting up and maintaining 'firewalls', which deny access to sensitive parts of the company's systems.

1.6.6 End-user applications development

An IC can help applications development by providing technical guidance to end-user developers and to encourage comprehensible and well-documented programs. Understandable programs can be maintained or modified more easily. Documentation provides a means of teaching others how the programs work. These efforts can greatly extend the usefulness and life of the programs that are developed.

2 Centralisation and decentralisation

FAST FORWARD

A **centralised** IS/IT department involves all IS/IT staff and functions being based out at a single central location, such as head office.

A **decentralised** IS/IT department involves IS/IT staff and functions being spread out throughout the organisation.

We now look at how the IS/IT department could be structured. There are two main options – centralised or decentralised.

Key term

A **centralised** IS/IT department involves all IS/IT staff and functions being based out at a single central location, such as head office.

A **decentralised** IS/IT department involves IS/IT staff and functions being spread out throughout the organisation.

There is no single 'best' structure for an IS/IT department – an organisation should consider its IS/IT requirements and the merits of each structure.

2.1 Advantages and disadvantages of a centralised IS/IT department

Possible **advantages** of a centralised IS/IT department include the following.

(a) Assuming centralised processing is used, there is only one set of files. Everyone uses the same data and information.

(b) It gives better security/control over data and files. It is easier to enforce standards.

(c) Head office is in a better position to know what is going on.

(d) There may be economies of scale available in purchasing computer equipment and supplies.

(e) Computer staff are in a single location, and more expert staff are likely to be employed. Career paths may be more clearly defined.

Disadvantages of a centralised IS/IT department.

(a) Local offices might have to wait for IS/IT services and assistance.
(b) Reliance on head office. Local offices are less self-sufficient.
(c) A system fault at head office will impact across the organisation.

2.2 Advantages and disadvantages of a decentralised IS/IT department

Advantages of a decentralised IS/IT department.

(a) Each office can introduce an information system specially **tailored** for its individual needs. Local changes in business requirements can be taken into account.

(b) Each office is more self-sufficient.

(c) Offices are likely to have quicker access to IS/IT support/advice.

(d) A decentralised structure is more likely to facilitate accurate IS/IT cost/overhead allocations.

Disadvantages of a decentralised IS/IT department.

(a) Control may be more difficult – different and uncoordinated information systems may be introduced.

(b) Self-sufficiency may encourage a lack of co-ordination between departments.

(c) Increased risk of data duplication, with different offices holding the same data on their own separate files.

3 Accounting issues

FAST FORWARD

Providing and maintaining information systems to deliver good quality information involves significant expenditure. There are three broad possibilities when **accounting for costs** related to information systems.

- IS costs are treated as an **administrative overhead**
- IS costs are **charged out at cost**
- IS costs are **charged out at market rates**

Providing and maintaining information systems to deliver good quality information involves significant expenditure. The costs incurred are summarised in the following table.

Capital costs	Revenue costs (one-off)	Revenue costs (ongoing)
• Hardware purchase • Cabling • System installation	• System development costs eg programmer and analyst fees, testing costs, file conversion costs etc • Initial training costs • Any redundancy costs attributable to the new system	• IS/IT staff costs • Communication and transmission costs • Power • Maintenance and support • Ongoing training • Consumables eg paper, printer ink, floppy disks, CDs

The organisation must account for the costs incurred providing and maintaining information systems. The IS charging system should encourage the efficient use of IS/IT resources. There are three broad possibilities when accounting for costs related to information systems.

- IS costs are treated as an **administrative overhead**
- IS costs are **charged out at cost**
- IS costs are **charged out at market rates**

3.1 Information technology as an administrative overhead

Under this system IT/IS costs are treated as a general administrative expense, and are not allocated to user departments.

Advantages of this approach are:

(a) It is simple and cheap to administer, as there is no charge out system to operate.

(b) May encourage innovation and experimentation as user-departments are more likely to demand better quality systems if they will not bear any cost.

(c) The relationship between IS staff and user departments is not subject to conflict over costs.

Disadvantages of this approach are:

(a) User departments may make unreasonable (and economically unjustifiable) demands.

(b) Any inefficiencies within the IS/IT department are less likely to be exposed – as user departments will not be monitoring cost levels.

(c) User departments may accept sub-standard service, as it is 'free'.

(d) A true picture of user departments financial performance is not obtained – as significant costs attributable to that department are held in a central pool.

3.2 Information technology charged out at cost

A cost-based charge out involves IS/IT costs being allocated to user departments. Costs may be allocated according to methods such as: cost per transaction processed; cost per page; cost per hour of programmer's and/or analyst's time; cost per number of terminals/workstations; cost per unit of CPU time.

However, collecting and analysing the detailed information required to allocate costs using these indicators can be time-consuming, and therefore costly. For the sake of simplicity therefore, the allocation across user departments may be based on a relatively simple measure such as an estimate of IS/IT use.

The **advantages** of re-charging IS/IT costs to user departments, at cost, are:

(a) Simpler than charging at market value – the amount recharged is the total IS/IT costs incurred.

(b) User departments are encouraged to consider the cost of their usage of IT services.

(c) Encourages efficiency within the IS/IT department as excessive recharges are likely to result in complaints from other departments.

The **disadvantages** of re-charging IS/IT costs to user departments include the following.

(a) Inefficiencies in the IS/IT department are merely passed on to users. This could be avoided if the department is only permitted to recharge budgeted or standard costs.

(b) The basis for recharging must be realistic – or users will feel that costs recharged are unfair which could lead to conflict.

(c) It may be difficult to choose a realistic basis to allocate the costs.

Under both the central overhead approach and the charge-out-at-cost approach the IS function is treated as a cost centre. This can influence the way in which information systems and technology are viewed within an organisation – it encourages the view that they are a drain on resources rather than tools in the quest for competitive advantage.

3.3 Market-based charge out methods

Under market-based methods, the IS/IT department acts as a profit centre. It sets its own prices and charges for its services with the aim of making a profit.

Advantages of the market-based charge out method include:

(a) User departments have the right to demand external standards of service. If the service provided by the IT department is sub-standard, it should be given the chance to improve – with the ultimate sanction of users choosing an outside supplier.

(b) It encourages an entrepreneurial attitude. IT managers are in charge of a department that could make a profit – this should help motivation.

(c) Efficiency and innovation within the IS/IT department is encouraged, as the more efficient the department is, and the more services users buy, the greater the profit will be. Bonuses for IT staff could be based on departmental profit.

(d) A true picture of user departments financial performance is able to be obtained – as the IS/IT costs charged to each department are based on market-rates.

Disadvantages of the market-based charge out method include:

(a) It can be difficult to decide on the charge out rate, particularly if there is no comparable service provider outside the organisation.

(b) If users feel rates are excessive, they may reduce their usage to below optimal levels, and relationships between the IS/IT department and user departments may become strained.

(c) Even if the service provided is poor, it may not be in the organisation's interest for user departments to buy from outsiders: the IS function's fixed costs still have to be covered, and there may result an under-use of resources available within the organisation. Also, a coherent approach to IS/IT should be taken – this would be difficult if a range of suppliers were used across the organisation.

3.3.1 Establishing the IS/IT function as a separate company

The concept of establishing the IS/IT department as a profit centre can be taken a step further – the IS/IT function could become a separate company, with a **separate legal entity**.

User departments within the 'main' company would **purchase IS/IT services** from the separate IS/IT company, and ideally should be free to change suppliers if service or value levels are sub-standard.

The new IS/IT company can also offer its services to other organisations – with the aim of increasing revenue and profit.

The advantages and **disadvantages of market-based charge out methods** covered earlier also apply to situations where a separate company has been set up.

Additional advantages include:

(a) The opportunity for increased revenue and profit.
(b) Increased career opportunities for IS/IT staff.
(c) Opportunities for economies of scale if the company grows.

Additional disadvantages include:

(a) IS/IT staff may lose touch with main company operations.

(b) Increased administration required for the additional company.

(c) The standard of service provided to the main company may suffer, as the focus switches to new clients.

(d) Setting appropriate prices for new clients may be difficult – tasks may not be similar to those undertaken within the original company.

4 Other organisational issues

4.1 Organisation structure

The structure of the **organisation** and the structure of the **organisations information systems** are **related** issues. Organisations that disperse decision making power to local offices will require an effective local management information system.

4.2 Constant change

A reliance on IS/IT commits an organisation to **continual change**. The pace of technological change is rapid. Computer systems – both hardware and software – are likely to be superseded after a few years.

4.3 Interoperability

Interoperability refers to the ability for systems to **share and exchange information** and facilities with other systems regardless of the technology platform or service provider. Interoperability implies an ability to cope with a variety of data structures, and the easy transfer of skills between applications and technologies.

4.4 Backward compatibility

A new version of a program is said to be backward compatible if it can **use files and data created with an older version** of the same program. Computer hardware is said to be backward compatible if it can run the same software as previous models.

Backward compatibility is important because it eliminates the need to start afresh when upgrading. In general, manufacturers try to keep their products backward compatible. Sometimes, however, it is necessary to sacrifice backward compatibility to take advantage of new technology.

4.5 Legacy system

FAST FORWARD

A **legacy system** is an old, outdated system which continues to be used because it is difficult to replace.

The main reason(s) legacy systems continue to be used often include the cost of replacing it, and the significant time and effort involved in introducing a new system.

Legacy systems often **require specialised knowledge** to maintain them in a condition suitable for operation. This may leave an organisation exposed should certain staff leave the organisation.

Legacy systems may also require data to be in a **specific**, maybe unusual **format**. This can cause **compatibility problems** if other systems are replaced throughout an organisation.

File conversion issues are common when replacing legacy systems, for example:

- Establishing the formats of data files held on the legacy system
- Assessing the data held for accuracy and completeness
- Automated file conversion procedures may not be applicable due to system compatibility and data issues
- Ensuring transferred data is available in the required format for all applications that access it

4.6 Open systems

Organisations develop computerised systems over a period of time, perhaps focusing on different functions at different times. The **ease with which systems interact with each other** is important for organisation efficiency. Examples of inefficiencies caused by systems incompatibility include:

(a) Hardware supplied by different manufacturers that can not interact.

(b) Data duplicated in different areas of the business as separate systems can not use the same source.

(c) Software that is unable to interact with other packages.

Open systems aim to ensure compatibility between different systems. An open systems infrastructure supports organisation-wide functions and allows interoperability of networks and systems. Authorised users are able to access applications and data from any part of the system.

5 Outsourcing

FAST FORWARD

Outsourcing is the contracting out of specified operations or services to an external vendor. There are various outsourcing options available, with different levels of control maintained 'in-house'. Outsourcing has **advantages** (eg use of highly skilled people) and **disadvantages** (eg lack of control).

Key term

Outsourcing is the contracting out of specified operations or services to an external vendor.

5.1 Types of outsourcing

There are four **broad classifications** of outsourcing, as described in the following table.

Classification	Comment
Ad-hoc	The organisation has a short-term requirement for increased IS/IT skills. An example would be employing programmers on a short-term contract to help with the programming of bespoke software.
Project management	The development and installation of a particular IS/IT project is outsourced. For example, a new accounting system. (This approach is sometimes referred to as **systems integration**.)
Partial	Some IT/IS services are outsourced. Examples include hardware maintenance, network management or ongoing website management.
Total	An external supplier provides the vast majority of an organisation's IT/IS services; eg third party owns or is responsible for IT equipment, software and staff.

5.2 Levels of service provision

The degree to which the provision and management of IS/IT services are transferred to the third party varies according to the situation and the skills of both organisations.

(a) **Time-share**. The vendor charges for access to an external processing system on a time-used basis. Software ownership may be with either the vendor or the client organisation.

(b) **Service bureaux** usually focus on a specific function. Traditionally bureaux would provide the same type of service to many organisations eg payroll processing. As organisations have developed their own IT infrastructure, the use of bureaux has decreased.

(c) **Facilities management (FM)**. The terms 'outsourcing' and 'facilities management' are sometimes confused. Facilities management traditionally involved contracts for premises-related services such as cleaning or site security.

In the context of IS/IT, facilities management involves an outside agency managing the organisation's IS/IT facilities. All equipment usually remains with the client, but the responsibility for providing and managing the specified services rests with the FM company. FM companies operating in the UK include Accenture and Cap Gemini.

The following table shows the main features of each of the outsourcing arrangements described earlier.

	Outsourcing arrangement		
Feature	Timeshare	Service bureaux	Facilities Management (FM)
Management responsibility	Mostly retained	Some retained	Very little retained
Focus	Operational	A function	Strategic
Timescale	Short-term	Medium-term	Long-term
Justification	Cost savings	More efficient	Access to expertise; higher quality service provision. Enables management to concentrate on the areas where they do possess expertise.

5.3 Organisations involved in outsourcing

5.3.1 Facilities management companies

FM arrangements were covered in section 5.2(c).

5.3.2 Software houses

Software houses concentrate on the provision of **'software services'**. These services include feasibility studies, systems analysis and design, development of operating systems software, provision of application program packages, 'tailor-made' application programming, specialist systems advice, and so on. For example, a software house might be employed to write a computerised system for the London Stock Exchange.

5.3.3 Consultancy firms

Some consultancy firms work at a fairly **high level**, giving advice to management on the **general approach** to solving problems and on the types of system to use. Others specialise in giving more particular systems advice, carrying out feasibility studies and recommending computer manufacturers/software houses that will supply the right system. When a consultancy firm is used, the terms of the contract should be agreed at the outset.

The use of consultancy services enables management to learn directly or indirectly from the experience of others. Many larger consultancies are owned by big international accountancy firms; smaller consultancies may consist of one– or two-person outfits with a high level of specialist experience in one area.

The following categories of **consulting activity** have been identified by *Beaumont* and *Sutherland*.

(a) **Strategic studies**, involving the development of a business strategy or an IS strategy for an organisation.

(b) **Specialist studies**, where the consultant provides a high level of expertise in one area, for example Enterprise Resource Management software.

(c) **Project management**, involving supervision of internal and external parties in the completion of a particular project.

(d) **Body-shopping**, where the necessary staff, including consultants, project managers, systems analysts and programmers, for a project are identified.

(e) **Recruitment**, involving the supply of permanent or temporary staff.

5.3.4 Hardware manufacturers and suppliers

Computer manufacturers or their designated suppliers will provide the **equipment** necessary for a system. They will also provide, under a **maintenance contract**, engineers who will deal with any routine servicing and with any breakdown of the equipment.

Case Study

The retailer Sears outsourced the management of its vast information technology and accounting functions to Accenture. First year *savings* were estimated to be £5 million per annum, growing to £14 million in the following year, and thereafter. This is clearly considerable, although re-organisation costs relating to redundancies, relocation and asset write-offs are thought to be in the region of £35 million. About 900 staff were involved: under the transfer of undertakings regulations (which protect employees when part or all of a company changes hands), Accenture was obliged to take on the existing Sears staff. This provided new opportunities for the staff who moved, while those who remained at Sears are free to concentrate on strategy development and management direction.

5.4 Developments in outsourcing

Outsourcing arrangements are becoming increasingly flexible to cope with the ever-changing nature of the modern business environment. Three trends are:

(a) **Multiple sourcing**. This involves outsourcing different functions or areas of the IS/IT function to a range of suppliers. Some suppliers may form alliances to present a stronger case for selection.

(b) **Incremental approach**. Organisations progressively outsource selected areas of their IT/IS function. Possible problems with outsourced services are solved before progressing to the next stage.

(c) **Joint venture sourcing**. This term is used to describe an organisation entering into a joint venture with a supplier. The costs (risks) and possible rewards are split on an agreed basis. Such an arrangement may be suitable when developing software that could be sold to other organisations.

(d) **Application Service Providers (ASP)**. ASPs are third parties that manage and distribute software services and solutions to customers across a Wide Area Network. ASPs could be considered the modern equivalent of the traditional computer bureaux.

5.5 Managing outsourcing arrangements

Managing outsourcing arrangements involves deciding what will be outsourced, choosing and negotiating with suppliers and managing the supplier relationship.

When considering whether to outsource a particular service the following questions are relevant.

(a) Is the system of strategic importance? Strategic IS are generally not suited to outsourcing as they require a high degree of specific business knowledge that a third party IT specialist can not be expected to possess.

(b) Can the system be relatively isolated? Functions that have only limited interfaces are most easily outsourced eg payroll.

(c) Do we know enough about the system to manage the outsourced service agreement? If an organisation knows very little about a technology it may be difficult to know what constitutes good service and value for money. It may be necessary to recruit additional expertise to manage the relationship with the other party.

(c) Are our requirements likely to change? Organisations should avoid tying themselves into a long-term outsourcing agreement if requirements are likely to change.

5.5.1 Service Level Agreement

A key factor when choosing and negotiating with external vendors is the contract offered and subsequently negotiated with the supplier. The contract is sometimes referred to as the **Service Level Contract** (SLC) or **Service Level Agreement** (SLA).

The key elements of the contract are described in the following table.

Contract element	Comment
Timescale	When does the contract expire? Is the timescale suitable for the organisation's needs or should it be renegotiated?
Service level	The contract should clearly specify minimum levels of service to be provided. Penalties should be specified for failure to meet these standards. Relevant factors will vary depending on the nature of the services outsourced but could include: • Response time to requests for assistance/information • System 'uptime' percentage • Deadlines for performing relevant tasks
Exit route	Arrangements for an exit route, addressing how transfer to another supplier, or the move back in-house, would be conducted.
Software ownership	Relevant factors include: • Software licensing and security • If the arrangement includes the development of new software who owns the copyright?
Dependencies	If related services are outsourced the level of service quality agreed should group these services together.
Employment issues	If the arrangement includes provision for the organisation's IT staff to move to the third party, employer responsibilities must be specified clearly.

The contract provides the framework for the **relationship** between the organisation and the service provider.

Question

Outsourcing

Do any organisations with which you are familiar use outsourcing? What is the view of outsourcing in the organisation?

Answer

One view is given below.

The PA Consulting Group's annual survey of outsourcing found that 'on average the top five strategic outsourcers out-performed the FTSE by more than 100 per cent over three years; the bottom five under-performed by more than 66%'.

However the survey revealed that of those organisations who have opted to outsource IT functions, only five per cent are truly happy with the results. A spokesman for the consultants said that this is because most people fail to adopt a proper strategic approach, taking a view that is neither long-term nor broad enough, and taking outsourcing decisions that are piecemeal and unsatisfactory.

This lack of prescience is compounded by a failure to take a sufficiently rigorous approach to selection, specification, contract drafting and contract management.

The survey found that a constant complaint among many of those interviewed is the lack of ability of outsourcing organisations to work together.

Twenty-five per cent of those asked would bring the functions they had outsourced back in-house if it were possible.

5.6 The advantages and disadvantages of outsourcing

5.6.1 Advantages of outsourcing

The **advantages** of outsourcing are as follows.

(a) Outsourcing can remove uncertainty about **cost**, as there is often a long-term contract where services are specified in advance for a **fixed price**. If computing services are inefficient, the costs will be borne by the FM company. This is also an incentive to the third party to provide a high quality service.

(b) Long-term contracts (maybe up to ten years) encourage **planning** for the future.

(c) Outsourcing can bring the benefits of **economies of scale**. For example, a FM company may conduct research into new technologies that benefits a number of their clients.

(d) A specialist organisation is able to retain **skills and knowledge**. Many organisations would not have a sufficiently well-developed IT department to offer IT staff opportunities for career development. Talented staff would leave to pursue their careers elsewhere.

(e) New skills and knowledge become available. A specialist company can **share** staff with **specific expertise** between several clients. This allows the outsourcing company to take advantage of new developments without the need to recruit new people or re-train existing staff, and without the cost.

(f) **Flexibility** (contract permitting). Resources may be able to be scaled up or down depending upon demand. For instance, during a major changeover from one system to another the number of IT staff needed may be twice as large as it will be once the new system is working satisfactorily.

An outsourcing organisation is more able to arrange its work on a **project** basis, whereby some staff will expect to be moved periodically from one project to the next.

5.6.2 Disadvantages of outsourcing

Some possible **drawbacks** are outlined below.

(a) It is arguable that information and its provision is an **inherent part of the business** and of management. Unlike office cleaning, or catering, an organisation's IT services may be too important to be contracted out. Information is at the heart of management.

(b) A company may have highly **confidential information** and to let outsiders handle it could be seen as **risky** in commercial and/or legal terms.

(c) If a third party is handling IS/IT services there is no onus upon internal management to keep up with new developments or to suggest new ideas. Consequently, opportunities to gain

competitive advantage may be missed. Any new technology or application devised by the third party is likely to be available to competitors.

(d) An organisation may find itself **locked in** to an unsatisfactory contract. The decision may be very difficult to reverse. If the service provider supplies unsatisfactory levels of service, the effort and expense the organisation would incur to rebuild its own computing function or to move to another provider could be substantial.

(e) The use of an outside organisation does not encourage awareness of the potential **costs** and benefits of IS/IT within the organisation. If managers cannot manage in-house IS/IT resources effectively, then it could be argued that they will not be able to manage an arrangement to outsource effectively either.

Chapter Roundup

- At the head of the information systems/information technology function will be either the IS/IT manager, or the **IS/IT director**. This person will be responsible for:
  - IS/IT strategy development
  - IS/IT risk management
  - Overseeing the steering committee
  - The IS/IT infrastructure
- The general purpose of an IS/IT **steering committee** is to make decisions relating to the future use and development of IS/IT by the organisation.
- A key information systems role is that of **database administrator**. A database administrator is responsible for all data and information held within an organisation.
- **Information centres**, sometimes referred to as **support centres**, are particularly useful in organisations which use distributed systems and so are likely to have hardware, data and software scattered throughout the organisation. The IC provides a centralised source of support and co-ordination.
- A **centralised** IS/IT department involves all IS/IT staff and functions being based out at a single central location, such as head office.
- A **decentralised** IS/IT department involves IS/IT staff and functions being spread out throughout the organisation.
- Providing and maintaining information systems to deliver good quality information involves significant expenditure. There are three broad possibilities when **accounting for costs** related to information systems.
  - IS costs are treated as an **administrative overhead**
  - IS costs are **charged out at cost**
  - IS costs are **charged out at market rates**
- A **legacy system** is an old, outdated system which continues to be used because it is difficult to replace.
- **Outsourcing** is the contracting out of specified operations or services to an external vendor. There are various outsourcing options available, with different levels of control maintained 'in-house'. Outsourcing has **advantages** (eg use of highly skilled people) and **disadvantages** (eg lack of control).

Quick Quiz

1 'It is essential that an information systems director has exceptional 'hands-on' computer programming skills'. TRUE or FALSE?

2 List four responsibilities of an IS/IT steering committee.

3 List three advantages of a decentralised IS/IT department.

4 List three disadvantages of a decentralised IS/IT department.

5 What does the 'open systems' concept aim to achieve?

6 Define 'legacy system'.

7 'Information systems that are strategically important should be outsourced to ensure those working with these systems have excellent technical knowledge'. TRUE or FALSE?

8 List four advantages of outsourcing the IS/IT function.

9 List four disadvantages of outsourcing the IS/IT function.

10 What would a SLA contain?

Answers to Quick Quiz

1 FALSE. An IS/IT director requires a wide range of skills including technical know-how, general management ability, a keen sense of business awareness and a good understanding of the organisations' operations. A knowledge of programming could be useful (as part of 'technical know-how), but actual hands-on skills would not be essential.

2 [Four of]

Ensuring IS/IT activities comply with IS/IT strategy
Ensuring IS/IT activities compliment the overall organisation strategy
Ensuring resources committed to IS/IT are used effectively
Monitoring IS/IT projects
Providing leadership and guidance on IS/IT

3 [Three of]

Each office can introduce an information system specially tailored for its individual needs.
Local offices are more self-sufficient.
Offices are likely to have quicker access to IS/IT support/advice.
A decentralised structure is more likely to facilitate accurate IS/IT cost/overhead allocations.

4 Three disadvantages are described below.

Control may be more difficult – different and uncoordinated information systems may be introduced.
Self-sufficiency may encourage a lack of co-ordination between departments.
Increased risk of data duplication, with different offices holding the same data on their own separate files.

5 Open systems aim to ensure compatibility between different systems. An open systems infrastructure supports organisation-wide functions and allows interoperability of networks and systems.

6 A legacy system is an old outdated system which continues to be used, but no-longer meets the information requirements of the organisation.

7 FALSE. Strategic IS are generally not suited to outsourcing as they require a high degree of specific business knowledge that a third party IT/IS specialist can not be expected to possess.

8 [Four of]

Cost control – services are specified in advance for a fixed price.

Certainty – long-term contracts allow greater certainty in planning for the future.

Economies of scale. Several organisations will employ the same company.

Skills and knowledge are retained within the specialist company who can offer staff career development.

New skills and knowledge become available. A specialist company can share staff with specific expertise between several clients.

Flexibility – resources employed can be scaled up or down depending upon demand.

9 [Four of]

An organisation's IS services may be too important to be contracted out. Information is at the heart of management.

Risky – confidential or commercially sensitive information could be leaked.

Opportunities may be missed to use IS/IT for competitive advantage – there is no onus upon internal management to keep up with new developments and have new ideas.

Locked in – an organisation may be locked into a contract with a poor service provider.

Hard to reverse – the effort and expense an organisation would have to incur to rebuild its own computing function and expertise would be enormous.

Outsourcing does not encourage an awareness of the potential costs and benefits of IT amongst managers.

10 The Service Level Agreement (SLA) or Service Level Contract (SLC) is a vital aspect of any outsourcing arrangement. It should specify minimum levels of service, arrangements for an exit route, transfer arrangements and dispute procedures.

Now try the question below from the Exam Question Bank

Number	Level	Marks	Time
Q19(a),(b),(c)	Examination	10	18 mins

Feasibility studies

4

Topic list	Syllabus reference
1 The feasibility study	1 (e)
2 Key areas of feasibility	1 (e)
3 Investment appraisal techniques	1 (e)
4 The feasibility study report	1 (e)

Introduction

In this chapter we look at the **purpose** and **objectives** of a **feasibility study**.

A feasibility study should be carried out before a new information systems project is undertaken to assess the technical, commercial, operational and social feasibility of the new undertaking.

Remember when reading this chapter that the nature and scale of a feasibility study will depend to a large extent on the **size** and **nature** of the project being considered.

Study guide

Part 1.5 – Feasibility study

- Explain the purpose and objectives of a feasibility study
- Evaluate the technical, operational, social and economic feasibility of the proposed project
- Describe and categorise the benefits and costs of the proposed project
- Apply appropriate investment appraisal techniques to determine the economic feasibility of a project
- Define the typical content and structure of a feasibility study report

Exam guide

The purpose and conduct of a feasibility study is a likely exam topic. In particular, the different areas of feasibility (technical, operational, social and economic) are regularly examined. In the past, questions related to cost benefit analysis have required a discussion of the relevant techniques rather than requiring candidates to perform calculations.

1 The feasibility study

FAST FORWARD

A **feasibility study** is a formal study to decide whether a project is viable. When considering an information systems project the study would investigate the type of system that could be developed to meet the needs of the organisation, and if it is possible to produce such a system within the relevant constraints.

Key term

A **feasibility study** is a formal study to decide what type of system can be developed which best meets the needs of the organisation.

1.1 The feasibility study team

A feasibility study team should be appointed to carry out the study (although individuals might be given the task in the case of smaller projects).

(a) Members of the team should be drawn from the **departments affected by the project**.

(b) At least one person must have a **detailed knowledge of computers and systems design** (in a small concern it may be necessary to bring in a systems analyst from outside.

(c) At least one person should have a **detailed knowledge of the organisation** and in particular of the workings and staff of the departments affected. Managers with direct knowledge of how the current system operates will know what the **information needs** of the system are, and whether any proposed new system (for example an off-the-shelf software package) will do everything that is wanted. They are also most likely to be in a position to recognise **improvements that can be made in the current system.**

(d) It is possible to hire **consultants** to carry out the feasibility study, but their **lack of knowledge about the organisation** may adversely affect the usefulness of their proposals.

(e) Before selecting the members of the study group, the steering committee must ensure that they possess **suitable personal qualities**, eg the ability to be **objectively critical**.

(f) All members of the study group should ideally have some knowledge of information technology and systems design. They should also be encouraged to read as widely as possible and take an **active interest in current innovations.**

With larger projects it may well be worthwhile for a small firm to employ a **professional systems analyst** and then appoint a management team to work with the analyst.

1.2 Identifying and selecting IS projects

A planned approach is needed when identifying and selecting new information systems projects. The following actions should be considered.

(a) IS projects almost always utilise IT. IT is critical to the success of many organisations. This means that an **IT strategy** should form a **core part of the overall corporate strategy** and should be developed/updated whenever the organisation's strategy is reviewed or as otherwise necessary. IT needs can then be identified in the context of **overall business needs**.

(b) Because IT is critical, it requires adequate **representation at senior management level**. It is no longer suitable for IT to be under the control of the MD, FD or computer centre manager. It really needs a separate Board level person responsible, such as an **Information Director** or an **IS director**. This will help to ensure that IT is given adequate consideration at strategic level.

(c) The IT development can no longer function as a subsystem of accounting, administration or finance. It should be given **separate departmental or functional status** in the organisation with its own reporting lines and responsibilities.

(d) Once the IT department has been set up, its **funding** must be considered. A simplistic approach would be to treat it as an overhead; this is simple but inefficient. There are various approaches possible to the recovery of IT costs from user departments, and the IT department may even operate as a commercial concern providing services to third parties at a profit.

(e) A **strategic plan for the use of IT** should be developed. This should take in separate elements such as information technology and information systems. It should also acknowledge the importance of the organisation's information resource.

(f) If new computer systems are to be introduced regularly, the organisation may set up a **steering committee** to oversee **systems development**. A steering committee can also be set up for a one-off project. The role of the steering committee includes approving or rejecting individual projects and where appropriate submitting projects to the Board for approval. The composition and determination of terms of reference for the steering committee must be agreed.

(g) The **approach** of the organisation to individual projects must be decided. Will it follow the traditional **life cycle** or will it use a **methodology**? Commercial methodologies impose discipline on the development process.

(h) Procedures for **evaluating and monitoring performance** both during and after a project need to be put in place. Many methodologies require formal sign-off of each stage, but this does not obviate the need for good project management or for post-implementation evaluation.

(i) Details of the **systems development procedures** must be agreed. If a commercial methodology is used, many of these procedures will be pre-determined. Areas to be considered include the approach to **feasibility studies**, methods of **cost-benefit analysis**,

design specifications and conventions, development **tools** and **techniques**, **reporting** lines, contents of standard **invitations to tender**, drawing up of **supplier conditions** and procedures for **testing** and **implementation**.

1.3 Conducting the feasibility study

Some of the work performed at the feasibility study stage may be similar to work performed later on in the development of the project. This is because both processes include the need to define the current situation or problem.

A **feasibility study** should be carried out before undertaking an information systems project because a new or amended system may:

(a) Be complicated and costly.

(b) Disrupt operations during development and implementation (eg staff and management time).

(c) Have far reaching consequences in a way an organisation conducts future business.

(d) Impact on organisation strategy and structure.

1.3.1 Terms of reference

The **terms of reference for a feasibility study** group may be set out by a steering committee, the information director or the board of directors, and might consist of:

(a) To investigate and report on an existing system, its procedures and costs.
(b) To define the systems requirements.
(c) To establish whether these requirements are being met by the existing system.
(d) To establish whether they could be met by an alternative system.
(e) To specify performance criteria for the system.
(f) To recommend the most suitable system to meet the system's objectives.
(g) To prepare a detailed cost budget, within a specified budget limit.
(h) To prepare a draft plan for implementation within a specified timescale.
(i) To establish whether the hoped-for benefits could be realised.
(j) To establish a detailed design, implementation and operating budget.
(k) To compare the detailed budget with the costs of the current system.
(l) To set the date by which the study group must report back.
(m) To decide which operational managers should be approached by the study group.

The remit of a feasibility study may be narrow or wide. The feasibility study team must engage in a substantial effort of **fact finding**.

1.3.2 Problem definition

In some circumstances the **'problem'** (for example the necessity for a real-time as opposed to a batch processed application) may be quite **exact**, in others it may be characterised as **'soft'** (related to people and the way they behave).

The problem definition stage should result in the production of a set of documents which define the problem.

(a) A set of **diagrams** representing, in overview:

(i) The current physical flows of data in the organisation (**documents**).
(ii) The activities underlying them (**data flows**).

(b) A description of all the people, jobs, activities and so on (**entities**) that make up the system, and their relationship to one another.

(c) The **problems/requirements** list established from the terms of reference and after consultation with users.

1.3.3 The problems/requirements list

The problems/requirements list or catalogue can cover, amongst other things, the following areas.

(a) The data **input** to the current system.
(b) The nature of the **output** information (contents, timing etc).
(c) Methods of **processing**.
(d) The expected **growth** of the organisation and so **future volumes** of processing.
(e) The systems **control** in operation.
(f) **Staffing** arrangements and organisational **structure**.
(g) The **operational costs** of the system.
(h) **Type of system** (batch, on-line).
(i) **Response times**.
(j) Current organisational **problems**.

1.3.4 Option evaluation

This stage involves suggesting a number of **options** for a new system, evaluating them and recommending one for adoption. It concludes with a final **feasibility study report**.

Step 1 Create the **base constraints** in terms of expenditure, implementation and design time, and system requirements, which any system should satisfy.

(a) **Operations** (for example faster processing, larger volumes, greater security, greater accuracy, better quality, real-time as opposed to other forms of processing).

(b) Information **output** (quality, frequency, presentation, eg GUIs, database for managers, EIS facilities).

(c) **Volume of processing**.

(d) **General system requirements** (eg accuracy, security and controls, audit trail, flexibility, adaptability).

(e) **Compatibility/integration** with existing systems.

Step 2 Create outlines of **project options**, describing, in brief, each option. The number will vary depending on the complexity of the problem, or the size of the application, but is typically between three and six.

Step 3 Assess the **impact** each proposal has on the work of the relevant user department and/or the organisation as a whole.

Step 4 **Review** these proposals with users, who should indicate those options they favour for further analysis.

1.3.5 System justification

A new system should not be recommended unless it can be justified. The justification for a new system would have to come from:

(a) An evaluation of the **costs and benefits** of the proposed system, and/or
(b) Other **performance criteria**.

2 Key areas of feasibility

FAST FORWARD

There are four key areas in which a project must be feasible if it is to be selected. It must be justifiable on **technical, operational, social and economic** grounds.

There are four key areas of feasibility:

- Technical feasibility
- Operational feasibility
- Social feasibility
- Economic feasibility

2.1 Technical feasibility

The requirements, as defined in the feasibility study, must be technically achievable. This means that any proposed solution must be capable of being implemented using available hardware, software and other technology. Technical feasibility considerations could include the following.

- **Volume** of transactions which can be processed within a given time.
- **Capacity** to hold files or records of a certain size.
- **Response times** (how quickly the computer does what you ask it to).
- **Number of users** which can be supported without deterioration in the other criteria.

2.2 Operational feasibility

Operational feasibility is a key concern. If a solution makes technical sense but **conflicts with the way the organisation does business**, the solution is not feasible. Thus an organisation might reject a solution because it forces a change in management responsibilities, status and chains of command, or does not suit regional reporting structures, or because the costs of redundancies, retraining and reorganisation are considered too high.

2.3 Social feasibility

An assessment of social feasibility will address a number of areas, including the following.

- **Personnel** policies
- Redrawing of **job specifications**
- Threats to **industrial relations**
- Expected **skills requirements**
- **Motivation**

2.4 Economic feasibility

Any project will have economic costs and economic benefits. Economic feasibility has three strands.

(a) The benefits must justify the costs.

(b) The project must be the 'best' option from those under consideration for its particular purpose.

(c) The project must compete with projects in other areas of the business for funds. Even if it is projected to produce a positive return and satisfies all relevant criteria, it may not be chosen because other business needs are perceived as more important.

2.4.1 The costs of a proposed system

In general the best cost estimates will be obtained for systems bought from an **outside vendor** who provides a cost quotation against a specification. Less concrete cost estimates are generally found with development projects where the work is performed by the organisation's own employees.

The costs of a new system will include costs in a number of different categories.

Cost	Example
Equipment costs	• Computer and peripherals • Ancillary equipment • The initial system supplies (disks, tapes, paper etc)
Installation costs	• New buildings (if necessary) • The computer room (wiring, air-conditioning if necessary)
Development costs	These include costs of measuring and analysing the existing system and costs of looking at the new system. They include software/consultancy work and systems analysis and programming. Changeover costs, particularly file conversion, may be very considerable.
Personnel costs	• Staff training • Staff recruitment/relocation • Staff salaries and pensions • Redundancy payments • Overheads
Operating costs	• Consumable materials (tapes, disks, stationery etc) • Maintenance • Accommodation costs • Heating/power/insurance/telephone • Standby arrangements, in case the system breaks down

2.4.2 Capital and revenue costs

The distinction between capital costs and revenue costs is important.

(a) The costs-benefit analysis of a system ought to include **cash flows and DCF**.

(b) The annual charge against profits shown in the financial accounts is of interest to **stakeholders.**

Capital items will be capitalised and then depreciated, and revenue items will be expensed as incurred as a regular annual cost.

In practice, **accounting treatment** of such development costs may **vary widely** between organisations depending on their accounting policies and on agreement with their auditors.

Question **System costs**

Draw up a table with three headings: capital cost items, one-off revenue cost items and regular annual costs. Identify at least three items to be included under each heading. You may wish to refer back to the preceding paragraphs for examples of costs.

Answer

Capital cost items	'One-off' revenue cost items	Regular annual costs
Hardware purchase costs	Consultancy fees	Operating staff salaries/wages
Software purchase costs	Systems analysts' and programmers' salaries	Data transmission costs
Purchase of accommodation (if needed)	Costs of testing the system (staff costs, consumables)	Consumable materials
Installation costs (new desks, cables, physical storage etc)	Costs of converting the files for the new system	Power
	Staff recruitment fees	Maintenance costs
		Cost of standby arrangements
		Ongoing staff training

2.4.3 The benefits of a proposed system

The benefits from a proposed new system must also be evaluated. Possible examples are outlined below

(a) **Savings** because the **old system** will no longer be operated. Savings may include:

  (i) Savings in **staff costs**.
  (ii) Savings in **other operating costs**, such as consumable materials.

(b) Extra **savings** or revenue benefits because of the improvements or enhancements that the **new system** should bring:

  (i) Possibly **more sales revenue** and so additional contribution.

  (ii) **Better stock control** (with a new stock control system) and so fewer stock losses from obsolescence and deterioration.

  (iii) Further savings in **staff time**, resulting perhaps in reduced future staff growth.

(c) Possibly, some one-off revenue benefits from the **sale of equipment** which the existing system uses, but which will no longer be required. Second-hand computer equipment does not have a high value, however! It is also possible that the new system will use **less office space**, and so there will be benefits from selling or renting the spare accommodation.

Some benefits might be **intangible**, or impossible to give a money value to.

(a) Greater **customer satisfaction**, arising from a more prompt service (eg because of a computerised sales and delivery service).

(b) Improved **staff morale** from working with a 'better' system.

(c) **Better decision making** is hard to quantify, but may result from better MIS, DSS or EIS.

3 Investment appraisal techniques

FAST FORWARD

One of the most important elements of the feasibility study is the **cost-benefit analysis**. Costs include equipment costs, installation costs, development costs, personnel costs and running costs. Benefits are usually more intangible, but include cost savings, revenue benefits and qualitative benefits.

A **Cost-benefit analysis relating to** the development of information systems is complicated by the fact that many system **cost elements** are **poorly defined** and that **benefits** can often be highly **qualitative** and **subjective** in nature.

FAST FORWARD

There are three principal methods of evaluating the **economic viability** of a project: Payback, Accounting Rate of Return and Discounted Cash Flow.

There are three principal methods of evaluating the economic viability of a project.

Method	Comment
Payback period	This method of investment appraisal calculates the length of time a project will take to recoup the initial investment; in other words how long a project will take to pay for itself. The method is based on cash flows.
Accounting rate of return	This method, also called return on investment, calculates the profits that will be earned by a project and expresses this as a percentage of the capital invested in the project. The higher the rate of return, the higher a project is ranked. This method is based on accounting results rather than cash flows.
Discounted cash flow (DCF)	This is a method which may be sub-divided into two approaches. (a) Net present value (NPV), which considers all relevant cash flows associated with a project over the whole of its life and adjusts those occurring in future years to 'present value' by discounting at a rate called the 'cost of capital'. (b) Internal rate of return (IRR), which involves comparing the rate of return expected from the project calculated on a discounted cash flow basis with the rate used as the cost of capital. Projects with an IRR higher than the cost of capital are worth undertaking.

Before looking at each of these methods in turn it is worth considering one **problem** common to all of them, that of **uncertainty**. Estimating **future** cash flows and other benefits cannot be done with complete accuracy, particularly as the future period under consideration may as long as five or even ten years.

It is therefore important that decision makers should consider how **variations** in the estimates **might affect their decision**.

Exam focus point

It is unlikely that you would have to perform an investment appraisal calculation in the examination for Paper 2.1. It is more likely that you would be required to demonstrate your understanding of the techniques – and comment on possible difficulties applying these techniques to an investment in an information system.

3.1 The payback method

FAST FORWARD

The **Payback** method calculates the length of time a project will take to recoup the initial investment.

Key term

The **payback period** is the length of time required before the total cash inflows received from the project is equal to the original cash outlay. In other words, it is the length of time the investment takes to pay itself back.

3.2 Example: Payback

The payback method has obvious disadvantages. Consider the case of two projects for which the following information is available.

	Project P	*Project Q*
	£	£
Cost	100,000	100,000
Cash savings		
Year 1	10,000	50,000
2	20,000	50,000
3	60,000	10,000
4	70,000	5,000
5	80,000	5,000
	240,000	120,000

Solution

Project Q pays back at the end of year two and Project P not until early in year four. Using the payback method Project Q is to be preferred, but this ignores the fact that the total profitability of Project P (£240,000) is double that of Q.

Despite the disadvantages of the payback method it is **widely used in practice**, though often only as a **supplement** to more sophisticated methods.

Besides being simple to calculate and understand, the argument in its favour is that its use will tend to **minimise** the effects of **risk** and **help liquidity**. This is because greater weight is given to **earlier cash flows** which can probably be **predicted more accurately** than distant cash flows.

3.3 Accounting rate of return

FAST FORWARD

The Accounting Rate of Return (**ARR**) method, also called return on investment, expresses the profits that will be earned by a project as a percentage of the capital invested.

A project may be assessed by calculating the accounting rate of return (ARR) and comparing it with a pre-determined target level. Various formulae are used, but the important thing is to be **consistent** once a method has been selected.

A common formula for ARR is:

Accounting rate of return is calculated as follows

$$\text{ARR} = \frac{\text{Estimated average profits}}{\text{Estimated average investment}} \times 100\%$$

3.4 Example: ARR

Caddick Limited is contemplating a computerisation project and has two alternatives. Based on the ARR method which of the two projects would be recommended?

	Project X	*Project Y*
Hardware cost	£100,000	£120,000
Estimated residual value	10,000	£15,000
Estimated life	5 years	5 years
Estimated future cost savings per annum before depreciation	£19,000	£21,800

Solution

It is first necessary to calculate the average profits (net savings) and average investment over the life of the project (five years in this example).

	Project X	*Project Y*
	£	£
Total savings before depreciation (eg £19,000 pa × 5 years)	95,000	109,000
Total depreciation	90,000	105,000
Total savings after depreciation	5,000	4,000
Average savings per annum (5 years so divide by 5)	1,000	800
Value of investment initially	100,000	120,000
Less eventual scrap value	(10,000)	(15,000)
	90,000	105,000
Average investment per annum (5 years so divide by 5)	18,000	21,000

The accounting rates of return are as follows. Project X would therefore be chosen.

$$\text{Project X} = \frac{£1{,}000}{£18{,}000} = 5.56\%$$

$$\text{Project Y} = \frac{£800}{£21{,}000} = 3.8\%$$

The return on investment is a measure of (accounting) profitability and its major **advantages** that it can be obtained from **readily available accounting data** and that its meaning is **widely understood**.

Its major **shortcomings** are that it is based on accounting profits rather than cash flows and that it fails to take account of the **timing** of cash inflows and outflows. For example, in the problem above cash savings in each year were assumed to be the same, whereas management might favour higher cash inflows in the **early years**. Early cash flows are less risky and they improve liquidity. This might lead them to choose a project with a lower ARR.

3.5 Discounted cash flow (DCF)

FAST FORWARD

Discounted Cash Flow (**DCF**) may be sub-divided into two approaches. Net Present Value (**NPV**) considers expected future cash flows but discounts future flows by the 'cost of capital'.

Key term

Discounted cash flow or DCF is a technique of evaluating capital investment projects, using **discounting arithmetic** to determine whether or not they will provide a satisfactory return.

A typical investment project involves a payment of capital for fixed assets at the **start** of the project and then there will be profits coming in from the investment over a number of years. When the system goes live, there will be **running costs** as well. The benefits of the system should exceed the running costs, to give net annual benefits.

DCF recognises that there is a **'time value'** or interest cost and **risk** cost to investing money, so that the expected benefits from a project should not only pay back the costs, but should also yield a satisfactory return. Only **relevant** costs are recognised: accounting conventions like depreciation, which is not a real cash flow, are ignored.

£1 is now worth more than £1 in a year's time, because £1 now could be used to earn interest by the end of year 1. Money has a lower and lower value, the further from 'now' that it will be earned or paid. With DCF, this time value on money is allowed for by converting cash flows in future years to a smaller, **present value**, equivalent.

3.6 Example: NPV

A DCF evaluation, using NPV analysis, of a proposed computer project might be as follows.

Project: new network system for administration department		
Development and hardware purchase costs (all incurred over a short time)		£150,000
Operating costs of new system, expressed as cash outflows per annum		£55,000
Annual savings from new system, expressed as cash inflow		£115,000
Annual net savings (net cash inflows)		£60,000
Expected system life	4 years	
Required return on investment	15% pa	

Solution

The calculation of NPV is performed as follows.

Year	*Cost/Savings*	*Discount factor at 15% (from NPV tables)*	*Present value at 15%*
	£		£
0	(150,000)	1.000	(150,000)
1	60,000	0.870	52,200
2	60,000	0.756	45,360
3	60,000	0.658	39,480
4	60,000	0.572	34,320
		Net present value of the project	21,360

In this example, the present value of the expected benefits of the project exceed the present value of its costs, all discounted at 15% pa, and so the project is financially justifiable because it would be expected to earn a yield greater than the minimum target return of 15%. Payback of the development costs and hardware costs of £150,000 would occur after 2½ years.

One disadvantage of the NPV method is that it involves complicated maths and this might make it **difficult to understand** Also, it is difficult in practice to determine the true **cost of capital.**

3.7 Internal rate of return (IRR)

FAST FORWARD

Internal Rate of Return (**IRR**) compares the rate of return expected from the project calculated on a discounted cash flow basis with the rate used as the cost of capital. Projects with an IRR higher than the cost of capital are considered to be worth undertaking.

The internal rate of return methods of DCF involves two steps.

(a) Calculating the **rate of return** which is expected from a project.

(b) **Comparing** the rate of return with the **cost of capital**.

If a project earns a higher rate of return than the cost of capital, it will be worth undertaking (and its NPV would be positive). If it earns a lower rate of return, it is not worthwhile (and its NPV would be negative). If a project earns a return which is exactly equal to the cost of capital, its NPV will be 0 and it will only just be worthwhile.

The manual method of calculating the rate of return is sometimes considered to be rather 'messy' and unsatisfactory because it involves some guesswork and approximation, but **spreadsheets** can do it with speed and precision.

Question

Investment appraisal techniques

Draw up a table which identifies, for each of payback, ARR and NPV, two advantages and two disadvantages.

Answer

Method	Advantages	Disadvantages
Payback	(1) Easy to calculate (2) Favours projects that offer quick returns	(1) Ignores cash flows after payback period (2) Only a crude measure of timing of a project's cash flows.
ARR	(1) Easy to calculate (2) Easy to understand	(1) Doesn't allow for timing of inflows/outflows of cash (2) Subject to accounting conventions.
NPV	(1) Uses relevant cost approach by concentrating on cash flows (2) Represents increase to company's wealth, expressed in present day terms	(1) Not easily understood by laymen. (2) Cost of capital may be difficult to calculate.

4 The feasibility study report

FAST FORWARD

Once each area of feasibility has been investigated a number of possible projects may be put forward. The results are included in a **feasibility report**.

Once each area of feasibility has been investigated a number of possible projects may be put forward. The results of the study should be compiled into a report that makes a recommendation regarding future action (eg a new system, modify the existing system, or to remain with the status quo).

The feasibility study report may be submitted to the organisation's steering committee for consideration – or perhaps to the likely project manager (this will depend upon the size and nature of the project and the preferences of the organisation.

A typical feasibility study report may include the following sections.

- Terms of reference
- Description of existing system
- System requirements
- Details of the proposed system(s)
- Cost/benefit analysis
- Development and implementation plans
- Recommendations as to the preferred option

Exam focus point

Candidates in June 2003 were asked to explain how the economic feasibility of a systems development project could be determined.

Chapter Roundup

- A **feasibility study** is a formal study to decide whether a project is viable. When considering an information systems project the study would investigate the type of system that could be developed to meet the needs of the organisation, and if it is possible to produce such a system within the relevant constraints.
- There are four key areas in which a project must be feasible if it is to be selected. It must be justifiable on **technical, operational, social and economic** grounds.
- One of the most important elements of the feasibility study is the **cost-benefit analysis**. Costs include equipment costs, installation costs, development costs, personnel costs and running costs. Benefits are usually more intangible, but include cost savings, revenue benefits and qualitative benefits.
- There are three principal methods of evaluating the **economic viability** of a project: Payback, Accounting Rate of Return and Discounted Cash Flow.
- The **Payback** method calculates the length of time a project will take to recoup the initial investment.
- The Accounting Rate of Return (**ARR**) method, also called return on investment, expresses the profits that will be earned by a project as a percentage of the capital invested.
- Discounted Cash Flow (**DCF**) may be sub-divided into two approaches. Net Present Value (**NPV**) considers expected future cash flows but discounts future flows by the 'cost of capital'.
- Internal Rate of Return (**IRR**) compares the rate of return expected from the project calculated on a discounted cash flow basis with the rate used as the cost of capital. Projects with an IRR higher than the cost of capital are considered to be worth undertaking.
- Once each area of feasibility has been investigated a number of possible projects may be put forward. The results are included in a **feasibility report**.

Quick Quiz

1 List three reasons why an organisation considering the implementation of a new information system should undertake a feasibility study.

2 What four areas should a feasibility study ensure a project is feasible in?

3 Define 'the payback period'.

4 Give three reasons why is it difficult to place a monetary value on the benefits of an information system.

5 List the contents of a typical feasibility study report.

Answers to Quick Quiz

1 A feasibility study should be undertaken when considering a new information system because new systems can:

Be complicated and cost a great deal to develop.
Be disruptive during development and implementation.
Have far-reaching consequences in a way an organisation conducts its business or is structured.

2 Technical, Operational, Social and Economic.

3 The payback period is the length of time required before the total cash inflows received from the project is equal to the original cash outlay.

4 Many benefits are intangible and hard to measure eg better quality decision-making. Many benefits will accrue in the future – it is difficult to accurately account for the time value of money. Many benefits are uncertain, for example a system may provide competitive advantage depending on what systems competitors introduce.

5 A typical report might include:

(a) Terms of reference.
(b) Description of existing system.
(c) System requirements.
(d) Details of the proposed system.
(e) Cost/benefit analysis.
(f) Development and implementation plans.
(g) Recommendations as to the preferred option.

Now try the questions below from the Exam Question Bank

Number	Level	Marks	Time
Q2(a)	Examination	10	18 mins
Q5(a)	Examination	10	18 mins
Q6	Examination	20	36 mins

The project manager and project stakeholders

5

Topic list	Syllabus reference
1 What is a project?	1 (f)
2 The project manager	1 (f)
3 The project team	1 (f)
4 Project stakeholders	1 (f)

Introduction

This chapter will introduce the subject of project management, explain what project management is and outline what a **project manager** does.

Later in the chapter we look at how a **project team** should be put together, and examine the **stakeholders** of a project and the relationships between them.

Project management tools and techniques will be covered in Chapter 6.

Study guide

Part 1.6 – Project initiation

- Identify the roles and responsibilities of staff who will manage and participate in the project
- Define in detail the role and responsibilities of the project manager
- Explain the concept of a flat management structure and its application to project-based systems development

Exam guide

It is highly likely that a reasonable proportion of the exam scenario questions will be based around an information systems project.

1 What is a project?

To understand project management it is necessary to first define what a project is.

Key term

A **Project** is 'an undertaking that has a beginning and an end and is carried out to meet established goals within cost, schedule and quality objectives'. (Haynes, *Project Management*)

FAST FORWARD

A **project** often has the following characteristics:

- A defined beginning and end
- Resources allocated specifically to them
- Intended to be done only once (although similar separate projects could be undertaken)
- Follow a plan towards a clear intended end-result
- Often cut across organisational and functional lines.

In general, the work organisations undertake involves either **operations** or **projects**. Operations and projects are planned, controlled and executed. So how are projects distinguished from 'ordinary work'?

Projects	Operations
Have a defined beginning and end	On-going
Have resources allocated specifically to them, although often on a shared basis	Resources used 'full-time'
Are intended to be done only once (eg organising the Year 2005 London Marathon – the 2006 event is a separate project)	A mixture of many recurring tasks
Follow a plan towards a clear intended end-result	Goals and deadlines are more general
Often cut across organisational and functional lines	Usually follows the organisation or functional structure

Common examples of projects include:

- Producing a new product, service or object
- Changing the structure of an organisation
- Developing or modifying a new information system
- Implementing a new information system

FAST FORWARD

Project management is the combination of systems, techniques, and people used to control and monitor activities undertaken within the project. A project will be deemed successful if it is completed at the specified level of **quality**, **on time** and within **budget**.

1.1 What is project management?

Key term

Project management involves co-ordinating the resources necessary to complete the project successfully (ie on time, within budget and to specification).

The objective of project management is a successful project. A project will be deemed successful if it is completed at the **specified level of quality**, **on time** and **within budget**.

Objective	Comment
Quality	The end result should conform to the project specification. In other words, the result should achieve what the project was supposed to do.
Budget	The project should be completed without exceeding authorised expenditure.
Timescale	The progress of the project must follow the planned process, so that the 'result' is ready for use at the agreed date. As time is money, proper time management can help contain costs.

1.1.1 The challenges of project management

Managing a project presents a variety of **challenges**. Some common challenges are outlined in the following table.

Challenge	Comment
Teambuilding	The work is carried out by a team of people often from varied work and social backgrounds. The team must 'gel' quickly and be able to communicate effectively with each other.
Planning	Many possible problems may be avoided by careful design and planning prior to commencement of work.
Problem solving mechanisms	There should be mechanisms within the project to enable unforeseen problems to be resolved quickly and efficiently.
Delayed benefit	There is normally no benefit from a project until the work is finished. This means that significant expenditure is being incurred for no immediate benefit – this can be a source of pressure.
Dealing with specialists	Project managers often have to deal competently and realistically with specialists at differing stages of the project.
Potential for conflict	Projects often involve several parties with different interests. This may lead to conflict.

Project management ensures responsibilities are clearly defined and that resources are **focussed** on specific objectives. The **project management process** also provides a structure for communicating within and across organisational boundaries.

All projects share similar features and follow a similar process. This has led to the development of **project management tools and techniques** that can be applied to all projects, no matter how diverse. For example, with some limitations similar processes and techniques can be applied to whether building a major structure or implementing a company-wide computer network.

All projects require a person who is ultimately responsible for delivering the required outcome. This person is the **project manager**.

2 The project manager

FAST FORWARD

The person who takes ultimate responsibility for ensuring the desired result is achieved on time and within budget is the **project manager**.

Some project managers have the job title 'Project Manager'. These people usually have one major responsibility: the project. Most people in business will have 'normal work' responsibilities outside their project goals – which may lead to conflicting demands on their time. Anybody responsible for a project (large or small) is a project manager.

Key terms

The person who takes ultimate responsibility for ensuring the desired result is achieved on time and within budget is the **Project Manager**.

The way in which a project manager co-ordinates a project from initiation to completion, using project management and general management techniques, is known as the **Project Management process.**

2.1 Project management v operations management

The role a project manager performs is in many ways similar to those performed by other managers. There are however some important differences, as shown in the following table.

Project manager	Operations manager
Are often 'generalists' with wide-ranging backgrounds and experience levels	Usually specialists in the areas managed
Oversee work in many functional areas	Relate closely to technical tasks in their area
Facilitate, rather than supervise team members	Have direct technical supervision responsibilities

2.2 Duties of the project manager

FAST FORWARD

Duties of the project manager include: Planning, teambuilding, communication, co-ordinating project activities, monitoring and control, problem-resolution and quality control.

The duties of a project manager are summarised below.

Duty	Comment
Outline planning	Project planning (eg targets, sequencing) • Developing project targets such as overall costs or timescale needed (eg project should take 20 weeks). • Dividing the project into activities and placing these activities into the right sequence, often a complicated task if overlapping. • Developing a framework for the procedures and structures, manage the project (eg decide, in principle, to have weekly team meetings, performance reviews etc).
Detailed planning	Work breakdown structure, resource requirements, network analysis for scheduling. (Covered in Chapter 6.)
Teambuilding	Build cohesion and team spirit.
Communication	The project manager must let superiors know what is going on, and ensure that members of the project team are properly briefed.

Duty	Comment
Co-ordinating project activities	Between the project team and users, and other external parties (eg suppliers of hardware and software).
Monitoring and control	The project manager should estimate the causes for each departure from the standard, and take corrective measures.
Problem-resolution	Even with the best planning, unforeseen problems may arise.
Quality control	There is often a short-sighted trade-off between getting the project out on time and the project's quality.

An effective project management process helps project managers maintain control of projects and meet their responsibilities.

2.3 The responsibilities of a project manager

A project manager has responsibilities to both management and to the project team.

2.3.1 Responsibilities to management

- Ensure resources are used efficiently – strike a balance between cost, time and results
- Keep management informed with timely and accurate communications
- Manage the project to the best of his or her ability
- Behave ethically, and adhere to the organisation's policies
- Maintain a customer orientation (whether the project is geared towards an internal or external customer) – customer satisfaction is a key indicator of project success

2.3.2 Responsibilities to the project and the project team

- Take action to keep the project on target for successful completion
- Ensure the project team has the resources required to perform tasks assigned
- Help new team members integrate into the team
- Provide any support required when members leave the team either during the project or on completion

2.4 The skills required of a project manager

FAST FORWARD

Project managers require the following **skills**: Leadership and team building, organisational ability, communication skills (written, spoken, presentations, meetings), some technical knowledge of the project area and inter-personal skills.

To meet these responsibilities a project manager requires a wide range of skills. The skills required are similar to those required when managing a wider range of responsibilities. The narrower focus of project management means it is easier to make a judgement as to how well these skills have been applied.

Type of skill	How the project manager should display the type of skill
Leadership and team building	Be **enthusiastic** about what the project will achieve. Be **positive** (but realistic) about all aspects of the project. Understand where the project fits into the '**big picture**'. **Delegate** tasks appropriately – and not take on too much personally. Build team spirit through encouraging **co-operation**. Do not be restrained by organisational structures – a high tolerance for ambiguity (lack of clear-cut authority) will help the project manager.
Organisational	Ensure all project **documentation** is clear and distributed to all who require it. Use project **management tools** to analyse and monitor project progress.
Communication	**Listen** to project team members. Use **persuasion** to coerce reluctant team members or stakeholders to support the project. Ensure management is kept **informed** and is never surprised.
Technical	By providing (or at least providing access to) the technical **expertise** and experience needed to manage the project.
Personal	Be **flexible**. Circumstances may develop that require a change in plan. Show **persistence**. Even successful projects will encounter difficulties that require repeated efforts to overcome. Be **creative**. If one method of completing a task proves impractical a new approach may be required. **Patience** is required even in the face of tight deadlines. The 'quick-fix' may eventually cost more time than a more thorough but initially more time-consuming solution.

2.5 Leadership styles and project management

As in other forms of management, different project managers have different styles of leadership. There is no 'best' leadership style, as individuals suit and react to different styles in different ways. The key is adopting a style that suits both the project leader and the project team.

Managers will usually adopt a style from the range shown in the following diagram.

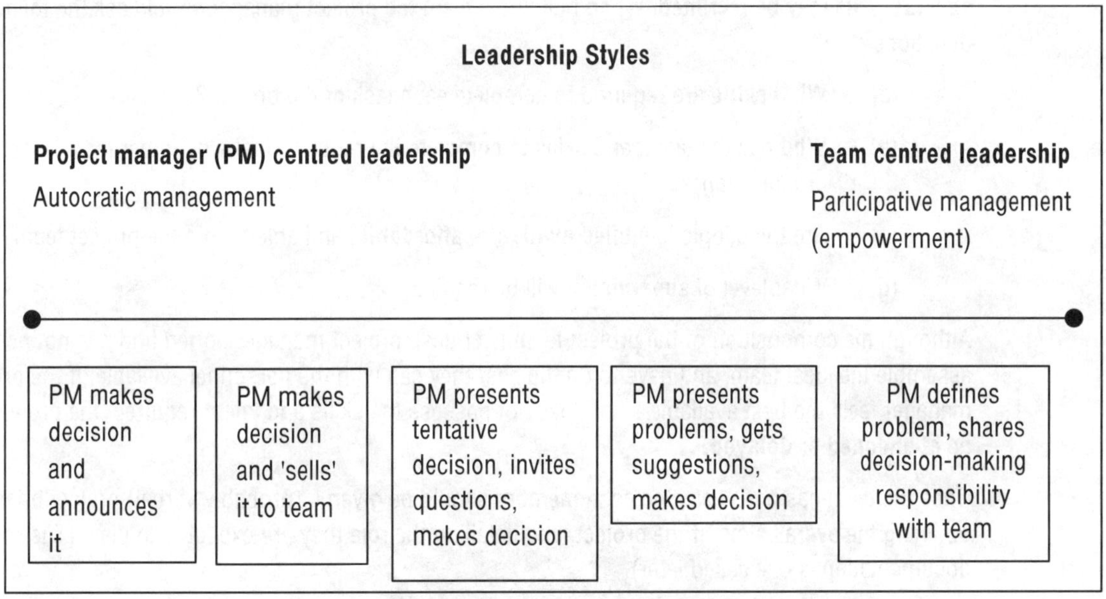
Leadership Styles
Project manager (PM) centred leadership
Autocratic management
Team centred leadership
Participative management (empowerment)
PM makes decision and announces it
PM makes decision and 'sells' it to team
PM presents tentative decision, invites questions, makes decision
PM presents problems, gets suggestions, makes decision
PM defines problem, shares decision-making responsibility with team

The leadership style adopted will affect the way decisions relating to the project are made. Although an autocratic style may prove successful in some situations (eg 'simple' or 'repetitive' projects), a more consultative style has the advantage of making team members feel more a part of the project. This should result in greater **commitment**.

Not all decisions will be made in the same way. For example, decisions that do not have direct consequences for other project personnel may be made with no (or limited) consultation. A **balance** needs to be found between ensuring decisions can be made efficiently, and ensuring adequate consultation.

The type of people that comprise the project team will influence the style adopted. For example, professionals generally dislike being closely supervised and dictated to. (Many non-professionals dislike this too!) Some people however prefer to follow clear, specific instructions and not have to think for themselves.

Project management techniques encourage **management by exception** by identifying, from the outset, those activities which might threaten successful completion of a project.

3 The project team

3.1 Building a project team

FAST FORWARD

Project **success** depends to a large extent on the **team members** selected.

Key term

The **Project Team** comprises the people who report directly or indirectly to the project manager.

Project success depends to a large extent on the team members selected. The ideal project team achieves project completion on time, within budget and to the required specifications – with the minimum amount of direct supervision from the project manager.

3.1.1 Project team composition

The team will comprise individuals with **differing skills and personalities**. The project manager should choose a balanced team that takes advantage of each team member's skills and compensates elsewhere for their weaknesses.

The project team will normally be drawn from existing staff, but highly recommended **outsiders with special skills** may be recruited. When building a team the project manager should ask the following questions.

(a) **What skills** are required to complete each task of the project?

(b) **Who** has the talent and skills to complete the required tasks (whether inside or outside the organisation)?

(c) Are the people identified **available**, **affordable**, and able to join the project team?

(d) What level of **supervision** will be required?

Although the composition of the project team is critical, project managers often find it is not possible to assemble the ideal team, and have to do the best they can with the personnel available. If the project manager feels the best available team does not possess the skills and talent required, the project should be **abandoned or delayed.**

Once the team has been selected each member should be given a (probably verbal) project briefing, outlining the overall aims of the project, and detailing the role they are expected to play. (The role of documentation is discussed later).

3.1.2 Project team performance

The performance of the project team will be enhanced by the following.

- Effective communication
- All members being aware of the team's purpose and the role of each team member
- Collaboration and creativity among team members
- Trusting, supportive atmosphere in group
- A commitment to meeting the agreed schedule
- Innovative/creative behaviour
- Team members highly interdependent, interface effectively
- Capacity for conflict resolution
- Results orientation
- High energy levels and enthusiasm
- An acceptance of change

Collaboration and **interaction** between team members will help ensure the skills of all team members are utilised, and should result in 'synergistic' solutions. Formal (eg meetings) and informal channels (eg e-mail links, a bulletin board) of **communication** should be set up to ensure this interaction takes place.

Team members should be responsible and accountable. The project manager should provide **regular updates** on project progress and timely **feedback** on team and individual performance.

3.1.3 Effective team management

Most **effective project managers** display the ability to:

- Select the right people
- Connect them to the right cause
- Solve problems that arise
- Evaluate progress towards objectives
- Negotiate resolutions to conflicts
- Heal wounds inflicted by change

3.2 Managing conflict

FAST FORWARD

Wherever there is a potential for conflict a **process to resolve** it should be established before the conflict occurs.

It is inevitable when people from wide-ranging backgrounds combine to form a project team that **conflict** will occasionally occur. Some conflicts may actually be **positive**, resulting in fresh ideas and energy being input to the project. Other conflicts can be **negative** and have the potential to bring the project to a standstill.

An open exchange of views between project personnel should be encouraged as this will help ensure all possible courses of action and their consequences are considered. The project manager should keep in touch with the relationships of team members and act as a conciliator if necessary.

Ideally, conflict should be harnessed for productive ends. Conflict can have **positive effects** such as those listed below.

- Results in better, well thought-out ideas
- Forces people to search for new approaches
- Causes persistent problems to surface and be dealt with
- Forces people to clarify their views
- Causes tension which stimulates interest and creativity

3.2.1 Negotiation techniques

FAST FORWARD

Most conflicts that arise during a project should be able to be resolved using **negotiation** and **resolution** techniques.

When conflict occurs the project manager should avoid displaying bias and adopt a logical, ordered approach towards achieving resolution. The following principles should be followed.

- Focus on the problem, not the personalities
- Define the problem carefully
- Try to develop options that would result in mutual gain
- Look for a wide variety of possible solutions

3.2.2 Resolution techniques

Ideally the conflict will be resolved by the parties involved **agreeing** on a course of action. In cases where insufficient progress towards a resolution has occurred the project manager should attempt to bring about a resolution.

The project manager should employ the following **techniques** in an attempt to resolve the conflict.

(a) Work through the problem using the **negotiation techniques** described above.

(b) Attempt to establish a **compromise** – try to bring some degree of satisfaction to all parties through give and take.

(c) Try to **smooth out any differences** and downplay the importance of any remaining differences.

(d) Emphasise areas of **agreement**.

(e) If all else fails, and resolution is vital, the project manager should force the issue and **make a decision**. He or she should emphasise to all parties that their commitment to the project is appreciated, and that the conflict should now be put behind them.

3.3 A computerised information system project team

Much of the work of a dedicated IS department is likely to be **project-based**. This has lead to many organisations organising the IS department according to a **flat** structure that recognises that multi-talented individuals will adopt **different roles** at **different times** – rather than occupying a particular 'status'. Staff are selected from a pool of those currently available, and perform different roles depending upon demand.

To operate such a system the organisation needs to devise a remuneration system that recognises **skills** and work done rather than status.

We cover the systems development process in depth later in this Text. In the context of explaining the roles **of analysts** and **programmers**, developing a computer system can be divided into two parts.

(a) **Designing** a system to perform the tasks the user department wants to be performed – to the user's specification. This is the task of the **systems analyst**.

(b) **Writing the software** – this is the job of the programmer.

3.3.1 Systems analysts

In general terms, the tasks of the systems analyst are as follows.

Systems analysis – involves carrying out a methodical study of a **current system** (manual or computerised) to establish:

(a) What the current system **does**.

(b) Whether it does what it is **supposed to do**.

(c) What the user department would **like it to do**, and so what the required objectives of the system are.

Systems design – having established what the proposed system objectives are, the next stage is to design a system that will **achieve these objectives**.

Systems specification – in designing a new system, it is the task of the systems analyst to **specify** the system in detail.

This involves identification of inputs, files, processing, output, hardware, costs, accuracy, response times and controls.

The system design is spelled out formally in a document or manual called the **systems specification** (which includes a program specification for each program in the system).

The analyst will often also have overall responsibility **systems testing**.

Once installed, the analyst will keep the system under **review**, and control system **maintenance** with the co-operation of **user** departments.

3.3.2 Programmers

Programmers write the programs. This involves:

(a) Reading the **system specification** and understanding it.

(b) Recognising what the processing requirements of the program are, in other words, **defining the processing problem in detail**.

(c) Having defined and analysed the processing problem, **writing the program** in a programming language.

(d) Arranging for the program to be **tested**.

(e) Identifying **errors** in the program and getting rid of these 'bugs' – ie **debugging** the program.

(f) Preparing full documentation for each program within the system.

3.4 Controlling the team

The project manager is responsible for overall control of the project team.

There are two types of control strategies related to supervision.

(a) **Behaviour control** deals with the behaviour of team members. In other words, control is exercised through agreed procedures, policies and methodologies.

(b) **Output control** is where management attention is focused on results, more than the way these were achieved.

Handy writes of a **trust-control dilemma** in which the sum of trust + control is a constant amount:

$T + C = Y$

Where T = the trust the superior has in the subordinate, and the trust which the subordinate feels the superior has in him;

C = the degree of control exercised by the superior over the subordinate;

Y = a constant, unchanging value.

Any increase in C leads to an equal decrease in T; that is, if the manager retains more 'control' or authority, the subordinate will immediately recognise that he or she is being trusted less. If the superior wishes to show more trust in the subordinate, this can only be done by reducing C, that is by delegating more authority.

3.4.1 Span of control

Span of control or 'span of management', refers to the **number of subordinates** or team members responsible to a person.

Classical theorists suggest:

(a) There are physical and mental limitations to a manager's ability to control people, relationships and activities.

(b) There should be tight managerial control from the top of an organisation downward. The span of control should be restricted to allow maximum control.

Project managers may control very large teams. On large projects management layers will be required between the overall project manager and team members. The appropriate span of control will depend on:

(a) **Ability of the manager**. A good organiser and communicator will be able to control a larger number. The manager's workload is also relevant.

(b) **Ability of the team members**. The more experienced, able, trustworthy and well-trained subordinates are, the easier it is to control larger numbers.

(c) **Nature of the task**. It is easier for a supervisor to control a large number of people if they are all doing routine, repetitive or similar tasks.

(d) The **geographical dispersal** of the subordinates, and the **communication system** of the organisation.

3.4.2 Flat management structures

FAST FORWARD

The wide range of people and skills required to successfully complete a systems development project has led to the acceptance of **flat management structures** being the most appropriate for this process.

The span of control has implications for the 'shape' of a project team and of an organisation overall. An organisation with a narrow span of control will have more levels in its management hierarchy – the organisation will be narrow and **tall**. A tall structure reflects tighter supervision and control, and lengthy chains of command and communication.

A team or organisation of the same size with a wide span of control will be wide and **flat**. The flat organisation reflects a greater degree of delegation – the more a manager delegates, the wider the span of control can be.

The wide range of people and skills required to successfully complete a systems development project has led to the acceptance of flat management structures being the most appropriate for this process.

The justification is that by empowering team members (or removing levels in hierarchies that restrict freedom), not only will the job be done more effectively but the people who do the job will get more out of it.

Project team members must be **flexible** to be able to respond quickly to specific and varied customer demands. Team members must therefore be committed.

The following steps may help increase commitment.

(a) Develop **identification** with the team and the project by means of:

- Communications
- Participation
- Team member ideas
- Financial bonuses

(b) Ensure that people **know what they have to achieve** and are aware of how their performance will be measured against agreed targets and standards.

(c) Introduce a **reward system**, which relates at least partly to individual performance.

(d) Treat team members **as human beings**, not machines.

Exam focus point

A question in the December 2004 exam required candidates to explain what is meant by a flat structure and why such a structure is appropriate to an information systems department.

4 Project stakeholders

Key term

Project stakeholders are the individuals and organisations who are involved in or may be affected by project activities.

We have already looked at the role of the **Project Manager** and the **Project Team**. Other key stakeholders are defined as follows.

Key terms

Project sponsor is accountable for the resources invested into the project and responsible for the achievement of the project's business objectives. The sponsor may be owner, financier, client etc., or their delegate.

Project support team is a term used to designate the personnel working on a project who do not report to the project manager administratively.

Users are the individual or group that will utilise the end product, process (system), or service produced by the project.

Risk manager. For large projects it may be necessary to appoint someone to control the process of identifying, classifying and quantifying the risks associated with the project.

Quality manager. For large projects it may be necessary to appoint someone to write the quality plan and develop quality control procedures.

Project stakeholders should all be **committed towards a common goal** – successful project completion. The Project Plan (covered in Chapter 6) should be the common point of reference that states priorities and provides cohesion.

However, the individuals and groups that comprise the stakeholders all have different roles, and therefore are likely to have different points of view. There is therefore the potential for **disagreements** between stakeholder groups.

4.1 Managing stakeholder disputes

The first step is to establish a **framework** to predict the potential for disputes. This involves **risk management**, since an unforeseen event (a risk) has the potential to create conflict, and dispute management – implementing dispute resolution procedures that have minimal impact on costs, goodwill and project progress. (Risk management is covered in Chapter 6.)

One approach to dispute management strategy is to organise affairs in a way that minimises exposure to the risk of disputes. This means employing effective management techniques throughout all areas of operation.

4.1.1 Dispute resolution processes

Resolution is the solution of a conflict. **Settlement** is an arrangement, which brings an end to the conflict, but does not necessarily address the underlying causes.

Wherever there is a potential for conflict, a **process to resolve** it should be established before the conflict occurs.

We have already discussed negotiation and resolution techniques in the context of project team conflict. Many of the principles discussed previously can be applied to stakeholder conflicts, although the relative positions of the stakeholders involved can complicate matters.

Conflict between project stakeholders may be resolved by:

- **Negotiation** (perhaps with the assistance of others)
- **Partnering**
- **Mediation**
- A third party neutral may judge or intervene to **impose a solution**

On very large projects a **Disputes Review Board** (DRB) may be formed. This may comprise persons directly involved in the project engaged to maintain a 'watching brief' to identify and attend upon disputes as they arise.

Usually there is a procedure in place which provides for the DRB to make an 'on the spot' decision before a formal dispute is notified so that the project work can proceed, and that may be followed by various rights of review at increasingly higher levels.

In practice, disputes are often resolved by the acceptance of the view of the party that has the most financial 'clout' in the project. In such a situation mediation and negotiation may only deliver an outcome which is a reflection of the original power imbalance.

Chapter Roundup

- A **project** often has the following characteristics:
  - A defined beginning and end
  - Resources allocated specifically to them
  - Intended to be done only once (although similar separate projects could be undertaken)
  - Follow a plan towards a clear intended end-result
  - Often cut across organisational and functional lines
- **Project management** is the combination of systems, techniques, and people used to control and monitor activities undertaken within the project. A project will be deemed successful if it is completed at the specified level of **quality**, **on time** and within **budget**.
- The person who takes ultimate responsibility for ensuring the desired result is achieved on time and within budget is the **project manager**.
- **Duties** of the project manager include: Planning, teambuilding, communication, co-ordinating project activities, monitoring and control, problem-resolution and quality control.
- Project managers require the following **skills**: Leadership and team building, organisational ability, communication skills (written, spoken, presentations, meetings), some technical knowledge of the project area and inter-personal skills.
- Project **success** depends to a large extent on the **team members** selected.
- Wherever there is a potential for conflict a **process to resolve** it should be established before the conflict occurs.
- Most conflicts that arise during a project should be able to be resolved using **negotiation** and **resolution** techniques.
- The wide range of people and skills required to successfully complete a systems development project has led to the acceptance of **flat management structures** being the most appropriate for this process.

Quick Quiz

1 What is a successful project?

2 List four areas a project manager should be skilled in.

3 Who is the project sponsor?

4 Project management techniques encourage management by exception. TRUE or FALSE?

5 Why is it generally accepted that project teams involved in information systems implementations, and IS/IT departments should have a flat management structure?

6 List four ways a dispute between project stakeholders could be settled.

Answers to Quick Quiz

1 One that is completed on time, within budget and to specification.

2 [Four of] Leadership, team building, organisational, communication, technical, personal.

3 The project sponsor may be the owner, financier, client etc., or their delegate. The sponsor is accountable for the resources invested into the project and responsible for the achievement of the project's business objectives.

4 TRUE.

5 A tall structure reflects tighter supervision and control, and lengthy chains of command and communication. A flat structure reflects a greater degree of empowerment and flexibility. As IS/IT projects and departments involve people with a wide range of skills, it is felt that flat management structures that allow flexibility are most appropriate.

6 Negotiation (perhaps with the assistance of others)

Partnering
Mediation
A neutral third party may intervene and impose a solution

The material in this chapter is tested in Q16 from the Exam Question Bank – attempt this question **after studying Chapter 6**.

Number	Level	Marks	Time
Q16 (attempt after studying Chapter 6)	Examination	20	36 mins

Project phases and management tools

Topic list	Syllabus reference
1 The project life cycle	1 (g)
2 Management tools and techniques	1 (f), 1 (g), 1 (h)
3 Project management software	1 (i)
4 Documentation and reports	1 (f), 1 (g), 1 (h)
5 Risk management	1 (d)
6 Information systems projects – common problems	1 (h), 3 (l)

Introduction

In this chapter we study the stages a project moves through from initiation to completion. Be aware that other books may refer to **project stages** with different names or may include more or fewer stages. This does not mean one description is incorrect. The principles behind the process and techniques are more important than the labels used.

Later in the chapter we study the various **management tools and techniques** used in project management – covering areas such as project documentation and risk management.

Study guide

Part 1.4 – Organising information systems; structural issues

- Discuss the meaning and need for a risk management process

Part 1.6 – Project initiation

- Define the content and structure of the terms of reference
- Describe the typical contents of a Project Quality Plan and explain the need for such a plan

Part 1.7 – Project planning

- Assist in splitting the project into its main phases
- Participate in the breakdown of work into lower-level tasks
- Assist in the estimation of the time taken to complete these lower-level tasks
- Define dependencies between lower-level tasks
- Construct and interpret a project network
- Construct and interpret a Gantt Chart

Part 1.8 – Project monitoring and control

- Describe methods of monitoring and reporting progress
- Define the reasons for slippage and how to deal with slippage when it occurs
- Discuss the reasons for changes during the project and the need for a project change procedure
- Reflect the effects of progress, slippage and change requests on the project plan
- Discuss the particular problems of planning and controlling Information Systems projects

Part 1.9 – Software support for project management

- Define the meaning of a project management software package and give a brief list of representative products
- Describe a range of features and functions that a project management software package may provide
- Explain the advantages of using a project management software package in the project management process

Part 3.27 – Relationship of management, development process and quality

- Explain the time/cost/quality triangle and its implications for information systems projects

Exam guide

Ensure you are able to apply project management tools and techniques. Network analysis and Gantt charts are highly examinable.

1 The project life cycle

A successful project relies on two activities – **planning** first, and then **doing**. These two activities form the basis of every project.

Projects can be divided into several phases to provide better management control. Collectively these phases comprise the **project life cycle**.

Key term

> The term **project life cycle** refers to the major time periods through which any project passes. Each period may be identified as a phase and further broken down into stages.

Although the principles of the project life cycle apply to all projects, the number and name of the phases identified will vary depending on what the project aims to achieve, and the project model referred to.

When studying Project Management it is convenient to give generic names to the phases of the **project life cycle**. Remember though, in '**real' situations** (or in examination questions!) the model can be modified to suit circumstances.

The diagram below shows a generic model of the **five main phases of a project**.

The phases of a project

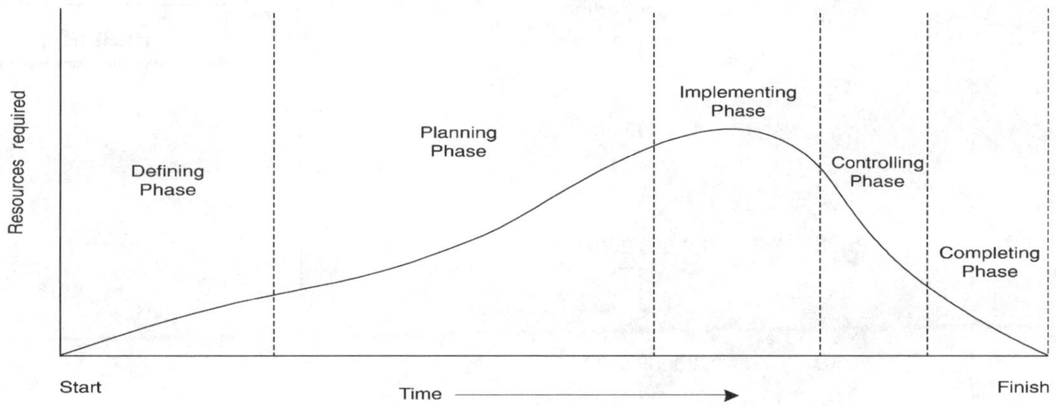

As shown on the diagram, resource use (such as funds and staff hours required) is relatively low at the start of the project, higher towards the end and then drops rapidly as the project draws to a close.

The cost of making changes to the project increases the further into the life cycle the project has progressed.

1.1 Project phases and stages

FAST FORWARD

> A project typically passes through five **phases**: defining, planning, implementing, controlling and completing. The number and sequence of **stages of a project** will vary across organisations.

The phases of a project can be broken down into a number of **stages**. Again, the number of stages identified varies depending on type of project and the conventions of the organisation undertaking the project.

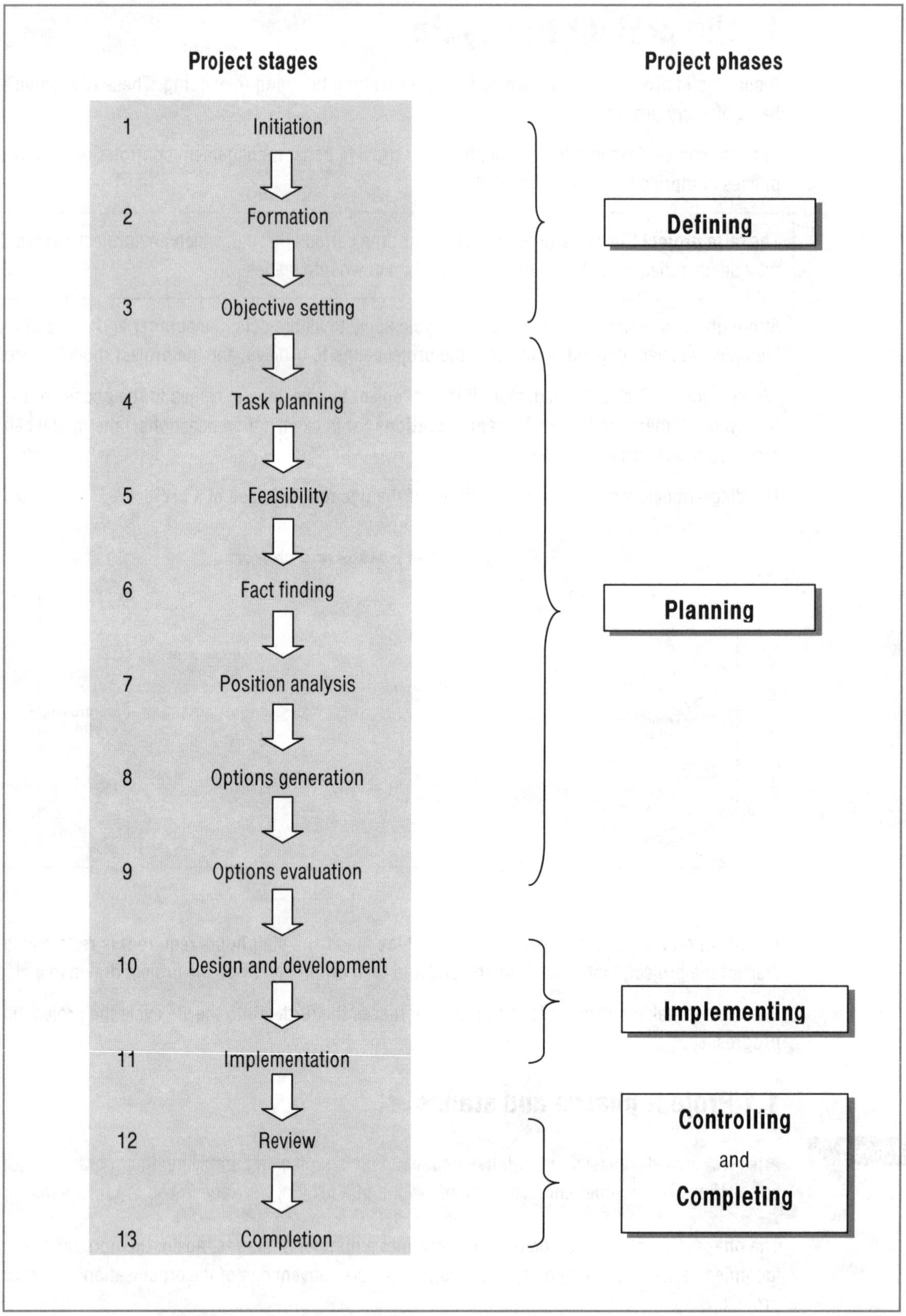

We now will look at each of these phases and stages.

1.2 Defining Phase

Key term

> The **defining phase** of a project is concerned with deciding whether a project should begin and committing to do so.

1.2.1 Initiation stage

Key term

Project initiation describes the beginning of a project at which point certain management activities are required to ensure that the project is established with clear reference terms and an appropriate management structure.

Projects originate from someone attempting to resolve a **problem**, or seeing an **opportunity** to do something new.

It is often not clear precisely what the problem is. The project team should study, discuss and **analyse** the problem, from a number of different aspects (eg technical, financial).

Not all ideas will result in viable projects. A 'reality test' should be applied to all ideas. This is not a detailed feasibility study, and is intended to eliminate only concepts that are **obviously not viable**. For example, a small construction company should not waste resources investigating the possibility of submitting a tender to build the second channel tunnel.

At the start of a project, a **Project Initiation Document (PID)** may be drawn up, setting out the **terms of reference** for the project. Typical contents might include.

(a) The **business objectives**. Projects should not be undertaken simply for their own sake: the business advantages should be clearly identified and be the first point of reference when progress is being reviewed, to make sure that the original aim is not lost sight of.

(b) Probable **project objectives**, stated in a general manner.

(c) The **scope** of the project: what it is intended to cover and what it is not.

(d) **Constraints**, such as maximum amount to be spent and interim and final deadlines.

(e) The **ultimate customer** of the project, who will resolve conflicts as they occur (for example between two different divisions who will both be using the new system) and finally accept it.

(f) The **resources** that will be used – staff, technical resources, finance.

(g) An **analysis of risks** inherent in the project and how they are to be avoided or reduced (for example, the consequences of replacing the old sales ledger system and only discovering after the event that the new one does not work).

(h) A preliminary **project plan** (targets, activities and so on) and details of how the project is to be organised and managed (see the next section).

(i) **Purchasing and procurement policy**, perhaps specifying acceptable suppliers and delivery details.

1.2.2 Formation stage

The formation stage involves selecting the personnel who will be involved with the project. First to be selected is usually the **Project Manager** (whose role was discussed in Chapter 5). and the **Project Board**.

The project manager should **select and build the project team**. This process was explained in Chapter 5.

1.2.3 Objective setting stage

Before specific objectives can be set it is necessary to establish more general **project goals**. Clear goals and objectives give team members **quantifiable targets** to aim for. This should improve motivation and performance, as attempting to achieve a challenging goal is more inspiring than simply being told 'do your best.'

The **overall project goal** or project definition will be developed. On complex projects it is likely that the goal will require be written in stages, with each definition being more detailed and refined than before. The project goal might be defined in a:

- Contract
- Product specification
- Customer's specification

Key terms

A **goal** is a result or purpose that is determined for a project. Goals are broader than objectives.

An **objective** is a specific project outcome required – including required resources and timing.

Objectives are developed from broad goals. In an accounting software installation project a project goal could be 'to produce timely and accurate management accounting reports.' An objective of the same project could be 'to have the nominal ledger system live and fully operational by November 1 200X.'

Project objectives should be **SMART**:

- **S**pecific – so all involved are working towards the same end
- **M**easurable – how will success be measured
- **A**greed upon – by all team members and stakeholders
- **R**ealistic – to motivate goals and objectives must be achievable
- **T**ime-bound – a date must be allocated to provide focus and aid priority setting
- Allocated – in terms of responsibility

1.3 Planning Phase

Key term

The **planning phase** of a project aims to devise a workable scheme to accomplish the overall project goal.

1.3.1 Task planning stage

After the project team is in place and project goals and objectives have been set, the project should be broken down into **manageable tasks**. This process is often referred to as **Work Breakdown Structure (WBS)**. A brief overview of the process follows. We cover WBS in greater detail later in this chapter.

Key terms

A **task** is an individual unit of work that is part of the total work needed to accomplish a project.

An **activity** is a set of tasks that are carried out in order to create a deliverable.

A **deliverable** is another name for a required outcome (eg product, service, document etc) from a project.

By breaking the project down into a series of manageable tasks it is easier to determine the skills needed to complete the project. A **task list** should be produced showing what tasks need to be done and the work sequences necessary.

Building a task list for a complex project can be an involved and lengthy process. It can be difficult deciding what constitutes a task, and where one task ends and another begins.

Tasks should be:

(a) **Clear**. Eg Design the layout of the fixed asset depreciation schedule.

(b) **Self-contained**. No gaps in time should be apparent on work-units grouped together to form a task. All work-units within a task should be related.

1.3.2 Feasibility and fact finding stage

Once all the tasks have been defined a basic **network diagram** can be developed, together with a **complete list of resources** required. Network diagrams are covered later in this chapter.

A more realistic judgement as to the **feasibility** of the project can now be made. Earlier feasibility decisions, such as a pre-project feasibility study, have been fairly general. Feasibility concerns now are more specific – such as whether initial time and cost estimates are realistic.

Fact finding may have been performed substantially during a pre-project feasibility study –as covered in Chapter 4.

The activities carried out will differ depending on the nature of the project. For information systems projects the fact finding exercise would take the form of a systems investigation. This process is covered in Chapter 8.

1.3.3 Position analysis, options generation and options evaluation stages

Once the current position has been clearly established options can be generated with the aim of utilising the internal strengths identified.

The general management technique of **SWOT analysis** can be applied to establish the current position, generate available options and evaluate those options.

Key terms

SWOT analysis is a process that aims to determine:

What **Strengths** do we have? (How can we take advantage of them?)

What **Weaknesses** do we have? (How can we minimise them?)

What **Opportunities** are there? (How can we capitalise on them?)

What **Threats** might prevent us from getting there? (eg Technical obstacles.)

A **strengths and weaknesses analysis** should identify:

(a) Strengths the organisation has that the project may be able to exploit.

(b) Organisational weaknesses that may impact on the project. Strategies will be required to improve these areas or minimise their impact.

The **strengths** and **weaknesses** analysis has an **internal** focus. The identification of shortcomings in skills or resources could lead to a decision to purchase from outsiders or to train staff.

An **external appraisal** is required to identify **opportunities** which can be exploited by the company and also to anticipate environmental **threats** (a declining economy, competitors' actions, government legislation, industrial unrest etc) against which the company must protect itself.

The internal and external appraisals of SWOT analysis will be brought together.

(a) Major **strengths** and profitable opportunities can be **exploited** especially if strengths and opportunities are matched with each other.

(b) Major **weaknesses** and threats should be **countered**, or a contingency strategy or corrective strategy developed.

The elements of the SWOT analysis can be summarised and shown on a **cruciform chart**. The following chart relates to a project that proposes to install a new computerised accounting system.

1.3.4 Example: New computerised accounting system

STRENGTHS	WEAKNESSES
£1 million of funds allocated Willing and experienced workforce	Workforce has very limited experience of computerised systems Seems to be an expectation that the new system will 'do everything'
THREATS	**OPPORTUNITIES**
The software vendor is rumoured to be in financial trouble and may 'disappear' Choosing a poor system will result in increased risk of system failure	Chance to introduce compatible systems in other departments at a later date Later integration with e-commerce functions is possible

One **potential strategy** identified as a result of this SWOT analysis is explained below.

Significant benefits can be obtained from the project, which should be able to achieve its aims within the £1 million budgeted.

Assurances should be sought from the software vendor as to their future plans and profitability. Contractual obligations should be obtained in regard to this. If the rumours are justified, either another supplier should be approached or the possibility of employing the original vendor's staff on a contract basis could be explored. *(This is an example of an alternative strategy coming out of the SWOT analysis.)*

The end users of the system must be involved in all aspects of system design. Training of staff must be thorough and completed before the system 'goes live'. Management and users must be educated as to what the system will and will not be able to do.

A contingency plan should be in place for repairing or even replacing hardware at short notice.

1.4 Implementing Phase

Key term

> The **implementing phase** is concerned with co-ordinating people and other resources to carry out the project plan.

1.4.1 Design and development stage

The design and development stage is where the actual product, service or process that will be the end result of the project is worked on.

The activities carried out in this stage will vary greatly depending on the type of project. For example, in a software implementation this is when the programming of the software would take place, in a construction project the building design would be finalised.

1.4.2 Implementation stage

After the process, service or product has been developed it will be implemented or installed so it is available to be used.

If the project involves a new system or process, a period of parallel running alongside the existing system or process may be carried out. This enables results to be checked, and any last-minute problems to be ironed out before the organisation is fully reliant on the new system or process.

1.5 Controlling Phase

Key term

The **controlling phase** is concerned with ensuring project objectives are met by monitoring and measuring progress and taking corrective action when necessary.

1.5.1 Review stage

Actual performance should be reviewed against the objectives identified in the project plan. If performance is not as expected, control action will be necessary.

1.6 Completing Phase

Key term

Completion involves formalising acceptance of the project and bringing it to an orderly end.

1.6.1 Completion stage

Following installation and review there should be a meeting of the Project Board to:

- Check that all products are complete and delivered
- Check the status of any outstanding requests for change
- Check all project issues have been cleared
- Approve the project completion report
- Arrange for a post-implementation review

2 Management tools and techniques

FAST FORWARD

Various **tools and techniques** are available to plan and control projects including the Project Plan Project Budget, Work Breakdown Structure, Gantt charts, Network Analysis, Resource Histogram and specialist software.

2.1 The Project Budget

Key term

Project budget. The amount and distribution of resources allocated to a project.

Building a project budget should be an orderly process that attempts to establish a realistic estimate of the cost of the project. There are two main methods for establishing the project budget; **top-down** and **bottom-up**.

2.1.1 Top-down budgeting

Top-down budgeting describes the situation where the budget is imposed 'from above'. Project Managers are allocated a budget for the project based on an estimate made by senior management. The figure may prove realistic, especially if similar projects have been undertaken recently. However the technique is often used simply because it is quick, or because only a certain level of funding is available.

2.1.2 Bottom-up budgeting

In **bottom-up budgeting** the project manager consults the project team, and others, to calculate a budget based on the tasks that make up the project. Work breakdown structure (WBS) is a useful tool in this process. WBS is explained later in this section.

The budget may express all resources in monetary amounts, or may show money and other resources – such as staff hours. A monetary budget is often used to establish the current cost variance of the project. To establish this we need:

(a) **The Actual Cost of Work Performed (ACWP)**. This is the amount spent to date on the project.

(b) **The Budgeted Cost of Work Scheduled (BCWS)**. The amount that was budgeted to be spent to this point on scheduled activities.

(c) **The Budgeted Cost of Work Performed (BCWP)**. This figure is calculated by pricing the work that has actually been done – using the same basis as the scheduled work.

BCWP – ACWP = The **cost variance** for the project.

BCWP – BCWS = The **schedule variance** for the project.

Budgets should be presented for approval and **sign-off** to the stakeholder who has responsibility for the funds being used.

It may be decided that a project costs more than the value of expected benefits. If so, scrapping the project is a perfectly valid option. In such cases the budgeting process has highlighted the situation before too much time and effort has been spent on an unprofitable venture.

During the project actual expenditure is tracked against budget on either a separate **Budget Report,** or as part of a regular **Progress Report.** We will be looking at project documentation and reports later in this chapter.

2.2 Work breakdown structure (WBS)

Key term

Work breakdown structure is the analysis of the work of a project into different units or tasks. WBS:

(a) Identifies the work that must be done in the project.
(b) Determines the resources required.
(c) Sequences the work done, to allocate resources in the optimum way.

Work breakdown structure is used as a starting point for many project management functions including budgeting and **scheduling**. As a simple example of WBS, **wiring** a house can be **sub-divided** into connecting the mains, fitting light sockets and power points etc. Dealing with the foundations involves digging, filling, area marking, damp proofing and disposal of soil.

The process of work breakdown continues until the smallest possible sub-unit is reached. Digging the foundations for example would be analysed so that the number of labour hours needed, and hence the cost, could be determined. *Lock* recommends giving each sub-unit of work a code number to enable resources to be obtained and the work to be planned.

2.2.1 WBS and estimates of expenditure

WBS can be used in devising estimates. From the WBS it is possible to compile a complete list of **every task** that is going to attract expenditure.

Collating the various costs identified with each task has several benefits:

(a) Provides a useful **cost analysis** for various business functions.
(b) Assists **cost control**.
(c) Provides evidence, in any dispute with the client, that the costs are reasonable.

Estimates (and therefore budgets) cannot be expected to be 100% accurate. Business **conditions may change**, the project plan may be amended or estimates may simply prove to be incorrect.

Any **estimate** must be accompanied by some **indication of expected accuracy**.

Estimates can be **improved** by:

- **Learning** from past mistakes
- Ensuring sufficient design **information**
- Ensuring as **detailed a specification as possible** from the customer
- Properly **analysing the job** into its constituent units

The overall level of cost estimates will be influenced by:

(a) **Project goals**. If a high level of quality is expected costs will be higher.

(b) **External vendors**. Some costs may need to be estimated by outside vendors. To be realistic these people must understand exactly what would be expected of them.

(c) **Staff availability**. If staff are unavailable, potentially expensive contractors may be required.

(d) **Time schedules**. The quicker a task is required to be done the higher the cost is likely to be – particularly with external suppliers.

2.3 Gantt charts

A Gantt chart, named after the engineer Henry Gantt who pioneered the procedure in the early 1900s, is a horizontal bar chart used to plan the **time scale** for a project and to estimate the amount of **resources** required.

The Gantt chart displays the **time relationships** between tasks in a project. Two lines are usually used to show the time allocated for each task, and the actual time taken.

A simple Gantt chart, illustrating some of the activities involved in a network server installation project, follows.

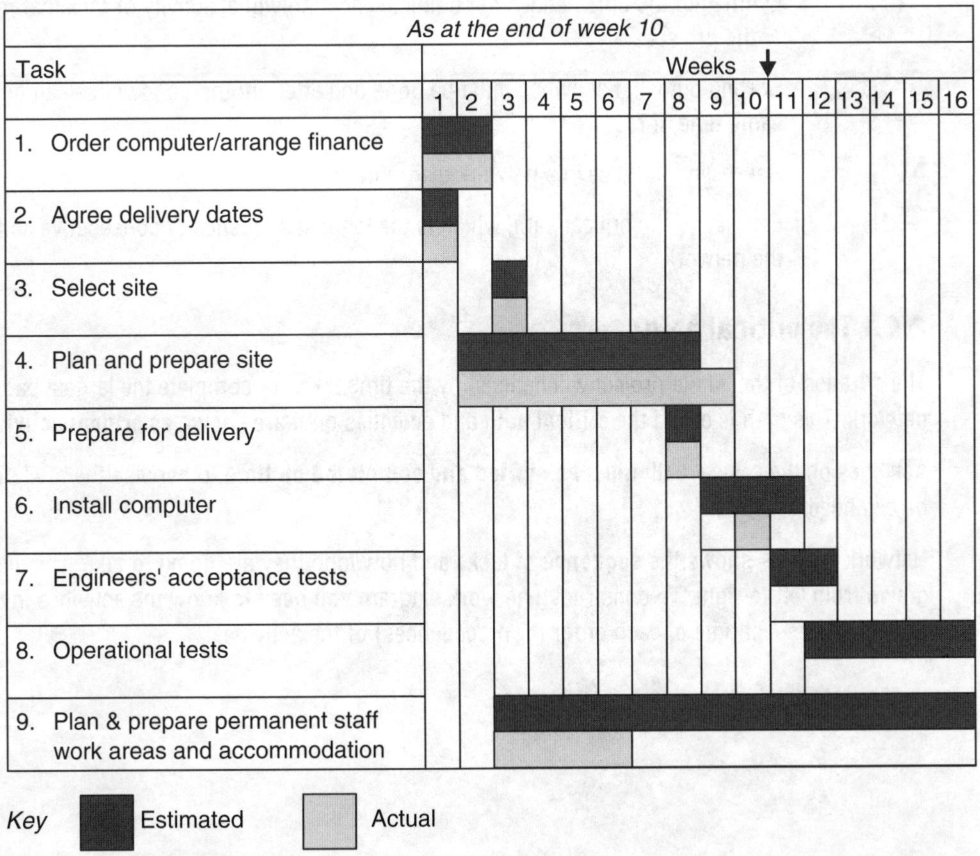

The chart shows that at the end of the tenth week Activity 9 is running behind schedule. More resources may have to be allocated to this activity if the staff accommodation is to be ready in time for the changeover to the new system.

Activity 4 had not been completed on time, and this has resulted in some disruption to the computer installation (Activity 6), which may mean further delays in the commencement of Activities 7 and 8.

A Gantt chart does not show the interrelationship between activities as clearly as a **network diagram** (covered later in this chapter). A combination of Gantt charts and network analysis will often be used for project planning and resource allocation.

2.4 Network analysis

Network analysis, also known as **Critical Path Analysis** (CPA), is a useful technique to help with planning and controlling large projects, such as construction projects, research and development projects and the computerisation of systems.

Key term

Network analysis requires breaking down the project into tasks with estimated durations and establishing a logical sequence. This enables the minimum possible duration of the project to be found.

CPA aims to ensure the progress of a project, so the project is completed in the **minimum amount of time**.

It pinpoints the tasks which are on the **critical path**, ie those tasks which, if delayed beyond the allotted time, would **delay the completion** of the project as a whole. The technique can also be used to assist in allocating resources such as labour and equipment.

Critical path analysis is quite a simple technique. The events and activities making up the whole project are represented in the form of a **diagram**. Drawing the diagram or chart involves the following steps.

Step 1 Estimating the time needed to complete each individual activity or task that makes up a part of the project.

Step 2 Sorting out what activities must be done one after another, and which can be done at the same time, if required.

Step 3 Representing these in a network diagram.

Step 4 Estimating the critical path, which is the longest sequence of consecutive activities through the network.

2.4.1 The critical path

The duration of the whole project will be fixed by the time taken to complete the largest path through the network. This path is called the **critical path** and activities on it are known as **critical activities**.

Activities on the critical path **must be started and completed on time**, otherwise the total project time will be extended.

Network analysis shows the **sequence** of tasks and how long they are going to take. The diagrams are drawn from left to right. To construct a network diagram you need to know the activities involved in a project, the expect time of each order (or precedences) of the activities.

2.4.2 Example

The table below shows the Activities, time scales and precedences of a particular project. This information could be used to construct the network diagram shown below the table.

Activity	Expected time	Preceding activity
A	3	–
B	5	–
C	2	B
D	1	A
E	6	A
F	3	D
G	3	C, E

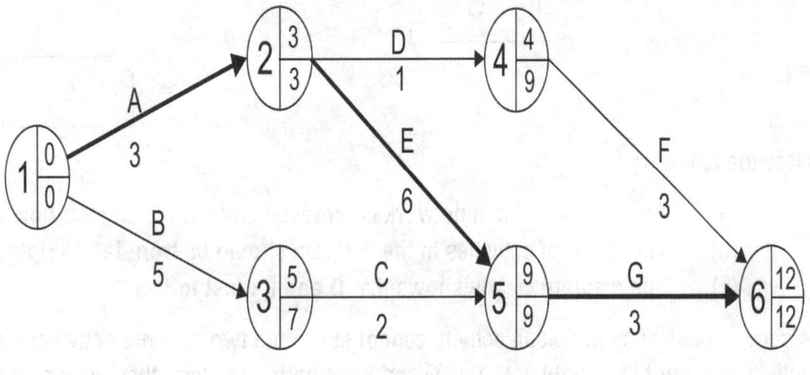

Points to note from the diagram:

(a) **Events** (eg 1 and 2) are represented by circles. **Tasks** (eg A) connect events.

(b) The **critical path** may be shown by drawing a small vertical line through the arrow or by making arrows on the critical path thicker. The critical path is the longest (in terms of time) path through the network – which is the **minimum amount of time** that the project will take.

(c) It is the convention to note the **earliest** start date of any task in the **top right hand corner** of the circle.

(d) We can then work **backwards** identifying the **latest** dates when tasks could start. These we insert in the **bottom right quarter** of the circle.

The **critical path** in the diagram above is AEG.

Note the **float time** of five days for Activity F. Activity F can begin any time between days 4 and 9, thus giving the project manager a degree of flexibility.

The diagram above uses **'Activity on line'** notation – as Activities are shown on the lines or arrows that connect events.

2.4.3 Activity-on-node presentation

Network diagrams may also be drawn using Activity-on-node presentation which is similar in style to that used by the **Microsoft Project** software package.

2.4.4 Example: Activity on Node

Suppose that a project includes three activities, C, D and E. Neither activity D nor E can start until activity C is completed, but D and E could be done simultaneously if required.

This would be represented as follows.

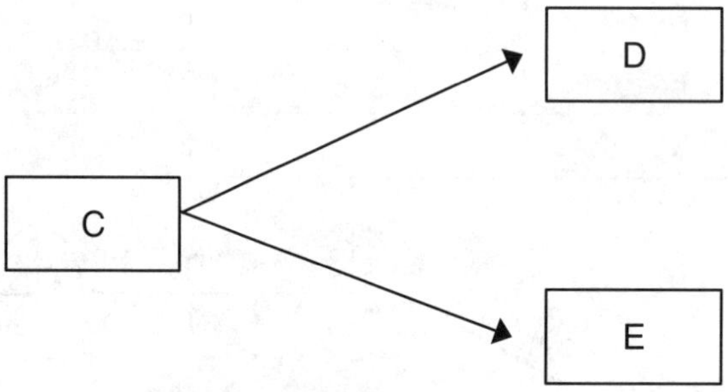

Note the following.

(a) An **activity** within a network is represented by a rectangular box. (Each box is a **node**.)

(b) The **'flow'** of activities in the diagram should be from **left to right**.

(c) The diagram clearly shows that **D and E must follow C.**

A second possibility is that an activity cannot start until two or more activities have been completed. If activity H cannot start until activities G and F are both complete, then we would represent the situation like this.

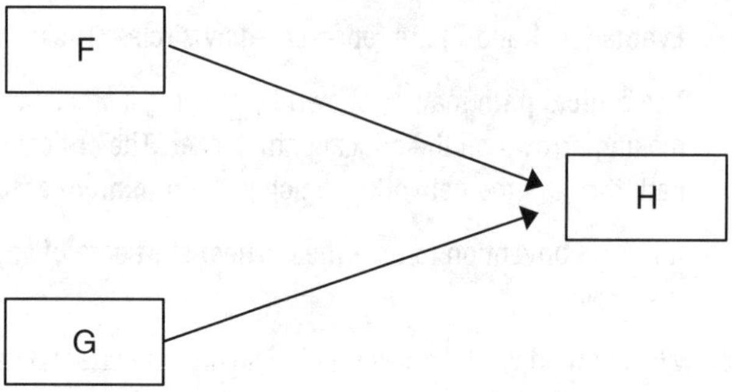

In some conventions an extra node is introduced at the start and end of a network. This serves no purpose (other than to ensure that all the nodes are joined up), so we recommend that you do not do it.

Just in case you ever see a network presented in this way, both styles are shown in the next example.

2.5 Example showing start and end nodes

Draw a diagram for the following project. The project is finished when both D and E are complete.

Activity	*Preceding activity*
A	–
B	–
C	A
D	B & C
E	B

The first solution that follows excludes start and end nodes – the second solution includes them.

Solution

2.5.1 Microsoft Project style

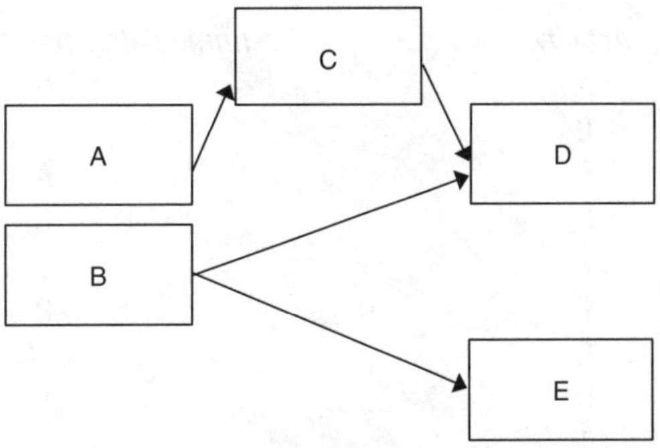

2.5.2 With start and end nodes

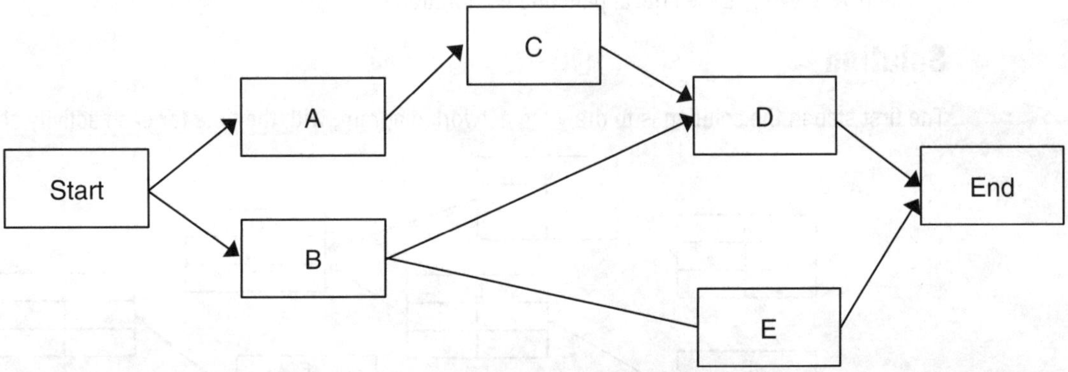

Any network can be analysed into a number of different paths or routes. A path is simply a sequence of activities which can take you from the start to the end of the network.

In the example above, there are just three possible routes or paths (based on the precedences given earlier).

(a) A C D.
(b) B D.
(c) B E.

2.6 Showing the duration of activities

The time needed to complete each individual activity in a project must be estimated. This **duration** may be shown within the node as follows. The meaning of the other boxes is explained later.

Task A	
ID	6 days

Note that there are a range of acceptable notation styles for network diagrams. You should learn the principles of the technique so you are able to interpret diagrams presented in a variety of formats (with an explanatory key).

2.7 Example: The critical path

Activity	*Immediately preceding activity*	*Duration (weeks)*
A	–	5
B	–	4
C	A	2
D	B	1
E	B	5
F	B	5
G	C, D	4
H	F	3
I	F	2

(a) What are the paths through the network?

(b) What is the critical path and its duration?

Solution

The first step in the solution is to draw the network diagram, with the time for each activity shown.

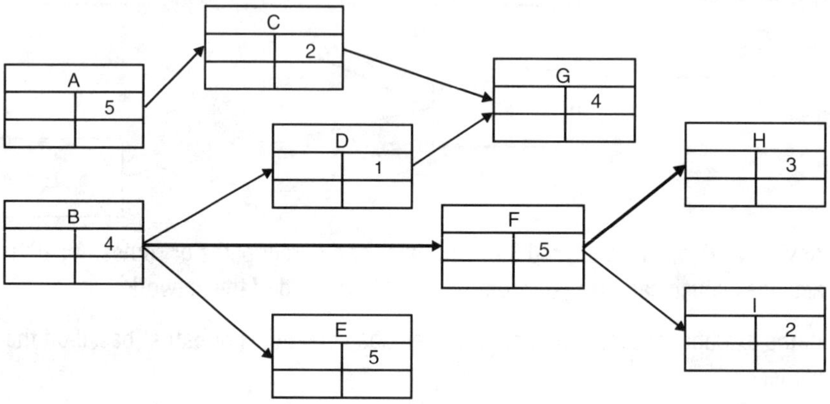

We could list the paths through the network and their overall completion times as follows.

Path	*Duration (weeks)*	
A C G	(5 + 2 + 4)	11
B D G	(4 + 1 + 4)	9
B E	(4 + 5)	
B F H	(4 + 5+ 3)	2
B F I	(4 + 5 + 2 + 0)	1

The critical path is the longest, **BFH**, with a duration of 12 weeks. This is the **minimum time needed** to complete the project.

The **critical path** may be indicated on the diagram by drawing **thick** (or **double-line**) arrows, or by the addition of one or two small vertical lines through the arrows on the critical path. In Microsoft Project the arrows and the nodes are highlighted in red.

Listing paths through the network in this way should be easy enough for small networks, but it becomes a **long and tedious task** for bigger and more complex networks. This is why **software packages** are used in real life.

Conventionally it has been recognised as useful to calculate the **earliest and latest times for activities to start or finish**, and show them on the network diagram. This can be done for networks of any size and complexity.

Project management software packages offer a much larger variety of techniques than can easily be done by hand. Microsoft Project allows **each activity** to be assigned to any one of a variety of types: 'start as late as possible', 'start as soon as possible', 'finish no earlier than a particular date', 'finish no later than a particular date', and so on.

In real life, too, activity times can be shortened by working **weekends and overtime**, or they may be constrained by **non-availability of essential personnel**. In other words with any more than a few activities the possibilities are mind-boggling, which is why software is used. Nevertheless, a simple technique is illustrated in the following example.

2.8 Example: Earliest and latest start times

One way of showing earliest and latest **start** times for activities is to divide each event node into sections. This is similar to the style used in Microsoft Project except that Project uses real dates, which is far more useful, and the bottom two sections can mean a variety of things, depending what constraints have been set.

These sections record the following things.

(a) The **name** of the activity, for example Task A. This helps humans to understand the diagram.

(b) An **ID number** which is unique to that activity. This helps computer packages to understand the diagram, because it is possible that two or more activities could have the same name. For instance two bits of research are done at different project stages might both be called 'Research'.

(c) The **duration** of the activity.

(d) The **earliest start time**. Conventionally for the first node in the network, this is time 0.

(e) The **latest start time**.

(**Note**. Don't confuse start times with the **'event'** times that are calculated when using the **activity-on-arrow** method, even though the approach is the same.)

<table>
<tr><td colspan="2">Task D</td></tr>
<tr><td>ID number:
4</td><td>Duration:
6 days</td></tr>
<tr><td>Earliest start:
Day 4</td><td>Latest start:
Day 11</td></tr>
</table>

2.8.1 Earliest start times

To find the earliest start times, always start with activities that have no predecessors and give them an earliest starting time of 0. In the example we have been looking at, this is week 0.

Then work along each path from **left to right** through the diagram calculating the earliest time that the next activity can start. For example, the earliest time for activity C is week 0 + 5 = 5. The earliest time activities D, E and F can start is week 0 + 4 = 4.

To calculate an activity's earliest time, simply look at the box for the **preceding** activity and add the bottom left figure to the top right figure. If **two or more** activities precede an activity take the **highest** figure as the later activity's earliest start time: it cannot start before all the others are finished!

2.8.2 Latest start times

The latest start times are the latest times at which each activity can start **if the project as a whole is to be completed in the earliest possible time**, in other words in 12 weeks in our example.

Work backwards from **right to left** through the diagram calculating the latest time at which the activity can start, if it is to be completed at the latest finishing time. For example the latest start time for activity H is 12 – 3 = week 9 and for activity E is 12 – 5 = week 7.

Activity F might cause difficulties as two activities, H and I, lead back to it.

(a) Activity H must be completed by week 12, and so must start at week 9.

(b) Activity I must also be completed by week 12, and so must start at week 10.

(c) Activity F takes 5 weeks so its latest start time F is the either 9 – 5 = week 4 or 10 – 5 = week 5. However, if it starts in week 5 it not be possible to start activity H on time and the whole project will be delayed. We therefore take the **lower** figure.

The final diagram is now as follows.

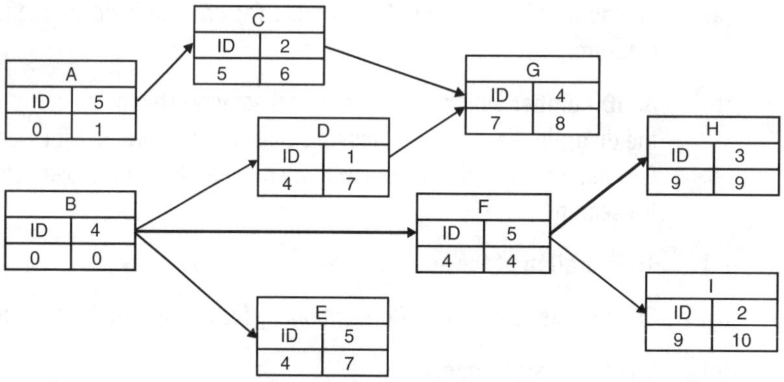

Critical activities are those activities which must be started on time, otherwise the total project time will be increased. It follows that each event on the critical path must have the same earliest and latest start times. The critical path for the above network is therefore **B F H**.

2.9 Criticisms of critical path/network analysis

The following criticisms are often made in relation to network analysis.

(a) It is not always possible to devise an effective WBS for a project.

(b) **It assumes a sequential relationship** between activities. It assumes that once Activity B starts after Activity A has finished. It is not very good at coping with the possibility that an activity 'later' in the sequence may be relevant to an earlier activity.

(c) There are **problems in estimation**. Where the project is completely new, the planning process may be conducted in conditions of relative ignorance.

(d) Although network analysis plans the use of resources of labour and finance, it **does not appear to develop plans for contingencies, other than crashing time**.

(e) CPA **assumes a trade-off between time and cost.** This may not be the case where a substantial portion of the cost is **indirect overheads** or where the direct labour proportion of the total cost is limited.

2.10 Example: Network analysis and Gantt charts

This example is provided as an illustration of how Gantt charts may be used to manage resources efficiently. A company is about to undertake a project about which the following data is available.

Activity	*Preceded by activity*	*Duration Days*	*Workers required*
A	–	3	6
B	–	5	3
C	B	2	4
D	A	1	4
E	A	6	5
F	D	3	6
G	C, E	3	3

There is a multi-skilled workforce of nine workers available, each capable of working on any of the activities. Draw the network to establish the duration of the project and the critical path. Then draw a Gantt chart, using the critical path as a basis, assuming that jobs start at the earliest possible time.

Solution

Here are the diagrams.

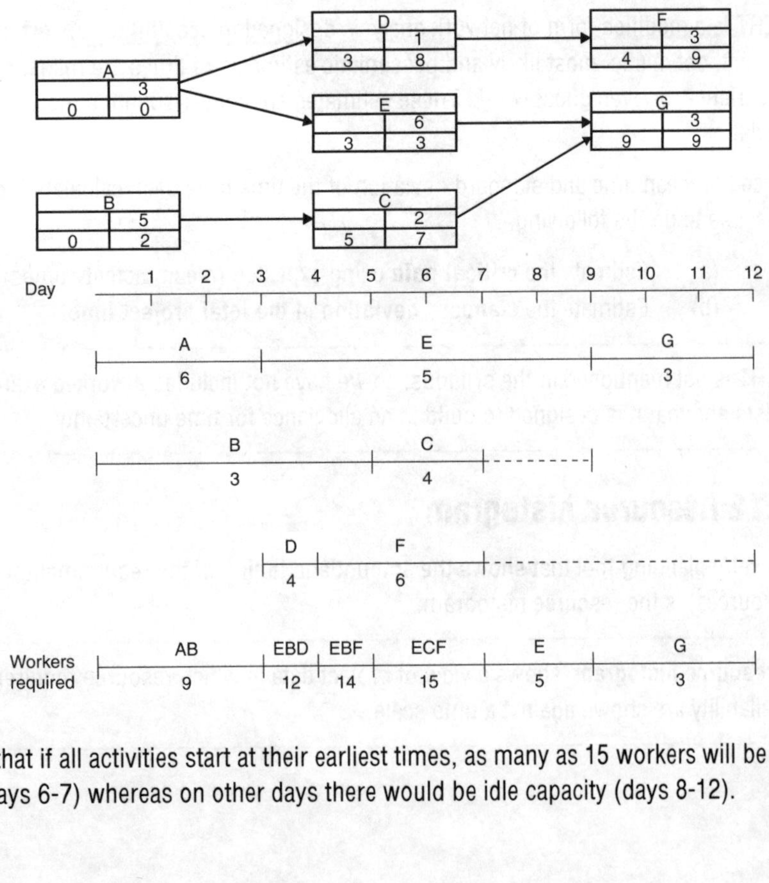

It can be seen that if all activities start at their earliest times, as many as 15 workers will be required on any one day (days 6-7) whereas on other days there would be idle capacity (days 8-12).

The problem can be reduced, or removed, by using up spare time on non-critical activities. Suppose we **deferred the start** of activities D and F until the latest possible days. These would be days 8 and 9, leaving four days to complete the activities by the end of day 12.

The Gantt chart would be redrawn as follows.

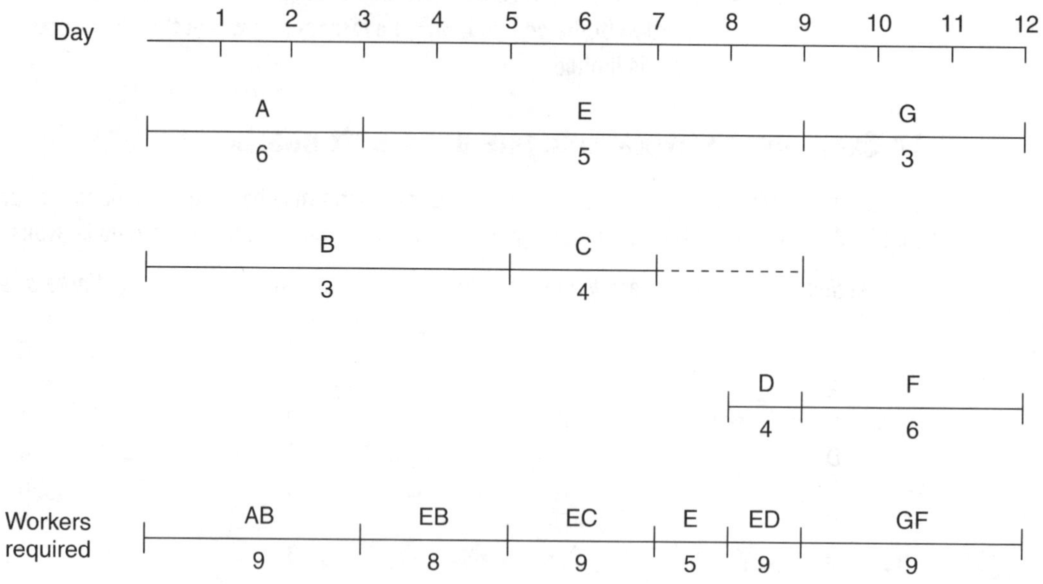

2.11 Project evaluation review technique (PERT)

Project evaluation and review technique (PERT) is a technique for allowing for uncertainty in determining project duration. Each task is assigned a best, worst, and most probable completion time estimate. These estimates are used to determine the average completion time. The average times are used to establish the critical path and the standard deviation of completion times for the entire project.

PERT is a modified form of network analysis designed to account for **uncertainty**. For each activity in the project, optimistic, most likely and pessimistic estimates of times are made, on the basis of past experience, or even guess-work. These estimates are converted into a mean time and also a standard deviation.

Once the mean time and standard deviation of the time have been calculated for each activity, it should be possible to do the following.

(a) Estimate the **critical path** using expected (mean) activity times.
(b) Estimate the **standard deviation of the total project time**.

Exam focus point

PERT is not mentioned in the syllabus, so we have not included a worked example. Just be aware that it exists and that it is designed to build in an allowance for time uncertainty.

2.12 Resource histogram

A useful planning tool that shows the amount and timing of the requirement for a resource (or a range of resources) is the resource histogram.

Key term

A resource histogram shows a view of project data in which resource requirements, usage, and availability are shown against a time scale.

A simple resource histogram showing programmer time required on a software development program is shown below.

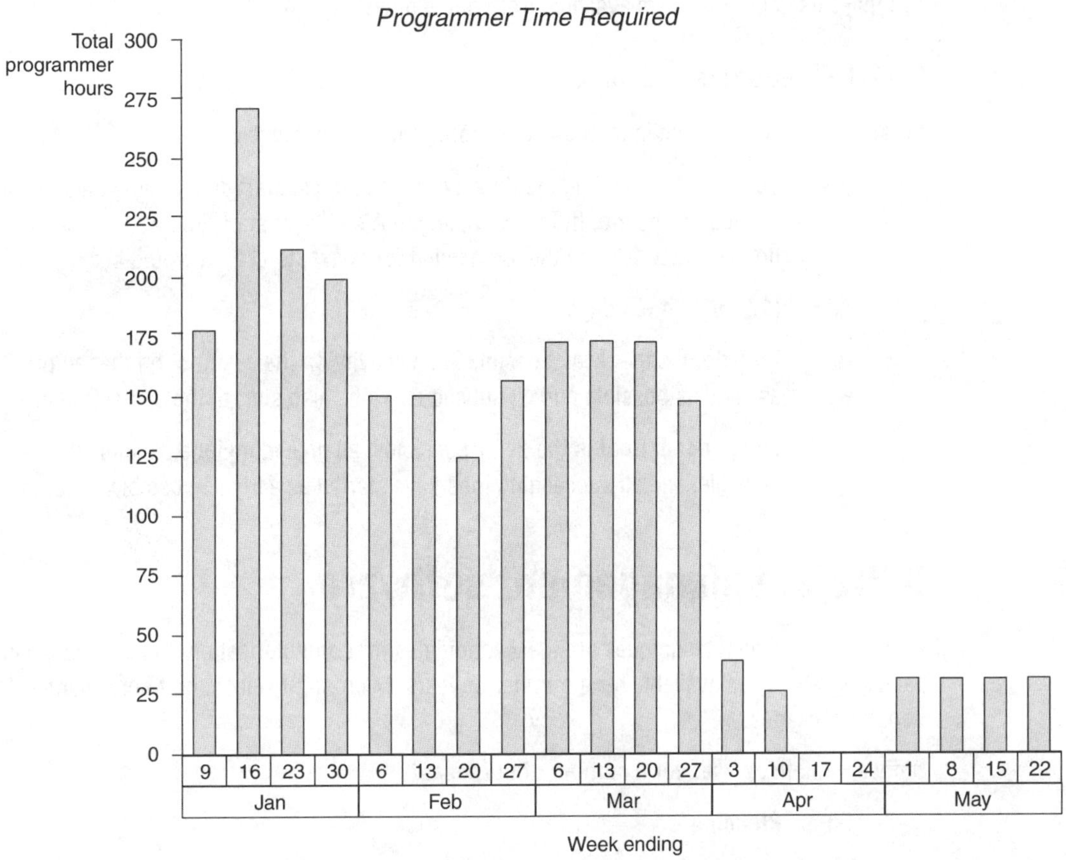

Some organisations add another bar (or a separate line) to the chart showing resource availability. The chart then shows any instances when the required resource hours exceed the available hours. Plans should then be made to either obtain further resource for these peak times, or to re-schedule the work plan. Alternately the chart may show times when the available resource is excessive, and should be re-deployed elsewhere. An example follows.

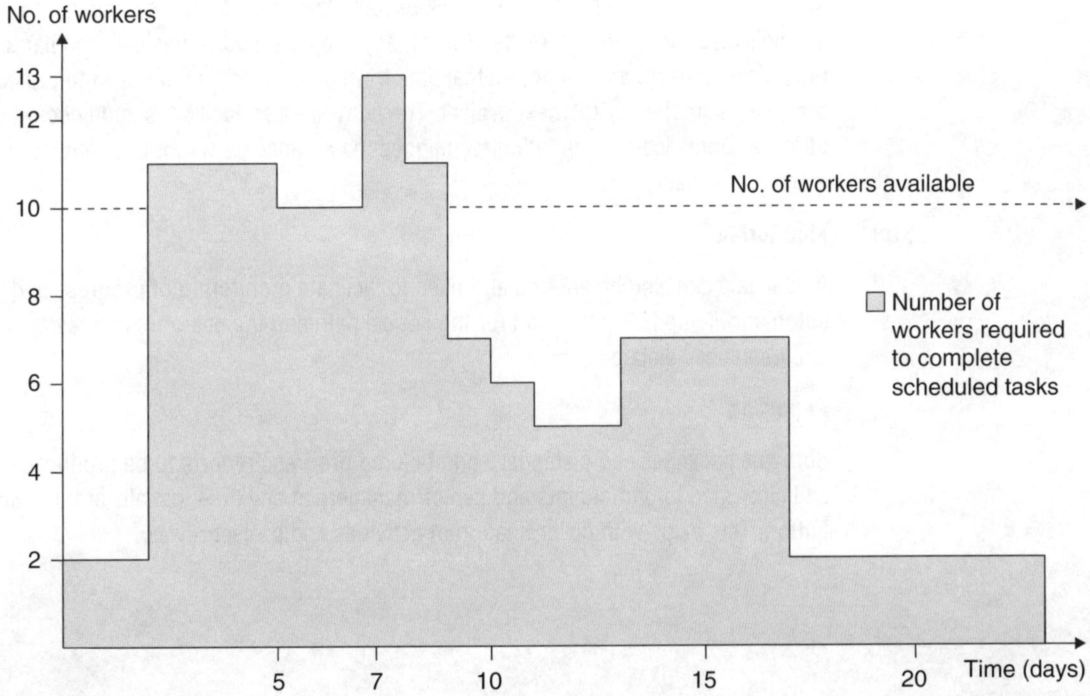

The number of workers required on the seventh day is 13. Can we re-schedule the non-critical activities to reduce the requirement to the available level of 10? We might be able to re-arrange activities so that we can make use of the workers available from day 9 onwards.

2.12.1 Float times and costs

Float time is the time built in to allow for unforeseen circumstances.

(a) **Total float** on a job is the time available (earliest start date to latest finish date) *less* time needed for the job. If, for example, job A's earliest start time was day 7 and its latest end time was day 17, and the job needed four days, total float would be:

$(17 - 7) - 4 = 6$ days

(b) **Free float** is the delay possible in an activity on the assumption that all preceding jobs start as early as possible and all subsequent jobs also start at the earliest time.

(c) **Independent float** is the delay possible if all preceding jobs have finished as late as possible, and all succeeding jobs have started as early as possible.

3 Project management software

Project management techniques are ideal candidates for computerisation. Project management software packages have been available for a number of years. Microsoft Project and Micro Planner X-Pert are two popular packages.

Software might be used for a number of purposes.

(a) **Planning**

Network diagrams (showing the critical path) and Gantt charts (showing resource use) can be produced automatically once the relevant data is entered. Packages also allow a sort of 'what if?' analysis for initial planning, trying out different levels of resources, changing deadlines and so on to find the best combination.

(b) **Estimating**

As a project progresses, actual data will become known and can be entered into the package and collected for future reference. Since many projects involve basically similar tasks (interviewing users and so on), actual data from one project can be used to provide more accurate estimates for the next project. The software also facilitates and encourages the use of more sophisticated estimation techniques than managers might be prepared to use if working manually.

(c) **Monitoring**

Actual data can also be entered and used to facilitate monitoring of progress and automatically updating the plan for the critical path and the use of resources as circumstances dictate.

(d) **Reporting**

Software packages allow standard and tailored progress reports to be produced, printed out and circulated to participants and senior managers at any time, usually at the touch of a button. This helps with co-ordination of activities and project review.

3.1 What input data is required?

Most project management packages feature a process of identifying the main steps in a project, and breaking these down further into specific tasks.

A typical project management package requires four **inputs**.

(a) The length of **time** required for each activity of the project.
(b) The **logical relationships** between each activity.
(c) The **resources** available.
(d) **When** the resources are available.

3.2 Advantages of project management software packages

The **advantages** of using project management software are summarised below.

Advantage	Comment
Enables quick re-planning	Estimates can be **changed many times** and a new schedule produced almost instantly. Changes to the plan can be reflected immediately.
Document quality	Well-presented plans give a **professional** impression and are easier to understand.
Encourages constant progress tracking	The project manager is able to compare **actual** progress against **planned** progress and investigate problem areas promptly.
What if? analysis	Software enables the effect of various scenarios to be calculated quickly and easily. Many project managers conduct this type of analysis using **copies** of the plan in separate computer files – leaving the actual plan untouched.

Another advantage is that the software is able to analyse and present the project information in a number of ways. The views available within Microsoft Project are shown in the following illustration – on the drop down menu.

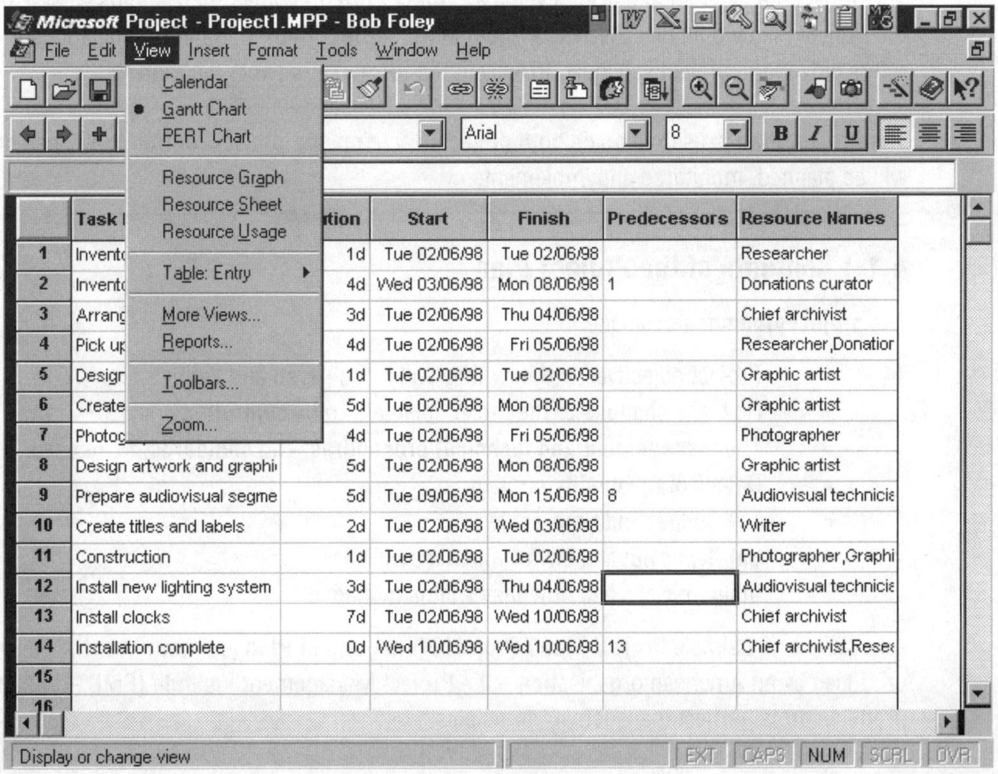

3.3 Disadvantages of project management software packages

Two **disadvantages** of project management software are:

(a) Some packages are difficult to use.

(b) Some project managers become so interested in producing perfect plans that they spend too much time producing documents and not enough time managing the project.

Exam focus point

> The June 2003 exam required candidates to describe three features of project management software that would assist the planning and monitoring of the project.

4 Documentation and reports

FAST FORWARD

> Project **documentation** plays an important part in project control and communication.

We will now look at the main **documents and reports** used in project management. The name allocated to documents will vary across different organisations. What is constant is the need for clear and relevant documentation that helps monitor and control the project.

Remember that reports are **not a substitute for one-on-one communication**. Too many (or too lengthy) reports will result in **information overload**.

When outlining possible content of documents some duplication of items occurs. This does not mean that information should be repeated, but that the information may appear in one or other of the documents depending on the format adopted by the organisation.

It is likely that the Project Initiation Document will evolve until it is ultimately incorporated into the Project Management Plan, sometimes referred to as the Project Quality Plan.

4.1 The Project Plan

The project manager should also develop a **Project Plan**. In some organisations what is described here as the Project Plan would be called the **Project Management Plan**. In other organisations the Project Plan refers only to the project schedule, usually in the form of a network diagram.

Key term

> The **Project Plan** is used to guide both project execution and project control. It outlines how the project will be planned, monitored and implemented.

4.1.1 Contents of the Project Plan

The **project plan** should include:

- Project objectives and how they will be achieved and verified
- How any **changes** to the project plan are to be **controlled**
- The **management and technical procedures**, and **standards**, to be used
- Details of the **quality** strategy
- The **budget** and **time-scale**
- **Safety**, health and environmental policies
- Inherent **risks** and how they will be managed

An example of a simple **Project Plan / Project Management Plan** is shown over the page. This plan was produced by an American organisation – the Project Management Institute (PMI) – to manage a project to produce formal project management principles.

The Project Plan **evolves** over time. A high level plan for the whole project and a detailed plan for the current and following stage is usually produced soon after project start-up. At each subsequent stage a detailed plan is produced for the following stage and if required, the overall project plan is revised

4.1.2 Project Quality Plan

An important element of the overall Project Plan is the Project Quality Plan.

Key term

The **Project Quality Plan** outlines the quality strategy to be followed and links this to any formal quality management approach the organisation has chosen to follow.

There is no generally accepted format for a quality plan – in fact **the distinction between a project management plan and a quality plan is becoming increasingly blurred**.

A **Project Quality Plan** may include a number of elements, for example; project **overview**, project **organisation** and **management**, project **requirements**, **development/production methods**, **quality management**, **risk** management and **procurement**.

For example, the organisation and management section of the Project Quality Plan would include details of the **roles** and **responsibilities** of stakeholders involved in managing the project. This might include members of the project board, the project sponsor, project manager, project team, contact people in the client organisation, formal reporting procedures, planning, monitoring and control methods.

Other sections of the Project Quality Plan will depend upon the nature of the project. For example, a software project Quality Plan may include a section dealing with **configuration management**, containing details of:

- Version control – how software version numbering issues are dealt with
- Change control – covering how changes are identified, evaluated and implemented correctly

We look at quality assurance in the systems development process more detail in Chapter 11.

Case Study

Project Management Plan	
Project Name	The full name of this project is 'Project Management Principles.'
Project Manager	The project manager is Joe Bloggs. The project manager is authorised to (1) initiate the project, (2) form the project team and (3) prepare and execute plans and manage the project as necessary for successful project completion.
Purpose/ Business Need	This project addresses a need for high-level guidelines for the project management profession through the identification and presentation of project management principles. The project sponsor and accepting agent is the Project Management Institute (PMI) Standards Program Team (SPT). The principal and beneficial customer is the membership of PMI. Principles are needed to provide high-level context and guidance for the profession of project management. These Principles will provide benefit from the perspectives of practice, evaluation, and development.
Product Description and Deliverables	The final deliverable of this project is a document containing a statement of project management Principles. The text is to be fully developed and ready for publication. As a research and development project, it is to be approached flexibly in schedule and resource requirements, with an initially proposed publication date of June 2001.
Project Management	The project team will use project methodology consistent with PMI Standards. The project is to be managed with definitive scope and acceptance criteria fully established as the project progresses and the product is developed.

Project Management Plan	
Assumptions, Constraints and Risks	The project faces some increased risk that without a clearly prescribed definition of a Principle, standards for product quality will be more difficult to establish and apply. To mitigate this risk, ongoing communication between the project team and the project sponsor on this matter will be required.
Resources	The PMI Standards Program Team (SPT) is to provide the project team with the following. **Financial**. SPT will provide financial resources as available. The initial amount for the current year is $5,000. The project manager must not exceed the allocated amount, and notify the SPT when 75% of the allocation has been spent. **Explanation of Standards Program**. SPT will provide guidance at the outset of the project, updates as changes occur, and clarifications as needed. **Personnel / Volunteers**. SPT will recruit volunteer team members from within the membership of PMI through various media and liaisons. The project team is to consist of no less than ten members, including the project manager. General qualifications to be sought by SPT in recruiting will be: **Mandatory** • Acceptance of project plan • Demonstrated capability for strategic, generalised or intuitive thinking • Capability to write clearly on technical subject matter for general audiences • Capability to work co-operatively with well developed interpersonal skills • Be conversant in English and be able to use telephone and Internet email telecommunications **As possible** • Time availability (Team members may contribute at different levels. An average of approximately five to ten hours per month is desired.) • Diversity (Team members collectively may represent diverse nationalities, types of organisations or corporate structure, business sectors, academic disciplines, and personal experience) • Travel (As determined mutually by the project sponsor and manager, some travel for face-to-face meetings may be requested)
Approach	The project will progress through the following phases. **Phase 1: Team formation** – Recruit and orient volunteer team members. Establish procedures and ground rules for group process and decision-making. **Phase 2: Subject Matter Clarification** – Identify and clarify initial scope and definitions of project subject matter. **Phase 3a: Exploration** – Begin brainstorming (through gathering, sharing, and discussion) of data and views in unrestricted, non-judgmental process. **Phase 3b: Selection** – Conclude brainstorming (through evaluation and acceptance or rejection) of collected data and views. As the conclusion to this phase, the SPT will review as an interim deliverable the selection made by the project team. **Phase 4: Development** – Conduct further research and discussion to develop accepted subject matter. **Phase 5: Articulation** – Write a series of drafts to state the accepted and developed subject matter as appropriate for the project business need and product description.

Project Management Plan	
Approach (continued)	**Phase 6: Adoption** – Submit product to SPT for the official PMI standards approval and adoption process. Revise product as needed. **Phase 7: Closeout** – Perform closure for team and administrative matters. Deliver project files to SPT.
Acceptance	The project manager will submit the final product and any interim deliverables to the Standards Program Team (SPT) for formal acceptance. The SPT may (1) accept the product as delivered by the project team, or (2) return the product to the team with a statement of specific requirements to make the product fully acceptable. The acceptance decision of the SPT is to be provided to the project manager in writing.
Change Management	Requests for change to this plan may be initiated by either the project sponsor or the project manager. All change requests will be reviewed and approved or rejected by a formal proceeding of the Standards Program Team (SPT) with input and interaction with the project manager. Decisions of the SPT will be documented and provided to the project manager in writing. All changes will be incorporated into this document, reflected by a new version number and date.
Communication and Reporting	The project manager and team will communicate with and report to the PMI Standards Program Team as follows. **Monthly Status Reports** – Written monthly status and progress reports are to include: • Work accomplished since the last report • Work planned to be performed during the next reporting period • Deliverables submitted since the last report • Deliverables planned to be submitted during the next reporting period • Work tasks in progress and currently outside of expectations for scope, quality, schedule or cost • Risks identified and actions taken or proposed to mitigate • Lessons Learned • Summary statement for posting on PMI Web site **Monthly Resource Reports** – Written monthly resource reports are to include: **Financial resources** • Total funds allocated • Total funds expended to date • Estimated expenditures for the next reporting period • Estimated expenditures for entire project to completion **Human resources** • List of all volunteer team members categorised by current involvement (i.e., active, new (pre-active), inactive, resigned) • Current number of new and active volunteer team members • Estimated number of volunteer team members needed for project completion

	Project Management Plan
Communication and Reporting (continued)	**Milestone and Critical Status Reports** – Additional status reports are to be submitted as mutually agreed upon by SPT and the project manager and are to include at least the following items. • Milestone Status Reports are to include the same items as the Monthly Status reports, summarised to cover an entire project phase, period since the last milestone report, or entire project to date. • Critical Status Reports are to focus on work tasks outside of expectations and other information as requested by SPT or stipulated by the project manager.

Plan Acceptance	Signature and Date	
By PMI Standards Program Team	____________________ Fred Jones – PMI Technical Research & Standards Manager	12 July 1999
By Project Manager	____________________ Joe Bloggs – PMI Member	20 July 1999

The contents of the plan will vary depending on the complexity of the project.

The contents page and introduction from a detailed Project Plan relating to a software implementation project at a call centre follow. (These plans are shown to provide practical examples – you do not need to learn the details of the plans – what you need for the exam is a general understanding of possible approaches to project documentation.)

Case Study

Extract from a call centre software implementation – Project Plan

CONTENTS

Page

SECTION 1

INTRODUCTION		
1a	**Purpose of the Project Plan** The purpose of this Plan is to define the working relationship between Project Team (PT) and the Manager, Customer Centres Group (MCCG). It details the level of service to be provided by Project Team to the client and the associated cost. If the nature of the project changes, or if situations develop which indicate a need for modification, then this plan will be altered accordingly in consultation with the Client. This Plan details key process steps (milestones), the methods for delivering these steps, and responsibilities of the project manager, project owner (client), and project team representatives.	
1b	**Project Objective** To develop and fully support a call centre environment that promotes the achievement of '80% of all incoming calls resolved at the first point of contact.'	
1c	**Project Deliverable** To deliver to the MCCG, fully commissioned and operational system upgrades as defined within this project plan, including an appropriately skilled call centre team, by 15 April 2001 at an estimated Project Team cost of £123,975.	

Note: Only the contents page and introduction of this comprehensive plan are reproduced here.

4.2 Progress report

Key term

A **progress report** shows the current status of the project, usually in relation to the planned status.

The frequency and contents of progress reports will vary depending on the length of the project and the progress being made.

The report is a **control tool** intended to show the discrepancies between where the project is, and where the plan says it should be.

A common form of progress uses two columns – one for **planned** time and expenditure and one for **actual**.

Any additional content will depend on the format adopted. Some organisations include only the 'raw facts' in the report, and use these as a basis for discussion regarding reasons for variances and action to be taken, at a project review meeting.

Other organisations (particularly those involved in long, complex projects) produce more comprehensive progress reports, with more explanation and comment.

The progress report should also include an updated budget status – perhaps showing the cost and schedule variance explained earlier in this chapter.

4.2.1 Milestones

The progress report should monitor progress towards key **milestones.**

Key term

A **milestone** is a significant event in the project, usually completion of a major deliverable.

Another way of monitoring progress that could be included in a progress report is a milestone slip chart.

The milestone slip chart compares planned and actual progress towards project milestones. Planned progress is shown on the X-axis and actual progress on the Y-axis. Where actual progress is slower than planned progress **slippage** has occurred.

A milestone slip chart is shown below.

Milestone slip chart

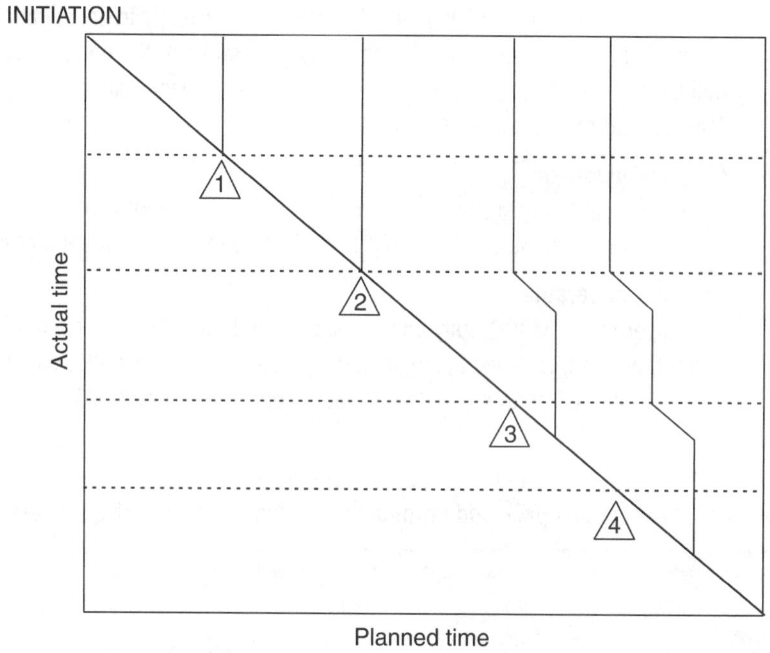

On the chart above milestones are indicated by a triangle on the diagonal planned progress line. The vertical lines that meet milestones 1 and 2 are straight – showing that these milestones were achieved on time.

At milestone 3 some slippage has occurred. The chart shows that further slippage occurred between milestones 3 and 4. This is shown by the fact that the vertical line for milestone 4 intersects the diagonal line further to the right of the triangle 4 than was the case for milestone 3.

We look at ways of dealing with slippage later in this chapter.

4.3 Completion report

Key term

The **completion report** summarises the results of the project, and includes client sign-off.

On project completion the project manager will produce the **Completion Report.** The main purpose of the completion report is to document (and gain client sign-off for) the end of the project.

The report should include a **summary** of the project outcome. The completion report should contain:

(a) Project objectives and the outcomes achieved.

(b) The final project budget report showing expected and actual expenditure (If an external client is involved this information may be sensitive – the report may exclude or 'amend' the budget report).

(c) A brief outline of time taken compared with the original schedule.

The completion report will also include provision for any **on-going issues** that will need to be addressed after completion. Such issues would be related to the project, but not part of the project. (If they are part of the project the project is not yet complete!) An example of an on-going issue would be a procedure for any 'bugs' that become apparent **after** a new software program has been tested and approved.

Responsibilities and procedures relating to any such issues should be laid down in the report.

The manager may find it useful to distribute a provisional report and request **feedback**. This should ensure the version presented for client sign-off at the completion meeting is acceptable to all parties.

A more detailed review of the project and the system follows a few months after completion, the post-completion audit.

4.4 The post-completion audit

Key term

The **post-completion audit** is a formal review of the project that examines the lessons that may be learned and used for the benefit of future projects.

The audit looks at all aspects of the project with regard to two questions.

(a) Did the end result of the project meet the **client's expectations**?

- The actual **design** and **construction** of the end product
- Was the project achieved **on time**?
- Was the project **completed within budget**?

(b) Was the **management of the project** as successful as it might have been, or were there bottlenecks or problems? This review covers:

(i) Problems that might occur on future projects with similar characteristics.

(ii) The performance of the team individually and as a group.

In other words, any project is an opportunity to learn how to manage future projects more effectively.

The post-completion audit should involve **input from the project team**. A simple questionnaire could be developed for all team members to complete, and a reasonably informal meeting held to obtain feedback. On what went well (and why), and what didn't (and why).

With information systems projects the post-completion audit may be conducted as part of the post-implementation review (covered later in this Text). Strictly speaking, a **post-completion audit** would **include** a detailed review of the **project management process,** while the **post-implementation review** is concerned mainly with the **resulting system.**

4.4.1 Post-completion audit report

The **post-completion audit report** should contain the following.

(a) A **summary** should be provided, emphasising any areas where the structures and tools used to manage the project have been found to be **unsatisfactory**.

(b) A **review** of the end result of the project should be provided, and compared against the results expected. Reasons for any significant **discrepancies** between the two should be provided, preferably with suggestions for how any future projects could **prevent these problems recurring**.

(c) A **cost-benefit review** should be included, comparing the forecast costs and benefits identified at the time of the feasibility study with actual costs and benefits.

(d) **Recommendations** should be made as to any steps which should be taken to **improve** the project management procedures used.

4.4.2 Using post-completion audit information

Lessons learnt that relate to the way the **project was managed** should contribute to the smooth running of future projects.

A starting point for any new project should be a **review** of the documentation of any **similar projects** undertaken in the past.

5 Risk management

FAST FORWARD

Risk management is concerned with identifying such and putting in place policies to eliminate or reduce these risks.

Projects and other undertakings carry an element of risk, for example the risk of an inappropriate system being developed and implemented.

The identification of risks involves an overview of the project to establish what could go wrong, and the consequences.

5.1 Risk management process

Risk management may be viewed as a six-stage process:

Stage 1 Plan risk management approach.

Stage 2 Identify and record risks, for example in a **risk register**.

Stage 3 Assess risks and record this assessment.

Stage 4 Plan and record risk responses.

Stage 5 Carry out risk reduction actions.

Stage 6 Review the risk management approach.

5.2 Risk assessment process

The likelihood and consequences of risks can be plotted on a matrix – as follows.

Risk Assessment Matrix

Potential impact			
High	M	H	VH
Med	L	M	H
Low	VL	L	M
	Low	*Med*	*High*

Threat Likelihood

5.3 Contingency plan

For each risk on the risk register it should be recorded what approach will be taken to deal with the risk.

Developing a risk **contingency plan** that contains strategies for risks that fall into the VH quadrant should have priority, followed by risks falling into the two H quadrants. Following the principle of **management by exception**, the most efficient way of dealing with risks outside these quadrants may be to do nothing unless the risk presents itself.

5.4 Dealing with risk

Dealing with **risk** involves four strategies.

(a) **Avoidance**: the factors which give rise to the risk are removed.

(b) **Reduction** or **mitigation**: the potential for the risk cannot be removed but analysis has enabled the identification of ways to reduce the incidence and / or the consequences.

(c) **Transference**: the risk is passed on to someone else – or is perhaps financed by an insurer.

(d) **Absorption**: the potential risk is accepted in the hope or expectation that the incidence and consequences can be coped with if necessary.

Risk management is a continuous process. Procedures are necessary to regularly review and reassess the risks documented in the risk register.

Exam focus point

The June 2003 exam examined risk management in the context of purchasing software.

6 Information systems projects – common problems

It is not uncommon for information systems projects to be years late, wildly over budget, and produce a system that does not meet user requirements.

A number of factors can combine to produce these expensive disasters – some are discussed in the following paragraphs.

6.1 Problems due to project managers

IS project managers were often **technicians**, not managers. Technical ability for IS staff is no guarantee of management skill – an individual might be a highly proficient analyst or programmer, but **not a good manager**.

The project manager has a number of **conflicting requirements**.

(a) The **systems manager**, usually the project manager's boss, wants the project **delivered on time**, to specification and within budget.

(b) **User** expectations may be misunderstood, ignored or unrealistic.

(c) The project manager has to plan and supervise the work of **analysts** and **programmers** and these are rather different roles.

The project manager needs to develop an **appropriate management style**. What he or she should realise is the extent to which the project will fail if users are not consulted, or if the project team is unhappy. As the project manager needs to encourage participation from users, an excessively authoritarian style is not suitable.

6.2 Other factors

Some other common factors are identified below.

(a) The project manager may accept **an unrealistic deadline** – the timescale is fixed early in the planning process. User demands may be accepted as deadlines before sufficient consideration is given to the realism of this.

(b) **Poor or non-existent planning** is a recipe for disaster. Unrealistic deadlines would be identified much earlier if a proper planning process was undertaken.

(c) A lack of **monitoring** and **control**.

(d) Users **change their requirements**, resulting in costly changes to the system as it is being developed.

(e) **Poor time-tabling and resourcing**. It is no use being presented on day 1 with a team of programmers, when there is still systems analysis and design work to do. The development and implementation of a computer project may take a considerable length of time (perhaps 18 months from initial decision to operational running for a medium-sized installation); a proper plan and time schedule for the various activities must be drawn up.

6.3 Time, cost and quality

A project is affected by a number of factors, often in **conflict** with each other.

(a) **Quality** of the system required, in terms of basic system requirements.

(b) **Time**, both to complete the project, and in terms of the opportunity cost of time spent on this project which could be spent on others.

(c) **Costs** and resources allocated to the project.

The balance between the constraints of time, cost and quality will be different for each project.

(a) If a system aims to provide competitive advantage then time will tend to be the dominant factor.

(b) If safety is paramount (eg an auto-pilot system) then quality will be most important.

(c) If the sole aim of a project is to meet administrative needs that are not time dependent, then cost may be the dominant factor.

The relationship can be shown as a triangle.

The Time/Cost/Quality Triangle

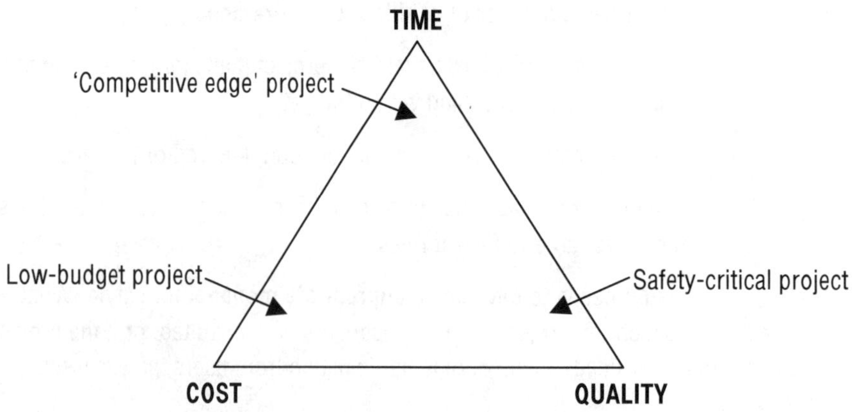

The balance of time, cost and quality will influence decision making throughout the project – for example whether to spend an extra £5,000 to fix a problem completely or only spend £1,000 on a quick fix and implement a user work-around?

6.4 Dealing with slippage

'Slippage' or slipping behind schedule is a common problem.

When a project has slipped behind schedule there are a range of options open to the project manager. Some of these options are summarised in the following table.

Action	Comment
Do nothing	After considering all options it may be decided that things should be allowed to continue as they are.
Add resources	If capable staff are available and it is practicable to add more people to certain tasks it may be possible to recover some lost ground. Could some work be subcontracted?
Work smarter	Consider whether the methods currently being used are the most suitable – for example could prototyping be used.
Replan	If the assumptions the original plan was based on have been proved invalid a more realistic plan should be devised.
Reschedule	A complete replan may not be necessary – it may be possible to recover some time by changing the phasing of certain deliverables.
Introduce incentives	If the main problem is team performance, incentives such as bonus payments could be linked to work deadlines and quality.
Change the specification	If the original objectives of the project are unrealistic given the time and money available it may be necessary to negotiate a change in the specification.

6.5 Project change procedure

Some of the reactions to slippage discussed above would involve changes that would significantly affect the overall project. Other possible causes of changes to the original project plan include:

- The availability of new technology
- Changes in personnel
- A realisation that user requirements were misunderstood
- Changes in the business environment
- New legislation eg Data protection

The **earlier** a change is made the **less expensive** it should prove. However, changes will cost time and money and should not be undertaken lightly.

When considering a change **an investigation** should be conducted to discover:

- The consequences of **not** implementing the proposed change.
- The impact of the change on **time, cost** and quality.
- The expected costs and benefits of the change.
- The risks associated with the change, and with the status-quo.

The process of ensuring that proper consideration is given to the impact of proposed changes is known as **change control.**

Changes will need to be implemented into the project plan and communicated to all stakeholders.

Case Study

WHY CAN'T WE BUILD SOFTWARE LIKE WE BUILD BUILDINGS?

Introduction

The software development industry has a reputation for poor project performance. This makes many organisations reluctant to undertake large development projects.

The Project Manager's Responsibility

The project manager plays the same role within a software development as they would in a construction project: their aim is to finish the job within time and cost to the quality required.

Get the Right Person for the Job

Just imagine that you have built a garden shed and a passer-by compliments you on your achievement. The passer-by then asks since you've made such a good job of the shed would you build a new three-bedroom house. After all, it will utilise the same materials, just more of them. It's not very likely is it?

Yet many people learned how to use a PC-based database development application such as Microsoft Access, Dbase, or Paradox, and then went on to build 'commercial' systems. In many cases these were not designed to be commercial systems, they just started as a useful place to store information, then grew until they became a vital source of information.

Appropriate Methodology

Every size of building project requires its own set of processes to most cost effectively complete. Software is no different. Applying skyscraper standards to a house will be expensive and result in over-engineering. When setting up a software development project the same rules apply. Select the right methodology and ensure that your developer is experienced with this methodology.

Reusable Components

When building, there is little point in designing non-standard sizes into a building then trying to fit standard components into the design. These components are often as simple as the garage or interior doors, but could well include items which cannot easily be built on site, such as sealed unit double glazing.

In the software industry, the reuse of code or objects is a relatively recent development. As with buildings, if you are going to use existing components, the design must be created in such a way as to accommodate them. In the early years of software development these components would be simple subroutines which could be copied into the code to perform simple tasks such as date verification. More recently the advent of commercially successful component infrastructures such as CORBA, the Internet, ActiveX or Java Beans, has triggered a whole industry of off-the-shelf components for various domains, allowing you to buy and integrate components rather than developing them all in-house. Reusability shifts software development from programming software (a line at time) to composing software (by assembling components) just as a modern builder does not fabricate their own material but assembles the delivered components.

Responsibility of the Project Manager

The project manager is key to the success of any project and must be able to manage both people and other resources. The key role of the manager is not simply in monitoring progress but is in fixing things when they go wrong. This is the case in both industries.

Create the Environment

The project manager can create a little bit of 'project magic' by establishing a project environment which allows project participants to operate effectively and co-operatively. This type of project environment is significantly more effective than an aggressive environment.

Issue Resolution

In the building industry, the issues that arise are more likely to be physical in nature. If a team is gathered around a hole in the ground or a piece of building which doesn't quite fit, they can start to suggest solutions by measuring, drawing or simply explaining what they think will fix it.

In the software industry, the issues that arise are more likely to be abstract. However, the need for the sponsor to understand the problem is just as important. Any explanation that can be given in terms which mere mortals can understand is worth far more than the exact technical definition, especially if the Sponsor is required to make a decision on how to resolve the issue.

Conclusion

The use of modern methodologies and modelling techniques allows much of the risk of software development to be reduced. The rigorous use of CASE tools applies standards which are as close to regulations the software industry has at present. The development environments, frameworks and object libraries of software developers are gaining in sophistication to a point where many of the risks are already written out of a new development.

It may take a few years to come to terms with the international implications of electronic commerce over the Internet. The changes in taxable revenue of having a business process independent of location will have far-reaching effects. This is likely to be the next challenge of the technology industry.

Adapted from a paper prepared by Synergy International 1999

Chapter Roundup

- A project typically passes through five **phases**: defining, planning, implementing, controlling and completing. The number and sequence of **stages of a project** will vary across organisations.
- Various **tools and techniques** are available to plan and control projects including the project plan, project budget, Work Breakdown Structure, Gantt charts, network analysis, resource histogram and specialist software.
- Project **documentation** plays an important part in project control and communication.
- **Risk management** is concerned with identifying such and putting in place policies to eliminate or reduce these risks.

A diagram 'rounding-up' project management follows the answers to the Quick Quiz.

Quick Quiz

1. List five typical phases of a project.
2. What would you expect a Project Initiation Document to contain?
3. What is Work Breakdown Structure?
4. What is the purpose of a Gantt chart?
5. What is the project quality plan used for?
6. Why do many project managers prefer to use project management software?
7. Briefly outline the relationship between quality, cost and time in the context of an information systems project.
8. What should the risk management process achieve?

Answers to Quick Quiz

1. Defining, Planning, Implementing, Controlling, Completing.
2. Contents could include: Project objectives, the scope of the project, overall budget, final deadlines, the ultimate customer, resources, risks inherent in the project, a preliminary project plan (targets, activities and so on) and details of how the project is to be organised and managed.
3. Work Breakdown Structure (WBS) is the process of breaking down the project into manageable tasks.
4. A Gantt chart displays the time relationships between tasks in a project. It is a horizontal bar chart used to estimate the amount and timing of resources required.
5. The Project Quality Plan is used to guide both project execution and project control. It outlines how the project will be planned, monitored and implemented.
6. A project management software package saves time and produces high quality output. As with all software, it is dependant on the quality of the data fed into the package – the length of time required for each activity of the project, the logical relationships between each activity, the resources available and when the resources are available.
7. The quality of information system produced is dependant upon (among other things) the time available to develop the system and the resources (ie cost) available to the project. Insufficient time and / or resources will have an adverse effect on the quality of system produced.
8. The risk management process should identify and quantify the risks associated with the project, and decide on how the risks should be managed.

Now try the questions below from the Exam Question Bank

Number	Level	Marks	Time
Q6	Examination	20	36 mins
Q9	Examination	20	36 mins
Q16(b)	Examination	8	14 mins
Q19(d), (e)	Examination	10	18 mins

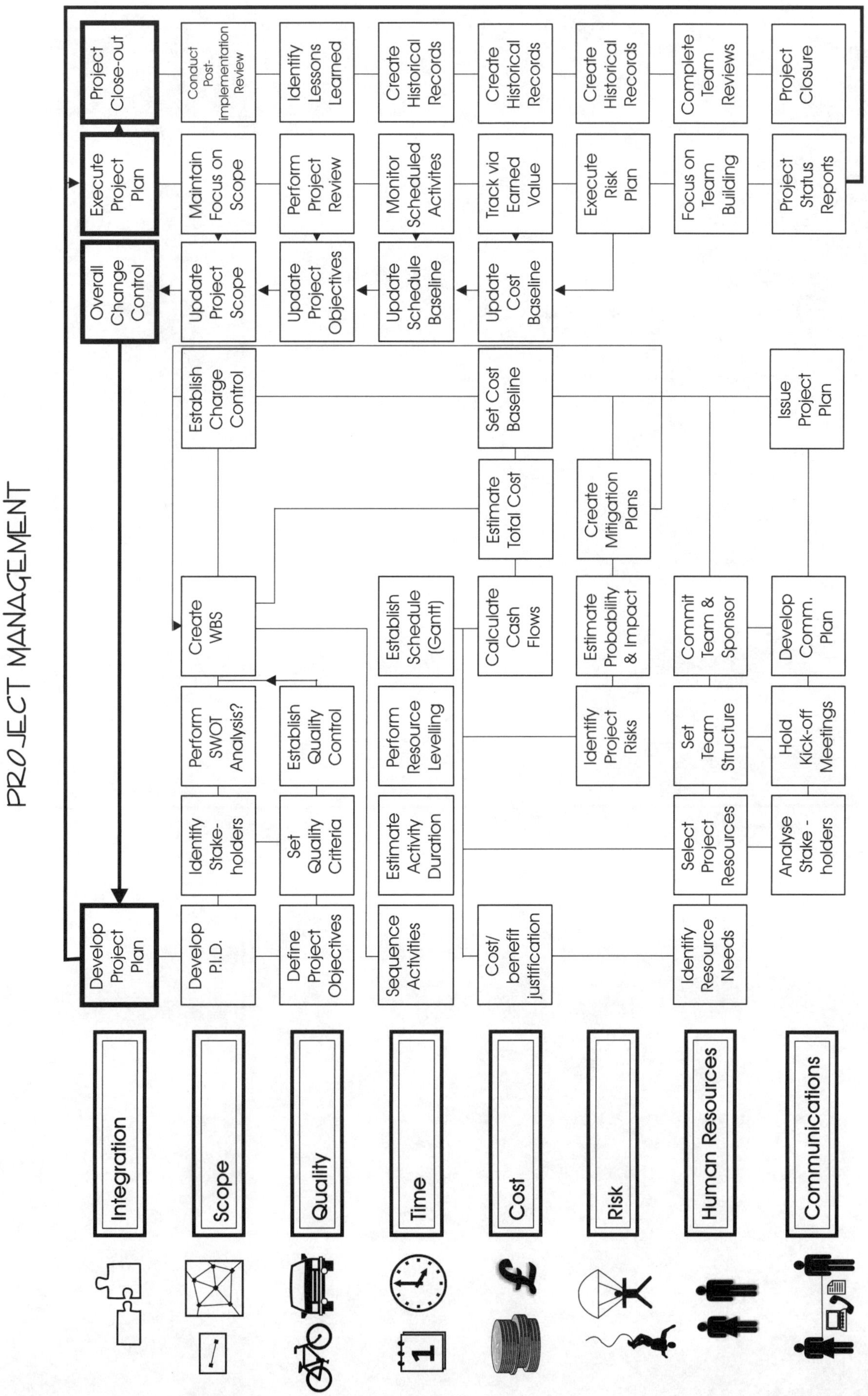
PROJECT MANAGEMENT
Integration
Scope
Quality
Time
Cost
Risk
Human Resources
Communications
Develop Project Plan
Overall Change Control
Execute Project Plan
Project Close-out
Develop P.I.D.
Identify Stake-holders
Perform SWOT Analysis?
Create WBS
Establish Charge Control
Update Project Scope
Maintain Focus on Scope
Conduct Post-implementation Review
Define Project Objectives
Set Quality Criteria
Establish Quality Control
Update Project Objectives
Perform Project Review
Identify Lessons Learned
Sequence Activities
Estimate Activity Duration
Perform Resource Levelling
Establish Schedule (Gantt)
Update Schedule Baseline
Monitor Scheduled Activites
Create Historical Records
Cost/ benefit justification
Calculate Cash Flows
Estimate Total Cost
Set Cost Baseline
Update Cost Baseline
Track via Earned Value
Create Historical Records
Identify Project Risks
Estimate Probability & Impact
Create Mitigation Plans
Execute Risk Plan
Create Historical Records
Identify Resource Needs
Select Project Resources
Set Team Structure
Commit Team & Sponsor
Focus on Team Building
Complete Team Reviews
Analyse Stake - holders
Hold Kick-off Meetings
Develop Comm. Plan
Issue Project Plan
Project Status Reports
Project Closure

Part B
Designing information systems

7

The information systems development process

Topic list	Syllabus reference
1 Systems development lifecycles	2 (a), 3 (i)
2 The waterfall model	2 (a)
3 The spiral model	2 (a)
4 Systems development methodologies	2 (a)
5 Software support for the systems development process	2 (f), 2 (i)
6 User involvement	2 (a)

Introduction

In this chapter we consider the **approaches to systems development** which may be used on Information Systems projects. These approaches are often referred to as **lifecycle models**.

The two approaches we look at in detail are those identified in the ACCA Study Guide; the **waterfall approach** and the **spiral approach**.

Later we look at how **methodologie**s can assist the development process. The chapter concludes by exploring the impact of **software development tools**.

Study guide

Part 2.10 – The information system development process

- Define the participants in the systems development process
- Describe the waterfall approach to systems development and identify its application in a representative systems development methodology
- Describe the spiral approach to systems development and identify its application in a representative systems development methodology
- Discuss the relative merits of the waterfall and spiral approaches including an understanding of hybrid approaches that include elements of both

Part 2.15 – External design

- Explain how prototyping may be used in defining external design

Part 2.18 – Software support for the systems development process

- Define a CASE tool and give a brief list of representative products
- Describe a range of features and functions that a CASE tool may provide
- Explain the advantages of using a CASE tool in the systems development process
- Define a Fourth Generation Language and give a brief list of representative products
- Describe a range of features and functions that a Fourth Generation Language may provide
- Explain how a Fourth Generation Language contributes to the prototyping process

Part 3.27 – Relationship of management, development process and quality

- Describe the relationship between project management and the systems development process (also see Chapter 5)

Exam guide

Examination questions could focus on the impact of modern developments (such as CASE tools) on the development process. Questions may also draw on your project management knowledge.

1 Systems development lifecycles

Key term

> The term '**systems development lifecycle'** describes the stages a system moves through from inception until it is discarded or replaced.

In the context of information systems projects a **distinction** can be made between the **project lifecycle** and the **systems development lifecycle**. As a project has a definite end it is unlikely that **ongoing maintenance** would be included in the scope of a project, but falls within our definition of the system development lifecycle.

In the early days of computing, systems development was **piecemeal**, involving automation of existing procedures rather than forming part of a planned strategy. The development of systems was **not properly planned**. The consequences were often poorly designed systems, which cost too much to make and which were not suited to users' needs.

This led to the development of systems development lifecycle models. Among the first models was one developed by the National Computing Centre in the 1960s. This **disciplined approach** to systems development identified several stages of development.

Stage	Comment
Identification of a problem or opportunity	This involves an analysis of the organisation's information requirements.
Feasibility study	This involves a review of the existing system and the identification of a range of possible alternative solutions. A feasible (technical, operational, economic, social) solution will be selected – or a decision not to proceed made. We covered feasibility studies, in detail, in Chapter 4.
Systems investigation	A fact finding exercise which investigates the existing system to assess its problems and requirements and to obtain details of data volumes, response times and other key indicators.
Systems analysis	Once the workings of the existing system have been documented, they can be analysed. This process examines why current methods are used, what alternatives might achieve the same, or better, results, and what performance criteria are required from a system.
Systems design	This is a technical phase which considers both computerised and manual procedures, addressing, in particular, inputs, outputs, program design, file design and security. A detailed specification of the new system is produced.
Systems implementation	This stage carries development through from design to operations. It involves acquisition (or writing) of software, program testing, file conversion or set-up, acquisition and installation of hardware and 'going live'.
Review and maintenance	This is an ongoing process which ensures that the system meets the objectives set during the feasibility study, that it is accepted by users and that its performance is satisfactory.

In the early 1970s a similar systems development lifecycle model was published by *Royce* – the waterfall model. The sequential approach described by the National Computing Centre and the waterfall model is sometimes referred to as the **'traditional approach'**.

FAST FORWARD

The term **'systems development lifecycle'** describes the stages a system moves through from inception until it is discarded or replaced. Traditional lifecycle models such as *Royce's* **waterfall model** break the systems development process into **sequential stages** – with the output from a stage forming the input to the following stage.

2 The waterfall model

Royce's waterfall model (like the National Computing Centre model) breaks the systems development process into sequential stages – with the output from a stage forming the input to the following stage. The model is shown in the following diagram.

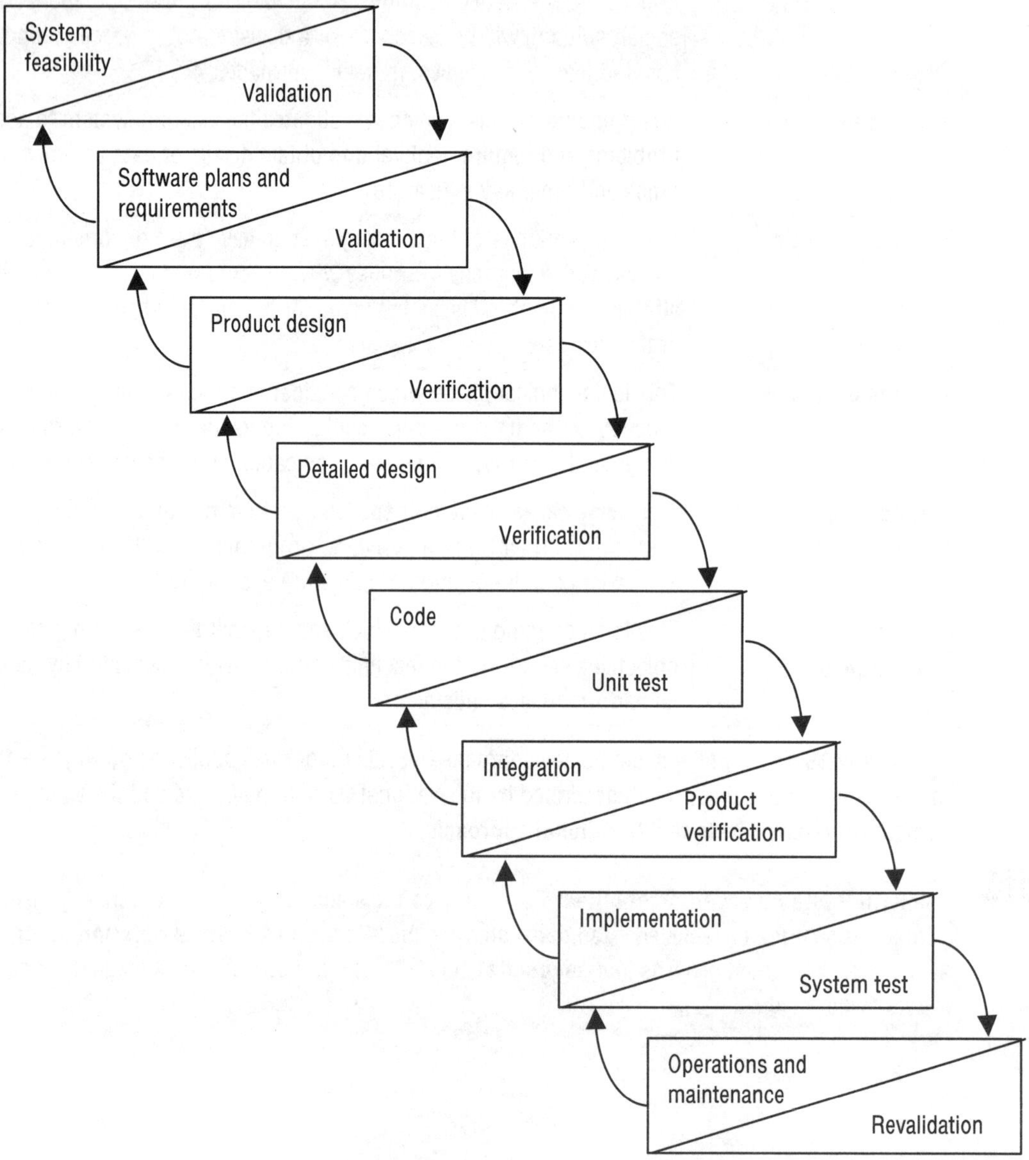

As shown on the diagram, each stage is divided into two parts – the actual work associated with the stage followed by a procedure to check what has been done. **Verification** in this context is concerned with ensuring required specifications have been met ('Have we built the system in the correct way?'). **Validation** is concerned with ensuring the system is fit for its operational role ('Have we built the correct product?').

The term 'waterfall model' is now used to describe any system development model that is made up of a number of sequential stages – regardless of the name given to the stages. It works reasonably well where the system requirements are well understood by users and developers.

2.1 Drawbacks of the waterfall approach

The waterfall approach is an efficient means of computerising existing procedures within easily defined processing requirements. It produces systems modelled on the manual systems they are replacing.

Sequential models restricted user input throughout much of the process. This often resulted in substantial and costly modifications late in the development process. It becomes increasingly difficult and expensive to change system requirements the further a system is developed.

Time overruns were the norm. The sequential nature of the process meant a hold-up on one stage would stop development completely – contributing to time overruns. Time pressures and lack of user involvement often resulted in a poor quality system and blame for the developers.

Operations and maintenance are treated as if the activity had a distinct start and end. Maintenance is in fact on-going and open-ended. *Birrel* and *Ould* devised **The 'b' model** to address this issue.

The 'b' model

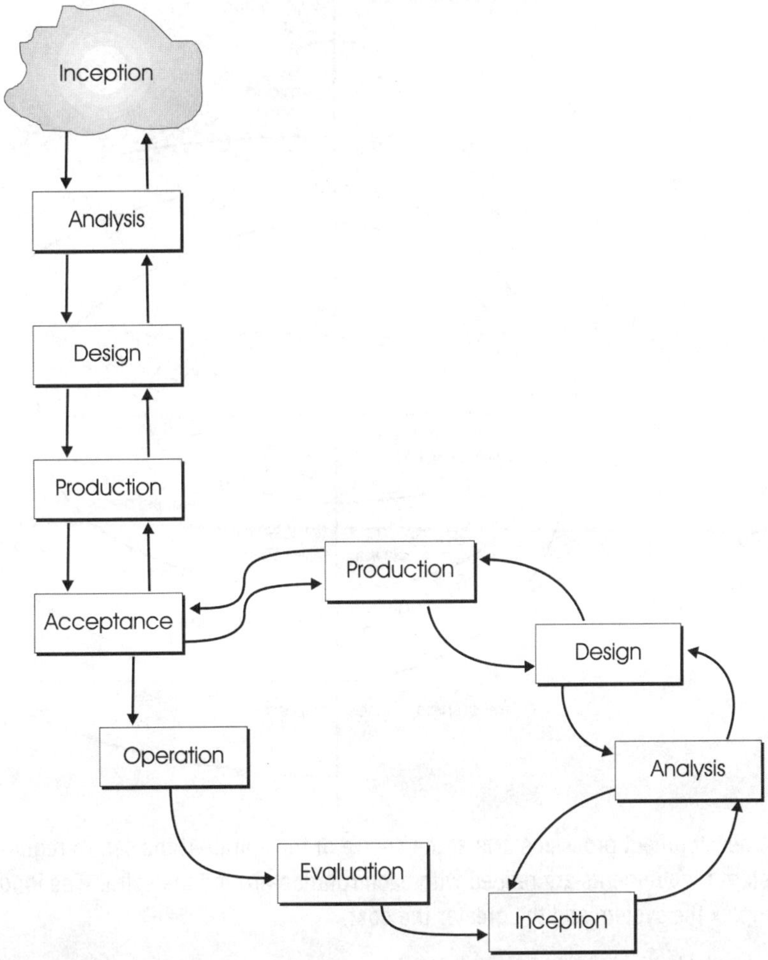

The 'b' model shows that enhancements or changes to the system (ie system maintenance) are made through a series of cycles that follow the same sequence as the original system development. Each change will go through the stages of feasibility, analysis, design production and operation.

3 The spiral model

FAST FORWARD

The **spiral approach** involves carrying out the same activities over a number of cycles in order to clarify requirements and solutions.

When developing systems where requirements are difficult to specify it is unrealistic to follow a sequential process which relies on getting things correct at each stage of development before starting subsequent activities. In these more complex situations the spiral approach is appropriate.

The spiral model represents an evolutionary approach to systems development. It involves carrying out the same activities over a number of cycles in order to clarify requirements and solutions.

The first spiral model was developed by *Boehm*. The model is shown below.

Boehm's spiral model

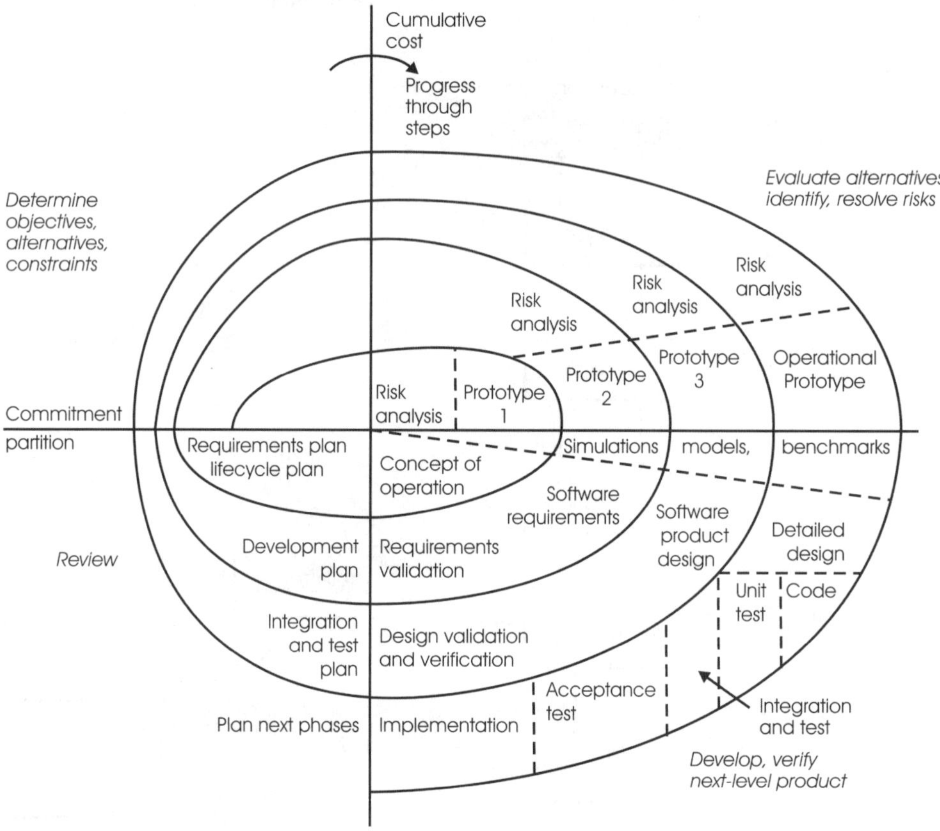

The development process starts at the centre of the spiral. At the centre requirements are not well defined. System requirements are refined with each rotation around the spiral. The longer the spiral, the more complex the system and the greater the cost.

The model Is divided into **four quadrants**.

(a) **Top left**

- Objectives determined
- Alternatives and constraints identified

(b) **Top right**

- Alternatives evaluated
- Risks identified and resolved

(c) **Bottom right**

- System development
- Covers the activities described in the waterfall model (including implementation)

(d) **Bottom left**

- The next phase in the development process is planned

Boehm's spiral model of system development includes the processes of objective setting and risk management that we have previously identified as key elements of project management.

The spiral approach aims to avoid the problems of the waterfall model (lack of user involvement, long delays). It is usually used in conjunction with prototyping which we look at later in this chapter.

4 Systems development methodologies

Another way to facilitate systems development is to use a systems development methodology.

Key term

A systems development **'methodology**' is a collection of procedures, techniques, tools and documentation aids which will help systems developers in their efforts to implement a new information system.

4.1 Characteristics of methodologies

Characteristic	Comment
Separation of logical and physical	The initial focus is on business benefits – on what the system will achieve (the logical design). Physical design and implementation issues are looked at later.
User involvement	User's information requirements determine the type of data collected or captured by the system. Users are involved throughout the development process.
Diagramatic documentation	Diagrams rather than text-based documentation are used as much as possible to ensure the focus is on what the system is trying to achieve – and to aid user understanding of the process.
Data driven	Most structured methods focus on data items regardless of the processes they are related to. The type of data within an organisation is less likely to change than either the processes which operate on it or the output information required of it.
Defined structure	Most methodologies prescribe a consistent structure to ensure a consistent and complete approach to the work. For example, the Structured Systems Analysis and Design Method (**SSADM**) suggests five modules: Feasibility, Requirements Analysis, Requirements Specification, Logical Systems Specification and Physical Design.

FAST FORWARD

A **methodology** is a collection of procedures, techniques, tools and documentation aids which are designed to help systems developers in their efforts to implement a new system. Methodologies are usually broken down into phases.

Jayaratna (*Understanding and Evaluating Methodologies,* 1994) estimates that there are **over 1,000 brand named methodologies** in use in the world. The Structured Systems Analysis and Design Method

(**SSADM**) was originally designed for use by the UK Government in 1980 – but is now widely used in many areas of business.

All methodologies seek to facilitate the **'best'** solution. But 'best' may be interpreted in a number of ways, such as **most rapid** or **least cost** systems. Some methodologies are highly **prescriptive** and require rigid adherence to stages whilst others are highly **adaptive** allowing for creative use of their components.

4.2 The stages of SSADM

SSADM covers five stages from the early and middle stages of the systems development process. SSADM refers to stages as modules.

Module	Comment
Feasibility study	SSADM may be adopted without conducting a feasibility study, or after a study has been conducted. If the study is conducted under SSADM, it focuses on investigating system requirements and conducting a cost-benefit analysis
Requirements analysis	Involves an analysis of current operations (for example through Data flow diagrams, which we cover in Chapter 8) followed by the development and presentation of options for the new system.
Requirements specification	This stage involves defining the data and processes that will be used in the new system. The systems specification document will be produced.
Logical system specification	This focuses initially on technical options for hardware and communications technology. Then the user interface and associated dialogue is designed. Logical rules for processing are established.
Physical design	The logical data structure is converted to actual physical data specifications, for example database specifications.

4.3 Choosing a methodology

In choosing the **most appropriate methodology**, an organisation must consider the following questions.

- How **open** is the system?
- To what extent does the methodology facilitate **participation**?
- Does it generate **alternative solutions**?
- Is it **well documented, tried, tested and proven** to work?
- Can **component 'tools'** be selected and used as required?
- Will it benefit from **computer aided tools** and **prototyping**?

Ultimately it is important to remember that whilst methodologies may be valuable in the development their use is a matter of great skill and experience. They **do not, by themselves, produce good systems solutions**.

4.4 Advantages and disadvantages of methodologies

The **advantages** of using a methodology are as follows.

(a) Detailed **documentation** is produced.

(b) **Standard methods** allow less qualified staff to carry out some of the analysis work, thus **cutting the cost** of the exercise.

(c) Using a standard development process leads to **improved system specifications**.

(d) Systems developed in this way are **easier to maintain and improve**.

(e) **Users are involved** with development work from an early stage and are required to sign off each stage.

(f) The emphasis on **diagramming** makes it easier for relevant parties, including users, to **understand** the system than if purely narrative descriptions were used.

(g) The structured framework of a methodology **helps with planning**. It defines the tasks to be performed, sets out when they should be done and identifies an end product. This allows control by reference to actual achievements rather than to estimates of progress.

(h) A logical design is produced that is **independent of hardware and software**.

(i) Techniques such as data flow diagrams, logical data structures and entity life histories **allow information to be cross-checked** between diagrams and ensure that the system delivered does what is required. These techniques are explained in Chapter 8.

The use of a methodology in systems development also has **disadvantages**.

(a) It has been argued that methodologies are ideal for analysing and documenting processes and data items at an operational level, but are perhaps **inappropriate for information of a strategic nature** that is collected on an ad hoc basis.

(b) Some are a little **too limited in scope**, being too concerned with systems design, and not with their impact on actual work processes or social context of the system.

(c) Arguably, methodologies encourage excessive documentation and **bureaucracy** and are just as suitable for documenting bad design as good.

5 Software support for the systems development process

There are a number of software tools that can be used to facilitate systems development process. We will examine three of the most widely used software tools – CASE tools, fourth generation languages and prototypes.

5.1 Computer aided software engineering (CASE) tools

Computer Aided Software Engineering tools are used in systems development to automate some development tasks, such as the production of documentation, and to provide an efficient tool to control developmental activities.

Key term

CASE tools are software tools used to automate some tasks in the development of information systems eg generating documentation and diagrams. The more sophisticated tools facilitate software prototyping and code generation.

FAST FORWARD

A **CASE tool** may be used to support the construction and maintenance of a system model – often allowing the construction of a prototype.

There are a range of CASE tools available. Some focus on certain phases of development such as analysis and design, others may be used throughout the complete development lifecycle.

The range of facilities offered by CASE tools are shown in the following table.

Stage of system development project	Possible use of CASE tools
Project initiation	Generate project schedules in various formats
Analysis and design	Produce diagrams eg flowcharts, DFDs, ERMs, ELHs Generate data dictionary
Design (logical and physical)	Produce system model diagrams Data structures Automate screen and report design
Implementation	Installation schedule Program code generator
Maintenance	Version control Change specification and tracking

CASE tools can be grouped into Upper CASE tools (sometimes referred to as analysts' workbenches) and Lower CASE tools (sometimes referred to as programmers' workbenches).

5.1.1 Upper CASE tools (analysts' workbenches)

Upper CASE tools are geared towards automating tasks associated with systems analysis. They include:

(a) **Diagramming tools** that automate the production of diagrams using a range of modelling techniques.

(b) **Analysis tools** that check the logic, consistency and completeness of system diagrams, forms and reports.

(c) A **CASE repository** that holds all data and information relating to the system. The **Data dictionary** records all data items held in the system and controls access to the repository. The dictionary will list all data entities, data flows, data stores, processes, external entities and individual data items.

5.1.2 Lower CASE tools (programmers workbenches)

Lower CASE tools are geared towards automating tasks later in the development process (after analysis and design). They include:

(a) **Document generators** that automate the production of diagrams using a range of modelling techniques.

(b) **Screen and report layout generators** that allow prototyping of the user-interface to be produced and amended quickly.

(c) **Code generators** that automate the production of code based on the processing logic input to the generator.

5.1.3 Advantages of using CASE tools

Advantages of CASE include the following.

(a) **Document/diagram preparation** and amendment is quicker and more efficient.

(b) **Accuracy of diagrams** is improved. Diagram drawers can ensure consistency of terminology and maintain certain standards of documentation.

(c) **Prototyping** (see later in this section) is made easier, as re-design can be effected very quickly.

(d) **Blocks of code can be re-used**. Many applications incorporate similar functions and processes; blocks of software can be retained in a library and used (or modified) as appropriate.

5.1.4 Examples of CASE tools

Examples of CASE tools include Select's SSADM Professional, Rational's ClearCase and AxiomSys from STG.

Example 1: Automated diagram production

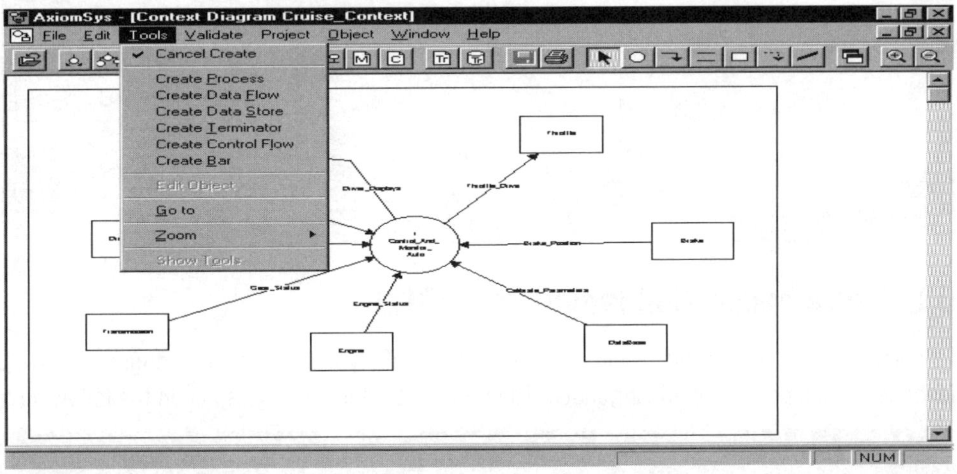

Example 2: Code generating and checking

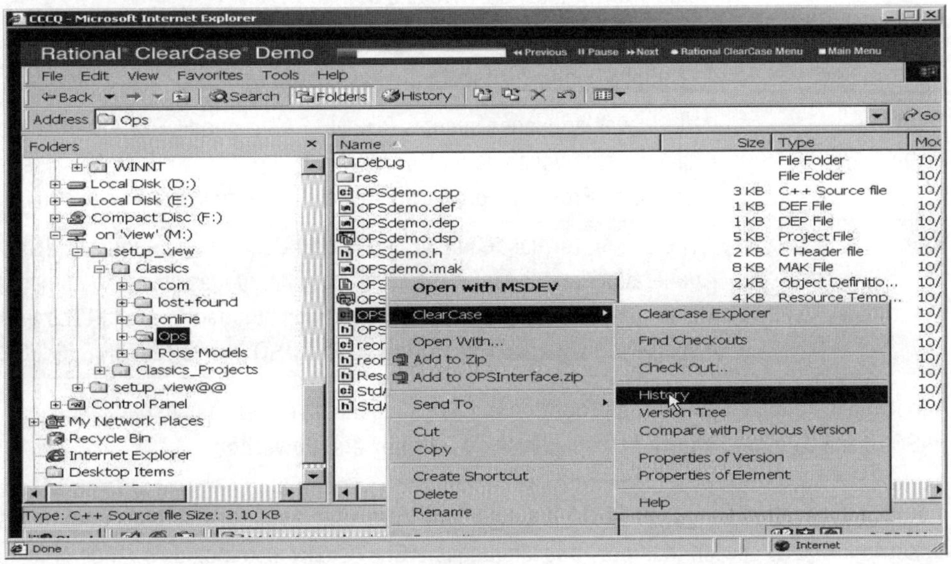

Example 3: Version/change control

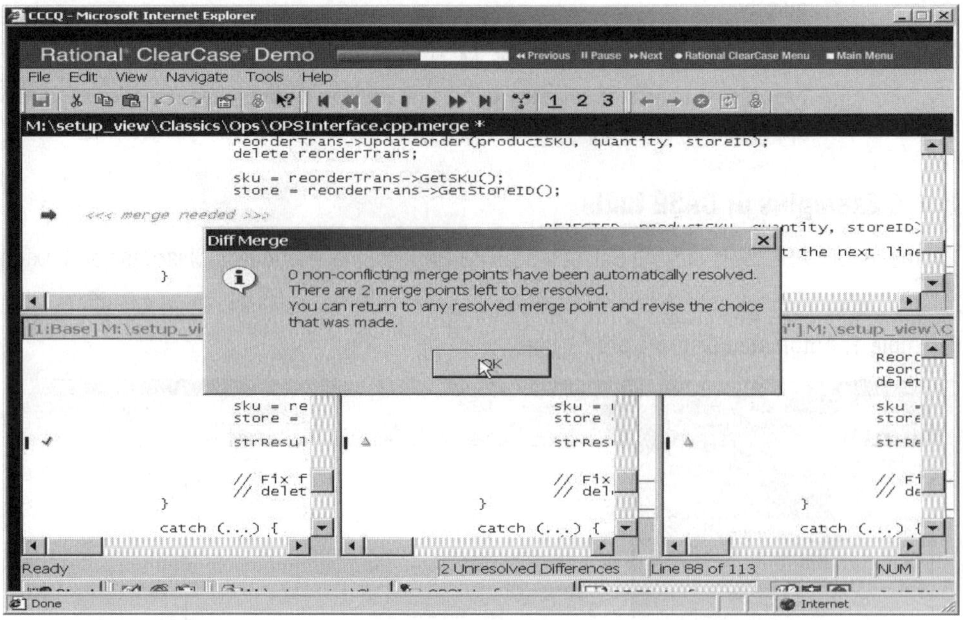

5.2 Fourth generation languages (4GLs)

As computer languages have developed over time, certain types of computer languages have become identified with a generation of languages. The four generations are explained in the following table.

Generation	Comment
First	Machine code. Program instructions were written for individual machines in binary form (a series of 1s and 0s).
Second	Assembly languages. Still machine specific, programs were written using symbolic code which made them easier to understand and maintain.
Third	High-level languages such as COBOL, BASIC and FORTRAN. These languages have a wider vocabulary of words, enabling commands to be closer to everyday language. Programs produced are able to be moved between similar computers.
Fourth	There is no formal definition of a Fourth Generation Language (4GL). Fourth-generation languages are programming languages closer to human languages than typical high-level or third generation languages. Most 4GLs use simple query language such as 'FIND ALL RECORDS WHERE NAME IS 'JONES'

A fourth generation language is a programming language that is easier to use than languages like COBOL, PASCAL and C++. Well known examples include **Informix** and **Powerhouse**.

Key term

A **Fourth Generation Language (4GL)** is a high-level computer language that uses commands that are closer to everyday speech than previous languages. 4GLs usually also include a range of features intended to automate software production.

FAST FORWARD

A **4GL** enables programs to be constructed more quickly and allows greater flexibility in the development process.

Most fourth generation languages use a graphical user interface. Icons, objects, help facilities, pull down menus and templates present programmers with the options for building the software. Sections of code are often treated as components, which may be used (maybe with slight modifications) in a variety of applications. A 4GL will often include the following features (many of these features could also be provided by a CASE tool).

- Relatively easy to learn and use
- Often centred around a database
- Includes a data dictionary
- Uses a relatively simple query language
- Includes facilities for screen design and dialogue box design
- Includes a report generator
- Code generation is often automated
- Documenting and diagramming tools

4GLs are often used to facilitate **object-oriented programming**. With object-oriented programming, programmers define the types of operations (functions) that can be applied to data structures (in programming, a data structure refers to a scheme for organising related pieces of information). In this way, the data structure becomes an object that includes both data and functions. In addition, programmers can create relationships between one object and another. For example, objects can inherit characteristics from other objects.

One of the principal advantages of object-oriented programming techniques over procedural programming techniques is that they enable programmers to create modules that do not need to be changed when a new type of object is added. A programmer can simply create a new object that inherits many of its features from existing objects. This makes object-oriented programs easier to modify (a group of objects with some common properties may be referred to as a **class**).

4GLs enable a more flexible approach to be taken to software production than under the traditional Systems Development Lifecycle. Using a 4GL, changes to the program design and to the code itself can be made relatively easily and quickly. This allows development to follow a pattern like the Spiral model, with users able to make amendments based on prototypes.

5.2.1 Examples taken from 4GLs

The following screenshots are taken from the Metamill 4GL.

Example 1: Automated diagram production

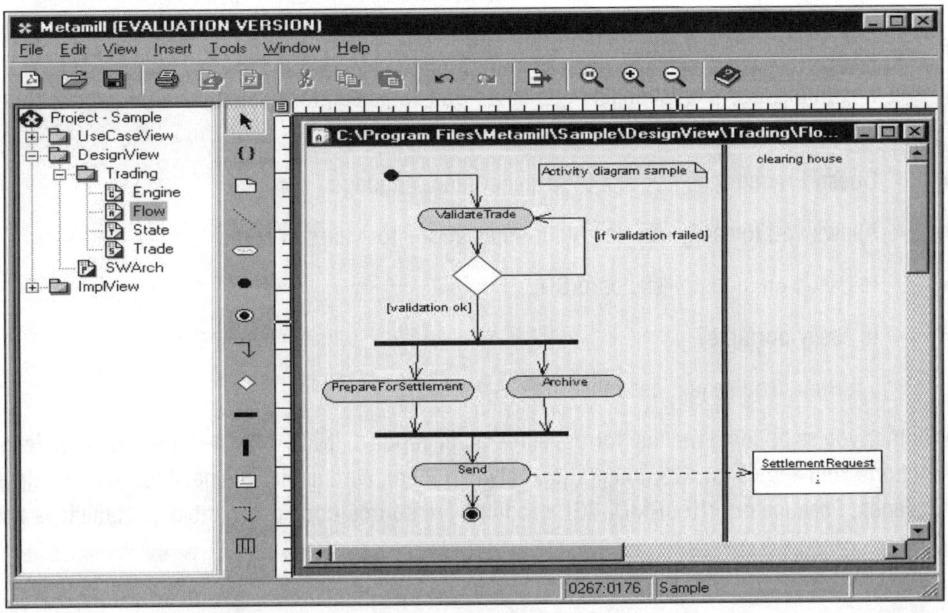

Example 2: Class properties window

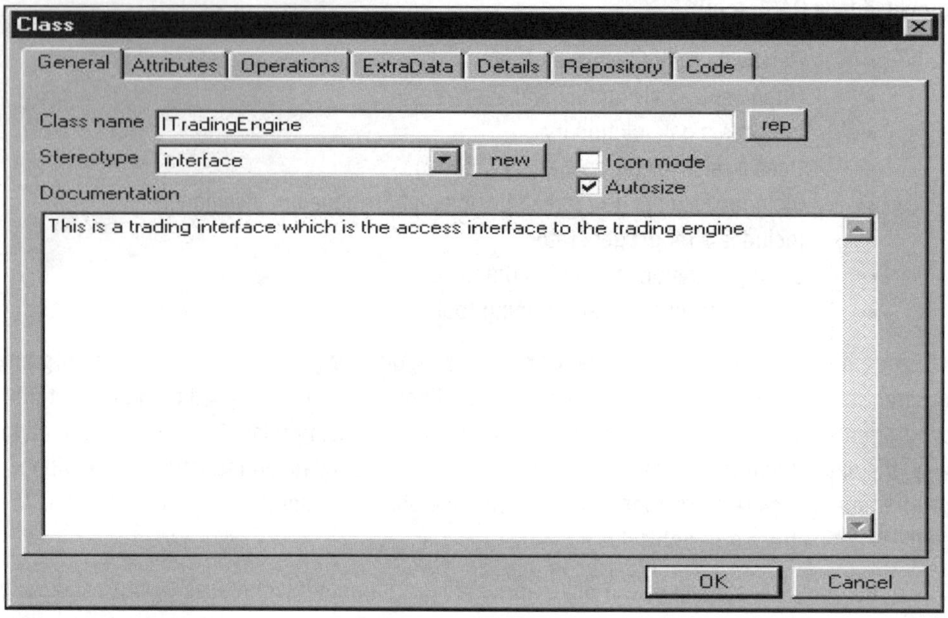

Case Study

The following is an extract from marketing material on the Informix website.

The INFORMIX-4GL Product Family, comprised of INFORMIX-4GL Rapid Development System, INFORMIX-4GL Interactive Debugger, and INFORMIX-4GL Compiler, is a comprehensive fourth-generation application development and production environment that provides power and flexibility without the need for third-generation languages like C or COBOL. INFORMIX-4GL version 4.1 provides more enhancements to the product line than any other release since 4GL was introduced in 1986 giving you more functionality than ever before!

Wouldn't you like to find a self-contained application development environment that:

- Provides rapid development and interactive debugging capabilities
- Offers high performance in the production environment
- Integrates all the functionality you could possibly need for building even the most complex applications
- Doesn't require the use of a third-generation language
- Allows you to easily maintain your applications for years to come
- Is based on industry-standard SQL
- Is easily portable?

Look no further. You've just described INFORMIX-4GL.

Whether you're building menus, forms, screens, or reports, INFORMIX-4GL performs all development functions, and allows for easy integration between them, eliminating the need for external development packages. Because our INFORMIX-4GL products are source-code compatible, portability is ensured.

5.3 Prototyping

The use of 4GLs, together with the realisation that users need to see how a system will look and feel to assess its suitability, have contributed to the increased use of **prototyping**.

Key term

A **prototype** is a model of all or part of a system, built to show users early in the design process how it is envisaged the completed system will appear.

As a simple example, a prototype of a formatted screen output from a system could be prepared using a graphics package, or even a spreadsheet model. This would describe how the screen output would appear to the user. The user could make suggested amendments, which would be incorporated into the next model.

FAST FORWARD

Prototyping enables programmers to write programs more quickly and allows the user to see a 'preview' of the system that is envisaged.

Using prototyping software, the programmer can develop **a working model of application program quickly**. He or she can then **check with the data user** whether the prototype program that has been designed appears to **meet the user's needs**, and if it doesn't it can be amended.

The prototyping process

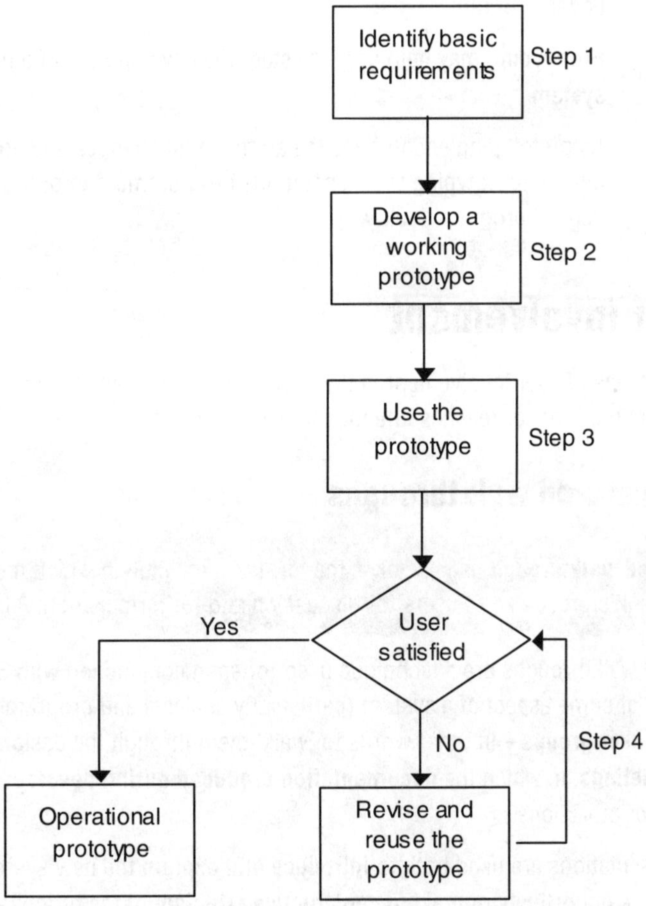

5.3.1 Advantages and disadvantages of prototyping

The **advantages** of prototyping.

(a) It makes it possible for programmers to present a 'mock-up' version of an envisaged system to users **before a substantial amount of time and money** have been committed. The user can judge the prototype before things have gone too far to be changed.

(b) The process facilitates the production of **'custom built' application software** rather than off-the-shelf packages which may or may not suit user needs.

(c) It makes **efficient use of programmer time** by helping programmers to develop programs more quickly. Prototyping may speed up the 'design' stage of the systems development lifecycle.

(d) A prototype does not necessarily have to be written in the language of what it is prototyping, so prototyping is not only a tool, but a **design technique**.

Disadvantages of prototyping.

(a) Some prototyping tools are **tied** to a particular make of **hardware**, or a particular **database system**.

(b) It is sometimes argued that prototyping tools are **inefficient** in the program codes they produce, so that programs are bigger and require more memory than a more efficiently coded program.

(c) Prototyping may help users to steer the development of a new system towards an **existing system**.

(d) As prototyping encourages the attitude that changes and amendments are likely, some believe prototyping tools encourage programmers to produce programs quickly, but to neglect program quality.

6 User involvement

The importance of user involvement in the development process cannot be over-estimated. This section looks at a number of approaches intended to ensure that the required level of involvement is achieved.

6.1 Structured walkthroughs

FAST FORWARD

A **structured walkthrough** usually takes the form of a meeting in which the output from a phase or stage of development is presented to users for discussion and for formal approval.

Structured walkthroughs are a technique used (often in conjunction with SSADM) by those responsible for the design of some aspect of a system (particularly analysts and programmers) to present their design to interested **user groups** – in other words to 'walk' them through the design. Structured walkthroughs are **formal meetings**, in which the **documentation produced during development is reviewed and checked** for errors or omissions.

These presentations are used both to **introduce and explain** the new systems to users and also to offer the users the opportunity of **making constructive criticism** of the proposed systems, and suggestions for further amendments/improvements, before the final systems specification is agreed.

Users are involved in structured walkthroughs because their knowledge of the desired system is more extensive than that of the systems development personnel. Walkthroughs are sometimes referred to as **user validation**.

6.1.1 The importance of signing off work

At the end of each stage of development, the resulting output is presented to users for their approval. There must be a **formal sign-off** of each completed stage before work on the next stage begins.

This **minimises reworking**, as if work does not meet user requirements, only the immediately preceding stage must be revisited. More importantly, it clarifies responsibilities and leaves little room for later disputes.

(a) If the systems developers fail to deliver something that both parties formally agreed to, it is the **developers' responsibility** to put it right, at their own expense, and compensate the user for the delay.

(b) If users ask for something extra or different, that was not formally agreed to, the developers cannot be blamed and **the user must pay** for further amendments and be prepared to accept some delay.

Question — **Benefits of a structured walkthrough**

What, besides identification of mistakes (errors, omission, inconsistencies etc), would you expect the benefits of a walkthrough to be?

(a) Users become involved in the systems analysis process. Since this process is a critical appraisal of their work, they should have the opportunity to provide feedback on the appraisal itself.

(b) The output from the development is shown to people who are not systems development personnel. This encourages its originators to prepare it to a higher quality and in user-friendly form.

(c) Because the onus is on users to approve design, they are more likely to become committed to the new system and less likely to 'rubbish' it.

(d) The process focuses on quality of and good practice in operations generally.

(e) It avoids disputes about who is responsible for what.

6.2 Joint applications development

FAST FORWARD

Joint Applications Development (JAD) describes a close partnership between users and developers.

Joint Applications Development (JAD) describes the partnership between users and system developers. JAD was originally developed by *IBM* to promote a more participative approach to systems development. The potential value to an organisation may be as follows.

(a) It creates a **pool of expertise** comprised of interested parties from all relevant functions.

(b) Reduced risk of systems being **imposed** by systems personnel.

(c) This **increases user ownership** and responsibility for systems solutions.

(d) Emphasises the **information needs of users** and their relationship to business needs and decision making.

There are a number of possible **risks** affecting the potential value of JAD.

(a) The relative **inexperience of many users** may lead to misunderstandings and possibly unreasonable expectations/demands on the system performance.

(b) The danger of **lack of co-ordination** leading to fragmented, individual, possibly esoteric information systems.

The shift of emphasis to applications development by end-users must be well managed and controlled. An organisation may wish to set up an **information centre** to provide the necessary support and co-ordination.

6.3 Rapid applications development

FAST FORWARD

Rapid Applications Development (RAD) combines a less structured approach to systems development with the use of modern software tools such as prototyping.

Rapid Applications Development (RAD) can be described as a quick way of building software. It combines a managed approach to systems development with the use of modern software tools such as **prototyping**. RAD also involves the **end-user** heavily in the development process.

RAD has become increasingly popular as the pace of change in business has increased. To develop systems that provide **competitive advantage** it is often necessary to build and implement the system quickly.

RAD can create **difficulties for the project manager** as RAD relies to a certain extent on a **lack of structure** and control.

6.4 User groups

User groups enable users to **share ideas and experience** relating to a particular product; usually a software package.

User groups can provide valuable insights and suggestions when system upgrades are being considered. We look at user groups in greater detail in Chapter 14.

Exam focus point

The June 2003 exam referred to a 'facilitated user workshop' to review a prototype. Don't be thrown by terminology that you may not have seen before, use common sense and the context to establish the likely meaning. A facilitated user workshop is simply a practical, hands-on meeting between developers and users (similar to a structured walkthrough).

Chapter Roundup

- The term **'systems development lifecycle'** describes the stages a system moves through from inception until it is discarded or replaced. Traditional lifecycle models such as *Royce's* **waterfall model** break the systems development process into **sequential stages** – with the output from a stage forming the input to the following stage.
- The **spiral approach** involves carrying out the same activities over a number of cycles in order to clarify requirements and solutions.
- A **methodology** is a collection of procedures, techniques, tools and documentation aids which are designed to help systems developers in their efforts to implement a new system. Methodologies are usually broken down into phases.
- A **CASE tool** may be used to support the construction and maintenance of a system model – often allowing the construction of a prototype.
- A **4GL** enables programs to be constructed more quickly and allows greater flexibility in the development process.
- **Prototyping** enables programmers to write programs more quickly and allows the user to see a 'preview' of the system that is envisaged.
- A **structured walkthrough** usually takes the form of a meeting in which the output from a phase or stage of development is presented to users for discussion and for formal approval.
- **Joint Applications Development (JAD)** describes a close partnership between users and developers.
- **Rapid Applications Development (RAD)** combines a less structured approach to systems development with the use of modern software tools such as prototyping.

Quick Quiz

1 List the seven stages identified in the National Computing Centre systems development lifecycle model.

2 What is the key feature of the waterfall model?

3 What shortcoming of the waterfall model did the 'b' model address?

4 What is the key feature of the spiral model?

5 Define 'systems development methodology'.

6 What would a CASE tool be used for?

7 Explain one advantage of prototyping.

8 Distinguish between JAD and RAD.

Answers to Quick Quiz

1 Identification of a problem or opportunity, Feasibility study, Systems investigation, Systems analysis, Systems design, Systems implementation, Review and maintenance.

2 The waterfall model, like the National Computing Centre model, breaks the systems development process into sequential stages, with the output from a stage forming the input to the following stage.

3 The 'b' model recognised that operations and maintenance are on-going.

4 The spiral approach involves carrying out the same activities over a number of cycles in order to clarify requirements and solutions.

5 A systems development 'methodology' is a collection of procedures, techniques, tools and documentation aids which will help systems developers in their efforts to implement a new information system.

6 A CASE tool is used to aid with system design and program coding.

7 Prototyping makes it possible for developers to present a 'mock-up' version of the envisaged system without committing too much time and effort. Users can then suggest improvements which can be incorporated in the actual system.

8 Joint Applications Development (JAD) describes the partnership between users and system developers. **Rapid Applications Development (RAD) is** a quick way of building software. It combines a managed approach to systems development with the use of modern software tools such as **prototyping** and **object oriented design methods**. As RAD involves the **end-user** heavily in the development process it is one example of JAD.

Now try the question below from the Exam Question Bank

Number	Level	Marks	Time
Q16(a)	Examination	12	21 mins

8

Systems analysis: User requirements

Topic list	Syllabus reference
1 Investigating user requirements	2 (b)
2 Process models (Data Flow Diagrams and Flowcharts)	2 (c)
3 A static structure model (Entity Relationship Model)	2 (d)
4 An event model (Entity Life History)	2 (e)
5 Structured English	2 (a), 2 (i)
6 Other system design issues	2 (c), 2 (d), 2 (e)

Introduction

We start this chapter with a look at some **common techniques of systems investigation**, including the use of **interviews** and **questionnaires**.

In the second half of the chapter we demonstrate the recording and **documenting tools** used during the analysis and design of information systems.

Study guide

Part 2.11 – Investigating and recording user requirements

- Define the tasks of planning, undertaking and documenting a user interview
- Identify the potential role of background research, questionnaires and special purpose surveys in the definition of requirements
- Explain the potential use of prototyping in the requirements definition
- Explain how requirements can be collected from current computerised information systems
- Discuss the problems users have in defining, agreeing and prioritising requirements

Part 2.12 – Documenting and modelling user requirements – processes

- Describe the need for building a business process model of user requirements
- Briefly describe different approaches to modelling the business processes
- Describe in detail the notation of one of these business process models
- Construct a business process model of narrative user requirements using this notation
- Explain the role of process models in the systems development process

Part 2.13 – Documenting and modelling user requirements – static structures

- Describe the need for building a business structure model of user requirements
- Briefly describe different approaches to modelling the business structure
- Describe in detail the notation of one of these business structure models
- Construct a business structure model of narrative user requirements using this notation
- Explain the role of structure models in the systems development process

Part 2.14 – Documenting and modelling user requirements – events

- Describe the need for building a business event model of user requirements
- Briefly describe different approaches to modelling the business events
- Describe in detail the notation of one of these business event models
- Construct a business event model of narrative user requirements using this notation
- Explain the role of event models in the systems development process

Exam guide

It is likely that the examination will require you to either draw a model representing a process, structure or event, or to interpret a diagram included in the examination paper.

1 Investigating user requirements

FAST FORWARD

During the **systems investigation** the project team examines the inputs, outputs, processing methods and volumes, controls, staffing and costs of the current system. This may involve fact finding by means of questionnaires, interviews, observation and reviewing documents.

The systems investigation is a detailed fact-finding exercise about the areas under consideration. It may be performed substantially during the feasibility study-depending upon the nature and size of the project.

The project team has to determine the inputs, outputs, processing methods and volumes of the current system. It also examines controls, staffing and costs and reviews the organisational structure. It should also consider the expected growth of the organisation and its future requirements.

The stages involved in this phase of the study are as follows.

(a) **Fact finding** by means of questionnaires, interviews, observation, reading handbooks, manuals, organisation charts, or from the knowledge and experience of members of the study team.

(b) **Fact recording** using flowcharts, decision tables, narrative descriptions, organisation and responsibility charts.

(c) **Evaluation**, assessing the strengths and weaknesses of the existing system.

At this phase, when the team is trying to discover the details of a system with which they may be unfamiliar, they will be interested in the organisational context of the system, as it is important to have an overall view of what the system does. Consequently, fact finding in a user department can cover a broad area, as demonstrated by a few examples, below. The emphasis in each area will be on the potential for **improvement**.

(a) **Plans and objectives.** Does the department have clear plans and objectives and are these consistent with the objectives of the organisation as a whole?

(b) **Organisation structure**. Is the structure geared towards achieving the department's objectives? Are responsibilities clearly delegated and defined?

(c) **Policies, systems and procedures**. How has the department established its current policies? Are they written down and formally reviewed? How does management ensure that policies are adhered to?

(d) **Personnel**. Are there adequate systems/procedures for job specifications and appraisals? Are there adequate systems for staff development and training?

(e) **Equipment and the office.** What is the general condition of office equipment? Is it used to full advantage?

(f) **Operations and control.** What exceptional cases are dealt with, and how are they dealt with? Are there bottlenecks in operations; if so, what can be done to ease them?

There are many items about which facts ought to be obtained, and so the systems investigators should begin by drafting a **checklist of points** before they start asking questions.

This 'top-down' approach **focuses first on management needs** and ignores operational needs until later on. Top management's needs in controlling the organisation are of great importance in systems design.

1.1 Interviews

FAST FORWARD

Interviews can be an effective method of fact finding. although they can be time consuming and therefore expensive.

Interviews with members of staff can be an effective method of fact finding. although they can be **time consuming** for the analyst, who may have several to conduct, and therefore expensive.

(a) In an interview, **attitudes** not apparent from other sources may be obtained.

(b) **Immediate clarification** can be sought to unsatisfactory/ambiguous responses.

(c) Interviews **require a response** – some staff may ignore a questionnaire.

(d) A well-conducted interview should provide staff with some reassurance regarding the upcoming change.

Some **guidelines** to consider when conducting fact-finding interviews are explained below.

(a) The interviewer may be dealing with many individuals each with different attitudes and personalities. The approach to each interview should be adapted to suit the individual interviewee.

(b) The interviewer should be **fully prepared**, having details of the interviewee's name and job position, and a plan of questions to ask.

(c) **Employees ought to be informed** before the interview that a systems investigation is taking place, and its **purpose explained**.

(d) The interviewer must ask questions at the **level appropriate** to the employee's position within the organisation.

(e) The interview should be allowed to develop into a **conversation** whereby the interviewee offers his opinions and suggestions, but the focus must remain on what the interview hopes to achieve.

(f) The interviewer must not **jump to conclusions** or confuse opinions with facts, accepting what the interviewee has to say (for the moment) and refraining from interrupting.

(g) The interviewer should gain the **interviewee's confidence** by explaining what is going on. This confidence may be more easily obtained by allowing the interview to take place on the interviewee's 'home ground' (desk or office). The purpose of note taking should also be explained.

(h) If possible, the interviewer may find it helps understanding to move **progressively** through the system, for example interviewing operational staff first, then supervisors, then managers.

(i) The interview should be **long** enough for the interviewer to obtain the information required and to ensure an understanding of the system, but **short** enough to ensure that concentration does not wander.

(j) The interview should be **concluded** by a resumé of its main points and the interviewer should **thank** the interviewee for their time.

Question

Fact finding interviews

Draw up a checklist of do's and don'ts for conducting fact-finding interviews.

Answer

A useful checklist for **guidance in conducting interviews** is suggested by Daniels and Yeates in *Basic training in systems analysis* as follows:

Do	Don't
Plan	Be late
Make appointments	Be too formal or too casual
Ask questions at the right level	Interrupt
Listen	Use technical jargon
Use the local terminology	Confuse opinion with fact
Accept ideas and hints	Jump to conclusions

Do	Don't
Hear both sides	Argue
Collect documents and forms	Criticise
Check the facts back	Suggest
Part pleasantly	

1.2 Questionnaires

FAST FORWARD

The use of **questionnaires** may be useful whenever a **limited** amount of **information** is required from a **large number of individuals**.

Questionnaires may be used as the **groundwork for interviews** with some respondents being interviewed subsequently. Alternatively, interviews may be carried out in one site/department, and questionnaires designed on the basis of experience and used elsewhere.

Many respondents find questionnaires **less imposing than interviews** and may therefore be more prepared to express their opinion.

(a) Employees ought to be informed of the questionnaire's **purpose**. This should remove any staff suspicion and hopefully ensure a good proportion of sensible responses.

(b) Question design is a very important issue. Questions should obtain the specific information necessary for the study, but should not be worded in such a way to influence the response given.

(c) Questionnaires must not be too long – a questionnaire of many pages is likely to end up in a 'pending' tray indefinitely, or worse, the bin.

(d) Staff may prefer **anonymity**. This should result in grater honesty, but has the disadvantage of preventing follow-up of uncompleted questionnaires, and of 'interesting' responses.

Questionnaires, by themselves, are useful for gathering specific information. In a systems development context, it is likely that further methods of gathering information, such as interview or observation, would also be required.

1.2.1 Designing a questionnaire

When designing a questionnaire, the following guidelines should be considered.

(a) Questionnaires should **not contain too many questions** (people tend to lose interest quickly and become less accurate in their answers).

(b) They should be **organised in a logical sequence**.

(c) Ideally, they should be designed so that each question can be answered with a limited range of answers, such as **'yes' or 'no'** or a 'tick' in a numbered box eg 1 = Strongly agree, 4 = Strongly disagree.

(d) They should be **tested independently** before being issued. This should enable the systems analyst to establish the effectiveness of the questions.

(e) Questionnaires should take into account the **sensitivity** of individuals in respect of any threat to their job security, change of job definition etc.

1.3 Observation

FAST FORWARD

Observation may be used to check facts obtained by interview or questionnaire. It may well be that staff work differently to the answers provided in interviews, and differently to written policies and procedures.

An analyst, after establishing the methods and procedures used in the organisation, may wish to undertake further investigation through **observing operations**.

The observer must remember that staff may act differently simply because they know they are being observed – this is a difficult problem to overcome as observing staff without their knowledge may not be **ethical**.

1.4 User workshops

FAST FORWARD

User workshops are often used in systems analysis to help establish and record user requirements.

A workshop is a meeting with the emphasis on **practical exercises.** User workshops are often used in systems analysis to help establish and record user requirements.

At a user workshop, user input is obtained by the analyst to analyse business functions and define the data associated with the current and future systems. An outline of the proposed new system is produced, which is used to design more detailed system procedures.

Depending on the complexity of the system, the workshop may devise a **plan for implementation**. More complex systems may conduct a workshop early in the design stage and hold a later workshop with the aim of producing a **detailed system model. Prototyping** may be used at such a workshop to prepare preliminary screen layouts.

User workshops should be facilitated by a **facilitator.** The facilitator co-ordinates the workshop activities with the aim of ensuring the objectives of the session are achieved.

The facilitator would most likely be a systems analyst with excellent **communication** and leadership skills. The skills of the person in this role are critical to the success of the workshop.

Many user workshops also utilise a **scribe**. The scribe is an active participant who is responsible for producing the outputs of the workshop. The scribe may use a **CASE tool** (explained in Chapter 7).

1.5 Document review

FAST FORWARD

An analysis of existing **system documentation** should help the analyst estimate future processing requirements and volumes.

The systems analyst must investigate the **documents** that are used in the system for input and output. One way of recording facts about document usage is the **document description form**, which is simply a standard form which the analyst can use to describe a document.

This may be a wide ranging investigation, using for example organisation charts, procedures manuals and standard operational forms.

One risk, however, is that **staff do not follow** documented policies and procedures or that these documents have **not been properly updated**. Document review should therefore be used in tandem with one or more other investigative techniques.

An analysis of documents, together with historical operational data, should help the analyst estimate future processing requirements and volumes.

1.6 Existing computerised systems

Existing computer systems can provide much information relevant to the requirements for a new computerised system. Areas where an existing system could provide useful information include:

- File structures
- Transaction volumes and processor speed
- Screen design
- User satisfaction and user complaints
- Help-desk/Information centre records
- Causes of system crashes

It is important to remember however that a duplicate of the existing system is not required. The aim is to produce a better system – which is likely to involve changes to existing working methods.

1.7 Requirements creep

If user requirements are investigated and established effectively, an accurate picture should be established of what the new system should achieve. This should prevent a common problem occurring later in the project, the problem of 'requirements creep'.

Requirements creep refers to the situation where users appear to change their requirements throughout the development process. Requirements creep may be due to actual changes in user requirements, but it is often caused by an inaccurate original system specification.

2 Process models (Data Flow Diagrams and Flowcharts)

FAST FORWARD

Process models may be used to model business systems. Two examples of process models are **dataflow diagrams** and **flowcharts**.

Business systems (which may include manual and computerised components) involve the input, processing and output of data. Process models may be used to model business systems and to show the movement and processing actions data is subjected to.

The production of a process diagram is often one of the first tasks in systems analysis – providing a basic understanding of how the system works. The syllabus refers to two process models, Data flow diagrams (DFDs) and flowcharts. We will look at both.

2.1 Data flow diagrams (DFD)

Four symbols are used in data flow diagrams as shown below.

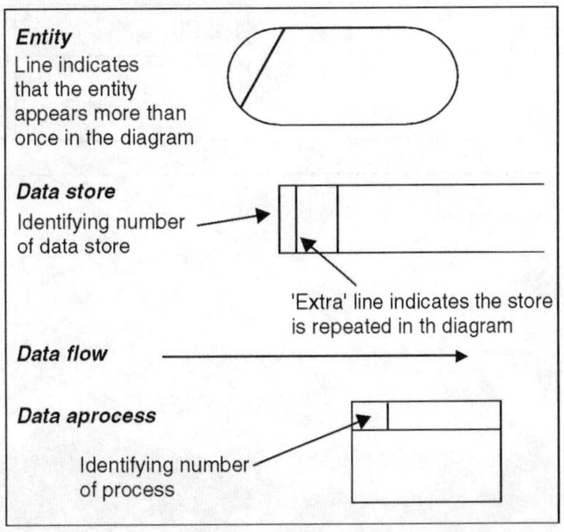

Key terms

An **external entity** is a **source** or **destination** of data which is considered **external to the system** (not necessarily external to the organisation). It may be people or groups who provide data or input information or who receive data or output information.

A **data store** is a point which receives a data flow and holds data. Most data stores would be either digital (ie computer files) or paper.

A **data flow** represents the movement or transfer of data from one point in the system to another.

Data processes involve data being used or altered. The processes could be manual, mechanised or computerised.

A data flow could 'physically' be anything – for example a letter, a telephone call, a fax, an e-mail, a link between computers, or a verbal statement. When a data flow occurs, a copy of the data transferred may also be retained at the transmitting point.

A process could involve changing the data in some way, or simply using the data. For example, a mathematical computation or a process such as sorting would alter data, whereas a printing data out does not change data – the process makes the same data available in a different form.

DFDs may be drawn to represent different levels of detail. The top level (least detailed) diagram would show one process only. The source of the data for this process, and its destination(s) are also shown. This type of diagram is known as a **Level 0 DFD**, or a Context diagram.

The Level 0 DFD may be 'exploded' into a more detailed data flow diagram, known as a **Level-1 DFD**. Further detail can be represented on a **Level-2 DFD**, and so on until all individual entities, stores, flows and processes are shown.

The diagram below illustrates how **levels of DFDs** are built up.

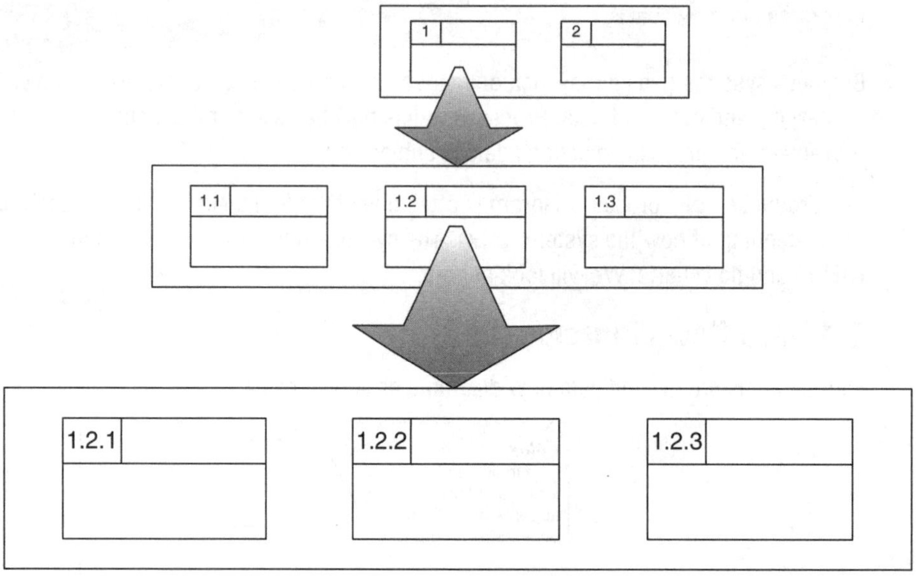

2.2 Example: Data flow diagram

The example used here is a system used for purchasing in a manufacturing company. Three data flow diagrams are shown; each is prepared to record a certain level of detail.

2.2.1 Level-0 DFD (context diagram)

The Level-0 DFD or context diagram would show the source of the purchasing process, its destination and the inputs and outputs. (Data stores are not shown on Context diagrams).

The central box represents the purchasing system as a whole. In this case only one external entity is shown. In some cases more than one entity will be required, but a context diagram will only ever show one process.

Note that we are only showing flows of data. The physical resources (the goods supplied) can be shown (by means of broad arrows ⇨), but this tends to overcomplicate the diagram.

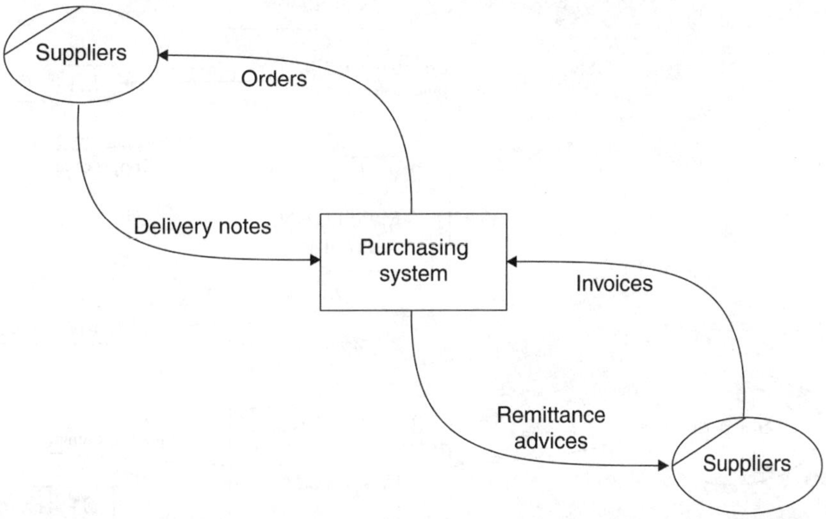

Exam focus point

> If you are required to draw on Data Flow Diagram in the exam the level of detail required may be established by the information you are asked to model.

2.2.2 Level 1 DFDs

Within the purchasing system as a whole in this organisation there are two **subsystems**: the **Stores department** places requests for purchases and accepts delivery of the goods themselves; the **Purchasing department** places orders, and receives and pays invoices.

A **Level-1 DFD** for the **purchasing department** is shown below.

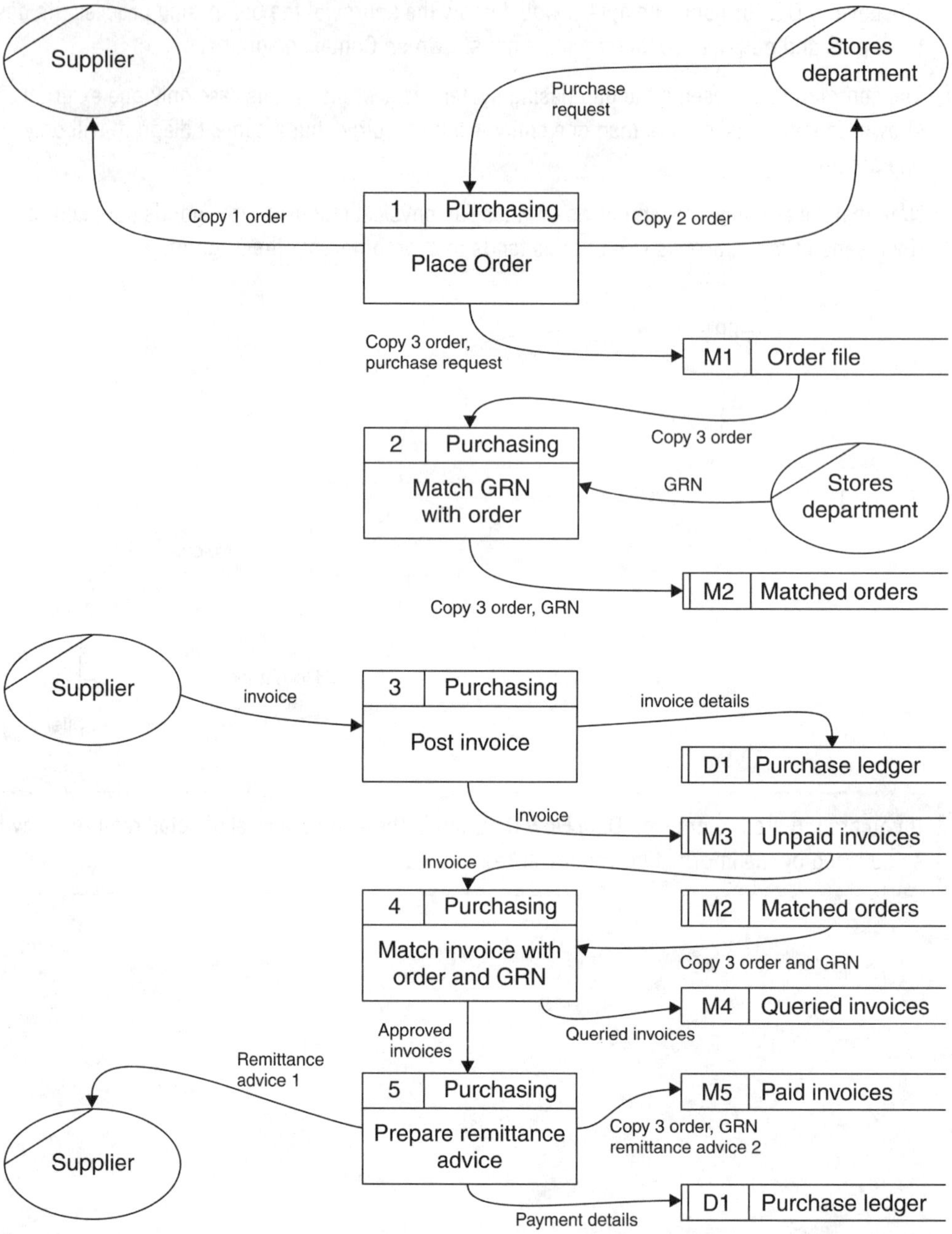

Note the following points.

(a) Some analysts prefer to also show a **system boundary**. This usually involves drawing a single line around the diagram enclosing everything except the Entities (ie all Entities would be shown outside the system boundary). This reflects the point-of-view that although Entities interact with the system, the focus of the model is the process that occurs inside the system boundary.

(b) If a boundary was added to the diagram above, the two Stores department entity symbols and the three Supplier entity symbols would be shown outside the system boundary. They may also be referred to as 'External entities' – this refers to being external to the process being focussed on rather than necessarily being external to the organisation. Other analysts prefer not to show a boundary – you should be aware of what the boundary is in case you are presented with a diagram that includes a boundary.

(c) Each process is numbered, but this is only for ease of identification: the numbers are not meant to show the strict sequence of events.

(d) Each process box has a heading, showing where the process is carried out or who does it. The description of the process should be a clear verb like 'prepare', 'calculate', 'check' (not 'process', which is too vague).

(e) The same entity or store may appear more than once on the same diagram (to prevent diagrams becoming overly complicated with arrows crossing each other). When this is done an additional line is put within the symbol. The supplier entity and several of the data stores have extra lines for this reason.

(f) Data stores are given a reference number (again sequence is not important). Some analysts like to use 'M' with this number if it is a **manual** store, and a 'D' if it is a digital or **computerised** store.

2.2.3 Level-2 DFDs

A **separate** DFD (Level-2) could be prepared for **each of the numbered processes** shown in the Level 1 DFD. This is known as decomposing a process.

For example, the diagram below shows the data flows for process 1, Place Order.

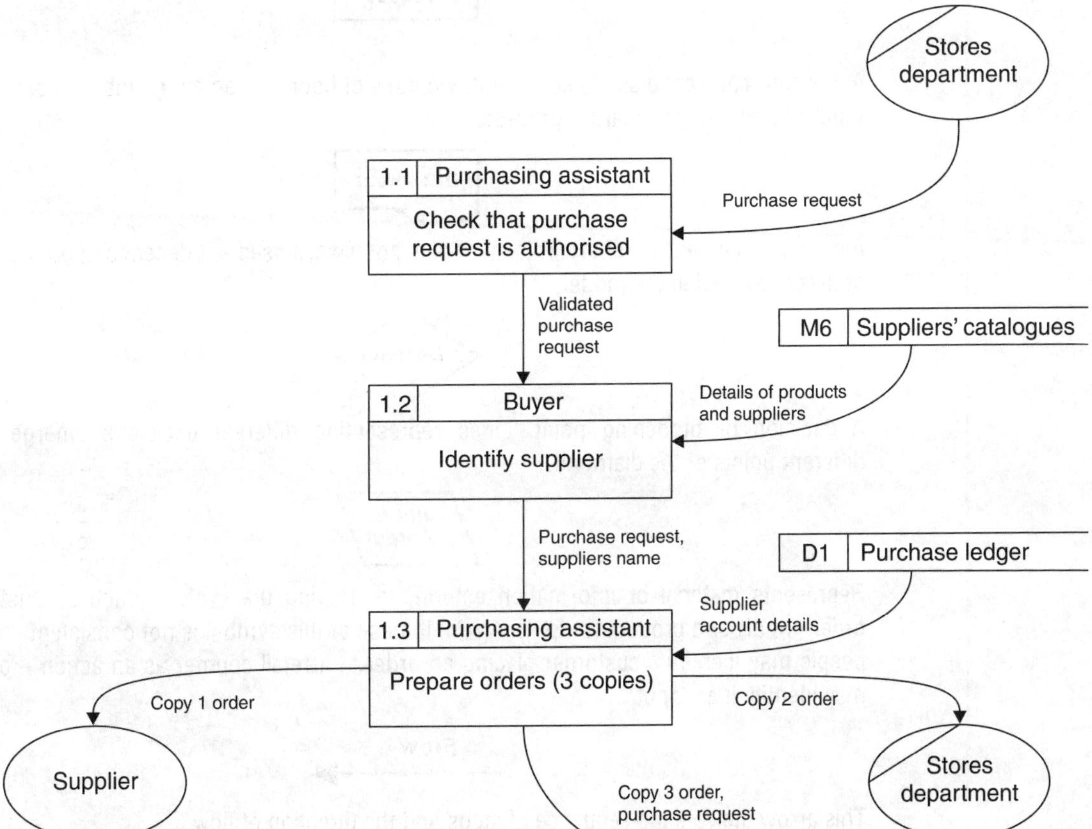

In turn, box 1.1 could be **further decomposed** in a Level-3 DFD, with processes 1.1.1, 1.1.2 and so on, and box 1.2 could be decomposed into processes 1.2.1, 1.2.2 etc.

2.3 Flowcharts

Flowcharts are another type of a process model. Flowcharts use special shapes to represent different types of actions or steps in a process. Lines and arrows show the sequence of the steps, and the relationships among them.

Below are examples of commonly used flowcharting symbols. You should remember though that different people and organisations may use different symbols, or may use only some of the symbols below. Factors such as the complexity of the process being modelled and simple personal preference play a part.

Exam focus point

In an examination, if you draw a flowchat you should provide a Key that explains the symbols you use. You should ensure your diagram is clear, logical – and able to be understood by the marker. Before the exam, ensure you are proficient in at least one of either DFDs or Flowcharts.

Flowcharting symbols

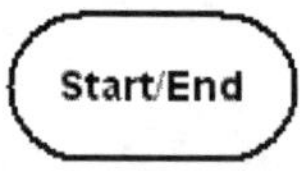

This symbol marks the starting or ending point of the system.

A box can represent a single step ('add two cups of flour'), or an entire sub-process ('make bread') within a larger process.

A printed document or report. This symbol is not always used – it depends upon the level of detail required in the model.

A decision or branching point. Lines representing different decisions emerge from different points of the diamond.

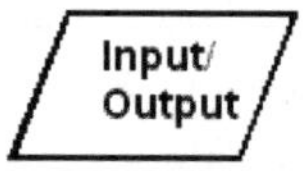

Represents material or information entering or leaving the system, such as customer order (input) or a product (output). Again, the use of this symbol is not consistent – some people may identify a customer placing an order at a retail counter as an action – others may identify it as Input.

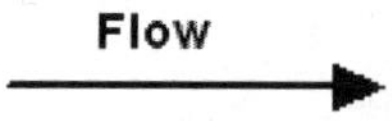

This arrow indicate the sequence of steps and the direction of flow.

2.4 Example: Flowchart

The following example shows how flowcharts may be used to model and re-design a process. Analysts studying the process of ordering at a fast-food chain noticed that may customers ordered a burger, fries and a drink. They decided they could streamline this process.

The 'before' and 'after' flowcharts follow. The flowcharts shown below include very little detail. More detailed models could be drawn if required – for example showing any receipt given to the customer and the customer leaving the counter. (In an examination the level of detail required would be able to be established from he information supplied.)

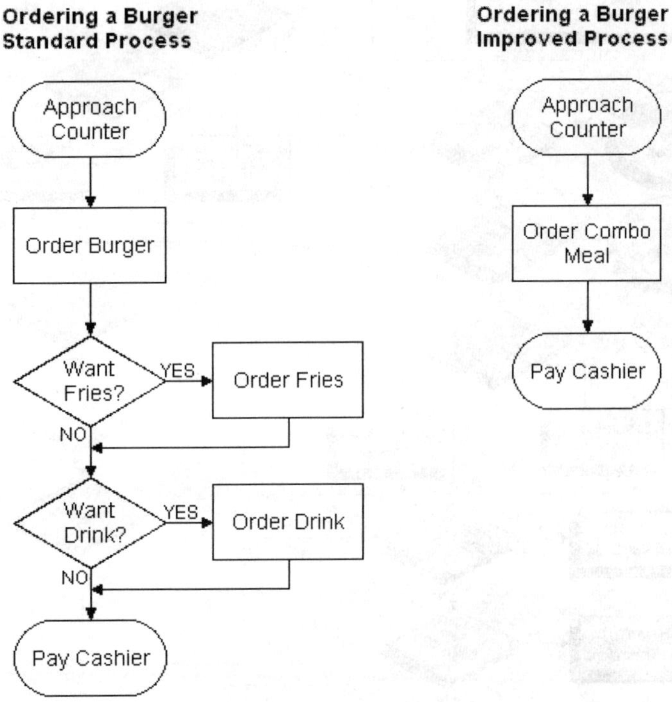

Exam focus point

There are some **variations in the use of flowcharting symbols**. For example, the chart above classifies 'Order Burger' as an Action. It could also justifiably be classified as an Input and a different symbol used.

In the examination always provide an explanatory **'key' explaining the notation used in your model**.

Case Study

This flowchart was produced for a US software vendor to model the process of processing telephone orders. (Note – 'Figure' is a US term meaning 'Calculate' eg 'Figure/Calculate the Grand Total'.)

Telephone Order Process

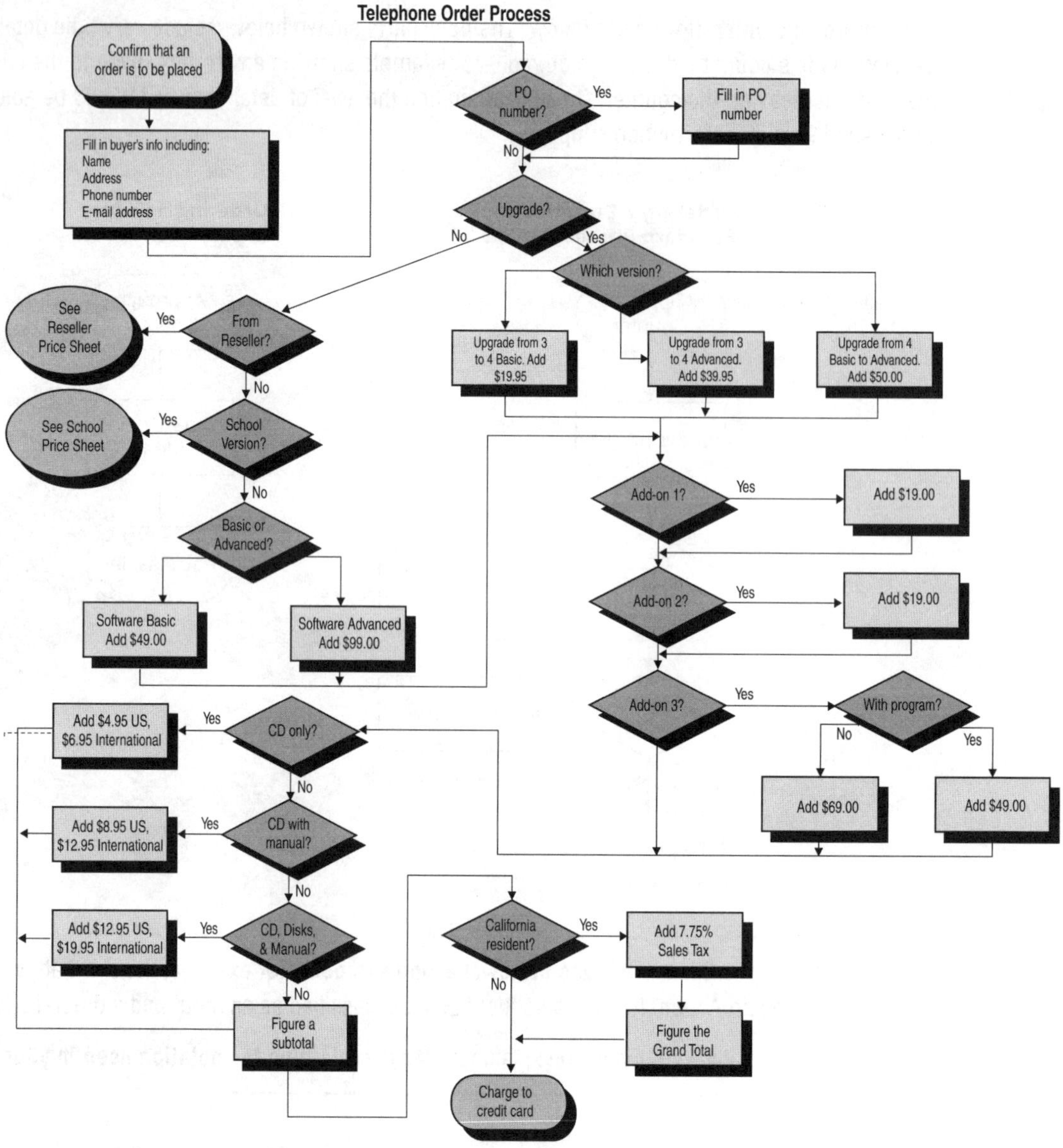

3 A static structure model (Entity Relationship Model)

FAST FORWARD

An **Entity Relationship Model** (ERM) (also known as an entity model or a logical data structure) provides an understanding of the logical data requirements of a system independently of the system's organisation and processes. An ERM is an example of a **Static structure model**.

An **entity**, as we have seen, is an item (a person, a job, a business, an activity, a product or stores item etc) about which information is stored.

Key term

An **Entity** is any item, role, object, organisation, activity or person that is relevant to the data held in a system.

An **attribute** is a characteristic or property of an entity. For a customer, attributes include customer name and address, amounts owing, date of invoices sent and payments received, credit limit etc.

Key term

An **Entity Relationship Model (ERM)** (also known as an **entity model** or a **logical data structure)** provides an understanding of the logical data requirements of a system independently of the system's organisation and processes.

FAST FORWARD

An ERM may show three main types of relationship:

- One-to-one relationship (1:1)
- One-to-many relationship (1:M), could be expressed as a Many-to-one relationship(M:1)
- Many-to-many relationship (M:M)

The following relationships may be identified between attributes and entities.

3.1 One-to-one relationship (1:1)

With a one-to-one relationship, an entity is related to only one of the other entity shown. For example, a one-to-one relationship exists between *company* and *finance director.* The model below shows one company which employs one finance director. (These diagrams are sometimes called Bachmann diagrams.)

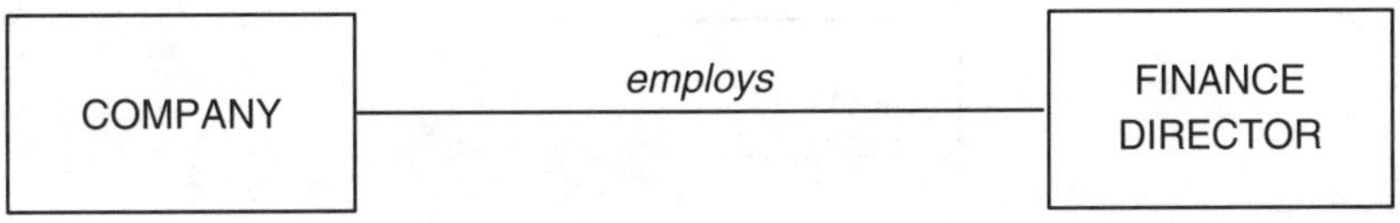

3.2 One-to-many relationship (1:M)

For example, the relationship **employs** also exists between *company* and *director.* The company employs more than one director.

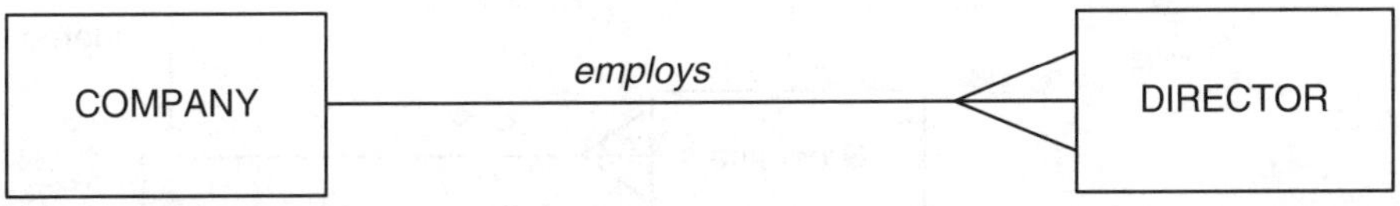

3.3 Many-to-one relationship (M:1)

This is really the same as the previous example, but **viewed from the opposite direction**. For example, many *sales managers* report to one *sales director.*

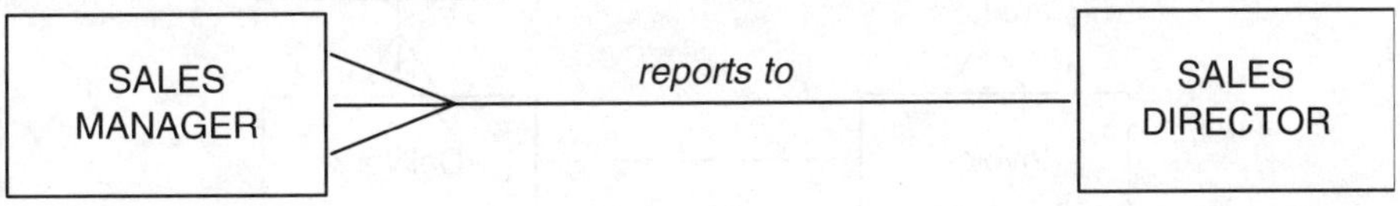

3.4 Many-to-many relationship (M:M)

The relationship between *product* and *part* is **many-to-many**. A product is composed of many parts, and a part might be used in many products.

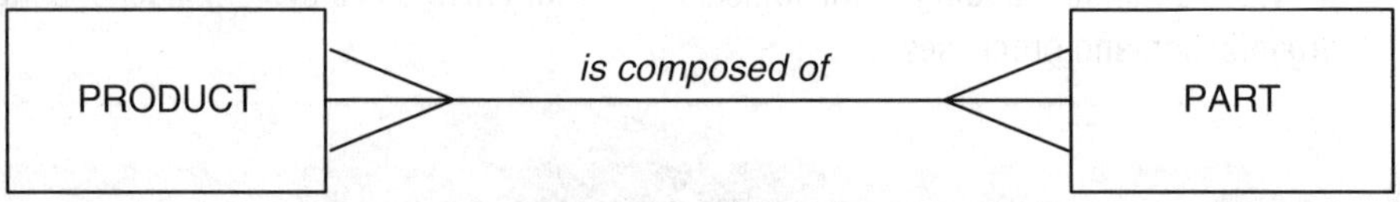

When analysing relationships the correct classification is important. If the one-to-many relationship customer order contains part numbers is incorrectly described as one-to-one, a system designed on the basis of this ERM might allow an order to be entered with one item and one item only.

3.5 Example: Building an ERM

A diagram modelling part of a warehousing and despatch system is shown below. This indicates that:

(a) A customer may make many orders.

(b) That an order form can contain several order lines.

(c) That each line on the order form can only detail one product, but that one product can appear on several lines of the order.

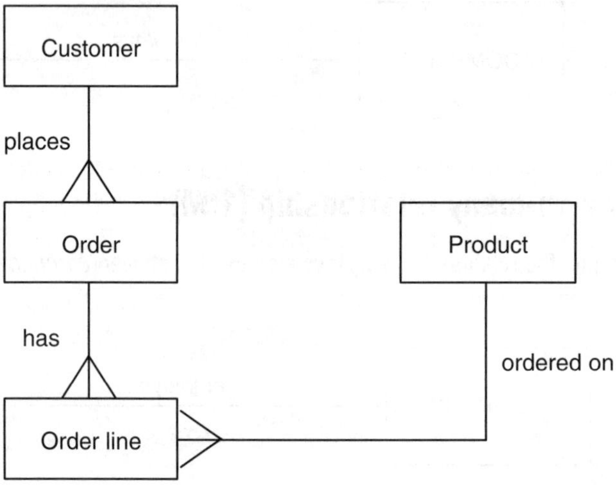

Another example of an entity model follows. Note the structure of the accompanying narrative (shown following the diagram).

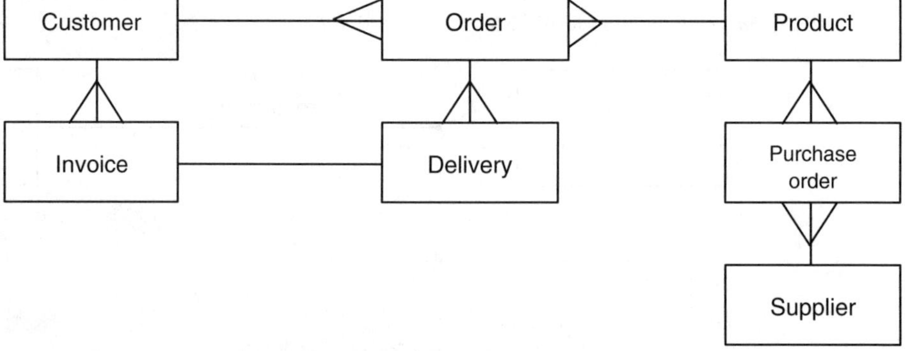

Entity	Relationship	Entity
Customer	Places many	Orders
Order	Has many	Deliveries
Product	Is ordered on many	Orders
Product	Is ordered on many	Purchase orders
Supplier	Receives many	Purchase orders
Invoice	Is for one	Delivery
Customer	Receives many	Invoices

4 An event model (Entity Life History)

As we have seen, **Entity Relationship Models** take a **static** view of data. We will now look at a modelling tool that focuses on **data processes**.

FAST FORWARD

An **Entity Life History** (ELH) documents the processes that happen to an entity. An ELH is a type of **Event model**.

Key term

An **Entity Life History (ELH)** is a diagram of the *processes* that happen to an *entity*. An entity life history gives a **dynamic** view of the data.

Data items do not always remain unchanged – they may come into existence by a specific operation and be destroyed by another. For example, a customer order forms part of a number of processes, and is affected by a number of different events. At its simplest, an entity life history displays the following structure.

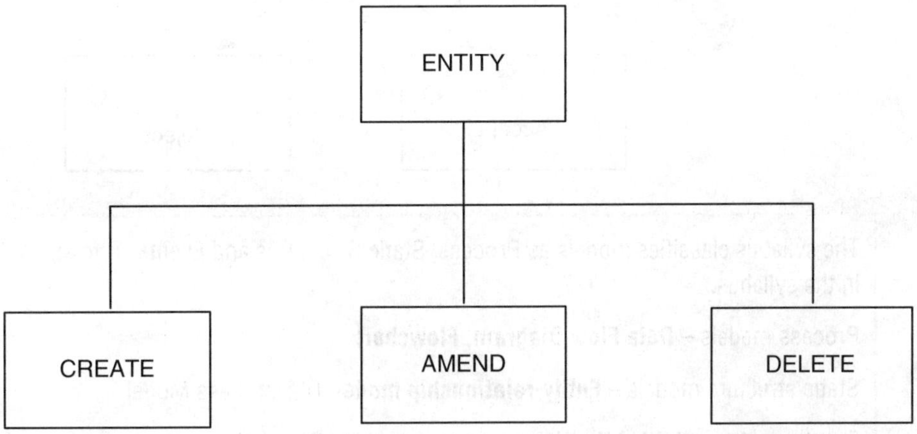

Entity life histories identify the various states that an entity can legitimately be in. It is really the functions and events which cause the state of the entity to change that are being analysed, rather than the entity itself.

The following notation rules are used for Entity life histories.

(a) Three symbols are used. The main one is a rectangular box. Within this may be placed an asterisk or a small circle, as explained below.

(b) At the top level the first box (the 'root node') shows the entity itself.

(c) At lower levels the boxes represent events that affect the life of the entity.

(d) The second level is most commonly some form of 'create, amend, delete', as explained earlier (or birth, life, death if you prefer). The boxes are read in **sequence** from top to bottom and left to right.

(e) If an event may affect an entity many times (**iteration**) this is shown by an **asterisk** in the top right hand corner of the box. A customer account, for example, will be updated many times.

(f) If events are alternatives (**selection**) – for example accept large order or reject large order – a **small circle** is placed in the top right hand corner.

Note the three types of process logic referred to above:

- Sequence
- Iteration (or repetition)
- Selection

Here is a very simple example.

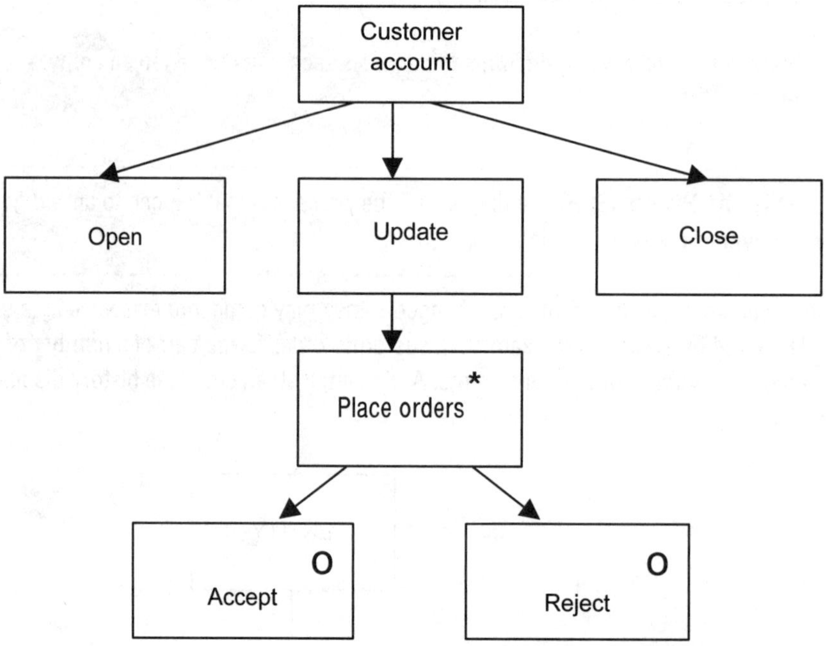

Exam focus point

> The syllabus classifies models as Process, Static Structures and Events. Two examples of each are named in the syllabus.
>
> Process models – **Data Flow Diagram**, **Flowchart**.
>
> Static structure models – **Entity-relationship model**, Object Class Model.
>
> Events models – **Entity Life History**, State Transition Diagram.
>
> The ACCA has stated that questions will be able to be answered using either one of the two examples provided for each type of model.

5 Structured English

FAST FORWARD

Structured English comprises a limited vocabulary of words that may be used to describe a process.

In systems development, the process depicted by a model could be described using Structured English as a step towards producing the actual program code.

There are several different kinds of Structured English, but they typically include the following features.

(a) It is more **like spoken English** than normal programming languages and so is easier for programmers and non-programmers to understand.

(b) It is much **more limited than normal speech**, as it has to follow a **strict logical order**.

(c) There is a **variety of conventions** for writing it.

Structured English uses **keywords** (eg IF, ADD) which, by some conventions, are written in capitals and have a **precise logical meaning** in the context of the narrative.

The logical order in which instructions are performed is sometimes expressed in indentation. There are **three basic logical structures**.

- Sequencing
- Selection
- Iteration or repetition

The **data elements** which are the subject of processing are, by some conventions, written in lower case and underlined.

5.1 Sequence instruction

Sequence instructions are followed once only. For example, the calculation of gross pay from hours worked and rate of pay could be written in structured English as shown below.

```
MULTIPLY hours worked by pay rate to get gross pay
```

5.2 Selection instruction

Most computer programs offer a number of **'choices'** and the consequent action taken depends on the choices being made. In structured English, a choice follows this structure.

```
IF
        THEN
ELSE
        THEN
ENDIF
```

For example, a company offers **discounts to trade customers only**. How would this be expressed in structured English?

```
IF the customer is a trade customer
   THEN give 10% discount
ELSE (customer is not trade customer)
   THEN no discount given
ENDIF
```

Sometimes, decisions are more complicated. Assume that the company only offers a 10% discount to trade customers who have been customers for over one year, but other trade customers receive a 5% discount.

```
IF the customer is a trade customer
          IF customer is customer over 1 year
          THEN 10% discount given
          ELSE 5% discount given
          ELSE (customer not a trade customer)
          THEN no discount given
ENDIF
```

One particular type of decision is a **CASE statement**. Cases are a special type of decision structure to indicate **mutually exclusive possibilities**.

A case structure is an alternative to the IF-THEN-ELSE-SO structure outlined above, which is satisfactory for making relatively simple decisions, but can become unwieldy when the decision becomes complex.

For example, we could have expressed the trade credit policy as follows.

```
IF customer a trade customer
          CASE     customer for more than one year
                   give 10% discount
          CASE     customer for less than one year
                   give 5% discount
END IF
```

5.3 Iteration or repetition

Sometimes a block or set of instructions may need to be **repeated** until a final condition is reached.

For example, assume we have called a given block out instructions the name Block 1. We wish these instructions to be executed until the number of records processed reaches 100. This requirement is a **condition**, which we can call condition 1. In structured English, this can be written as follows.

```
REPEAT
          Block 1
UNTIL
          Condition 1
```

Exam focus point

The syllabus does not mention Structured English specifically – so it is unlikely that you would be required to apply this technique. However, you may mention the technique, if it is relevant to the situation, when answering general systems design/development questions.

6 Other system design issues

6.1 Requirements specification

FAST FORWARD

Models of an existing system may be referred to when developing the **requirements specification** of a new system.

Developing a requirements specification involves the following activities.

(a) Detailed dataflow diagrams, flowcharts and other models are produced, and the **proposed** system compared with the **current** system to ensure that all necessary processing will be performed. If necessary, the diagrammatic models are modified.

(b) Specifications for **input** and **output** are prepared. These detail what appears on screen, or on documents. Prototyping could be used at this stage.

(c) Relational data analysis (**normalisation**) is performed on the input and output descriptions. This is to identify any entities that might not have been noticed, or drawn in enough detail, in the existing **logical data structure.** (Normalisation is a way of **analysing and simplifying the relationships** between items of data.)

(d) **Entity life histories** are drawn up, indicating what happens to each entity, ie what functions (processes) it is subjected to.

6.2 Logical design

Logical design involves describing the purpose of a system – **what the system will do**. Logical design does not include any specific hardware or software requirements – it is more concerned with the **processes** to be performed.

Models such as Data Flow Diagrams (for example) or written descriptions may be used to show and explain what a system will do. In some cases logical design may also include the identification of the main data files that will be required by the system (eg these may be established from a DFD).

6.3 Physical design

Physical design refers to the actual 'nuts and bolts' of the system – it includes technical specifications for the hardware and software required. Physical design involves the following tasks.

(a) **Initial physical design –** obtaining the design rules from the chosen system and applying them to the logical data design drawn up in the previous stages.

(b) Further define the **processing** required. For instance requirements for **audit, security and control** are considered, such as **controls over access** to the system; controls **incorporated within programs** (eg data validation, error handling); and **recovery procedures**, in case processing is interrupted.

(c) **Program specifications** are created. These provide in detail exactly what a particular program is supposed to achieve.

(d) Program specifications are assessed for their **performance** when implemented. It should be possible to estimate the times that programs will take to run.

(e) File and data specifications are **finalised**.

(f) **Operating instructions** are drawn up (user documentation). These will include such items as error correction and detailed instructions for operators and users (eg the sort of screen format that will appear).

Prototyping (covered in Chapter 7) may be used so that users can actually see what the system will look like and get a feel for how it will work.

6.4 Technical system options

The organisation will have to make choices concerning the specifications of the physical components of the new system.

There might be a number of options available so choices will need to be made regarding:

(a) **Hardware configuration** – for example mainframe, mini, PC; centralised or distributed processing; Internet connections.

(b) **Software** – use of an off the shelf package or a bespoke solution. This issue is covered in detail later in this Text.

Performance objectives for the system are then specified in detail so that these can be followed in the actual design of the system.

Chapter Roundup

- During the **systems investigation** the project team examines the inputs, outputs, processing methods and volumes, controls, staffing and costs of the current system. This may involve fact finding by means of questionnaires, interviews, observation and reviewing documents.
- **Interviews** can be an effective method of fact finding. although they can be time consuming and therefore expensive.
- The use of **questionnaires** may be useful whenever a **limited** amount of **information** is required from a **large number of individuals**.
- **Observation** may be used to check facts obtained by interview or questionnaire. Staff may work differently to the answers provided in interviews and specified in written policies and procedures.
- **User workshops** are often used in systems analysis to help establish and record user requirements.
- An analysis of existing **system documentation** should help the analyst estimate future processing requirements and volumes.
- **Process models** may be used to model business systems – usually at a fairly high level. Two examples of process models are **dataflow diagrams** and **flowcharts**.
- An **Entity Relationship Model** (ERM) (also known as an entity model or a logical data structure) provides an understanding of the logical data requirements of a system independently of the system's organisation and processes. An ERM is an example of a **Static structure model**.
- An **ERM** may show **three** main **types of relationship**:
  - One-to-one relationship (**1:1**)
  - One-to-many relationship (**1:M**), could be expressed as a Many-to-one relationship(**M:1**)
  - Many-to-many relationship (**M:M**)
- An **Entity Life History** (ELH) documents the processes that happen to an entity. An ELH is a type of **Event model**.
- **Structured English** comprises a limited vocabulary of words that may be used to describe a process.
- Models of an existing system may be referred to when developing the **requirements specification** of a new system.

Quick Quiz

1 List three advantages of conducting user interviews to establish user requirements, rather than sending users a written questionnaire.

2 List three advantages of using a written questionnaire to establish user requirements, rather than conducting user interviews.

3 Give two examples of a Process model.

4 What four symbols are used in data flow diagrams?

5 List the three types of relationship an Entity Relationship Model (ERM) may portray.

6 What three types of process logic may an Entity Life History (ELH) show?

7 Distinguish between logical design and physical design.

Answers to quick quiz

1 Any three of the following (you may have thought of other valid points). In an interview, attitudes not apparent from other sources may be obtained. Interviews allow immediate clarification to be sought to unsatisfactory/ambiguous responses. Interviews require a response – some staff may ignore a questionnaire. A well-conducted interview should provide staff with some reassurance regarding the upcoming change.

2 Any three of the following (you may have thought of other valid points). Using questionnaires allows focus to be maintained – interview discussions may lose focus. Questionnaires can be 100% anonymous. Questionnaires can be sent to widespread locations very cheaply. People may find questionnaires less imposing than interviews and may therefore be more prepared to express their opinion.

3 Dataflow diagrams and flowcharts.

4 The four symbols used in Data Flow Diagrams are:

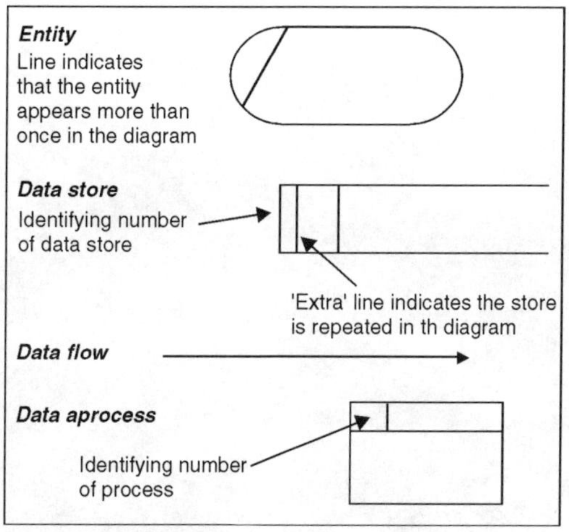

5 One-to-one (1:1), one-to-many (1:M) (or many-to-one M:1), and many-to-many (M:M).

6 Sequence, iteration, selection.

7 Logical design is concerned with the purpose and processes of the system. Physical design involves the physical aspects including hardware, software, data storage and presentation.

In general, the logical design is more relevant to the systems analyst while programmers will require details of physical design.

Now try the questions below from the Exam Question Bank

Number	Level	Marks	Time
Q4	Examination	20	36 mins
Q14	Examination	20	36 mins

9

External design

Topic list	Syllabus reference
1 External and internal system elements	2 (f)
2 Input devices	2 (f)
3 Output devices	2 (f)
4 The Human-Computer Interface	2 (f)
5 Input and output design	2 (f)

Introduction

The syllabus emphasises the issues surrounding **external design** – the parts of the system that the **user** interacts with.

In this chapter we look at how users interact with computer systems.

The issues covered are important both in the context of the syllabus and exam – and are particularly important when **designing information systems**. If a system is not relatively easy to use it is unlikely to gain **user acceptance**.

Study guide

Part 2.15 – External design

- Define the characteristics of a 'user-friendly' system
- Describe the task of external design and distinguish it from internal design
- Select appropriate technology to support output design
- Design effective output documents and reports
- Select appropriate technology to support input design
- Design effective inputs
- Describe how the user interface may be structured for ease of use

Exam guide

Questions related to external design may require you to comment on, or suggest improvements to, documents, screen displays or input procedures.

1 External and internal system elements

FAST FORWARD

External design refers to the elements of a computer system that the user can see. The **Human-Computer Interface (HCI)** includes all external elements of a system.

The distinction between external and internal elements of a computer system is a simple one – see the following definitions.

Key terms

External design refers to the elements of a computer system that the user can see.

Internal design refers to the elements of a computer system that the user does not see.

Accountants use computer systems extensively, and are often involved in system selection and implementation. However, accountants do not require an intimate knowledge of the internal workings of computer hardware and programs. This is reflected in the syllabus for this paper, which emphasises the elements of computer systems that the user interacts with – the external elements.

2 Input devices

2.1 Data collection and input

A computerised information system receives data and instructions via input devices, stores data and programs on storage devices and outputs processed data (information) using output devices. The system may also **interact** with other systems via communications devices.

Data must be input into a computer system in a form the computer is able to interpret. There are a number of various methods of data input. When **choosing a method of data input** for a given situation, **key considerations** are:

- Speed
- Accuracy
- Cost
- Volume of data\transactions
- System reliability
- Flexibility required

FAST FORWARD

Data input options include:

- Keyboard/mouse/track-ball
- Bar code readers
- Magnetic ink readers
- Scanners and OCR or OMR
- Magnetic stripe cards
- EPOS systems
- Smart cards
- Touch sensitive screens
- Voice recognition systems

Some common methods of input are explained in the following paragraphs.

2.2 The keyboard

Almost all computer terminals and personal computers include a keyboard based on the basic QWERTY typewriter keyboard.

Keyboard input is a **labour-intensive process**, but is the only suitable option in many circumstances eg producing a unique letter in which accuracy is vital.

2.3 The VDU or monitor

A VDU (visual display unit) or 'monitor' displays text and graphics. The screen's resolution is the number of pixels that are lit up. Higher resolution monitors have greater number of pixels – so each pixel is smaller providing greater detail.

2.4 Mouse

A **wheeled mouse** has a rubber ball protruding from its base. The mouse is moved over a flat surface, and as it moves, internal sensors pick up the motion and convert it into electronic signals which instruct the cursor on screen to move in the same direction.

The **optical mouse** has a small light-emitting diode (LED) that bounces light off the surface the mouse is moved across. The mouse contains sensors that convert this movement into co-ordinates the computer can understand.

A typical mouse has two or three buttons which can be pressed (clicked) to send specific signals. Some also have a wheel to facilitate scrolling up and down a screen display.

Similar to the mouse is the **trackball**, which is often found on laptop computers. Trackballs comprise a casing fixed to the computer, and a ball which protrudes upwards. The user moves the ball by hand. Other mobile computers use a touch sensitive pad for mouse functions; others have a tiny joystick in the centre of the keyboard.

2.5 Magnetic ink character recognition (MICR)

Magnetic ink character recognition (MICR) involves the recognition by a machine of special formatted **characters printed in magnetic ink**. The characters are read using a specialised reading device. The main advantage of MICR is its speed and accuracy, but MICR documents are expensive to produce. The main commercial application of MICR is in the banking industry – on cheques and deposit slips.

2.6 Optical mark reading (OMR)

Optical mark reading involves the **marking of a pre-printed form** with a ballpoint pen or typed line or cross in an appropriate box. The card is then read by an OMR device which senses the mark in each box using an electric current and translates it into machine code. Applications in which OMR is used include National Lottery entry forms (in the UK), and answer sheets for multiple choice questions.

2.7 Scanners and Optical Character Recognition (OCR)

A scanner is device that can read text or illustrations printed on paper and translate the information into a form the computer can use. A scanner works by digitising an image, the resulting matrix of bits is called a bit map.

Optical Character Recognition (OCR) software is used to translate the image into text.

2.8 Bar coding and EPOS

Bar codes are groups of marks which, by their spacing and thickness, indicate specific codes or values.

Electronic Point of Sale (EPOS) devices, which include bar code readers, enable retailers to record and manage stock movements and provide detailed sales information.

2.9 EFTPOS

Many retailers have now introduced EFTPOS systems (Electronic Funds Transfer at the Point of Sale). An EFTPOS terminal is used with a customers credit card or debit card to pay for goods or services. The customer's credit card account or bank account will be debited automatically. EFTPOS systems combine point of sale systems with electronic funds transfer.

2.10 Magnetic stripe cards

The standard magnetic stripe card contains machine-sensible data on a thin strip of magnetic recording tape stuck to the back of the card. The magnetic card reader converts this information into directly computer-sensible form. The widest application of magnetic stripe cards is as bank credit or service cards.

2.11 Smart cards

A smart card is a plastic card in which is embedded a microprocessor chip. A smart card would typically contain a memory and a processing capability. The information held on smart cards can therefore be updated (eg using a PC and a special device). The chip enables more effective security checks to be carried out.

2.12 Touch screens

A touch screen is a display screen that enables users to make selections by touching areas of the screen. Sensors, built into the screen surround, detect which area has been touched. These devices are widely used in vending situations, such as the selling of train tickets.

2.13 Voice recognition or Voice Data Entry (VDE)

Computer software has been developed that can convert speech into computer-sensible form via a microphone. Users are required to speak clearly and reasonably slowly.

Question — **Supermarket information system**

The next time you are at the supermarket check-out, think of the consequences of the operator simply scanning one bar code. What effect does this quick and simple action have?

Answer

(a) The price of the item is added to your bill.

(b) The supermarket stock 'number on shelf' is reduced by one, and if the predetermined minimum has been reached the 'shelf restock required' indicator will be activated.

(c) The overall stock on hand figure will be reduced, and if the minimum stock holding has been reached the 'reorder from supplier' indicator will be activated.

(d) The relevant accounting entries will be made, or be sent to a pending file awaiting the running of the month-end routine.

(e) Marketing information will be obtained – what time the purchase was made, what else was purchased and if your loyalty card was swiped – who purchased it.

You may have thought of others. The key point to grasp from this exercise is that **efficient information collection** can be achieved using appropriate technology.

3 Output devices

FAST FORWARD

The three most common methods of computer output are output to a **printer**, output to the **screen** and output to a **computer file**.

3.1 The choice of output medium

Choosing a suitable output medium depends on a number of factors.

Factor	Comment
Hard copy	Is a printed version of the output needed?
Quantity	For example, a VDU screen can hold a certain amount of data, but it becomes more difficult to read when information goes 'off-screen' and can only be read a 'page' at a time.
Speed	For example if a single enquiry is required it may be quicker to make notes from a VDU display.
Suitability for further use	**Output to a file** would be appropriate if the data will be processed further, maybe in a different system. Large volumes of reference data might be held on microfilm or microfiche.
Cost	The 'best' output device may not be justifiable on the grounds of cost – another output medium should be chosen.

3.1.1 Printers

Character printers, such as dot matrix printers, print a single character at a time. Dot matrix printers are less common today than in the past, but may still be found in some accounting departments. Their main drawback is their low-resolution. They are also relatively slow and noisy, but are relatively cheap to run.

Inkjet printers are small and relatively cheap. They work by sending a jet of ink on to the paper to produce the required characters – a line at a time. They produce print of a higher quality than dot matrix printers, and most models can print in colour. Running costs can be high.

Laser printers print a whole page at a time, rather than line by line. The quality of output with laser printers is very high. Compared with inkjet printers, running costs are relatively low.

3.1.2 The VDU

Screens were described earlier, as they are used together with computer keyboards for input. They can be used as an output medium, primarily where the volume of output is low, for example a single enquiry.

4 The Human-Computer Interface (HCI)

Key term

The **Human-Computer Interface** (HCI) includes all external elements of a system. Elements of the HCI include keyboard, mouse, VDU, screen layout and the dialogue between the user and the system.

The Human Computer Interface should be appropriate to the purpose of the system, the situation the system is used in and to users' levels of competency.

4.1 Human-computer dialogue

FAST FORWARD

The exchange of information between a computer system and a user is known as **human-computer dialogue**.

The screen provides 'feedback' for the user, allowing the system to be flexible, interactive and conversational. This dialogue between the system and the user is the key factor in how the system is operated. The term 'conversational mode' describes the continual dialogue between the user and the system.

Well-designed human-computer dialogue takes account of the following factors.

4.1.1 Usability

Usability includes all aspects that influence how easy a package is to use. Some key aspects of usability are described below.

(a) Data entry screens should be presented in a logical order. The sequence of tasks – screen should match the natural order a user would follow when performing these tasks.

(b) If an input form (source document) is used, the input screen should require items in the same order as the input form. Titles should be easy to read and should match the titles used on source documents.

(c) The screen layout should be clear. For example, input fields may be highlighted using colour. The position of the cursor should be clear. Dialogue language should be clear and concise. The meaning of icons and menu options should be obvious.

(d) Default entries should be provided for items such as the standard VAT rate. Defaults are used unless the user overwrites them – this can speed up data entry considerably.

(e) Consistency of screen layout and design enables user skills to be transferred between systems. Common features across different packages should reduce training costs.

(f) Users should always have options available that enable them to navigate around the system. Options should be available that allow users to abandon their current task, save work completed so far or exit from the system. There must always be clear instructions for how to proceed.

Exam focus point

A question in the December '2004 exam required candidates to explain usability requirements for three different sets of users.

4.1.2 On-screen help

Users should be able to access information that will help them understand what actions are required. Typically, if a user requires help, he or she requests it through the F1 key, or by selecting 'Help' from pull-down menu. The help provided should be context specific – it should relate to the current task the user is attempting. The traditional printed manual has been largely superseded by on-screen help.

Some software packages also include an on-line tutorial, which may be used to demonstrate a typical processing cycle.

4.1.3 Use of dialogue boxes and on-screen prompts

When options such as 'delete' or 'update' are used, user-friendly software should issue a warning confirming what has been requested. This gives the user a second chance to confirm that the command was intended and that the computer is indeed required to carry out the specified process.

4.1.4 Convenience

Many users find that they perform the same series of actions so frequently that it becomes tedious to click their way through menus and dialogue boxes. User-friendly software will recognise this and offer faster alternatives.

(a) 'Shortcut keys' (typically pressing the Ctrl key together with one or more other keys) can be assigned to standard actions.

(b) A series of commands can be automated in the form of a 'macro', which can be activated using a shortcut key or user-defined button.

(c) 'Wizards' may be developed to simplify tasks that otherwise would require detailed knowledge. For example, the Chart wizard provided in modern spreadsheet packages has simplified the previously complicated task of producing charts.

Question — **Software features**

Examine the menus and features of at least two software packages written for Microsoft Windows. What similarities do you notice?

Answer

Amongst the similarities are:

Common menu design eg drop-down menus, the File and Edit menus, Common function keys (F1 is 'help'). Common features eg Cut and Paste, use of toolbars, viewing options such as magnification, scroll bars etc.

4.2 Graphical user interfaces (GUI)

Because they are easier to use than character (text) based menu systems, most software today has a **Graphical User Interface (GUI)**.

A GUI involves the use of two design ideas and two operating methods which can be remembered by the abbreviation **WIMP**. This stands for '**W**indows, **I**cons, **M**ouse, **P**ull-down menu' and is an environment which offers a method of accessing the computer without using the keyboard. Dialogue is conducted through images rather than typed text.

Graphical user interfaces (GUIs) were designed to make computers more 'user-friendly'. They are now the most prominent method by which people and systems conduct dialogue.

FAST FORWARD

A Graphical User Interface (GUI) utilises WIMP methods.

4.2.1 Windows (the generic term rather than the operating system)

A window is a section of the on-screen display. Numerous 'windows' of flexible size, which can be opened and closed, may be available to the user at any one time. This enables **two or more documents to be viewed and edited** together, and sections of one to be inserted into another. For example, figures from a spreadsheet can be pasted directly into a word-processing document.

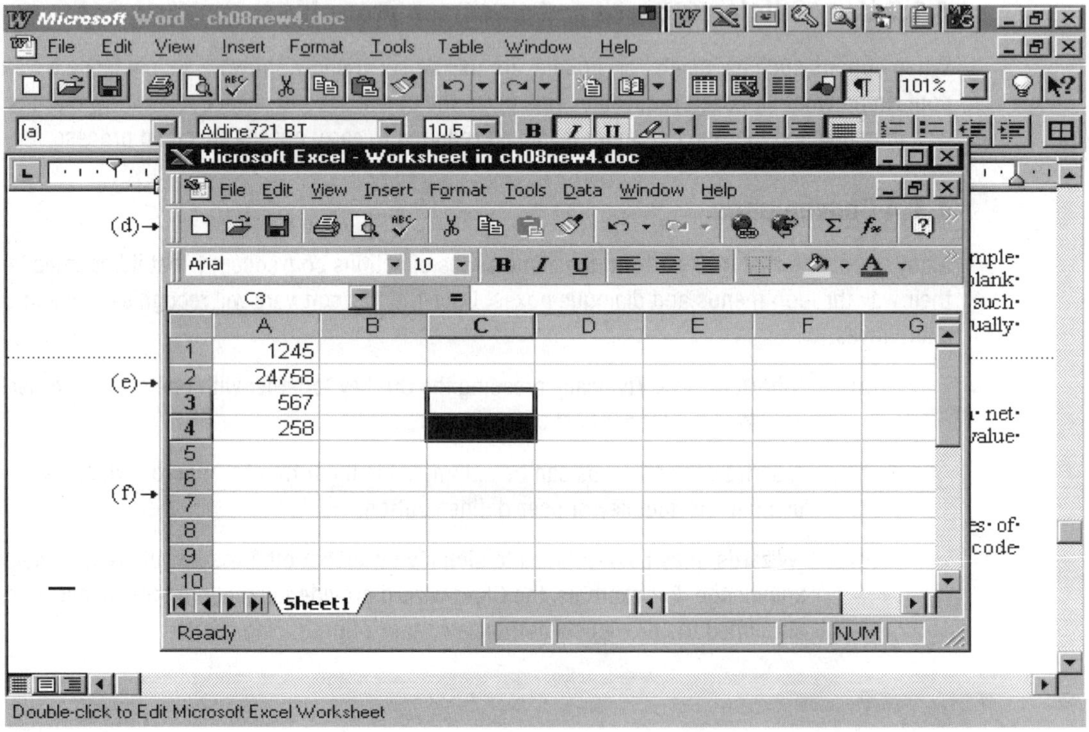

4.2.2 Icons

An icon is an image of an object used to represent a function or a file in an obvious way. For instance Windows based packages use a picture of a printer which is simply clicked to start the printing process. Another common icon is a waste paper bin to indicate the deletion of a document.

Both icons and windows are shown in the following illustration.

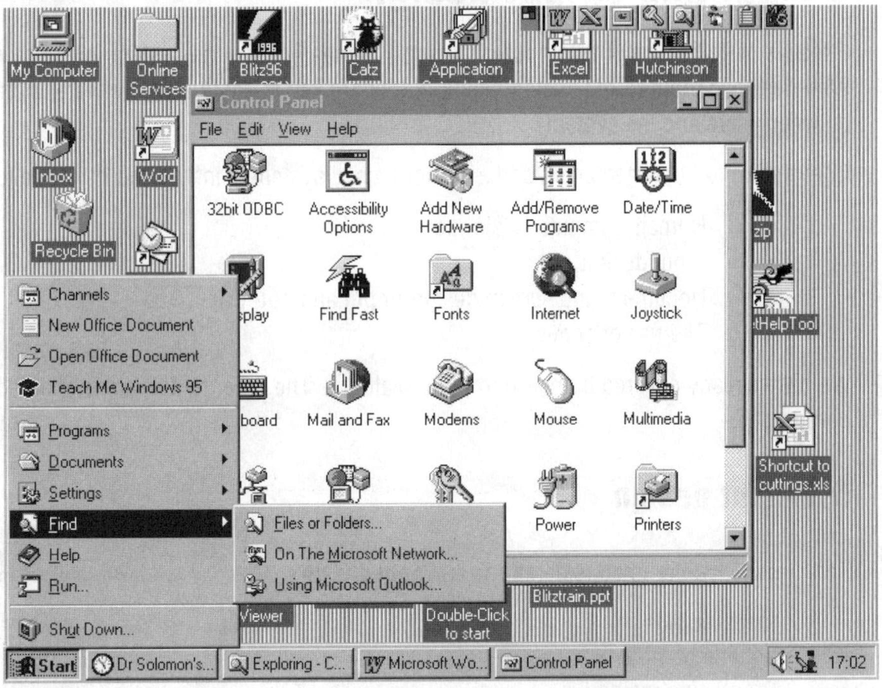

4.2.3 Mouse

We explained the physical workings of mice earlier. As a mouse moves around on the desktop a *pointer* (cursor) on the screen mimics its movements. A mouse can be used to pick out and activate an icon or button, to highlight a block of text for deletion/insertion, or to drag data from one place on the screen to another. It also has buttons which are clicked to execute the current command.

4.2.4 Pull-down menu

A 'menu-bar' is typically displayed along the top of a window. If a menu option is selected, a subsidiary menu is 'pulled-down' offering further choices. The following illustration shows the pull-down menu activated by selecting the Format option, and then the further options available within the Background option.

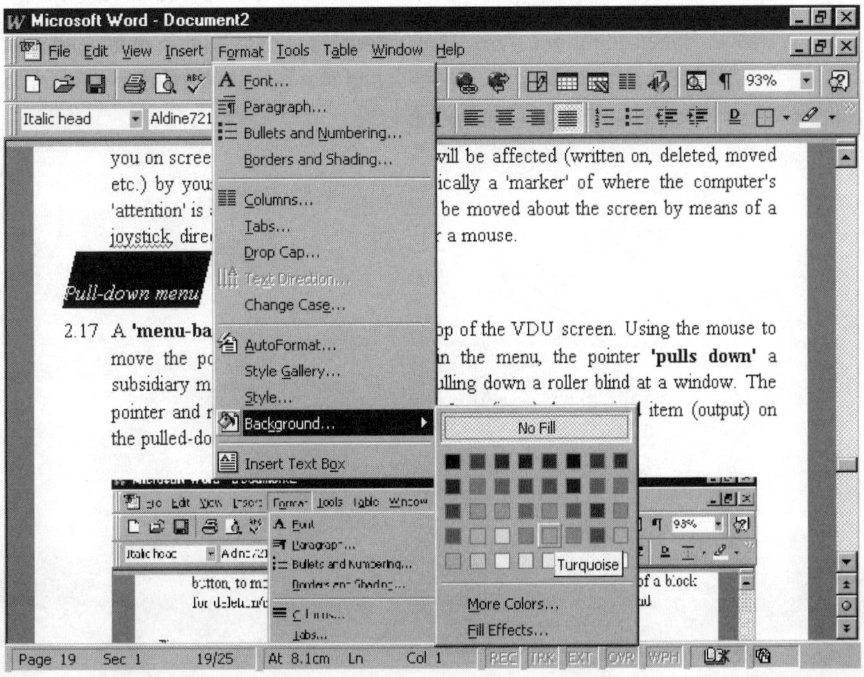

5 Input and output design

Effective performance of a computer system depends on how the system interacts with its environment. Well-designed input forms, dialogue and output are key to ensuring effective and efficient communication between users and the system.

Communication between users and a computerised system is influenced by the following factors:

- Human-computer dialogue
- Input design
- Document and screen design (input and output)
- The use of codes

We have already covered human-computer dialogue. The other factors are explained in the following paragraphs.

5.1 Input design

FAST FORWARD

There are a number of considerations for **input design**.

- Input method
- Volume of input
- Processing method
- The need for accuracy

Input design is concerned with data collection, data entry and data validation. There are a number of **considerations for input design**.

(a) What **data input method** will be used? Bar code readers or magnetic ink character readers may be able to be utilised.

(b) What **volumes** of input are expected? Large volumes of input are more likely to require automated input procedures.

(c) Does the system use **batch processing** or **real-time processing**. This will impact on the frequency and method of input.

(d) Will data be required to be **transcribed** from a source document?

(e) The need for **accuracy**. How extensive should built-in data validation checks be to ensure all data entered is input correctly, and that no data is missed or entered twice. We will look at input controls in Chapter 13.

5.2 Document and screen design (input and output)

The contents and design of a document or on-screen display depends on the purpose of the document or screen.

Document design comprises the following steps (these steps may also be adapted to the process of designing the on-screen layout).

Step 1 Determine the purpose of the document or screen.

Step 2 Determine the input needed to produce the required system output.

Step 3 Determine the layout by considering the order data will be input to the document or system.

Step 4 Decide the size of the document or display (eg for paper, is standard A4 suitable). Is one page/input screen sufficient, or would this be too cluttered given the amount of data/information the document will hold? Are multiple copies (possibly colour-coded) required?

Step 5 Devise a suitable title/heading which communicates the screen/document purpose/content.

Step 6 Determine what information can be included pre-printed (or as default values if designing an input screen) to reduce input requirements.

Step 7 Decide how the document will be controlled (eg serial numbers) and what authorisation is required before the document or input is processed.

5.2.1 Working documents and presentation documents

FAST FORWARD

There are two main categories of documents output from a computer system – **working documents** and **information presentation documents**.

There are two main categories of documents output from a computer system.

- Working documents, eg purchase orders, invoices, statements, credit notes
- Information presentation documents, eg management accounts, sales analysis reports

Working document design should focus on ensuring the document is functional. Many working documents are printed on pre-printed stationery eg invoices produced using popular accounting packages.

Information presentation documents, such as a report, should be clear and understandable. Reports should use a simple structure. An example, that could be adapted to suit the report requirements, would include:

- Meaningful Title
- Author name and position
- Purpose/Terms of Reference
- Procedure followed
- Findings
- Conclusion / Recommendations

Longer reports should use a hierarchy of headings to aid clarity. For example,

1	**Section heading**
1.1	Related paragraph
1.1 (a)	Related sub-paragraph

5.3 Codes

FAST FORWARD

Computers are able to organise and use data more efficiently if some data is expressed in the form of codes.

In a computer system, the use of codes saves storage space. For example, a product code could be stored on a computer record, rather than the full product description, and the description obtained from the product master file when required.

Codes also save user-time. For example a customer code may consist of four characters, which when input retrieve full customer name and address details.

Coding systems may include validation techniques such as the use of a check digit. We will look at data validation and verification in Chapter 13.

5.3.1 Types of coding systems

Types of coding systems include:

- **Sequenced**, eg 0001 Cars, 0002 Vans, 0003 Trucks
- **Grouped,** eg 1000-1999 types of car, 2000-2999 types of van, 3000-3999 types of truck
- **Faceted**, eg first digit vehicle type, second digit vehicle colour
- **Hierarchical** – multi-digit codes, often with decimal points, where digits to the right represent sub-sets of the digits to the left, eg the decimal coding system used in libraries
- **Mnemonic** – a mixture of alpha-numeric characters to signify characteristics of the items, eg this ACCA paper could be coded IS21

5.3.2 Characteristics of a good coding system

A **coding system** should be:

- Easy to use and remember
- Flexible, including the ability to expand
- Designed to avoid errors and confusion

Chapter Roundup

- **External design** refers to the elements of a computer system that the user can see. The **Human-Computer Interface (HCI)** includes all external elements of a system.
- **Data input options** include:
  - Keyboard/mouse/track-ball
  - Bar code readers
  - Magnetic ink readers
  - Scanners and OCR or OMR
  - Magnetic stripe cards
  - EPOS systems
  - Smart cards
  - Touch sensitive screens
  - Voice recognition systems
- The three most common **methods of computer output** are output to a printer, and output to the screen and output to a computer file.
- The exchange of information between a computer system and a user is known as **human-computer dialogue**.
- A **Graphical User Interface** (GUI) utilises **WIMP** methods.
- There are a number of considerations for **input design**.
  - Input method
  - Volume of input
  - Processing method
  - The need for accuracy
- There are two main categories of documents output from a computer system – **working documents** and **information presentation documents**.
- Computers are able to organise and use data more efficiently if some data is expressed in the form of **codes**.

Quick Quiz

1 What do the following abbreviations mean; OCR, OMR, EPOS, EFTPOS, MICR?

2 List five factors that could influence the choice of a suitable output medium.

3 What does HCI stand for? What are WIMP features?

4 Why are Graphical User Interfaces favoured by most users?

5 Suggest a simple report structure.

6 List five possible types of coding system.

Answers to Quick Quiz

1. Optical Character Recognition, Optical Mark Recognition, Electronic Point of Sale, Electronic Funds Transfer at Point of Sale, Magnetic Ink Character Recognition.

2. Five possibilities are; whether a printed version of the output is needed, the quantity of information to be output, how quickly the output is required, whether the output will be processed further, the cost.

3. Human-Computer Interface. WIMP features are features associated with modern software packages; Windows, Icons, Mouse, Pull-down menus.

4. Because they are considered more user-friendly than text based interfaces.

5. Meaningful Title
   Author name and position
   Purpose/Terms of Reference
   Procedure followed
   Findings
   Conclusion / Recommendations

6. Sequenced, grouped, faceted, hierarchical, mnemonic.

Now try the question below from the Exam Question Bank

Number	Level	Marks	Time
Q17	Examination	20	36mins

10

Software sources and selection

Topic list	Syllabus reference
1 Software sources	2 (f), 2 (g), 2 (h)
2 Invitations To Tender (ITT)	2 (g)
3 Evaluating supplier proposals	2 (h)
4 The advantages and disadvantages of bespoke and off-the-shelf software	2 (g)
5 Software contracts and licences	2 (h), 3 (b)

Introduction

In this chapter we look at the issues to be considered when **acquiring software** for information systems.

We start by looking at the options available when **sourcing software**, before examining the issues to consider when obtaining and evaluating **supplier proposals**.

The relative advantages and disadvantages of **bespoke** and **off-the-shelf** software are covered next – and the chapter concludes with an outline of **software licensing** issues.

Study guide

Part 2.16 – Developing a system to fulfil requirements

- Define the bespoke software approach to fulfilling the user's information systems requirements
- Briefly describe the tasks of design, programming and testing required in developing a bespoke systems solution
- Define the application software package approach to fulfilling the user's information systems requirements
- Briefly describe the tasks of package selection, evaluation and testing required in selecting an appropriate application software package
- Describe the relative merits of the bespoke systems development and application software package approaches to fulfilling an information systems requirement

Part 2.17 – Software package selection

- Describe the structure and content of an Invitation to Tender (ITT)
- Describe how to identify software packages and their suppliers that may potentially fulfil the information systems requirements
- Develop suitable procedures for distributing an ITT and dealing with subsequent enquiries and bids
- Describe a process for evaluating the application software package, the supplier of the package and the bid received from the supplier
- Describe risks of the application software package approach to systems development and how these might be reduced or removed

Part 3.20 – Legal compliance in information systems

- Explain the implications of software licences and copyright law in computer systems development
- Discuss the legal implications of software supply with particular reference to ownership, liability and damages

Exam guide

Ensure you have a thorough understanding of the Invitation to tender process and how a tender should be chosen. The issues surrounding bespoke and off-the-shelf software selection are also likely to be examined regularly.

1 Software sources

FAST FORWARD

An organisation has a range of options when sourcing software. The four main options are:

- A standard **off-the-shelf** package
- Amended standard package
- Standard package plus additions
- Have **bespoke** software written

An organisation has a range of options when sourcing software for information systems. The four main options are described in the following table.

Source	Comment
Standard off-the-shelf package	This is the simplest option. The organisation purchases and installs a ready-made solution.
Amended standard package	A standard package is purchased, but some customisation is undertaken so that the software meets the organisations requirements. This may require access to the source code.
Standard package plus additions	The purchased standard package is not amended itself, but additional software that integrates with the standard package is developed. This also may require access to the source code.
Bespoke package	Programmers write an application to meet the specific needs of the organisation. This can be a time-consuming and expensive process.

In this chapter we discuss the process and relative advantages of the two main options – purchasing an application off-the-shelf and developing a bespoke solution. The other two options include elements of both of these two main options.

Key terms

Bespoke software is designed for a specific user or situation. It may be written either 'in-house' by the IS department or externally by a software house.

An **off-the-shelf package** is one that is sold to a wide range of users. The package is written to handle requirements that are common to a wide range of organisations.

1.1 Choosing an application package off-the shelf

FAST FORWARD

Off-the-shelf software is produced to meet requirements that are common to many organisations. The software is likely to be available **immediately** and **cost significantly less** than bespoke solutions. However, as it has not been written specifically for the organisation, it may not meet all their requirements.

Off-the-shelf packages are generally available for functions that are likely to be performed similarly across a range of organisations eg accounting. The following table describes some of the factors to consider when choosing an off-the-shelf application package.

Factor	Comment
User requirements	Does the package fit the user's particular requirements? Matters to consider include data volumes, data validation routines, number of users and the reports available.
Processing times	Are the processing times fast enough? If response times to enquiries is slow, the user might consider the package unacceptable.
Factor	Comment
Documentation	Is there full and clear documentation for the user? A comprehensive user manual, a quick reference guide and on-line help should be considered.
Compatibility	Is the package compatible with existing hardware and software? Can data be exchanged with other related systems?

Factor	Comment
Controls	Access and security controls (eg passwords) should be included, as should processing controls that enable the accuracy of processing operations to be confirmed.
User-interface	Users are most affected by the user-interface design. The interface should be clear, logical, and consistent, and should follow standard interface conventions such as those used on most packages produced for use with the Microsoft Windows operating system.
Modification	Can the package be modified by the user – allowing the user to tailor it to meet their needs?
Support, maintenance and updates	The availability and cost of support, such as a telephone help-line, should be considered, as should the arrangements for updates and upgrades. This is particularly important if software is likely to be affected by changes in legislation eg a payroll package.
Cost	An organisation should aim to purchase a package that will meet their requirements. However, a package should not be purchased if the cost outweighs the value of the benefits it should bring.

1.2 Developing a bespoke application

FAST FORWARD

Bespoke software should be written so as to **match** the organisation's requirements exactly. However, the software is likely to be considerably **more expensive** than an off-the-shelf package. Bespoke software may be designed and written 'in-house' by the IS department, or externally by a software house.

Producing a bespoke software system involves all the tasks included in the software development and testing cycle.

The process is summarised in the diagram below, and explained in the table that follows.

The software development cycle

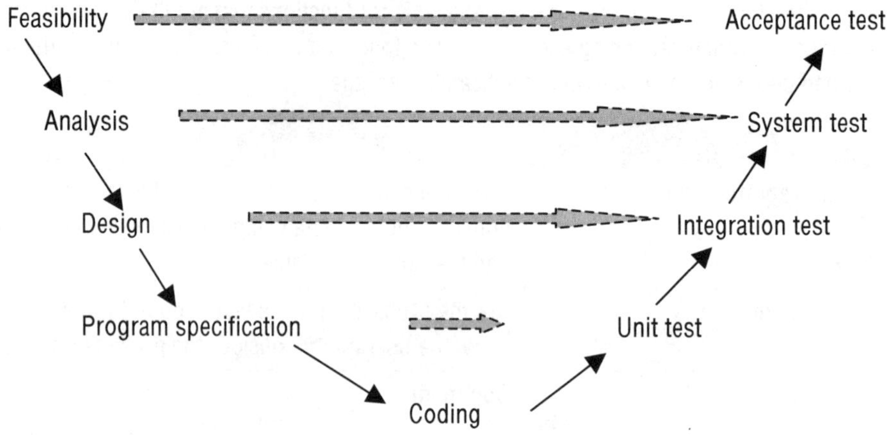

Stages of software development	Comment
Feasibility and analysis	The feasibility of software solutions would have usually been covered during the overall system feasibility study. An analysis of the software requirements should therefore be available.
Design and program specification	The software requirements are used to develop a systems design specification, which in turn is used to produce a detailed program specification. The specification would be used by in-house software developers, or would be distributed to software producers (as part of the invitation to tender – covered below).
Coding	Software producers will decide how to build the package, for example identifying parts of existing programs that may be used, and establishing what will need to be coded (ie written) from scratch. Prototyping may be used to help ensure user requirements are met.
Testing **Unit; Integration; System; Acceptance**	We cover all aspects of testing, in detail, in Chapter 11. Briefly though, Unit testing tests individual programs (or units) operating alone. Integration testing tests how two or more units of the software interact with each other. System testing tests the complete package and how it interacts with other software programs. User acceptance testing aims to ensure all user requirements included in the software specification have been met.

2 Invitations To Tender (ITT)

A number of suppliers may be invited to tender (bid) to supply specific software (the tendering procedure could also be used for hardware, or for a complete system).

Key term

An **Invitation To Tender** is a document that invites suppliers to bid for the supply of specified software, or hardware, or both.

There are a number of possible options available to identify possible suppliers who may be in a position to submit a realistic tender:

- **Trade magazines and websites** may include software advertisements and reviews
- **Computer consultants** may have experience and/or knowledge of suitable suppliers
- **Establish who supplies other similar organisations** – it is likely these suppliers could also meet the requirements of a similar organisation

FAST FORWARD

An organisation that requires bespoke software to be written may issue an **Invitation to Tender (ITT)** to a range of potential suppliers. The **contents of a typical invitation ITT** could include:

- Covering letter
- Instructions
- Detailed software requirements
- Details of development model/methodology
- Request for further details of the proposed software contract

The contents of a typical invitation to tender (ITT) are outlined in the following table. This format could be used when inviting tenders for bespoke or off-the-shelf software – although sections such as the development methodology would be shorter for off-the-shelf tenders, as this would refer only to any proposed amendments to the package.

ITT section	Comment
Covering letter	An ITT will include a letter inviting the supplier to tender. The letter should specify: • Contact names for queries relating to the tendering process and for technical queries • The closing date for submitting tenders
Instructions	Instructions to tenderers should specify the information required in a tender. Instructions are likely to require tenderers to specify: • Areas of their tender that do not comply with the software • specification provided, and the reasons why • The period of validity for the tender • The basis for calculating prices, whether prices are estimates or a quote • An indication of timescale – when work could start and an approximate completion date • Alternative ways of approaching parts of the software design than indicated in the requirements specification
Detailed software requirements	The ITT must include a detailed requirements specification so tenderers know exactly what they are tendering for. This should include: • The purpose of the system • The volume of data to be processed. • Processing requirements (including details of inputs andoutputs, and interfaces with other systems). • The number of locations and users requiring access. • The speed of processing required, eg response times. • Expected life of the system. • Possible upgrades or expansion anticipated. When submitting their bids, some potential suppliers may come up with alternative specifications – these must be fully explained.
Details of development model/ methodology	This section of the ITT requires tenderers to provide a description of the methodology or systems development model used to develop their software. The aim is to ensure that the supplier produces software using accepted development techniques – reducing the possibility of poor quality software.
Request for details of the proposed software contract	The ITT document should request information from potential suppliers relating to the key terms of any future software contract. We cover software contracts later in this chapter.

3 Evaluating supplier proposals

Once vendor proposals have been obtained, they should be evaluated against what was requested within the ITT. There are many factors that should be considered when evaluating proposals. The factors to consider fit into three general categories:

- **Technical**, how well does the proposal meet the specified technical requirements?
- **Support**, what after-sales support is included?
- **Cost**, what do we get for our money?

Some of the main factors to consider when evaluating supplier proposals are described in the following table. Some of the relevant points are the same as those considered when choosing off-the-shelf software.

Factor	Comment
Organisation needs	How well does the software meet the requirements of the organisation? If some requirements aren't met, how important are they – can they be satisfied through other means?
Speed	Can the system cope with data volumes; is response time affected by high data volumes?
Documentation	Is there full and clear documentation for the user, and a technical manual that would allow further development?
Compatibility	Is the package compatible with existing hardware and software? Can data be exchanged with other related systems?
Controls	Access and security controls (eg passwords) should be included, as should processing controls that enable the accuracy of processing operations to be confirmed.
User-friendly	Software should be relatively easy to use and tolerant to user errors. Menu structures should be logical, the software should follow standard user-interface conventions.
Modification	Can the package be modified by the user – allowing the organisation to tailor it to meet their specific needs?
Demonstration	A demonstration version of the software may be available – this should provide a good idea of how the finished product would look, feel and operate.
Training provided	Training is essential for the organisation to utilise the software effectively.
Support, maintenance and updates	The availability and cost of support, such as a telephone help-line, should be considered, as should the arrangements for updates and upgrades. This is particularly important if software is likely to be affected by changes in legislation eg a payroll package.
Conditions included in the software contract	The software contract includes terms relating to the actual supply and use of the software.
Supplier size, reputation and customer base	Software suppliers that have been in business for a reasonable amount of time, and who have an established client base, are more likely to remain in business – and therefore be in a position to provide support. References may be available from existing customers, attesting to the quality of software and support.
Cost	An organisation should aim to purchase a package that will meet their requirements. However, a package should not be purchased if the cost outweighs the value of the benefits it should bring.

3.1 Comparing supplier proposals

An organisation may receive a number of apparently viable tenders. Tenders are likely to have different strengths and weaknesses – a process to establish the 'best' tender needs to be established. Two common ways of comparing software or systems are benchmark tests and weighted ranking scores.

FAST FORWARD

Suppliers' proposals need to be evaluated, perhaps using **benchmark tests**. Other relevant factors include how well the software would meet **user requirements**, **user-friendliness**, **controls**, **compatibility** and **cost**. Supplier **reputation** and **reliability** should also be considered.

3.1.1 Benchmark tests

There are several factors involved in measuring the capability of a system. Benchmark tests are particularly useful to compare system speed and capacity.

Key term

Benchmark tests test how long it takes a machine and program to run through a particular routine or set of routines.

Benchmark tests are carried out to compare the performance of a piece of hardware or software against pre-set criteria. Typical criteria which may be used as benchmarks include speed of performance of a particular operation, acceptable volumes before a degradation in response times is apparent and the general user-friendliness of equipment. Benchmarks can cover subjective tests such as user-friendliness, although it may be harder to reach definitive conclusions.

For example, an organisation comparing accounting software packages may test a number of different packages on its own existing hardware to see which performed the best according to various predefined criteria (eg speed of response, ability to process different volumes of transactions, reporting capabilities and so on).

Once the performance of the software package under consideration has been evaluated, the acquiring organisation should consider other features of the proposal, possibly using a weighted ranking system.

3.1.2 Weighted ranking

Key term

A **weighted ranking** system involves establishing a number of factors important to a system, giving each factor a numerical weighting to reflect its importance, and using these weightings to calculate a score for each supplier (or software, or system).

FAST FORWARD

A **weighted ranking** scoring system may be used to evaluate software proposals from a number of different vendors.

The factors chosen to be used in the weighted ranking, and the relative importance of each factor will vary according to the purpose of the software/system under consideration. Judgements need to be made in the selection of criteria, the weightings applied to the criteria and the scores allocated. These judgements must be made by people who have a good understanding of the software/system requirements.

The following example shows how weighted ranking scores could be calculated.

Case Study

An organisation must chose between three software suppliers.

The decision-makers within the organisation have decided on the relevant criteria and weightings that will be used to judge the suppliers. This information is shown in the following model, together with the scores that have been allocated to each supplier.

Weighted ranking							
Ranking scale: 3 = best supplier, 1 = worst		**Supplier A software**		**Supplier B software**		**Supplier C software**	
Criteria	**Weight**	Rank	Weighted rank score	Rank	Weighted rank score	Rank	Weighted rank score
User friendliness	9	2	18	3	27	1	9
Cost	4	1	4	2	8	3	12
Controls/Security	8	1	8	3	24	2	16
Processing speed	7	3	21	2	14	1	7
Support	10	2	20	1	10	3	30
		Total score	**71**	**Total score**	**83**	**Total score**	**74**

The weighted ranking calculation shows that the software supplied by Supplier B appears to best meet the organisation's needs.

4 The advantages and disadvantages of bespoke and off-the-shelf software

4.1 Bespoke software

Bespoke software is written to meet the specific needs of an organisation.

4.1.1 Advantages of bespoke software

Advantages of having software specially written include the following.

(a) If it is well-written, the software should meet the organisation's specific needs.

(b) Data and file structures may be chosen by the organisation rather than having to meet the structures required by standard software packages.

(c) The company may be able to do things with its software that competitors cannot do with theirs. In other words it is a source of competitive advantage.

(d) Similar organisations may wish to purchase the software.

(e) The software should be able to be modified to meet future needs.

4.1.2 Disadvantages of bespoke software

Key **disadvantages** are:

(a) As the software is being developed from scratch, there is a risk that the package may not perform as intended.

(b) There is a greater chance of 'bugs'. Widely used off-the-shelf software is more likely to have had bugs identified and removed.

(c) Development will take longer than purchasing ready-made software.

(d) The cost is considerable when compared with a ready-made package.

(e) Support costs are also likely to be higher than with off-the-shelf software.

4.1.3 Overcoming the risks of bespoke development

Building a bespoke software application involves much time, effort and money. The risks associated with such an undertaking are that the resulting software:

- Does not meet user needs
- Does not interact as intended with other systems
- Is produced late
- Is produced over-budget

These risks can be minimised or overcome by:

(a) Good project management.

(b) Involving users at all stages of development.

(c) Ensuring in-house IT staff are able to maintain and support bespoke systems supplied from outside parties.

(d) Ensuring the ITT document includes details of all file structures required, and details of interfaces with other systems.

4.2 Off-the-shelf packages

Advantages of an off-the-shelf package

(a) The software is likely to be available immediately.

(b) A ready-made package will almost certainly cheaper because it is 'mass-produced''.

(c) The software is likely to have been written by software specialists and so should be of a high quality.

(d) A successful package will be continually updated by the software manufacturer.

(e) Other users will have used the package already, and a well-established package should be relatively free of bugs.

(f) Good packages are well-documented, with easy-to-follow user manuals or on-line help.

(g) Some standard packages can be customised to the user's specific needs (see below).

The **disadvantages** of ready-made packages are as follows.

(a) The organisation is purchasing a standard solution. A standard solution may not be well suited to the organisation's particular needs.

(b) The organisation is dependent on the supplier for maintenance of the package – ie updating the package or providing assistance in the event of problems. It is unlikely that the supplier would give access to the code that would allow organisations with the relevant expertise to amend the software themselves.

(c) Competitors may well use the same package, removing any chance of using IS/IT for competitive advantage.

4.3 Customised versions of standard packages

Standard packages can be customised so that they fit an organisation's specific requirements. This can be done by purchasing the source code of the package and making modifications in-house, or by paying the producer of the package to customise it.

Advantages of customisation are similar to those of producing a bespoke system, with the additional advantages that:

(a) Development time should be much quicker, given that most of the system will be written already.

(b) If the work is done in-house the organisation gains considerable knowledge of how the software works and may be able to 'tune' it so that it works more efficiently with the company's hardware.

Disadvantages of customising a standard package include the following.

(a) It may prove more costly than expected, because new versions of the standard package will also have to be customised.

(b) Customisation may delay delivery of the software.

(c) Customisation may introduce bugs that do not exist in the standard version.

(d) If done in-house, the in-house team may have to learn new skills.

(e) If done by the original manufacturer disadvantages such as those for off-the-shelf packages may arise.

4.4 Add-ons and programming tools

Two other ways of trying to give a computer user more flexibility with packages are:

(a) The sale of 'add-ons' to a basic package, which an organisation may purchase if the add-ons suit their particular needs.

(b) The provision of programming tools (such as fourth generation languages) with a package, which allows users to write amendments to the software (without having to be a programming expert).

5 Software contracts and licences

5.1 Software contracts

FAST FORWARD

The agreement to supply bespoke software should be formally laid out in a contract. **Software contracts** include provisions relating to matters such as warranty, ownership and liability.

The agreement to supply bespoke software should be formally laid out in a contract. The contract to supply the software is likely to include terms relating to:

(a) The cost, and what this figure does and does not include.
(b) Delivery date.
(c) Ownership of the source code, sometimes referred to as ownership rights.
(d) Right to make copies.
(e) Number of licensed users.
(f) Performance criteria, such as what the software will and will not do, processing speed.
(e) Warranty period.
(f) Support available.
(g) Arrangements for upgrades.
(h) Maintenance arrangements (maintenance is discussed in Chapter 14).

5.2 Software licences

FAST FORWARD

A **software licence** typically covers issues such as the number of users, right to copy and a limitation of liability.

Packaged software generally has a licence, the **terms** of which users are deemed to have agreed to the moment the package is unwrapped or a seal is broken.

A licence typically covers the following areas:

(a) **How many users** can use the software.

(b) Whether the software may be **modified**.

(c) In what circumstances the licence is **terminated**.

(d) A **limitation of liability** should the software contain bugs or be misused (in an 'exclusion clause'). This is a complex area that is still developing. The representations that the software supplier makes regarding the package's capabilities would also be taken into account in any legal dispute.

When a user purchases software they are merely buying the **right to use** the software in line with the terms and conditions within the licence agreement. The licence will be issued with the software, on paper or in electronic form. It contains the terms and conditions of use, as set out by the software publisher or owner of the copyright. A breach of the licence conditions usually means the owners' copyright has been infringed. In the UK, computer software is defined as a 'Literary Work' in the Copyright, Designs and Patents Act (1988).

5.2.1 Software piracy

The **unauthorised copying** of software is referred to as software **piracy**. If an organisation is using illegal copies of software, the organisation may face a civil suit, and corporate officers and individual employees may have criminal liability.

In the UK, remedies for civil copyright infringement may include damages to compensate the copyright owners for damage caused to their business, including reputation, and for loss of sales. Criminal penalties can include unlimited fines and two years' imprisonment or both.

The most common type of software misuse in a business setting is referred to as **Corporate Over-Use**. This is the installation of software packages on more machines than there are licences for. For example if a company purchases five single-user licences of a software program but installs the software on ten machines, then they will be using five infringing copies. If a company is running a large network and more users have access to a software program than the company has licences for, this too is Corporate Over-Use.

A grey area is the additional installation of programs on portable or laptop computers for use off-site. Generally speaking, if a person has a program installed on their desktop in the office and the **same person** has the same program on their laptop for off-site use, then this usually counts as one user under the licence rather than two. However, the terms in different licences may differ.

To ensure they **do not infringe copyright** organisations should:

- Make sure they receive and keep licences – these are valuable documents
- Track the number of users with access to licensed programs
- Periodically check all computers for unlicensed software
- Buy from reputable dealers
- Get a written quote listing hardware/software specification and version
- Require an itemised invoice giving details of all hardware and software supplied

In the UK, the Copyright, Designs and Patents Act 1998 specifically allows the making of back-up copies of software, but only providing it is for lawful use.

Extracts from a typical licence for an off-the-shelf package follow.

Case Study

Program & licence

(i) The "Program" means the licensed software programs as stored on the computer disks or compact disks included in this box.

(ii) This Licence permits you to **install the Program on a single personal computer (or single network, where you have purchased this version**) and install data onto the Program for a single set of data at any one time (unless, and to the extent that, you have purchased the relevant licence for multiple users and/or multiple sets of data from X Co Ltd), whether for a company, partnership, group, person or otherwise, in the course of which you may make one copy of the Program in any computer readable format for back-up purposes. The copyright design right and any other intellectual property rights in the source and object codes of this Program vest exclusively in X Co Ltd ("X Co Ltd").

(iii) The **Program may not be copied** without the express consent in writing of X Co Ltd under such terms as it shall determine. In particular, **the Program shall not be installed onto any additional network** (where you have purchased such version) **or onto any additional personal computer** including any lap-top or portable computer **without an additional user licence**, available at separate cost from X Co Ltd.

(iv) THIS LICENCE IS PERSONAL TO YOU. **YOU MAY NOT TRANSFER** OR PART WITH POSSESSION OF THE PROGRAMS OR SEEK TO SUB-LICENSE OR ASSIGN THIS LICENCE OR YOUR RIGHTS UNDER IT.

YOU MUST NOT MODIFY OR MERGE (EXCEPT BY A X CO LTD APPROVED DEALER, OR OTHERWISE WITH THE WRITTEN CONSENT OF X CO LTD), REVERSE ENGINEER OR DECOMPILE THE PROGRAM. YOU MUST NOT COPY THE PROGRAM EXCEPT AS EXPRESSLY PROVIDED IN (II) ABOVE. ANY BREACH OF THIS SUB-CLAUSE (IV) WILL AUTOMATICALLY TERMINATE YOUR LICENCE.

(v) X CO LTD DOES NOT WARRANT OR GUARANTEE THAT THE PROGRAM PERFORMS ANY PARTICULAR FUNCTION OR OPERATION WHICH MAY BE SUITABLE FOR YOUR REQUIREMENTS OTHER THAN MAY BE DISCLOSED IN RELEVANT DOCUMENTATION PUBLISHED BY X CO LTD.

Case Study

Federation Against Software Theft reports 12% increase

Reports of corporate under licensing are on the rise according to the latest figures issued by industry watchdog, the Federation Against Software Theft (FAST). In the year 2000 the organisation received in excess of 380 reports of under licensing within the business community, an annual increase of 12%.

According to FAST the figures indicate a number of trends year on year not least the increased impact of the organisation's awareness campaigns. These campaigns, aimed at educating everyone within the workforce, have increasingly focused on the criminality of under licensing and the impact it can have on business.

Over the past couple of years FAST and other trade bodies associated with protecting copyright, have made it far easier to report the illegal use of software within the business community. This has included a new Hotline facility, greater anonymity for those reporting under licensing and even the ability to report via the FAST web site.

Commenting on the rise in reports made to the Federation, Geoff Webster, CEO said: 'We believe these figures reflect a positive change in attitude towards how organisations in general are viewing software piracy as a serious business issue. Particularly within large organisations, board level executives are realising that software piracy can have a huge financial impact on the business if not dealt with properly.'

He continued: 'It is an interesting point to note that while software piracy and under licensing is in general in decline, according to the latest figures from the Business Software Alliance (BSA), the number of reports is on the rise. This can to my mind solely be attributed to a general increase in awareness of the issue. FAST believes that its educational and enforcement roles are working in tandem and working effectively.'

FAST, January 2001

Chapter Roundup

- An organisation has a range of options when sourcing software. The four main options are:
  - A standard **off-the-shelf** package
  - Amended standard package
  - Standard package plus additions
  - Have **bespoke** software written
- **Off-the-shelf software** is produced to meet requirements that are common to many organisations. The software is likely to be available **immediately** and **cost significantly less** than bespoke solutions. However, as it has not been written specifically for the organisation, it may not meet all their requirements.
- **Bespoke software** should be written so as to **match** the organisation's requirements exactly. However, the software is likely to be considerably **more expensive** than an off-the-shelf package. Bespoke software may be designed and written 'in-house' by the IS department, or externally by a software house.
- An organisation that requires bespoke software to be written may issue an **Invitation to Tender (ITT)** to a range of potential suppliers. The **contents of a typical invitation ITT** could include:
  - Covering letter
  - Instructions
  - Detailed software requirements
  - Details of development model/methodology
  - Request for further details of the proposed software contract
- Suppliers' proposals need to be evaluated, perhaps using **benchmark tests**. Other relevant factors include how well the software would meet **user requirements**, **user-friendliness**, **controls**, **compatibility** and **cost**. Supplier **reputation** and **reliability** should also be considered.
- A **weighted ranking** scoring system may be used to evaluate software proposals from a number of different vendors.
- The agreement to supply bespoke software should be formally laid out in a contract. **Software contracts** include provisions relating to matters such as warranty, ownership and liability.
- A **software licence** typically covers issues such as the number of users, right to copy and a limitation of liability.

Quick Quiz

1 List five factors to consider when choosing an off-the-shelf application package.

2 List eight stages of a typical software development project.

3 Why would an organisation issue an Invitation To Tender (ITT)?

4 What would you say is the main advantage of bespoke software?

5 What is the main disadvantage of bespoke software?

6 Briefly explain how a weighted ranking system works.

7 Define 'Corporate Over-Use'.

Answers to Quick Quiz

1 Any five of the following (you may have thought of other valid considerations). User requirements; Processing times; Documentation; Compatibility; Controls/security; User-interface; Modification; Support; Maintenance; Updates/upgrades; Cost.

2 Feasibility, Analysis, Design, Program specification, Coding, Unit test, Integration test, System test, Acceptance test.

3 To invite tenders (offers to supply) for the system specified in the ITT.

4 As it is written for a specific purpose, it should match user requirements very closely.

5 It's expensive when compared to off-the-shelf software.

6 A weighted ranking system involves establishing a number of factors important to a system, giving each factor a numerical weighting to reflect its importance, and using these weightings to calculate a score for each supplier (or software, or system).

7 The installation of software by more users than the organisation is licensed for.

Now try the question below from the Exam Question Bank

Number	Level	Marks	Time
Q3	Examination	20	36 mins

Part C
Evaluating information systems

11

Quality assurance and testing

Topic list	Syllabus reference
1 Quality software	3 (f)
2 Approaches to quality	3 (f)
3 External quality standards	3 (f)
4 Quality and information system development	3 (f)
5 Stages of testing	3 (a), 3 (e)
6 Methods of testing	3 (a), 3 (e)
7 Developing a testing strategy	3 (a), 3 (e)

Introduction

An information system that does not operate as intended is likely to cause **disruption** – and could potentially cost an organisation a great deal.

In this chapter, we explore how **quality assurance** and **testing** are employed in systems development to ensure the delivery of high **quality** systems that perform as users require them to.

Study guide

Part 3.22 – Quality assurance in the management and development process

- Define the characteristics of a quality software product
- Define the terms quality management, quality assurance and quality control
- Describe the V model and its application to quality assurance and testing
- Explain the limitations of software testing
- Participate in the quality assurance of deliverables in requirement specification using formal static testing methods
- Explain the role of standards and their application in quality assurance
- Briefly describe the task of unit testing in bespoke systems development

Part 3.23 – Systems and user acceptance testing

- Define the scope of systems testing
- Distinguish between dynamic and static testing
- Use a cause-effect chart (decision table) to develop an appropriate test script for a representative systems test
- Explain the scope and importance of performance testing and usability testing
- Define the scope and procedures of user acceptance testing
- Describe the potential use of automated tools to support systems and user acceptance testing

Part 3.27 – Relationship of management, development process and quality

- Describe the relationship between the systems development process and quality assurance

Exam guide

The 'V' **model** is particularly suited to examination questions as it links the systems development process with testing and quality issues.

1 Quality software

FAST FORWARD

In the context of software and information systems, **quality** may be defined as conformance to customer (user) needs.

The concept of quality is concerned with **'fitness for purpose'**.

Key term

In the context of software and information systems, **Quality** may be defined as conformance to customer (user) needs.

1.1 What is quality software?

High **quality software** should possess the following **characteristics.**

Characteristic	Comment
No major bugs	Whilst it is unrealistic to expect completely bug-free software, any bugs that significantly impact upon system effectiveness\efficiency should be fixed before a package is released.
Produced within budget	As with any purchase, software should be cost-effective. A realistic budget for good quality software that will satisfy user requirements should be set, and then kept to.
Produced on time	Software impacts upon organisational activities – it is important therefore that plans are able to be made for the introduction of new software. Delays to this schedule will cause disruption.
Meets user needs and specification	Quality software must meet the requirements of users. It is vital therefore that user requirements are stated clearly and accurately early in the development process. It should also be user-friendly.
Competitive and compatible with other products	Software production is a competitive market – a product that ignores trends in development is likely to become obsolete in a short period of time – and may not be compatible with other software packages.
Produced according to 'best' practices	There are widely accepted practices and procedures for producing software (eg documenting program design). There are also internationally recognised standards (issued by the International Standards Organisation) relating to software development. Using procedures that satisfies these standards should result in quality software.

2 Approaches to quality

FAST FORWARD

An organisation may attempt to maintain quality throughout their operations through one of, or a combination of, three approaches:

- Quality management
- Quality assurance
- Quality control

Key terms

Quality management is concerned with controlling activities with the aim of ensuring that products or services are fit for their purpose, and meet specifications. Quality management encompasses quality assurance and quality control.

Quality assurance schemes involve a supplier guaranteeing the quality of goods or services supplied. Procedures and standards are devised with the aim of ensuring defects are eliminated.

Quality control is concerned with checking and reviewing work that has been done. Quality control therefore has a narrower focus than quality assurance.

2.1 Quality management

Faulty output is costly – as it **wastes resources** and **damages relationships**. The essence of quality management is that quality should be 'built-in' to all processes and materials used within an organisation, with the ultimate aim of no sub-standard output.

Quality management focuses on the belief that quality is essential if an organisation is to prosper. Quality management, sometimes referred to as **Total Quality Management** or **TQM**, has been adopted as a **business philosophy**.

2.1.1 Principles of TQM

Principle	Comment
Prevention	It costs less, in the long run, to prevent defective production than to employ teams of inspectors, to scrap materials or to rework shoddy output.
Right first time	Defective production is worse than no production.
Zero defects	The aim should be no defects. In products with many components, the defect rates in components should be extremely small.
Eliminate waste	This includes time, materials and money spent on dealing with customer complaints.
Everybody's concern	Quality is not just the concern of the production department, but is a culture for the whole business.
Internal customers	Each part of an organisation acquires services from other parts of the organisation. User departments are thus internal customers.
Principle	Comment
Quality chains	Internal customers are linked in quality chains – they are dependent on the product/service they receive from, and pass on to, each other.
Continuous improvement	TQM is not a goal that is achieved, but a way of managing. Firms should continually seek ways to improve their performance.
Employee participation	As so much attention is paid to the production process itself, the production workforce has a vital role to play in managing and improving quality.
Teamwork	'Managing quality involves systems and techniques, and requires the identification of individuals with company success through teamwork' (*Holmes*).

(Mnemonic, using first words in bold above: Prevention Rightly Zaps and Eliminates Everybody's Ineffective Quality, and Continuously Encourages Teamwork.)

Holmes proposes an eight-stage model for **implementing quality management**.

Step 1 **Find out the problems** (eg from customers and employees).

Step 2 **Select action targets** from the number of improvement projects identified in *Step 1*, on the basis of cost, safety, importance, and feasibility (with current resources).

Step 3 **Collect data** about the problem.

Step 4 **Analyse data** by a variety of techniques to assess common factors behind the data, to tease out any hidden messages the data might contain.

Step 5 **Identify possible causes** (eg using brainstorming sessions). No ideas are ruled out of order.

Step 6 **Plan improvement action**. Significant help might be required.

Step 7 **Monitor the effects of the improvement**.

Step 8 **Communicate** the result.

2.2 Quality assurance

The term 'quality assurance' is used where a supplier guarantees the quality of goods or services they supply. Quality assurance programs usually involve a close relationship between supplier and customer, which may extend to allowing customer representatives to view and/or monitor production procedures.

Quality assurance emphasises the **processes and procedures** used to produce a product or service – the logic being that if these are tightly controlled and monitored the resulting product and service will be high quality. As quality has been 'built-in', the routine inspection of goods **after** production should not be required.

2.3 Quality control

Quality control focuses on the **product or service produced**, rather than the production procedures.

Quality control involves establishing standards of quality for a product or service, implementing procedures that are expected to produce products of the required standard in most cases and **monitoring output** to ensure sub-standard output is rejected or corrected.

2.4 The cost of quality

Quality involves four types of cost. These are explained below, with examples referring to the development of an information system.

(a) **Prevention costs** are costs incurred to ensure the work is done correctly – for example ensuring the system design is correct before beginning production. Prevention costs are the cost of avoiding poor quality.

(b) **Appraisal costs** are the costs of inspection and testing – for example design reviews, structured walkthroughs and program testing.

(c) **Internal failure costs** are the costs of correcting defects discovered before the system is delivered.

(d) **External failure costs**. These are costs arising to fix defects discovered after the system has been delivered.

However, operating to high quality standards and procedures should also produce **savings**. Expenditure on failure prevention can reduce the cost of failure. Another saving is the reduction in quality inspection costs..

3 External quality standards

FAST FORWARD

The most widely used **external quality standards** are those published by the International Organisation for Standardisation (ISO). ISO standards can be applied to many types of organisations – including those involved in producing software.

A number of organisations produce quality standards that can be applied to variety of organisations. The most widely used are those published by the **International Organisation for Standardisation (ISO)**. (You would reasonably assume that it ought to be IOS, but the term ISO was chosen because 'iso' in Greek means equal, and ISO wanted to convey the idea of organisations using **equivalent standards**.)

ISO standards can be applied to many types of organisations – including those involved in producing software. The standards are updated periodically. The ISO 9000 2000 series of standards consists of four primary standards: ISO 9000, ISO 9001, ISO 9004, and ISO 19011.

(a) ISO 9001:2000 contains ISO's new quality management system requirements. This is the standard you need to use if you wish to become certified (registered).

(b) ISO 9000:2000 and ISO 9004:2000 contain ISO's new quality management system guidelines. These standards explain ISO's approach to quality management – ISO 9000:2000 presents definitions and discusses terminology, while ISO 9004:2000 is a set of guidelines for improving performance. These two guideline standards help organisations implement quality management, but they are not intended to be used for certification purposes.

(c) ISO 19011. ISO 19011 is concerned with quality auditing standards.

3.1 What's the difference between being ISO certified/registered and being ISO compliant?

When a company claims that they are ISO 9000 certified or registered, they mean that an independent registrar has audited their quality system and certified that it meets the ISO 9001:2000 requirements (or the old ISO 9001:1994, 9002:1994, or 9003:1994 requirements). It means that a **registrar has given a written assurance** that ISO's quality management system standard has been met.

When an organisation says that they are ISO 9000 compliant, they mean that they have met ISO's quality system requirements, but have **not been formally certified** by an independent registrar. In effect, they are self-certified. Of course, an official Certificate does tend to carry more weight in the market place.

If an organisation that is certified or compliant, this does not indicate that their products and services meet ISO 9000 requirements. The ISO 9000 standards are **process standards**, not product standards. It is the processes that are use to produce that products or services that have been certified.

4 Quality and information system development

4.1 The 'V' model

FAST FORWARD

The **'V' model** shows the relationship between system **development**, **testing** and **quality** throughout a systems development project.

We discussed the stages involved in the design and implementation of systems, and models of system development, in Chapter 7.

An illustration of the V model follows. The 'V' refers to the **two legs** of the diagram – system design runs down the left leg of the V and testing runs up the right leg.

The 'V' Model

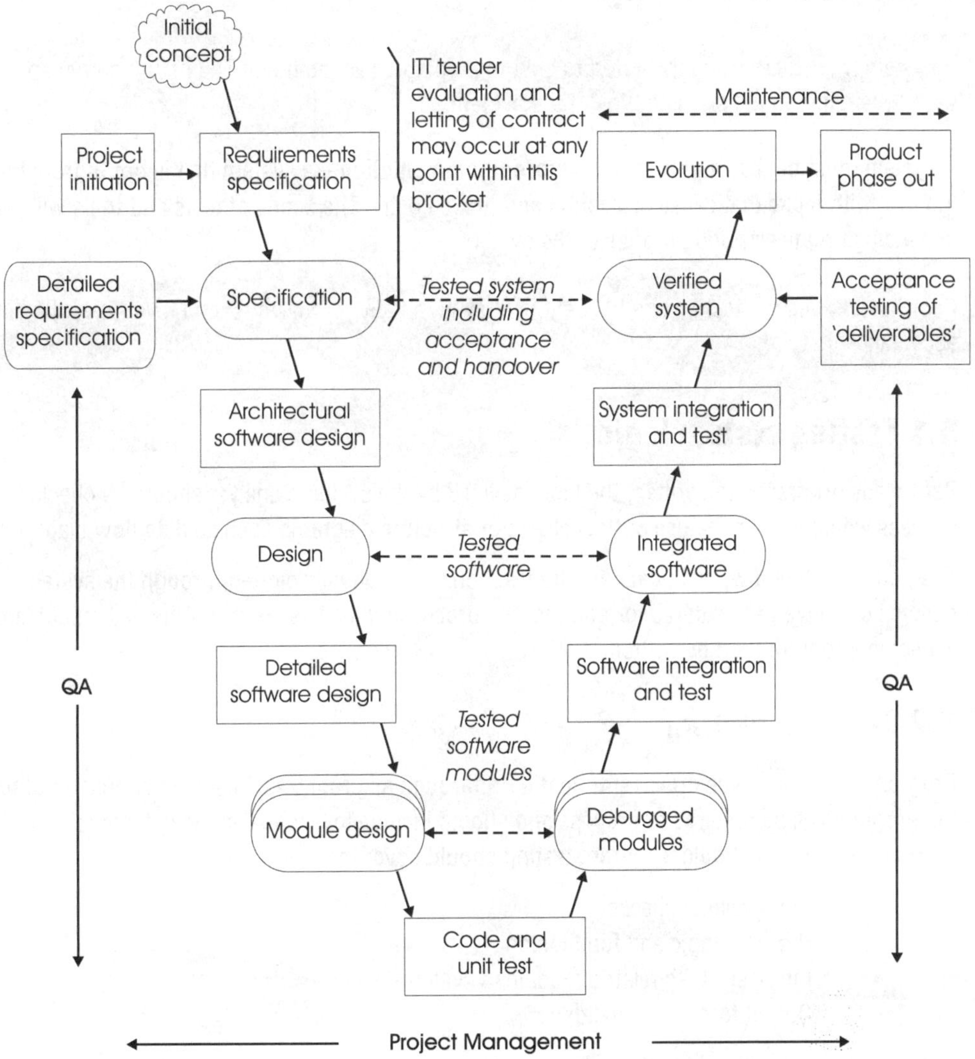

The left leg of the V shows the system development stages of analysis and design – including programming. The upward leg covers the assembly and testing phases and product delivery.

4.1.1 V model 'quality links'

The model shows **three links** between the left and right legs of the V. These links all refer to testing of some sort. We will look at testing in detail later in this chapter – the explanation below is provided to explain the role of the V model in system quality.

(a) Starting from the bottom point of the V travelling up the right leg, the first link is between 'debugged' modules (sections) of the system and the module design. This check ensures individual modules operate as intended.

(b) The second quality link checks the integrated software against the design specification for the integrated modules (ie how the modules operate together).

(c) At the top of the V is the final test of quality. The verified system is checked against the overall systems specification. This process includes user acceptance testing and system hand-over or sign-off.

5 Stages of testing

FAST FORWARD

A system must be thoroughly **tested** to ensure it operates as intended. The nature and scope of testing will vary depending on the size and type of the system.

A system must be **thoroughly tested before implementation** – a system that is not thoroughly tested may 'go live' with faults that cause disruption and prove costly. The scope of tests and trials will vary depending on the size and purpose of the system.

FAST FORWARD

Four basic stages of testing can be identified: system logic, program testing, system testing and user acceptance testing.

5.1 Testing system logic

Before any programs are written, the logic devised by the systems analyst should be checked. This process would involve the use of flow charts or structure diagrams such as data flow diagrams.

The path of different types of data and transactions are manually plotted through the system, to ensure all possibilities have been catered for and that the processing logic is correct. When all results are as expected, programs can be written.

5.2 Program testing

Program testing involves **processing test data** through all programs. Test data should be of the type that the program will be required to process and should include invalid/exceptional items to test whether the program reacts as it should. Program testing should cover the following areas:

- Input validity checks
- Program logic and functioning
- Interfaces with related modules \ systems
- Output format and validity

The testing process should be **fully documented** – recording data used, expected results, actual results and action taken. This documentation may be referred to at a later date, for example if program modifications are required.

Two types of program testing are unit testing and unit integration testing.

5.2.1 Unit testing and unit integration testing

Key terms

Unit testing means testing one function or part of a program to ensure it operates as intended.

Unit integration testing involves testing two or more software units to ensure they work together as intended. The output from unit integration testing is a debugged module.

Unit testing involves detailed testing of part of a program – refer back to the V model and you will see unit testing referred to at the lowest point of the V. If it is established during unit testing that a program is not operating as intended, the cause of the error must be established and corrected. Automated diagnostic routines, that step through the program line by line may be used to help this process.

Test cases should be developed that include test data (inputs), test procedures, expected results and evaluation criteria. Sets of data should be developed for both unit testing and integration testing. Cases should be developed for all aspects of the software.

5.3 System testing

When it has been established that individual programs and interfaces are operating as intended, overall system testing should begin. System testing has a wider focus than program testing. System testing should extend beyond areas already tested, to cover:

- Input documentation and the practicalities of input eg time taken
- Flexibility of system to allow amendments to the 'normal' processing cycle
- Ability to produce information on time
- Ability to cope with peak system resource requirements eg transaction volumes, staffing levels
- Viability of operating procedures

System testing will involve testing both before installation (known as off-line testing) and after implementation (on-line testing). As many problems as possible should be identified before implementation, but it is likely that some problems will only become apparent when the system goes live.

5.4 User acceptance testing

Key term

User acceptance testing is carried out by those who will use the system to determine whether the system meets their needs. These needs should have previously been stated as acceptance criteria. The aim is for the customer to determine whether or not to accept the system.

It is vital that users are involved in system testing to ensure the system operates as intended when used in its operating environment. Any problems identified should be corrected – this will improve system efficiency and should also encourage users to accept the new system as an important tool to help them in their work.

Users process test data, system performance is closely monitored and users report how they felt the system meets their needs. Test data may include some historical data, because it is then possible to check results against the 'actual' output from the old system.

6 Methods of testing

In the previous section we looked at system testing in four chronological stages. In this section we explain in greater detail how testing is **performed**. The terms used to describe testing procedures in this section are not prescriptive or mutually exclusive – a variety of techniques may be used to test different aspects of the same system.

6.1 Static testing and dynamic testing

FAST FORWARD

Software testing may be carried out in a **static environment** or a **dynamic environment**

Key terms

Static testing describes the process of evaluating a system or component based on its form, structure and content. The program or process is not executed or performed during static testing.

Dynamic testing. is testing that is performed by executing a program. It involves running the program and checking the results are as expected.

Both static and dynamic testing play an important role in software development. Static testing allows the program or part of program to be looked at in isolation – which means that other programs or parts of the system do not influence the test, and are not affected by the test. Many logical and coding errors are able to be found by simply checking and reviewing code.

However, it is only when actually running a program that some errors will be discovered. Dynamic testing will reveal any potential conflicts between the program and other elements of the system (hardware and software).

6.2 Test scripts and decision tables

FAST FORWARD

A **test script** is a document that lists all tests that a new piece of software will be subjected to.

It is likely that some tests from the script would be carried out by the **programmer**, and some by **users**. The script should include procedures for noting the results of the test, and for details of any suspected errors.

Decision tables (also known as cause-effect charts) are used as a method of demonstrating the effect of a process or action in a concise manner. Decision tables are useful in deciding what action to take if an error is identified when following a test script.

FAST FORWARD

Decision tables show the effect of a process, decision or action. They are often used in the context of system testing.

Before we look at an example in the context of system testing, we will work through a simple example to demonstrate the workings of a decision table. A decision table consists of four quadrants, as shown below.

Condition stub	Condition entry
Action stub	Action entry

6.3 Example : A simple decision table

Suppose you have to get out of bed at 8 am to enable you to get to work on time. You go to work on Monday to Friday only. If you woke up one Tuesday morning, checked the time – which is 8.02, your decision making process could be shown in the form of a decision table. An X marks the action you should take.

Conditions	Entry
Is it 8 o' clock yet?	Yes
Is it the weekend?	No
Actions	**Entry**
Get up	X
Stay in bed	

We can expand the table so that it takes account of all possible combinations of conditions and actions.

(a) Because a condition can only apply or not apply (Yes or No), the number of combinations (or 'rules') is 2^n, where n is the number of conditions.

In our example there are 2 conditions (n = 2) so the number of combinations is $2^2 = 4$. There are four columns.

	1	2	3	4
Is it 8 o' clock yet?				
Is it the weekend?				
Get up				
Stay in bed				

(b) The conditions can either have a Yes or No answer (Y or N).

(i) As there are **two** possible outcomes, fill **half** of each row with Ys and the other half with Ns. So, write in Y for the first half of the columns in row 1 (columns 1 and 2) and N for the other half (columns 3 and 4).

(ii) For row 2, write in Ys and Ns for **half** the number of columns of each group in the previous row. In this example row 1 has Ys in groups of twos, so row 2 will have Ys in groups of 1.

(iii) If there are more conditions continue **halving** for each row until you reach the final condition, which will always be consecutive Ys and Ns.

	1	2	3	4
Is it 8 o' clock yet?	Y	Y	N	N
Is it the weekend?	Y	N	Y	N
Get up				
Stay in bed				

(c) Now **consider what action** you would take if the condition(s) specified in each column applied. For column 1 it is 8 o'clock but it is the weekend so you can stay in bed. For column 2 it is 8 o' clock but it is not the weekend so you must get up. Explain the logic of columns 3 and 4 yourself.

	1	2	3	4
Is it 8 o' clock yet?	Y	Y	N	N
Is it the weekend?	Y	N	Y	N
Get up		X		
Stay in bed	X		X	X

(d) In more complicated problems you may find that there are some columns that do not have any Xs in the Action entry quadrant because **this combination of conditions is impossible**. We will show you how to deal with these columns later. The question below deals with the same situation in a slightly different manner – as the thought process used identified three conditions instead of two.

Question

Simple decision table

Jed decided to draw up a decision table demonstrating the decision-making process he executed when he woke up each day.

He identified 3 conditions, mirroring his early-morning thought processes, and 2 possible actions.

Conditions *Is it 8 o' clock yet? Is it a weekday? Is it the weekend?*

Actions *Get up. Stay in bed.*

Draw up and complete the decision table.

Answer

There are 3 conditions so there will be $2^3 = 8$ columns.

	1	2	3	4	5	6	7	8
Is it 8 o' clock yet?	Y	Y	Y	Y	N	N	N	N
Is it a weekday?	Y	Y	N	N	Y	Y	N	N
Is it the weekend?	Y	N	Y	N	Y	N	Y	N
Get up		X						
Stay in bed			X			X	X	

Columns 1, 4, 5 and 8 do not have any Xs because it cannot be both a weekday *and* a weekend. In more complex decision situations it may only become clear that certain combinations are impossible once the table has been drawn up.

In this example we could simplify the table by deleting columns 1, 4, 5 and 8. We then end up with the same decision table as the one we saw earlier (although with the columns in a different order).

Exam focus point

The logical nature of decision tables makes them an excellent way of defining the paths a process may pass through and predicting the outcome of these paths in advance. Examination questions are likely to test decision tables in the context of systems testing – as shown in the following example.

6.4 Example: Decision table and system testing

We will now apply decision tables in the context of system testing. Remember the basic principles shown in the earlier example:

- The **condition stub** specifies what is being tested
- The **condition entry** shows the outcome for the condition stub, in the form of Ys and Ns
- The **action stub** shows the range of possible actions
- The **action entry** shows when the action or actions that will be performed, in the form of Xs

An accounts payable module includes a facility for entering invoices.

A test script has been devised to ensure the checks built-in to the 'Value' field within the Invoice entry field are operating as intended.

Possible actions to be taken depending on the results of testing have been laid out in a decision table, as shown below.

Invoice entry screen: value field testing	**Rules**															
	1	**2**	**3**	**4**	**5**	**6**	**7**	**8**	**9**	**10**	**11**	**12**	**13**	**14**	**15**	**16**
Numeric values only	Y	Y	Y	Y	Y	Y	Y	Y	N	N	N	N	N	N	N	N
Positive values only	Y	Y	Y	Y	N	N	N	N	Y	Y	Y	Y	N	N	N	N
Maximum value 999,999.99	Y	Y	N	N	Y	Y	N	N	Y	Y	N	N	Y	Y	N	N
Field must not be empty	Y	N	Y	N	Y	N	Y	N	Y	N	Y	N	Y	N	Y	N
Test passed	X															
Amend exit condition for Invoice entry screen		X		X		X		X		X		X		X		X
Amend field properties - maximum value			X	X			X	X			X	X			X	X
Amend field properties - minimum value					X	X	X	X					X	X	X	X
Amend field properties - numeric only									X	X	X	X	X	X	X	X

6.5 Performance testing

FAST FORWARD

Tests can also be classified according to **what** they are testing – specifically **performance** and **usability**.

Key term

Performance testing is conducted to evaluate the compliance of a system or component with specified performance requirements.

The specific performance requirements which performance testing uses will vary depending on the nature of the system. The initial specification for the software should provide suitable performance testing criteria.

As it is possible that the demands placed on the system and software may increase over time, it is useful to know what **volume** of transactions the system can cope with. Performance testing is therefore taken a 'step-further', by increasing the volume of transactions input within a given timeframe to establish the volume of transactions or data the system can handle. This process is known as '**stress testing**' or '**load testing**'.

6.6 Usability testing

Key term

Usability testing is conducted to establish the relative ease with which users are able to learn and use a system.

Usability testing is vital as a system may look great on paper and perform well when tested by analysts and programmers, but prove inefficient when used by users in the required operating environment.

Usability testing has a slightly different emphasis than user acceptance testing. Usability testing is concerned with lessons that could be learned regarding system design, in order to produce a system that is easier to learn and use. It is possible to improve usability without actually changing system capabilities – by making something more user-friendly.

User acceptance testing is more specific – its purpose is to establish whether users are satisfied that the system meets the system specification when used in the actual operating environment.

6.7 Automated testing tools

Software testing can be very time consuming – often accounting for 30 percent of software development effort and budget. The need for thorough testing to achieve a quality product often conflicts with the requirement to produce the system on time and within budget.

FAST FORWARD

The need for more efficient testing has led to the development of **automated software testing**. Automated testing involves using computer programs that automatically run the software to be tested, and record the results.

Automated testing tools are sometimes referred to as **Computer Aided Software Testing** (**CAST**) tools. There are products available that can automate a variety of tasks, including:

- Executing various command combinations and recording the results
- Testing software in a variety of operating environments and comparing results
- The debugging of some 'obvious' programming errors
- Facilities to track and document all testing and quality assurance information

Automated testing routines may be written by the same organisation that is writing the software, or, a specialised software testing product could be used. The following illustration shows how a software error is recorded in the testing package produced by a prominent testing software provider – Rational.

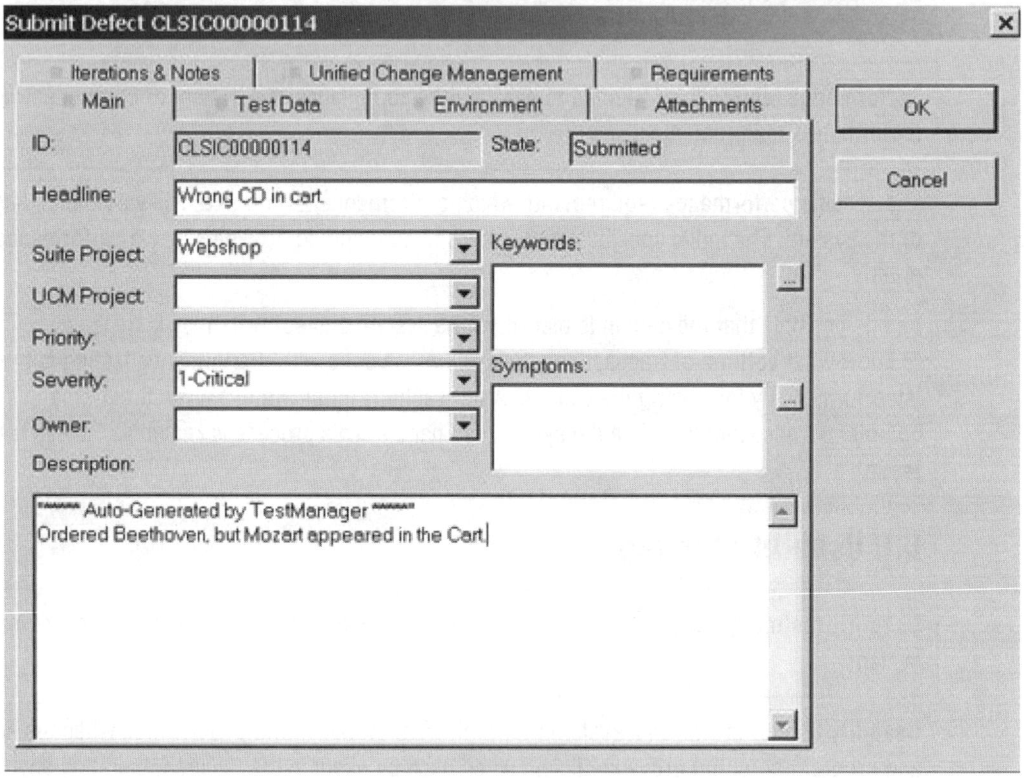

The facility provided by Rational to track software errors and testing is shown below.

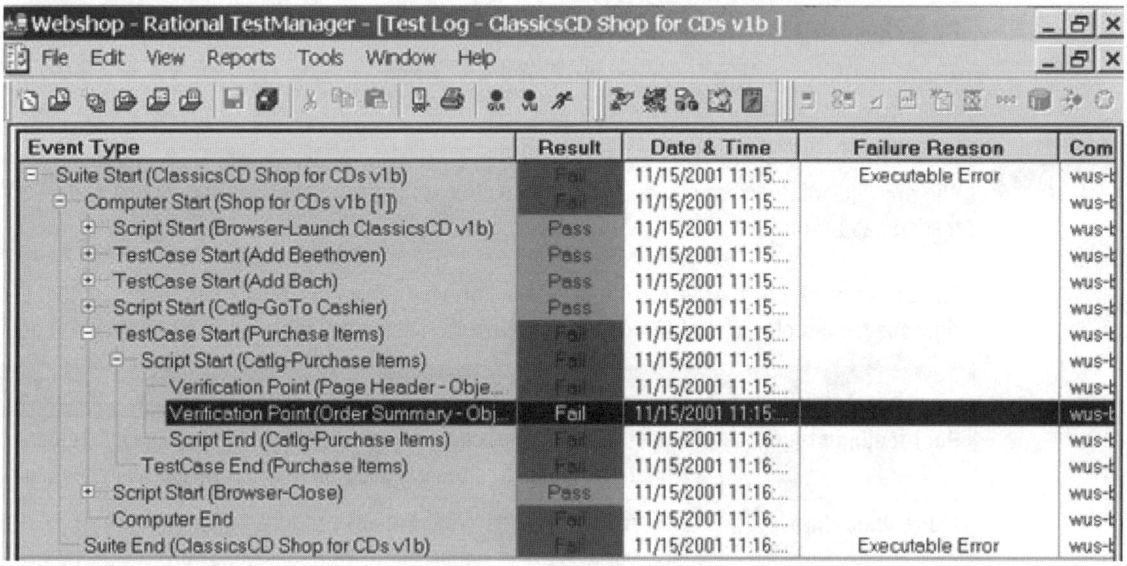

6.8 Beta versions

FAST FORWARD

Commercial software producers often carry out user acceptance testing through the use of **beta versions** of software.

A beta version is an almost finalised package, that has been tested in controlled conditions, but has not been used 'in the field'. Some users are prepared to use beta versions – and report any remaining bugs.

7 Developing a testing strategy

FAST FORWARD

To ensure a coherent, effective approach to testing, a **testing plan** should be developed.

As we have seen in this chapter, there are numerous testing stages and techniques available to system developers. This plan would normally form part of the overall software development quality plan.

A **testing strategy should cover the following areas**.

Testing strategy area	Comment
Strategy approach	A testing strategy should be formulated that details the approach that will be taken to testing, including the tests to be conducted and the testing tools/techniques that will be used.
Test plan	A test plan should be developed that states: • What will be tested • When it will be tested (sequence) • The test environment
Test design	The logic and reasoning behind the design of the tests should be explained.
Performing tests	Detailed procedures should be provided for all tests. This explanation should ensure tests are carried out consistently, even if different people carry out the tests.
Documentation	It must be clear how the results of tests are to be documented. This provides a record of errors, and a starting point for error correction procedures.

Testing strategy area	Comment
Re-testing	The re-test procedure should be explained. In many cases, after correction, all aspects of the software should be re-tested to ensure the corrections have not affected other aspects of the software.

FAST FORWARD

The presence of 'bugs' or errors in the vast majority of software/systems shows that software/system testing has **limitations**.

The presence of 'bugs' or errors in the vast majority of software/systems demonstrates that even the most rigorous testing plan is unlikely to identify all errors. The limitations of software testing are outlined below.

Limitation	Comment
Poor testing process	The test plan may not cover all areas of system functionality. Testers may not be adequately trained. The testing process may not be adequately documented.
Inadequate time	Software and systems are inevitably produced under significant time pressures. Testing time is often 'squeezed' to compensate for project over-runs in other areas.
Future requirements not anticipated	The test data used may have been fine at the time of testing, but future demands may be outside the range of values tested. Testing should allow for future expansion of the system.
Inadequate test data	Test data should test 'positively' – checking that the software does what it should do, and test 'negatively' – that it doesn't do what it shouldn't. It is difficult to include the complete range of possible input errors in test data.
Software changes inadequately tested	System/software changes made as a result of testing findings or for other reasons may not be adequately tested as they were not in the original test plan.

Exam focus point

A question in June 2003 required knowledge of how testing contributed to the quality of a software product.

Chapter Roundup

- In the context of software and information systems, **quality** may be defined as conformance to customer (user) needs.
- An organisation may attempt to maintain quality through one of, or a combination of, three approaches: **quality management**, **quality assurance** and **quality control**.
- The most widely used **external quality standards** are those published by the International Organisation for Standardisation (ISO). ISO standards can be applied to many types of organisations – including those involved in producing software.
- The **'V' model** shows the relationship between system development, testing and quality throughout a systems development project.
- A system must be thoroughly **tested** to ensure it operates as intended. The nature and scope of testing will vary depending on the size and type of the system.
- Four basic **stages of testing** can be identified: system logic, program testing, system testing and user acceptance testing.
- Software testing may be carried out in a **static environment** or a **dynamic environment**.
- A **test script** is a document that lists all tests that a new piece of software will be subjected to.
- **Decision tables** show the effect of a process, decision or action. They are often used in the context of system testing.
- Test can also be classified according to what they are testing – specifically performance and usability.
- The need for more efficient testing has led to the development of **automated software testing** using computer programs that automatically run the software to be tested, and record the results.
- Commercial software producers often carry out user acceptance testing through the use of **beta versions** of software.
- To ensure a coherent, effective approach to testing, a **testing plan** should be developed.
- The presence of 'bugs' or errors in the vast majority of software/systems shows that software/system testing has **limitations**.

Quick Quiz

1 List five characteristics of high quality software.

2 Define 'quality management', 'quality assurance' and 'quality control'.

3 Explain the three 'quality links' included in the V model.

4 List four different stages of testing applicable through a systems development project.

5 Define 'unit testing'.

6 Distinguish between 'static testing' and 'dynamic testing'.

7 Decision tables consist of four quadrants. Label the four quadrants below.

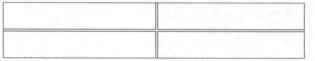

8 What is the purpose of user-acceptance testing?

9 What does CAST stand for?

10 List three reasons why software testing may not identify all bugs.

Answers to Quick Quiz

1 Possibilities include; no major bugs, produced within budget, produced on time, meets user needs and specification, competitive and compatible with other products, produced according to 'best' practices. You may have thought of others.

2 **Quality management** is concerned with controlling activities with the aim of ensuring that products or services are fit for their purpose, and meet specifications. Quality management encompasses quality assurance and quality control.

Quality assurance schemes involve a supplier guaranteeing the quality of goods or services supplied. Procedures and standards are devised with the aim of ensuring defects are eliminated.

Quality control is concerned with checking and reviewing work that has been done. Quality control therefore has a narrower focus than quality assurance

3 Starting from the bottom point of the V travelling up the right leg, the first link is between 'debugged' modules (sections) of the system and the module design. This check ensures individual modules operate as intended.

The second quality link checks the integrated software against the design specification for the integrated modules (ie how the modules operate together).

At the top of the V is the final quality link where the verified system is checked against the overall systems specification. This process includes user acceptance testing and system hand-over or sign-off.

4 Four basic stages of testing can be identified: system logic, program testing, system testing and user acceptance testing.

5 Unit testing means testing one function or part of a program to ensure it operates as intended.

6 Static testing describes the process of evaluating a system or component based on its form, structure and content. The program or process is not executed or performed during static testing.

Dynamic testing is testing that is performed by executing a program. It involves running the program and checking the results are as expected

7

Condition stub	Condition entry
Action stub	Action entry

8 User acceptance testing is carried out by those who will use the system to determine whether the system meets their needs. These needs should have previously been stated as acceptance criteria. The aim is for the customer to determine whether or not to accept the system.

9 Computer Assisted Software Testing.

10 Possibilities include; The test plan didn't cover all areas of system functionality; Testers not adequately trained; Not enough time dedicated to testing; Test data did not include the full range of values the system is required to process; Inadequate re-testing after software changes. You may have thought of others.

Now try the question below from the Exam Question Bank

Number	Level	Marks	Time
Q18	Examination	20	36 mins

12

Implementing systems

Topic list	Syllabus reference
1 Implementation strategy	3 (f)
2 Training	3 (f)
3 Documentation	3 (f)
4 File conversion	3 (a)
5 Changeover	3 (f)

Introduction

In this chapter we explore the issues surrounding **system implementation**.

Different implementation strategies are covered, and the options available when the time comes for the new system to 'go-live' are discussed.

This is a relatively short chapter, but the issues covered are popular topics for examination questions.

Study guide

Part 3.19 – Technical information system requirements

- Define and record performance and volume requirements of information systems
- Establish requirements for data conversion and data creation

Part 3.24 – Implementation issues and implementation methods

- Plan for data conversion and creation
- Discuss the need for training and suggest different methods for delivering such training
- Describe the type of documentation needed to support implementation and comment on ways of effectively organising and presenting this documentation
- Distinguish between parallel running and direct changeover and comment on the advantages and disadvantages of each

Part 3.27 – Relationship of management, development process and quality

- Describe the relationship between the systems development process and quality assurance

Exam guide

The different approaches to system changeover have proved popular in past examination questions.

1 Implementation strategy

FAST FORWARD

The implementation of a new computer system is a **complex task** that requires careful **planning**.

The implementation of a new computer system is a **complex task**, particularly with large systems. As with any complex task involving a number of related issues, **planning** is the key to success.

The **main steps involved** in a major computer **system installation** are **outlined below**. Note that this is only an example, the actual tasks and order will depend on the system being implemented and the organisation involved.

Step 1 Select location/site

Step 2 Choose and order hardware

Step 3 Design and write software (or purchase off-the shelf)

Step 4 Program testing

Step 5 Staff training

Step 6 Produce user documentation

Step 7 Produce systems documentation

Step 8 File conversion

Step 9 Testing (including user acceptance testing)

Step 10 System changeover (and further testing and training if required)

Software design and software/system testing have been covered in detail in previous chapters – the other main implementation issues are explained in the remainder of this chapter.

1.1 The importance of an effective implementation strategy

How the system implementation is conducted will have a significant impact on how users perceive the new system. A poorly planned implementation, that causes widespread disruption, is likely to result in users viewing the system negatively – which will hinder system operation.

It is important, therefore, that implementation procedures are designed so that likely problems are avoided and that unavoidable problems are managed to cause minimal disruption. Project management tools and techniques (covered in Chapters 5 and 6) are relevant here.

The introduction of a new system will change the way some people work, and will impact on established working relationships. To ensure staff support for change, users should be involved and kept informed at all stages of system development.

If the new system will result in some roles becoming redundant, management should handle these issues sensitively and openly. Re-training should be offered if other positions are available.

To get full value from a system, it is essential that staff are aware of what the systems capabilities are, and how these can be applied to help staff perform their roles. Training is the key to achieving this.

2 Training

FAST FORWARD

Staff should be involved and kept **fully informed** at all stages of system development and implementation. **Staff training** is essential to ensure that information systems are utilised to **their full potential**.

Staff training in the use of information systems and information technology is essential if the return on investment in IS/IT is to be maximised.

Training is not simply an issue that affects operational staff. Training in information technology **affects all levels** in an organisation, from senior managers learning how to use an executive information system for example, to accounts clerks learning how to use an accounting package.

Training will be needed when:

- A new system is implemented
- An existing system is significantly changed
- Job specifications change
- New staff are recruited
- Skills have been forgotten

FAST FORWARD

Training should be targeted to ensure those involved receive training relevant to the tasks they perform.

2.1 An overview of the role of training

A **systematic approach** to training is illustrated below. This relates to the role of training within an organisation as a whole – but also can be applied to training in an information systems context. Training is provided primarily to help the **organisation** achieve its **objectives**.

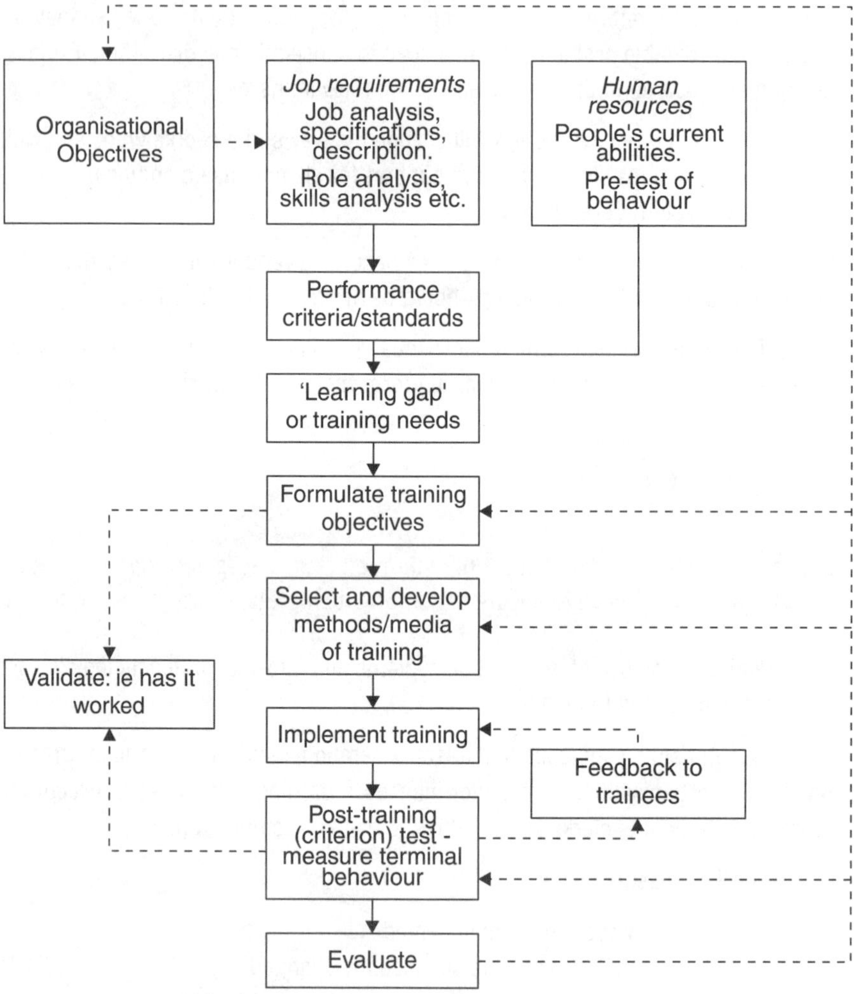

2.2 Establishing an individual's training needs

An individual's **training need** is generally defined as follows.

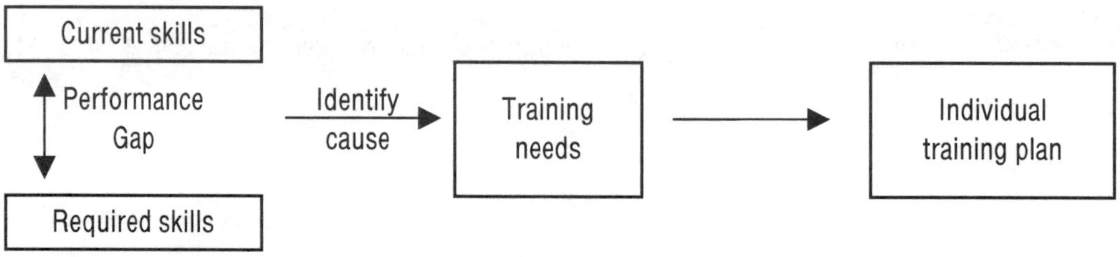

Training should be **evaluated** to make sure that it has worked. If not, the training need still exists and should be addressed perhaps using a refined or different approach.

2.3 Senior management training

Senior manager are most likely to require training in the use of Executive Support Systems and Decision Support Systems.

Senior managers may also require an a**wareness** of information technology in general, and **project management skills** to enable them to manage the acquisition and use of IS/IT within the organisation.

Training relevant to the management of information systems should therefore form part of a managers development plan.

2.4 Middle managers/supervisors training requirements

Staff operating at this level are likely to require a range of computing skills. They should be able to extract the information they require from various elements of the Management Information System.

Staff at this level should also be competent using 'office' type software (eg word-processing, spreadsheets, databases).

2.5 Operational staff

Operational staff are most likely to be involved in processing transactions. This could involve the use of bar-code readers (eg supermarket checkout operators), or keying into a transaction processing system.

Training should focus on the specific tasks the user is required to perform eg entering an invoice or answering a query.

2.6 Delivering training

FAST FORWARD

There area range of options available to **deliver training**

- Individual tuition 'at desk'
- Classroom course
- Computer based training (CBT)
- Case studies and exercises

There **options** available to **deliver training** are outlined below.

Training method	Comment
Individual tuition 'at desk'	A trainer could work with an employee observing how they use a system and suggesting possible alternatives
Classroom course	The software could be used in a classroom environment, using 'dummy' data.
Computer-based training (CBT)	Training can be provided using CDs, or via an interactive website.
Case studies and exercises	Regardless of how training is delivered, it is likely that material will be based around a realistic case study relevant to the user.
Software reference material	Users may find on-line help, built-in tutorials and reference manuals useful.

The **most suitable training method(s)** in a given situation will depend on the following factors:

- Time available
- Software complexity
- User skill levels
- Facilities available
- Budget

Exam focus point

A question in December 2004 required candidates to consider the advantages and disadvantages of a range of training options.

3 Documentation

Key term

Documentation includes a wide range of technical and non-technical books, manuals, descriptions and diagrams relating to the design, use and operation of a computer system. Examples include user manuals, hardware and operating software manuals, system specifications and program documentation.

FAST FORWARD

The **technical manual** is produced as a reference tool for those involved in producing and installing the system.

3.1 Technical manual

The technical manual is produced as a reference tool for those involved in producing and installing the system.

The technical manual should include the following:

- Contact details for the original developers
- System overview
- System specifications including performance details
- Hardware technical specification
- System objectives
- Flowcharts or Data Flow Diagrams
- Entity models and life histories
- Individual program specifications
- Data dictionary

The technical manual should be referred to when future modifications are made to the system. The technical manual should be updated whenever system changes are made.

3.2 User manual

FAST FORWARD

The **user manual** is used to explain the system to users.

The system should be documented from the point-of-view of **users**. User documentation is used to **explain** the system to users and in training. It provides a **point of reference** should the user have problems with the system. Much of this information **may be available on-line** using context-sensitive help eg 'Push F1 for help'.

3.2.1 User manual contents

The manual provides full documentation of the **operational procedures** necessary for the 'hands-on' running of the system. Amongst the matters to be covered by this documentation would be the following.

(a) **Systems set-up procedures**. Full details should be given for each application of the necessary file handling and stationery requirements etc.

(b) **Security procedures**. Particular stress should be placed on the need for checking that proper authorisation has been given for processing operations and the need to restrict use of machine(s) to authorised operators.

(c) **Reconstruction control procedures**. Precise instructions should be given in relation to matters such as back-up and recovery procedures to be adopted in the event of a systems failure.

(d) **System messages**. A listing of all messages likely to appear on the operator's screen should be given together with an indication of the responses which they should evoke.

(e) **Samples**, including input screens and reports.

When a system is developed in-house, the user documentation might be written by a systems analyst. However, it might be considered preferable for the user documentation to have some input from **users.** As user-documentation is intended to help users, it must be written in a way that users are able to understand. The aim is to **ensure the smooth operation of the system,** not to turn users into analysts.

As with the technical manual, the content of the user manual must be updated to reflect any system changes.

Exam focus point

Candidates in June 2003 were asked to describe the documentation they would expect from a software supplier.

4 File conversion

Key term

File conversion means converting **existing files** into a format suitable for the new system.

Most computer systems are based around files containing data. When a new system is introduced, files must be created that conform to the requirements of that system.

The various scenarios that file conversion could involve are outlined in the following table.

Existing data	Comment
Held in manual (ie paper) files	Data must be entered manually into the new system – probably via the use of input forms, so that data entry operators have all the data they require in one document. This is likely to be a time-consuming process.
Held in existing computer files	How complex the process is in converting the files to a format compatible with the new system will depend on various technical issues such as whether coding systems are changing. It may be possible to automate much of the conversion process.
Held in both manual and computer files	Two separate conversion procedures are required
Existing data is incomplete	If the missing data is crucial, it must be researched and made available in a format suitable for the new-system – or suitable for the file conversion process.

4.1 File conversion process

The file conversion process is shown in the following diagram, which assumes the original data is held in manual files.

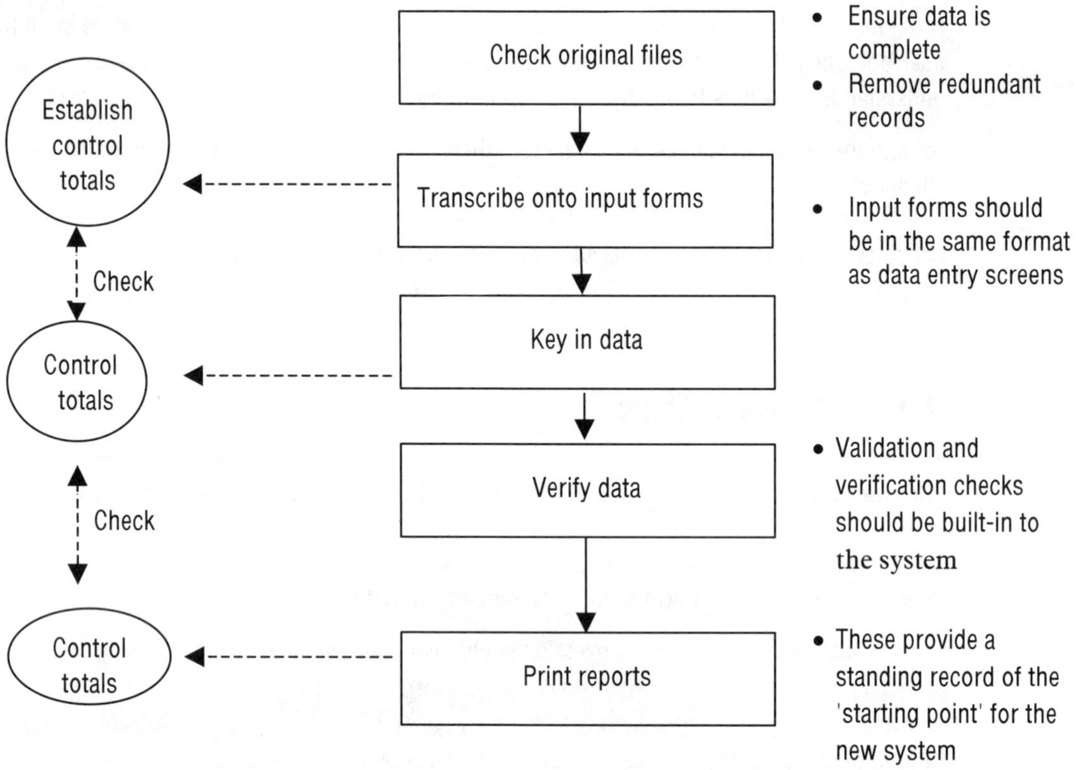

It is essential that the 'new' converted files are accurate. Various controls can be utilised during the conversion process.

(a) **One-to-one checking** between records on the old and new systems.

(b) **Sample checking**. Selecting and checking a sample of records, as there are too many to check individually.

(c) **Built-in data validation** routines in automated conversion processes.

(d) **Control totals** and **reconciliations**. These checks could include checking the total number of records, and the value of transactions.

Question — Data conversion

You have been asked to transfer 400 Sales Ledger manual record cards to a PC based system. The program menu has a record create option. Explain how you would set about this process, and the steps you would take to ensure that the task was completed successfully.

Answer

The steps that should be taken are as follows.

(a) Check the manual records, and remove any dead accounts.

(b) Assign account codes to each record, ideally with codes that incorporate a check digit.

(c) If necessary transcribe the data from the card records on to documents which can be used for copying from, for data input.

(d) Add up the number of accounts and the total value of account balances as control totals (perhaps using a spreadsheet).

(e) Select the record create option from the program menu and key the standing data and current data onto the new computer file. This should ideally be done at a quiet time, perhaps over a weekend.

(f) Input that is rejected by a data validation check should be re-keyed correctly.

(g) A listing of the records put on to file should be printed out. This listing should be checked for errors, ideally by someone who did not do the keying in. Errors should be reported, and corrected data keyed in to amend the data on file.

(h) The program should produce control totals of the number of records put on to the file, and the total value of account balances. These control totals should be checked against the pre-prepared control totals. Discrepancies should be investigated, and any errors or omissions put right.

(i) A back-up copy of the new file should be made.

(j) The file and the new system should then be ready for use.

5 Changeover

FAST FORWARD

There are four approaches to **changeover**: direct changeover, parallel running, pilot operations and phased changeover. These vary in terms of time required, cost and risk.

Once the new system has been fully and satisfactorily tested the changeover can be made. This may be according to one of four approaches.

- Direct changeover
- Parallel running
- Pilot operation
- Phased or 'staged' changeover

5.1 Direct changeover

The old system is **completely replaced** by the new system **in one move**.

This may be unavoidable where the two systems are substantially different, or where the costs of parallel running are too great.

While this method is comparatively **cheap** it is **risky** (system or program corrections are difficult while the system has to remain operational).

The new system should be introduced during **a quiet period**, for example over a bank holiday weekend or during an office closure.

5.2 Parallel running

The **old and new** systems are **run in parallel** for a period of time, both processing current data and enabling cross checking to be made.

This method provides a **degree of safety** should there be problems with the new system. However, if there are differences between the two systems cross-checking may be difficult or impossible.

There is a **delay** in the actual implementation of the new system, a possible indication of **lack of confidence,** and a need for **more staff** to cope with both systems running in parallel.

This cautious approach, if adopted, should be properly planned, and the plan should include:

(a) A firm **time limit** on parallel running.

(b) Details of **which data** should be **cross-checked**.

(c) Instructions on how **errors** are to be dealt with eg previously undiscovered errors in the old system.

(d) Instructions on how to report and act on any **major problems** in the new system.

5.3 Pilot operation

Pilot operation involves selecting part or parts of an organisation (eg a department or branch) to operate running the new system in parallel with the existing system. When the branch or department piloting the system is satisfied with the new system, they cease to use the old system. The new system is then piloted in another area of the organisation.

Pilot operation is **cheaper** and **easier to control** than running the whole system in parallel, and provides a **greater degree of safety** than does a direct changeover.

5.4 Phased changeover

Phased changeover involves selecting a complete section of the system for a direct changeover, eg in an accounting system the purchase ledger. When this part is running satisfactorily, another part is switched – until eventually the whole system has been changed.

A phased series of direct changeovers is less risky than a single direct changeover, as any problems and disruption experienced should be isolated in an area of operations.

The relative advantages and disadvantages of the various changeover methods are outlined in the following table.

Method	Advantages	Disadvantages
Direct changeover	Quick Minimal cost Minimises workload	Risky Could disrupt operations If fails, will be costly
Parallel running	Safe, built-in safety Provides way of verifying results of new system	Costly-two systems need to be operated Time-consuming Additional workload
Pilot operation	Less risky than direct changeover Less costly than complete parallel running	Can take a long time to achieve total changeover Not as safe as complete parallel running
Phased changeover	Less risky than a single direct changeover Any problems should be in one area – other operations unaffected	Can take a long time to achieve total changeover Interfaces between parts of the system may make this impractical

Chapter Roundup

- The implementation of a new computer system is a **complex task** that requires careful **planning**.
- Staff should be involved and kept **fully informed** at all stages of system development and implementation. **Staff training** is essential to ensure that information systems are utilised to **their full potential**.
- **Training** should be targeted to ensure those involved receive training relevant to the tasks they perform.
- There are a range of options available to **deliver training**
  - Individual tuition 'at desk'
  - Classroom course
  - Computer based training (CBT)
  - Case studies and exercises
- The **technical manual** is produced as a reference tool for those involved in producing and installing the system.
- The **user manual** is used to explain the system to users.
- There are four approaches to **changeover**: direct changeover, parallel running, pilot operations and phased changeover. These vary in terms of time required, cost and risk.

Quick Quiz

1 List the main steps involved in a major computer installation.

2 List five situations where training is required.

3 What factors are relevant when considering how training should be delivered?

4 Which method of system changeover is usually safest?

5 Which method of system changeover is probably most expensive?

6 Which method of system changeover is usually the riskiest?

7 Which method of system changeover is considered the cheapest?

Answers to Quick Quiz

1 Dynamic testing is testing that is performed by executing a program.

Step 1 Select location/site

Step 2 Choose and order hardware

Step 3 Design and write software (or purchase off-the shelf)

Step 4 Program testing

Step 5 Staff training

Step 6 Produce user documentation

Step 7 Produce systems documentation

Step 8 File conversion

Step 9 Testing (including user acceptance testing)

Step 10 System changeover (and further testing and training if issues arise)

2
- A new system is implemented
- An existing system is significantly changed
- Job specifications change
- New staff are recruited
- Skills have been forgotten

3 The time available, how the complex the software is, the existing user-skill level, the training facilities available and the cost.

4 Parallel running.

5 Parallel running.

6 Direct changeover.

7 Direct changeover.

Now try the question below from the Exam Question Bank

Number	Level	Marks	Time
Q13 (c)	Examination	10	18 mins

15

Security and legal compliance

Topic list	Syllabus reference
1 Security	3 (c)
2 Physical threats	3 (c)
3 Physical access control	3 (c)
4 Building controls into an information system	1 (a), 3 (c)
5 Privacy and data protection	3 (b)
6 Internet security issues	3 (c)
7 Information systems and the accountant	3 (i)

Introduction

Organisations are becoming increasingly **reliant on computerised information systems**.

It is vital therefore to ensure these systems are secure – to protect the information held on them, to ensure operations run smoothly, to prevent theft and to ensure compliance with legislation.

Security and legal issues crop up regularly in the examination.

Study guide

Part 1.4 – Organising information systems – structural issues

- Discuss the meaning and need for a disaster recovery plan

Part 3.19 – Technical information system requirements

- Discuss the need for archiving, backup and restore and other housekeeping functions
- Explain the need for a software audit trail and define the content of such a trail

Part 3.20 – Legal compliance in information systems

- Describe the principles, terms and coverage typified by the UK Data Protection Act
- Describe the principles, terms and coverage typified by the UK Computer Misuse Act

Part 3.21 – Implementing security and legal requirements

- Describe methods to ensure the physical security of IT systems
- Discuss the role, implementation and maintenance of a password system
- Explain representative clerical and software controls that should assist in maintaining the integrity of a system
- Describe the principles and application of encryption techniques
- Discuss the implications of software viruses and malpractice
- Discuss how the requirements of the UK Data Protection and UK Computer misuse legislation may be implemented

Part 3.27 – Relationship of management, development process and quality

- Explain the role of the accountant in information systems management, delivery and quality assurance

Exam guide

Data protection and privacy are extremely topical at the moment, as is Internet Security.

1 Security

FAST FORWARD

Security is the protection of data from accidental or deliberate threats and the protection of an information system from such threats.

1.1 The responsibilities of ownership

If you own **something that you value** – you **look after it**. **Information** is valuable and it deserves similar care.

Key term

> **Security**, in information management terms, means the **protection of data** from accidental or deliberate threats which might cause unauthorised modification, disclosure or destruction of data, and the **protection of the information system** from the degradation or non-availability of services.

Security refers to **technical** issues related to the computer system, psychological and **behavioural** factors in the organisation and its employees, and protection against the unpredictable occurrences of the **natural world**.

Security can be subdivided into a number of aspects.

(a) **Prevention**. It is in practice impossible to prevent all threats cost-effectively.

(b) **Detection**. Detection techniques are often combined with prevention techniques: a log can be maintained of unauthorised attempts to gain access to a computer system.

(c) **Deterrence**. As an example, computer misuse by personnel can be made grounds for disciplinary action.

(d) **Recovery procedures**. If the threat occurs, its consequences can be contained (for example checkpoint programs).

(e) **Correction procedures**. These ensure the vulnerability is dealt with (for example, by instituting stricter controls).

(f) **Threat avoidance**. This might mean changing the design of the system.

2 Physical threats

FAST FORWARD

Physical threats to security may be natural or man made. They include fire, flooding, weather, lightning, terrorist activity and accidental damage.

The **physical environment** quite obviously has a major effect on information system security, and so planning it properly is an important precondition of an adequate security plan.

2.1 Fire

Fire is the **most serious hazard** to computer systems. Destruction of data can be even more costly than the destruction of hardware.

A fire safety plan is an essential feature of security procedures, in order to prevent fire, detect fire and put out the fire. Fire safety includes:

- **Site preparation** eg fireproof materials, fire doors
- **Detection equipment** eg smoke detector alarms
- **Extinguishing equipment** eg sprinklers and extinguishers
- **Staff awareness** of fire safety procedures

2.2 Water

Water is a serious hazard. Flooding and water damage are often encountered following firefighting activities elsewhere in a building.

This problem can be countered by the use of waterproof ceilings and floors together with the provision of adequate drainage.

In some areas flooding is a natural risk, for example in parts of central London and many other towns and cities near rivers or coasts. Basements are therefore generally not regarded as appropriate sites for large computer installations.

2.3 Weather

Wind, rain and storms can all cause substantial **damage to buildings**. In certain areas the risks are greater, for example the risk of typhoons in parts of the Far East. Many organisations make heavy use of prefabricated and portable offices, which are particularly vulnerable.

Cutbacks in maintenance expenditure may lead to leaking roofs or dripping pipes, which can invite problems of this type, and maintenance should be kept up if at all possible.

2.4 Lightning

Lightning and electrical storms can play havoc with power supplies, causing power failures coupled with power surges as services are restored. Minute adjustments in power supplies may be enough to affect computer processing operations (characterised by lights which dim as the country's population turns on electric kettles following a popular television program).

One way of combating this is by the use of **uninterrupted (protected) power supplies.** This will protect equipment from fluctuations in the supply. Power failure can be protected against by the use of a **separate generator**.

2.5 Terrorist activity

Political terrorism is the main risk, but there are also threats from individuals with **grudges.**

In some cases there is very little that an organisation can do: its buildings may just happen to be in the wrong place and bear the brunt of an attack aimed at another organisation or intended to cause general disruption.

There are some avoidance measures that should be taken, however.

(a) **Physical access** to buildings should be controlled (see the next section).

(b) Organisations involved in controversial activities may consider moving into other lines of business.

(c) The organisation should consult with police and fire authorities about potential risks, and co-operate with their efforts to avoid them.

2.6 Accidental damage

People are a physical threat to computer installations: there can be few of us who have not at some time spilt a cup of coffee over a desk covered with papers, or tripped and fallen doing some damage to ourselves or to an item of office equipment.

Combating accidental damage is a matter of:

(a) Sensible **attitudes** to office behaviour.

(b) Good office **layout**.

Question — Fire and flooding

You are the financial controller of your organisation. The company is in the process of installing a mainframe computer, and because your department will be the primary user, you have been co-opted onto the project team with responsibility for systems installation. You have a meeting at which the office services manager will be present, and you realise that no-one has yet mentioned the risks of fire or flooding in the discussions about site selection. Make a note of the issues which you would like to raise under these headings.

Answer

(a) **Fire**. Fire security measures can usefully be categorised as preventative, detective and corrective. Preventative measures include siting of the computer in a building constructed of suitable materials and the use of a site which is not affected by the storage of inflammable materials (eg stationery, chemicals). Detective measures involve the use of smoke detectors. Corrective measures may include installation of a sprinkler system (water-based or possibly gas-based to avoid electrical problems), training of fire officers and good siting of exit signs and fire extinguishers.

(b) **Flooding**. Water damage may result from flooding or from fire recovery procedures. If possible, large installations should not be situated in basements.

3 Physical access control

FAST FORWARD

Physical access controls are designed to prevent **intruders** getting near to computer equipment and/or storage media.

Physical access controls including the following.

(a) **Personnel**, including receptionists and, outside working hours, security guards, can help control human access.

(b) **Door locks** can be used where frequency of use is low. (This is not practicable if the door is in frequent use.)

(c) Locks can be combined with:

   (i) A **keypad system**, requiring a code to be entered.
   (ii) A **card entry system**, requiring a card to be 'swiped'.

(d) Intruder **alarms**.

The best form of access control would be one which **recognised** individuals immediately, without the need for personnel or cards. However, machines which can identify a person's fingerprints or scan the pattern of a retina are **expensive**, so are used only in highly sensitive industries, eg defence.

It may not be cost effective or practical to use the same access controls in all areas. The **security requirements of different departments** should be estimated, and appropriate measures taken. Some areas will be very restricted, whereas others will be relatively open.

FAST FORWARD

Important aspects of physical access of control are **door locks** and **card entry systems**. Computer theft is becoming more prevalent as equipment becomes smaller and more portable.

3.1 Personal identification numbers (PINs)

In some organisations staff are allocated an individual **personal identification number**, or PIN, which identifies him or her to the system. Based on the security privileges allocated, the person will be **allowed** access to certain parts of a building, but prevented from accessing other areas.

3.2 Door locks

Conventional door locks are of value in certain circumstances, particularly where users are only required to pass through the door a **couple of times a day**. If the number of people using the door increases and the frequency of use is high, it will be difficult to persuade staff to lock a door every time they pass through it.

A 'good' lock must be accompanied by a **strong door**. Similarly, other points of entry into the room/complex must be as well protected, otherwise the intruder will simply use a **window** to gain access.

One difficulty with conventional locks is the matter of **key control**. Each person authorised to use the door will need a key. Cleaners and other contractors might also be issued with keys. Practices such as lending out keys or taking duplicate keys may be difficult to prevent.

One approach to this is the installation of **combination locks**, where a numbered keypad is located outside the door and access allowed only after the correct 'code', or sequence of digits has been entered. This will only be fully effective if users ensure the combination is kept confidential, and the combination is **changed** frequently.

3.3 Card entry systems

Card entry systems are a more sophisticated means of control than the use of locks, as **cards can be programmed** to allow access to certain parts of a building only, between certain times.

Cards allow a high degree of monitoring of staff movements; they can for example be used instead of clock cards to record details of time spent on site. Such cards can be incorporated into **identity cards**, which also carry the photograph and signature of the user and which must be 'displayed' at all times.

3.4 Computer theft

As computer equipment becomes **smaller** and **more portable**, it can be 'smuggled' out of buildings with greater ease. Indeed much equipment is specifically **designed for use off-site**.

A **log of all equipment** should be maintained. This may already exist in basic form as a part of the fixed asset register. The log should include the **make, model** and **serial number** of each item, together with some other organisation-generated code which identifies the **department** which owns the item, the **individual** responsible for the item and its **location**. Anyone taking any equipment off-site should book it out and book it back in.

Smaller items of equipment, such as laptop computers and floppy disks, should always be **locked securely away**. Larger items cannot be moved with ease and one approach adopted is the use of **bolts** to secure them to desks. This discourages 'opportunity' thieves. Larger organisations may also employ site security guards and install closed circuit camera systems.

Other possible precautions include the bolting of equipment to desks, and the locking away of CDs and other storage media.

Question — Security measures

You are the chief accountant at your company. Your department, located in an open-plan office, has five networked desktop PCs, two laser printers and a dot matrix printer.

You have just read an article suggesting that the best form of security is to lock hardware away in fireproof cabinets, but you feel that this is impracticable. Make a note of any alternative security measures which you could adopt to protect the hardware.

Answer

(a) 'Postcode' all pieces of hardware. Invisible ink postcoding is popular, but visible marking is a better deterrent. Soldering irons are ideal for writing on plastic casing.

(b) Mark the equipment in other ways. Some organisations spray their hardware with permanent paint, perhaps in a particular colour (bright red is popular) or using stencilled shapes.

(c) Hardware can be bolted to desks. If bolts are passed through the desk and through the bottom of the hardware casing, the equipment can be rendered immobile.

(d) Ensure that the organisation's standard security procedures (magnetic passes, keypad access to offices, signing in of visitors etc) are followed.

4 Building controls into an information system

FAST FORWARD

It is possible to **build controls** into a computerised information system. A balance must be struck between the degree of control and the requirement for a user friendly system.

Controls can be classified as:

- Security controls
- Integrity controls
- Contingency controls

4.1 Security controls

Key term

Security can be defined as 'The protection of data from accidental or deliberate threats which might cause unauthorised modification, disclosure or destruction of data, and the protection of the information system from the degradation or non-availability of services'.

(Lane: *Security of computer based information systems*)

Risks to data

- Human error
  - Entering incorrect transactions
  - Failing to correct errors
  - Processing the wrong files
- Technical error such as malfunctioning hardware or software
- Natural disasters such as fire, flooding, explosion, impact, lightning
- Deliberate actions such as fraud
- Commercial espionage
- Malicious damage
- Industrial action

4.2 Integrity controls

Key terms

Data integrity in the context of security is preserved when data is the same as in source documents and has not been accidentally or intentionally altered, destroyed or disclosed.

Systems integrity refers to system operation conforming to the design specification despite attempts (deliberate or accidental) to make it behave incorrectly.

Data will maintain its **integrity** if it is **complete** and **not corrupted**. This means that:

(a) The original **input** of the data must be controlled in such a way as to ensure that the results are complete and correct.

(b) Any **processing and storage** of data must maintain the completeness and correctness of the data captured.

(c) That reports or other **output** should be set up so that they, too, are complete and correct.

4.2.1 Input controls

Input controls should ensure the **accuracy, completeness and validity** of input.

(a) **Data verification** involves ensuring data entered matches source documents.

(b) **Data validation** involves ensuring that data entered is not incomplete or unreasonable. Various checks can be used, depending on the data type.

(i) **Check digits**. A digit calculated by the program and added to the code being checked to validate it eg modulus 11 method.

(ii) **Control totals**. For example, a batch total totalling the entries in the batch.

(iii) **Hash totals**. A system generated total used to check the reasonableness of numeric codes entered.

(iv) **Range checks**. Used to check the value entered against a sensible range, eg balance sheet account number must be between 5,000 and 9,999.

(v) **Limit checks**. Similar to a range check, but usually based on a upper limit eg must be less than 999,999.99.

Data may be **valid** (for example in the **correct format**) but still **not match source documents**.

4.2.2 Processing controls

Processing controls should ensure the **accuracy and completeness of processing**. Programs should be subject to development controls and to rigorous testing. Periodic running of test data is also recommended.

4.2.3 Output controls

Output controls should ensure the accuracy, completeness and security of output. The following measures are possible.

- Investigation and follow-up of error reports and exception reports
- Batch controls to ensure all items processed and returned
- Controls over distribution/copying of output
- Labelling of disks/tapes

4.2.4 Back-up controls

FAST FORWARD

A **back-up** and **archive** strategy should include:

- Regular back-up of data (at least daily)
- Archive plans
- A **disaster recovery** plan including off-site storage

Back-up controls aim to maintain system and data integrity. We have classified back-up controls as an integrity control rather than a contingency control (see later this section) because back-ups should part of the day-to-day procedures of all computerised systems.

Key term

Back-up means to make a copy in anticipation of future failure or corruption. A back-up copy of a file is a duplicate copy kept separately from the main system and only used if the original fails.

The **purpose of backing up data** is to ensure that the most recent usable copy of the data can be recovered and restored in the event of loss or corruption on the primary storage media.

In a well-planned data back-up scheme, a copy of backed up data is delivered (preferably daily) to a secure **off-site** storage facility.

A tape **rotation scheme** can provide a restorable history from one day to several years, depending on the needs of the business.

A well-planned **back-up and archive strategy** should include:

(a) A plan and schedule for the **regular back-up of critical data**.
(b) **Archive plans**.
(c) A **disaster recovery plan** that includes off-site storage.

Regular tests should be undertaken to **verify that data backed up can be successfully restored**.

The **intervals** at which back-ups are performed must be decided. Most organisations back up their data daily, but back-ups may need to be performed more frequently, depending on the nature of the data and of the organisation.

Even with a well planned back-up strategy some re-inputting may be required. For example, if after three hours work on a Wednesday a file becomes corrupt, the Tuesday version can be restored – but Wednesday's work will need to be re-input.

4.2.5 Archiving

A related concept is that of **archiving.** Archiving data is the process of moving (by copying) data from primary storage, such as a hard disk, to tape or other portable media for long-term storage.

Archiving provides a legally acceptable **business history**, while freeing up **hard disk space**. If archived data is needed, it can be restored from the archived tape to a hard disk. Archived data can be used to recover from site-wide disasters, such as fires or floods, where data on primary storage devices is destroyed.

How long data should be retained will be influenced by:

- Legal obligations
- Other business needs

Data stored for a long time should be tested periodically to ensure it is **still restorable** – it may be subject to **damage** from environmental conditions or mishandling.

4.2.6 Passwords and logical access systems

Key term

> **Passwords** are a set of characters which may be allocated to a person, a terminal or a facility which are required to be keyed into the system before further access is permitted.

Unauthorised persons may circumvent physical access controls. A **logical access system** can prevent access to data and program files, by measures such as the following.

- Identification of the user
- Authentication of user identity
- Checks on user authority

Virtually all computer installations use passwords. Failed access attempts may be logged. Passwords are not foolproof.

- Standard system passwords must be changed
- Passwords must never be divulged to others and must never be written down
- Passwords must be changed regularly – and changed immediately if it is suspected that the password is known by others
- Obvious passwords must not be used

4.2.7 Administrative controls

Personnel selection is important. Some employees are always in a position of trust.

- Computer security officer
- Senior systems analyst
- Database administrator

Measures to control personnel include the following.

- Careful recruitment
- Job rotation and enforced vacations
- Systems logs
- Review and supervision

For other staff, **segregation of duties** remains a core security requirement. This involves division of responsibilities into separate roles.

- Data capture and data entry
- Computer operations
- Systems analysis and programming

4.2.8 Audit trail

FAST FORWARD

> An audit trail shows who has accessed a system and the operations performed.

The original concept of an audit trail is to enable a manager or auditor to follow transactions stage-by-stage through a system to ensure that they had been processed correctly. The intention is to:

- **Identify errors**
- **Detect fraud**

Modern integrated computer systems have cut out much of the time-consuming stage-by-stage working of older systems, but there should still be some **means of identifying individual records** and the **input and output documents** associated with the processing of any individual transaction.

Key term

> An **audit trail** is a record showing who has accessed a computer system and what operations he or she has performed. Audit trails are useful both for maintaining security and for recovering lost transactions. Accounting systems include an audit trail component that is able to be output as a report.
>
> In addition, there are separate audit trail software products that enable network administrators to monitor use of network resources.

An audit trail should be provided so that every transaction on a file contains a **unique reference** (eg a sales system transaction record should hold a reference to the customer order, delivery note and invoice).

Typical contents of an accounting software package audit trail include the following items.

(a) A system generated **transaction number**.
(b) A meaningful reference number eg invoice number.
(c) Transaction type eg reversing journal, credit note, cashbook entry etc.
(d) Who input the transaction (user ID).
(e) Full **transaction details** eg net and gross amount, customer ID and so on.
(f) The **PC or terminal** used to enter the transaction.
(g) The **date** and **time** of the entry.
(h) Any additional reference or **narration** entered by the user.

4.2.9 Systems integrity with a PC

Possible **controls relevant to a stand-alone PC** are as follows.

(a) Installation of a **password** routine which is activated whenever the computer is booted up, and activated after periods of inactivity.

(b) The use of additional passwords on 'sensitive' files eg employee salaries spreadsheet.

(c) Any data stored on floppy disk, Zip-disk or CD should be locked away.

(d) **Physical access controls**, for example door locks activated by swipe cards or PIN numbers, to prevent access into the room(s) where the computers are kept. This is probably not feasible in an open plan office.

4.2.10 Systems integrity with a LAN

The main additional risk is the risk (when compared to a stand-alone PC) is the risk of a fault **spreading across the system**. This is particularly true of **viruses**. A virus introduced onto one machine could replicate itself throughout the network. All files coming in to the organisation should be scanned using **anti-virus software** and all machines should have anti-virus software running constantly.

A further risk, depending on the type of network configuration, is that an extra PC could be 'plugged in' to the network to gain access to it. The **network management software** should detect and prevent breaches of this type.

4.2.11 Systems integrity with a WAN

Additional issues, over and above those already described are related to the extensive communications links utilised by Wide Area Networks. Dedicated land lines for data transfer and encryption software may be required.

If **commercially sensitive data** is being transferred it would be necessary to specify high quality communications equipment and to use sophisticated network software to prevent and detect any security breaches.

4.3 Contingency controls

Key term

A **contingency** is an unscheduled interruption of computing services that requires measures outside the day-to-day routine operating procedures.

The preparation of a contingency plan (also known as a disaster recovery plan) is one of the stages in the development of an organisation-wide security policy. A contingency plan is necessary in case of a major **disaster,** or if some of the **security measures** discussed elsewhere **fail**.

A **disaster** occurs where the system for some reason breaks down, leading to potential **losses** of equipment, data or funds. The system **must recover as soon as possible** so that further losses are not incurred, and current losses can be rectified.

Question — **Cause of system breakdown**

What actions or events might lead to a system breakdown?

Answer

System breakdowns can occur in a variety of circumstances, for example:

(a) Fire destroying data files and equipment.
(b) Flooding.
(c) A computer virus completely destroying a data or program file or damaging hardware.
(d) A technical fault in the equipment.
(e) Accidental destruction of telecommunications links (eg builders severing a cable).
(f) Terrorist attack.
(g) System failure caused by software bugs which were not discovered at the design stage.
(h) Internal sabotage (eg logic bombs built into the software).

4.3.1 Disaster recovery plan

Any disaster recovery plan must provide for:

(a) **Standby procedures** so that some operations can be performed while normal services are disrupted.

(b) **Recovery procedures** once the cause of the breakdown has been discovered or corrected.

(c) **Personnel management** policies to ensure that (a) and (b) above are implemented properly.

4.3.2 Contents of a disaster recovery plan

FAST FORWARD

A disaster recovery plan must cover all activities from the initial response to a 'disaster', through to damage limitation and full recovery. Responsibilities must be clearly spelt out for all tasks.

The contents of a disaster recovery (or contingency plan) will include the following.

Section	Comment
Definition of responsibilities	It is important that somebody (a manager or co-ordinator) is designated to take control in a crisis. This individual can then delegate specific tasks or responsibilities to other designated personnel.
Priorities	Limited resources may be available for processing. Some tasks are more important than others. These must be established in advance. Similarly, the recovery program may indicate that certain areas must be tackled first.
Backup and standby arrangements	These may be with other installations, with a company that provides such services (eg maybe the hardware vendor); or reverting to manual procedures.
Communication with staff	The problems of a disaster can be compounded by poor communication between members of staff.
Public relations	If the disaster has a public impact, the recovery team may come under pressure from the public or from the media.
Risk assessment	Some way must be found of assessing the requirements of the problem, if it is contained, with the continued operation of the organisation as a whole.

The contingency plan is dependent on effective **back-up procedures** for data and software, and arrangements for replacement – and even alternative premises.

5 Privacy and data protection

FAST FORWARD

Privacy is the right of the individual not to suffer unauthorised disclosure of information.

Key term

Privacy is the right of the individual to control the use of information about him or her, including information on financial status, health and lifestyle (ie prevent unauthorised disclosure).

5.1 Why is privacy an important issue?

In recent years, there has been a growing fear that the ever-increasing amount of **information** about individuals held by organisations could be misused.

In particular, it was felt that an individual could easily be harmed by the existence of computerised data about him or her which was inaccurate or misleading and which could be **transferred to unauthorised third parties** at high speed and little cost.

In the UK the current legislation covering this area is the **Data Protection Act 1998**.

5.2 The Data Protection Act 1998

FAST FORWARD

The (UK) **Data Protection Act 1998** protects individuals about whom data is held. Both manual and computerised information must comply with the Act.

The Data Protection Act 1998 is an attempt to protect the **individual**. The terms of the Act cover data about individuals – **not data about corporate bodies**.

5.3 Definitions of terms used in the Act

In order to understand the Act it is necessary to know some of the technical terms used in it.

Key terms

Personal data is information about a living individual, including expressions of opinion about him or her. Data about organisations is not personal data.

Data users are organisations or individuals who control personal data and the use of personal data.

A **data subject** is an individual who is the subject of personal data.

5.4 The data protection principles

The UK Data Protection Act includes eight Data Protection Principles with which data users must comply.

DATA PROTECTION PRINCIPLES

Schedule 1 of the Act contains the data protection principles.

1 Personal data shall be processed fairly and lawfully and, in particular, shall not be processed unless:

   (a) At least one of the conditions in Schedule 2 is met (see paragraph 5.5.3 (c) later in this chapter).

   (b) In the case of sensitive personal data, at least one of the conditions in Schedule 3 is also met (see 5.5.3 (d)).

2 Personal data shall be obtained only for one or more specified and lawful purposes, and shall not be further processed in any manner incompatible with that purpose or those purposes.

3 Personal data shall be adequate, relevant and not excessive in relation to the purpose or purposes for which they are processed.

4 Personal data shall be accurate and, where necessary, kept up to date.

5 Personal data processed for any purpose or purposes shall not be kept for longer than is necessary for that purpose or those purposes.

6 Personal data shall be processed in accordance with the rights of data subjects under this Act.

7 Appropriate technical and organisational measures shall be taken against unauthorised or unlawful processing of personal data and against accidental loss or destruction of, or damage to, personal data.

8 Personal data shall not be transferred to a country or territory outside the European Economic Area unless that country or territory ensures an adequate level of protection for the rights and freedoms of data subjects in relation to the processing of personal data.

The Act has two main aims:

(a) To protect **individual privacy**. Previous UK law only applied to **computer-based** information. The 1998 Act applies to **all personal data, in any form.**

(b) To **harmonise data protection legislation** so that, in the interests of improving the operation of the single European market, there can be a **free flow of personal data** between the member states of the EU.

5.5 The coverage of the Act

Key points of the Act can be summarised as follows.

(a) **Data users** have to **register** under the Act with the **Data Protection Registrar**.

(b) **Individuals** (data subjects) are awarded certain **legal rights**.

(c) **Data holders** must adhere to the **data protection principles**.

5.5.1 Registration under the Act

The Data Protection Registrar keeps a Register of all data users. Only registered data users are permitted to hold personal data. The data user must only hold data and use data for the registered **purposes**.

5.5.2 The rights of data subjects

The Act establishes the following rights for data subjects.

(a) A data subject may seek **compensation** through the courts for damage and any associated distress caused by the **loss**, **destruction** or **unauthorised disclosure** of data about himself or herself or by **inaccurate data** about himself or herself.

(b) A data subject may apply to the courts for **inaccurate data** to be **put right** or even **wiped off** the data user's files altogether. Such applications may also be made to the Registrar.

(c) A data subject may obtain **access** to personal data of which he or she is the subject. (This is known as the 'subject access' provision.) In other words, a data subject can ask to see his or her personal data that the data user is holding.

(d) A data subject can **sue** a data user for any **damage or distress** caused to him by personal data about him which is **incorrect** or **misleading** as to matter of **fact** (rather than opinion).

5.5.3 Other features of the legislation

(a) Everyone has the right to go to court to seek redress for **any breach** of data protection law.

(b) Filing systems that are structured so as to facilitate access to information about a particular person now fall within the legislation. This includes systems that are **paper-based** or on **microfilm** or **microfiche**. Personnel records meet this classification.

(c) Processing of personal data is **forbidden** except in the following circumstances.

  (i) With the **consent** of the subject. Consent cannot be implied: it must be by freely given, specific and informed agreement.

  (ii) As a result of a **contractual arrangement.**

  (iii) Because of a **legal obligation.**

  (iv) To **protect the vital interests** of the subject.

  (v) Where processing is in the **public interest.**

  (vi) Where processing is required to exercise **official authority.**

(d) The processing of **'sensitive data'** is forbidden, unless express consent has been obtained. Sensitive data includes data relating to **racial origin**, **political opinions**, **religious beliefs**, physical or mental **health, sexual orientation** and **trade union** membership.

(e) If data about a data subject is **obtained from a third party** the data subject must be given.

  (i) The identity of the **controller** of the data.

  (ii) The **purposes** for which the data are being processed.

(iii) **What data** will be disclosed and **to whom.**
(iv) The existence of a right of subject **access** to the data.

(f) Data subjects have a right not only to have a **copy of data** held about them but also the right to know **why** the data is required.

Question — **Data protection**

(a) Your Managing Director has asked you to recommend measures that your company, which is based in the UK, could take to ensure compliance with data protection legislation. Suggest what measures should be taken.

(b) Watch the newspapers and the *ACCA Student Accountant* for details of developments in legislation.

Answer

(a) Measures could include the following.

- Obtain consent from individuals to hold any sensitive personal data you need.
- Supply individuals with a copy of any personal data you hold about them if so requested.
- Consider if you may need to obtain consent to process personal data.
- Ensure you do not pass on personal data to unauthorised parties.

6 Internet security issues

FAST FORWARD: Establishing organisational **links to the Internet** brings numerous **security dangers**.

There are a numbers of security issues associated with the Internet.

(a) Corruptions such as **viruses** on a single computer can spread through the network to all of the organisation's computers. (Viruses are described at greater length later in this section.)

(b) Disaffected employees have much greater potential to do **deliberate damage** to valuable corporate data or systems because the network could give them access to parts of the system that they are not really authorised to use.

(c) If the organisation is linked to an external network, persons outside the company (**hackers**) may be able to get into the company's internal network, either to steal data or to damage the system.

(d) Employees may **download inaccurate information** or imperfect or **virus-ridden software** from an external network. For example 'beta' (free trial) versions of forthcoming new editions of many major packages are often available on the Internet, but the whole point about a beta version is that it is not fully tested and may contain bugs that could disrupt an entire system.

(e) Information transmitted from one part of an organisation to another may be **intercepted**. Data can be 'encrypted' (scrambled) in an attempt to make it unintelligible to eavesdroppers, this is covered later in this section.

(f) The **communications link itself may break down or distort data**. The worldwide telecommunications infrastructure is improving thanks to the use of new technologies, and there are communications 'protocols' governing the format of data and signals transferred.

6.1 Hacking

Hacking involves attempting to gain unauthorised access to a computer system, usually through telecommunications links.

Hackers require only limited programming knowledge to cause large amounts of damage. The fact that billions of bits of information can be transmitted in bulk over the public telephone network has made it **hard to trace** individual hackers, who can therefore make repeated attempts to invade systems. Hackers, in the past, have mainly been concerned to **copy** information, but a recent trend has been their desire to **corrupt it**.

Phone numbers and passwords can be guessed by hackers using **electronic phone directories** or number generators and by software which enables **rapid guessing** using hundreds of permutations per minute.

Default passwords are also available on some electronic bulletin boards and sophisticated hackers could even try to 'tap' messages being transmitted along phone wires (the number actually dialled will not be scrambled).

6.2 Viruses

Key term

> A virus is a piece of software which infects programs and data and possibly damages them, and which replicates itself.

Viruses need an **opportunity to spread**. The programmers of viruses therefore place viruses in the kind of software which is most likely to be copied. This includes:

(a) Free software (for example from the Internet).

(b) Pirated software (cheaper than original versions).

(c) Games software (wide appeal).

(d) **E-mail attachments**. E-mail has become the most common means of spreading the most destructive viruses. The virus is often held in an attachment to the e-mail message. Recent viruses have been programmed to send themselves to all addresses in the user's electronic address book.

The main types of viruses (and related programs) are explained in the following table.

Type of virus/program	Explanation/Example
File viruses	File viruses infect program files. When you run an infected program the virus runs first, performs an unauthorised act and copies itself to another file or to another location (replicating itself).
Boot sector or 'stealth' viruses	The boot sector is the part of every hard disk and diskette which is read by the computer when it starts up. These 'stealth' viruses hide from virus detection programs by hiding themselves in boot records or files. If the boot sector is infected, the virus runs when the machine starts.
Trojan	A Trojan (or Trojan Horse) is a small program that performs an unexpected function. The trojan is hidden inside a 'valid' program. Trojans therefore act like a virus, but they aren't classified as a virus as they don't replicate themselves.
Logic bomb	A logic bomb is a program that is executed when a specific act is performed. The logic bomb then performs an unexpected function, often designed to cause damage.

Type of virus/program	Explanation/Example
Time bomb	A time bomb is a logic bomb activated at a certain time or date, such as Friday the 13th or April 1st.
Worm	A worm is a type of virus that can replicate (copy) itself and use memory, but cannot attach itself to other programs.
Dropper	A dropper is a program that installs a virus while performing another function.
Macro viruses	A macro virus is a piece of self-replicating code written in an application's 'macro' language. Many applications have macro capabilities including all the programs in Microsoft Office. The distinguishing factor which makes it possible to create a virus with a macro is the existence of auto-execute events. Auto-execute events are opening a file, closing a file, and starting an application. Once a macro is running, it can copy itself to other documents, delete files, and create general havoc. Melissa was a well publicised macro virus.

6.3 Protecting against viruses

The main protection against viruses is **anti-virus software**. Anti-virus software, such as McAfee or Norton's searches systems for viruses and removes any that are found. Anti-virus programs include an auto-update feature that enables the program to download profiles of new viruses, enabling the software to check for all **known** or existing viruses. Very new viruses may go undetected by anti-virus software (until the anti-virus software vendor updates their package – and the organisation installs the update).

Additional precautions include disabling floppy disk drives to prevent viruses entering an organisation via floppy disk. However, this can disrupt work processes. At the very least, organisations should ensure all files received via floppy disk and e-mail are virus checked.

External e-mail links can be protected by way of a **firewall** that may be configured to virus check all messages, and may also prevent files of a certain type being sent via e-mail (eg .exe files, as these are the most common means of transporting a virus).

6.4 Encryption and other safety measures

6.4.1 Encryption

Encryption aims to ensure the security of data during transmission. It involves the translation of data into secret code. To read an encrypted file, you must have access to a secret key or password that enables you to decrypt it. Unencrypted data is called plain text; encrypted data is referred to as cipher text.

Key term

Encryption involves scrambling the data at one end of the line, transmitting the scrambled data, and unscrambling it at the receiver's end of the line.

6.4.2 Authentication

Authentication is a technique of making sure that a message has come from an authorised sender. Authentication involves adding an extra field to a record, with the contents of this field derived from the remainder of the record by applying an algorithm that has previously been agreed between the senders and recipients of data.

6.4.3 Firewalls and dial-back security

Systems can have **firewalls** (which disable part of the telecoms technology) to prevent unwelcome intrusions into company systems, but a determined hacker may well be able to bypass even these.

Dial-back security operates by requiring the person wanting access to the network to dial into it identify themselves first. The system then dials the person back on their authorised number before allowing them access.

All attempted **violations of security** should be automatically **logged** and the log checked regularly. In a multi-user system, the terminal attempting the violation may be automatically disconnected.

6.5 Jokes and hoaxes

Some programs claim to be doing something destructive to your computer, but are actually 'harmless' jokes. For example, a message may appear suggesting that your hard disk is about to be reformatted. Unfortunately, it is **easy to over-react** to the joke and cause more damage by trying to eradicate something that is not a virus.

There are a number of common hoaxes, which are widely believed. The most common of these is **Good Times**. This hoax has been around for a couple of years, and usually takes the form of a virus warning about viruses contained in e-mail. People pass along the warning because they are trying to be helpful, but they are wasting the time of all concerned.

6.6 The Computer Misuse Act

FAST FORWARD

The (UK) **Computer Misuse Act 1990** was enacted to respond to the growing threat of **hacking** to computer systems and data.

The (UK) Computer Misuse Act 1990 made hacking and the deliberate infection of computer systems with viruses criminal offences. The Act defines three levels of hacking, as shown in the following table.

Crime	Explanation
Unauthorised access	This means that a hacker, who, knowing he or she is unauthorised, tries to gain access to another computer system. It is the **attempt** which is the crime: the hacker's success or failure is irrelevant.
Unauthorised access with the **intention** of committing another offence	This results in **stricter penalties** than unauthorised access alone.
Unauthorised **modification** of data or programs	In effect this makes the deliberate introduction of computer **viruses** into a system a **criminal offence**. Guilt is based on the **intention to impair** the operation of a computer or program, or prevent or **hinder access** to data.

Although the legislation was originally aimed at external unauthorised users of the system, it can also be applied to internal users.

Possible sources of evidence that could be used in a case brought under The Computer Misuse Act include software audit trails, communications link records, Internet Service Provider records and logs such as the operating system transaction log.

6.7 Denial of service attack

A fairly new threat, relating to Internet websites and related systems is the 'Denial of Service (DoS)' attack. A denial of service attack is characterised by an attempt by attackers to prevent legitimate users of a service from using that service. Examples include attempts to:

- 'Flood' or bombard a site or network, thereby preventing legitimate network traffic (major sites, such as Amazon.com and Yahoo! have been targeted in this way)
- Disrupt connections between two machines, thereby preventing access to a service
- Prevent a particular individual from accessing a service

7 Information systems and the accountant

FAST FORWARD

In many organisations the **accountant** plays an **important role** in the **IS/IT** function.

Depending on the size and structure of the organisation, the responsibility for ensuring an organisation's information systems operate efficiently and comply with relevant legislation may fall to the accountant. In other organisations these responsibilities may rest with the Company Secretary or the Information Systems Manager.

Historically, accountants have played an important role in information systems installations. The accounting function was often the first area of an organisation to be computerised and many organisations lacked specialist IS/IT staff.

As the importance of IS/IT has increased large and medium sized organisations have created specialist IS/IT departments. In many smaller organisations the accountant still has responsibility for information systems.

Even in larger organisations, the accountant still has an important role to play in the information systems function. Key areas include:

- Investment appraisal
- Cost-benefit analysis
- Internal audit requirements
- Performance measurement eg metrics
- Presenting user concerns (eg accounts department staff)
- Assessing usability

Chapter Roundup

- **Security** is the protection of data from accidental or deliberate threats and the protection of an information system from such threats.
- **Physical threats** to security may be natural or man made. They include fire, flooding, weather, lightning, terrorist activity and accidental damage.
- **Physical access control** attempts to stop **intruders** or other unauthorised persons getting near to computer equipment or storage media.
- Important aspects of physical access of control are **door locks** and **card entry systems**. Computer theft is becoming more prevalent as equipment becomes smaller and more portable.
- It is possible to **build controls into** a **computerised** information system. .A **balance** must be struck between the degree of control and the requirement for a user friendly system.
- A **back-up** and **archive** strategy should include:
  - Regular back-up of data (at least daily)
  - Archive plans
  - A **disaster recovery** plan including off-site storage
- An **audit trail shows who has accessed a system and the operations performed.**
- A disaster recovery plan must cover all activities from the initial response to a 'disaster', through to damage limitation and full recovery. Responsibilities must be clearly spelt out for all tasks.
- **Privacy** is the right of the individual not to suffer unauthorised disclosure of information.
- The (UK) **Data Protection Act 1998** protects individuals about whom data is held. Both manual and computerised information must comply with the Act.
  - Data users must **register** with the Data Protection Registrar and announce the uses to which the data will be put.
  - The Act contains eight **data protection principles**, to which all data users must adhere.
- Establishing organisational **links to the Internet** brings numerous **security dangers**.
- The (UK) **Computer Misuse Act 1990** was enacted to respond to the growing threat of **hacking** to computer systems and data
- In many organisations the **accountant** plays an **important role** in the **IS/IT** function.

Quick Quiz

1. List three physical access control methods.
2. List four risks to data.
3. What is the purpose of taking a back-up?
4. Why should certain duties be segregated between staff members?
5. List six possible items shown on an accounting package audit trail report.
6. What is 'personal data' under the (UK) Data Protection Act (1998)?
7. Does the (UK) Data Protection Act 1998 cover data held on manual system, on computerised systems or on both manual and computerised systems?

8 Briefly describe the process of encryption.

9 List the three levels of hacking referred to in the (UK) Computer Misuse Act 1990.

10 What is the most common method of spreading a virus?

Answers to Quick Quiz

1 Personnel (security guards), mechanical devices (eg keys), electronic devices (eg card-swipe systems, PIN keypads).

2 Human error
Hardware error
Software error
Deliberate actions
You may have come up with others.

3 To enable valid files to be restored in case of a future corruption or failure.

4 To reduce the opportunity for fraud and/or malicious damage.

5 [Six of]
Transaction number
Transaction date and time
User ID
Transaction type
Amount
Terminal/PC used to input
User entered description or narration

6 Information about a living individual.

7 Both.

8 Encryption involves scrambling data at one end of the communications link, transmitting the scrambled data, then receiving and unscrambling the data at the other end of the link.

9 Unauthorised access, unauthorised access with the intention of modification and finally unauthorised modification.

10 E-mail.

Now try the questions below from the Exam Question Bank

Number	Level	Marks	Time
Q8	Examination	20	36 mins
Q11	Examination	20	36 mins

14

Post-implementation issues

Topic list	Syllabus reference
1 Post-implementation review	3 (g)
2 Systems maintenance	3 (h)
3 End-user development and user groups	3 (h)
4 Evaluation	3 (g), 3 (i)
5 Computer-based monitoring	3 (g)
6 System performance	3 (g)

Introduction

In this final chapter we explore the issues surrounding the running of an Information System.

Throughout its life, a system should operate effectively and efficiently. To do this, the system needs to be **maintained** and its users need to be **supported**. The first half of this chapter looks at how this may be done.

We then look at the **evaluation process.** This aims to ensure the system continues to meet requirements.

Study guide

Part 3.25 – Post implementation issues

- Describe the metrics required to measure the success of the system
- Discuss the procedures that have to be implemented to effectively collect the agreed metrics
- Identify what procedures and personnel should be put in place to support the users of the system
- Explain the possible role of software monitors in measuring the success of the system
- Describe the purpose and conduct of an end-project review and a post-implementation review
- Describe the structure and content of a report from an end-project review and a post-implementation review

Part 3.26 – Change control in systems development and maintenance

- Describe the different types of maintenance that a system may require
- Explain the need for a change control process for dealing with these changes
- Describe a maintenance lifecycle
- Explain the meaning and problems of regression testing
- Discuss the role of user groups and their influence on system requirements

Part 3.27 – Relationship of management, development process and quality

- Discuss the need for automation to improve the efficiency and effectiveness of information systems management, delivery and quality assurance

Part 1.4 – Organising information systems – structural issues

- Discuss the relationship of information systems with end-users and the implications of the expectations and skills of end users

Exam guide

The purpose and conduct of the post-implementation review proved a popular examination topic under the previous syllabus – and is likely to remain so under this syllabus.

1 Post-implementation review

FAST FORWARD

A **post-implementation review** is carried out to see whether the targeted performance criteria have been met, and to review of costs and benefits. The review should culminate in the production of a **report**.

Post-implementation review should establish whether the objectives and targeted performance criteria have been met, and if not, why not, and what should be done about it.

In appraising the operation of the new system immediately after the changeover, comparison should be made between **actual and predicted performance**. This will include:

(a) Consideration of **throughput speed** (time between input and output).
(b) Use of computer **storage** (both internal and external).
(c) The number and type of **errors/queries**.
(d) The **cost** of processing (data capture, preparation, storage and output media, etc).

A special **steering committee** may be set up to ensure that post-implementation reviews are carried out, although the **internal audit** department may be required to do the work of carrying out the reviews.

The post-implementation measurements should **not be made too soon** after the system goes live, or else results will be abnormally affected by 'teething' problems, lack of user familiarity and resistance to change.

1.1 The post-implementation review report

The findings of a post-implementation review team should be formalised in a **report**.

(a) A **summary** of their findings should be provided, emphasising any areas where the system has been found to be **unsatisfactory**.

(b) A review of **system performance** should be provided. This will address the matters outlined above, such as run times and error rates.

(c) A **cost-benefit review** should be included, comparing the forecast costs and benefits identified at the time of the feasibility study with actual costs and benefits.

(d) **Recommendations** should be made as to any **further action** or steps which should be taken to improve performance.

2 Systems maintenance

2.1 Types of maintenance

FAST FORWARD

There are three types of systems maintenance. **Corrective** maintenance is carried out following a systems failure, **perfective** maintenance aims to make enhancements and **adaptive** maintenance takes account of anticipated changes in the processing environment.

There are three types of maintenance activity.

- Corrective – to fix a problem or failure
- Perfective – to improve ineffeciencies
- Adaptive – to fit the new environment

Key terms

Corrective maintenance is carried out when there is a systems failure of some kind, for example in processing or in an implementation procedure. Its objective is to ensure that systems remain operational.

Perfective maintenance is carried out in order to perfect the software, or to improve software so that the processing inefficiencies are eliminated and performance is enhanced.

Adaptive maintenance is carried out to take account of anticipated changes in the processing environment. For example new taxation legislation might require change to be made to payroll software.

The key features of system maintenance ought to be **flexibility** and **adaptability**.

(a) The system, perhaps with minor modifications, should cope with changes in the computer user's procedures or volume of business.

(b) The computer user should benefit from advances in computer hardware technology without having to switch to another system altogether.

2.2 The causes of systems maintenance

Besides environmental changes, three factors contribute to the need for maintenance.

Factor	Comment
Errors	However carefully and diligently the systems development staff carry out systems testing and program testing, it is likely that bugs will exist in a newly implemented system. The effect of errors can obviously vary enormously.
Constraints	Cost constraints may have meant that certain requested features were not incorporated. Time constraints may have meant that requirements suggested during development were ignored in the interest of prompt completion.
Changes in requirements	Although users should be consulted at all stages of systems development, problems may arise after a system is implemented because users may have found it difficult to express their requirements, or may have been concerned about the future of their jobs and not participated fully in development.
Poor documentation	If old systems are accompanied by poor documentation, or even a complete lack of documentation, it may be very difficult to understand their programs. It will be hard to update or maintain such programs. Programmers may opt instead to patch up the system with new applications using newer technology.

2.3 The systems maintenance lifecycle

Corrective and adaptive maintenance should be carried out **as and when** problems occur, but perfective maintenance may be carried out on a more scheduled system-by-system basis.

If maintenance requires major changes to bespoke software, this will involve all the tasks included in the software development and testing cycle – as explained in Chapter 10.

Systems should be built with a certain amount of flexibility that allows changes to be made in the future to cope with different demands. Changing a system carries the same risks associated with the initial system development. Any system changes should therefore pass through a formal change procedure.

2.4 System change procedure

Components of a formal system change procedure	
Purpose of the component	**Comment**
Raise the change request	This is a definition of the required change in business functionality. It is usually specified in business terms. For example, 'the ability to support three regions rather than one'. The reason for the required change should be specified, with business benefits defined and quantified.
Evaluate the impact of the requested change	The change is investigated and the time and cost taken to develop, test and implement the change is estimated. This time and cost must take into account the total impact of the change on the system. The cost of the change is compared with the benefits that it will bring (defined in the previous stage) and if the decision is taken to proceed, then a priority is allocated to the change.

Components of a formal system change procedure	
Purpose of the component	**Comment**
Specify the change request	A detailed specification for the change is prepared by the systems developer. This detailed specification must be developed in consultation with, and subsequently signed off by, user representatives.
Program and unit testing the change	Programmers write the program code, and then unit testing is carried out.
Regression, system and acceptance testing	Following unit testing, the amended program is tested in a realistic environment. (Regression testing is explained later in this section.)
Implement the change	Following user acceptance testing, the changes are implemented on the live system.

2.5 In-house maintenance

With **large computer systems**, developed by the organisation itself, **in-house** systems analysts and programmers might be given the responsibility for **software** maintenance.

2.5.1 Good practice

To ensure that maintenance is carried out efficiently, the principles of **good programming practice** should be applied.

(a) Any change must be **properly authorised** by a manager in the user department (or someone even more senior, if necessary).

(b) The new program requirements must be **specified in full and in writing**. These specifications will be prepared by a systems analyst. A programmer should use these specifications to produce an amended version of the program.

(c) In developing a new program version, a programmer should keep **working papers**. He or she can refer back to these papers later to check in the event that there is an error in the new program or the user of the program asks for a further change in the program.

(d) The new program version should be **tested** when it has been written. A programmer should prepare test data and establish whether the program will process the data according to the specifications given by the systems analyst.

(e) **Provisions** should be made for **further program amendments** in the future. One way of doing this is to leave space in the program instruction numbering sequence for new instructions to be inserted later. For example, instructions might be numbered 10,20,30,40 etc instead of 1,2,3,4.

(f) A **record** should be kept of **all program errors** that are found during 'live' processing and of the corrections that are made to the program.

(g) Each **version** of a program (versions that are produced with processing modifications or corrections to errors) should be **separately identified**, to avoid a mix-up about what version of a program should be used for 'live' operating.

2.5.2 Regression testing

A problem with systems development and maintenance is that it is **hard to predict all the effects of a change** to the system.

A 'simple' software change in one area of the system may have unpredicted effects elsewhere. It is important therefore to carry out **regression testing**.

Key term

> **Regression testing** involves the retesting of software that has been modified to fix 'bugs'. It aims to ensure that the bugs have been fixed **and** that no other previously working functions have failed as a result of the changes.

Regression testing involves **repeating system tests** that had been executed correctly before the recent changes were made.

Only the changes expected as a result of the system maintenance should occur under the regression test – other changes could be due to errors caused by the recent change.

Problems with regression testing include:

- Deciding on the extent of testing required
- Envisaging all areas possibly effected
- Convincing users and programmers that the tests are necessary

2.6 Off-the-shelf software maintenance

With ready-made software, the **software house** or **supplier** is likely to issue a new version of a package if significant changes are required.

2.6.1 Maintenance contracts

There is also likely to be an **agreement** between the supplier of software and the customer for the provision of a **software support service**. A maintenance contract typically includes the following services.

(a) **Help**

When a customer runs into difficulties operating the system help will initially be given by a **telephone 'hot line'**. If a telephone call does not resolve the problem, the software expert may arrange to visit the customer's premises (within a period of time agreed in the contract), although this would be rare for standard packages.

(b) **Information**

Extra information about using the package may be provided through factsheets or a magazine sent free to subscribers. This may include **case studies** showing how other users have benefited from using the package in a particular way and **technical tips** for common user problems

(c) **Updates**

Free updates are provided to **correct errors** in part of a package, or if there is something **inevitable** that will mean that some aspect of a package **has to be changed**. For example payroll software has to reflect the latest Finance Act.

(d) **Upgrades**

When the **whole package** is revised the contract often provides for subscribers to get the new version at a heavily **discounted price**. Upgrades usually include **new features** not found in the previous versions or updates.

(e) **Legal conditions**

There will be provisions about the **duration** of the contract and in what circumstances it terminates, about the **customer's obligations** to use the software in the way it was intended to be used, on the right sort of hardware, and not to make illegal copies. The **liability of the supplier** will also be set out, especially regarding consequential loss.

2.7 Hardware maintenance

Computer **hardware** should be kept serviced and maintained too. Maintenance services are provided by:

- The computer **manufacturers**
- **Third-party** maintenance companies

Maintenance of hardware can be obtained:

- On a **contract** basis
- On an **ad hoc** basis

3 End-user development and user groups

3.1 End-user development

End-user computing has been fuelled by the introduction of **PCs** to user departments, by **user-friendly software**, and by **greater awareness** of computers and what they can do.

Key term

> **End-user development** is the direct, hands-on development of computer systems by users.

Accounts staff designing and using complex **spreadsheet models** is an example of end-user computing.

Many users who develop their own applications have **little or no formal training** in programming, consequently their programs might be extremely crude and virtually incomprehensible.

While these programs may work they will be very **difficult to modify** and they will very often be the personal property of the individual who developed the system, with **no wider use**. This is undesirable from the organisation's viewpoint: a great deal of time and energy is going into producing inefficient programs which are unusable by anyone other than their developer.

Other disadvantages are as follows:

(a) The risk from the elimination of the **separation of the functions of user and analyst**.

(b) The risk from **limits on user ability** to identify correct and complete requirements for an application.

(c) The risk from **lack of user knowledge and acceptance of application quality assurance procedures** for development and operation.

(d) The risk from **unstable user systems**.

(e) The risk from encouraging **private information systems**.

(f) The risk from permitting **unstructured information systems development**.

3.2 User groups

FAST FORWARD

User groups enable personnel who come into contact with a particular system to meet and share their views.

The concept of user groups has existed in the computer industry for some time.

Key term

A **user group** is a forum for users of particular hardware or, more usually, software, so that they can **share ideas and experience**.

User groups are usually set up either by the software manufacturers themselves (who use them to **maintain contact** with customers and as a source of **new product ideas**) or by groups of users. The term is used most commonly with users of packaged software.

Users of a particular package can meet, or perhaps exchange views over the **Internet** to discuss solutions, ideas or 'short cuts' to improve productivity. An (electronic) newsletter service might be appropriate, based on views exchanged by members, but also incorporating ideas culled from the wider environment by IT specialists.

Sometimes user groups are set up **within** individual organisations. Where an organisation has written its own application software, or is using tailor-made software, there will be a very **small knowledge base** initially, and there will obviously not be a national user group, because the application is unique.

'Interested parties', including, as a minimum, representatives from the **IT department** and **users** who are familiar with different parts of the system can attend monthly or quarterly **meetings** to discuss the **operation** of the system, make **suggestions for improvements** (such as the production of new reports or time-tabling of processing) and raise any **queries**.

Question

End user computing

The increased use of PCs and wide availability of sophisticated general purpose packages have resulted in more responsibility for information systems being transferred to end-users. What problems may this result in for organisations?

Answer

Here are some suggestions.

(a) Lack of formal training could result in inefficient or even 'faulty' systems.

(b) User requests for assistance that overwhelm the IS/IT department.

(c) Lack of user knowledge or concern may lead to inadequate controls being built into the system.

(d) Lack of integration across the organisation with many users developing systems to suit themselves.

(e) Poor maintainability of user-developed systems as only the person that developed it understands it

(f) Lack of centralised management of resources.

(g) A lack of understanding of the organisations use of IS/IT may develop – it becomes difficult to see the 'big picture'.

4 Evaluation

FAST FORWARD

A system can be **evaluated** by reference to technical, operational, social and economic factors.

In most systems there is a constant need to maintain and improve applications and to keep up to date with technological advances and changing user requirements. A system should therefore be **reviewed** after implementation, and periodically, so that any unforeseen problems may be solved and to confirm that it is achieving the desired results.

The system should have been designed with clear, specified **objectives**, and justification in terms of **cost-benefit analysis** or other **performance criteria**.

Just as the feasibility of a project is assessed by reference to **technical, operational, social and economic factors**, so the same criteria can be used for evaluation. We need not repeat material that you have covered earlier, but here are a few pointers.

4.1 Cost-benefit review

A cost-benefit review is similar to a cost-benefit analysis, except that **actual** data can be used.

For instance when a large project is completed, techniques such as **DCF appraisal** can be performed **again**, with actual figures being available for much of the expenditure.

Question — Cost and benefits

A cost-benefit review might categorise items under the five headings of direct benefits, indirect benefits, development costs, implementation costs and running costs.

Give two examples of items which could fall to be evaluated under each heading.

Answer

Direct benefits might include reduced operating costs, for example lower overtime payments.

Indirect benefits might include better decision-making and the freeing of human 'brainpower' from routine tasks so that it can be used for more creative work.

Development costs include systems analysts' costs and the cost of time spent by users in assisting with fact-finding.

Implementation costs would include costs of site preparation and costs of training.

Running costs include maintenance costs, software leasing costs and on-going user support.

4.2 Efficiency and effectiveness

FAST FORWARD

Efficiency is a measure of how well **resources** have been utilised irrespective of the purpose for which they are employed. **Effectiveness** is a measure of whether the organisation has achieved its **objectives**.

In any evaluation of a system, two terms recur. Two key reasons for the introduction of information systems into an organisation are to improve the **efficiency** or the **effectiveness** of the organisation.

Key term

> **Efficiency** can be measured by considering the resource **inputs** into, and the **outputs** from, a process or an activity.

An activity uses **resources** such as staff, money and materials. If the same activity can be performed using **fewer resources**, for example fewer staff or less money, or if it can be completed **more quickly**, the efficiency of the activity is improved. An improvement in efficiency represents an improvement in **productivity**.

Automation of an organisation's activities is usually expected to lead to greater efficiency in a number of areas.

(a) The **cost** of a computer system is lower than that of the manual system it replaces, principally because jobs previously performed by human operators are now carried out by computer.

(b) The **accuracy** of data information and processing is improved, because a computer does not make mistakes.

(c) The **speed** of processing is improved. Response times, for example in satisfying customer orders, are improved.

Key term

> **Effectiveness** is a measurement of how well the organisation is achieving its **objectives**.

Effectiveness is a **more subjective** concept than efficiency, as it is concerned with factors which are less easy to measure. It focuses primarily on the relationship of the organisation with its environment. For example, automation might be pursued because it is expected that the company will be more effective at **increasing market share** or at satisfying **customer needs**.

Computing was originally concerned with the automation of **'back office'** functions, usually aspects of data processing. Development was concerned with improving **efficiency**.

Recent trends are more towards the development of **'front office'** systems, for example to improve an organisation's decision-making capability or to seek competitive advantage. This approach seeks to improve the **effectiveness** of the organisation.

4.3 Metrics

Key term

> **Metrics** are quantified measurements used to measure system performance.

The use of **metrics** enables **system quality** to be **measured** and the early identification of problems.

Examples of metrics include system response time, the number of transactions that can be processed per minute, the number of bugs per hundred lines of code and the number of system crashes per week.

Metrics should be devised that **suit the system in question** – those given above are simply typical examples.

Many facets of system quality are **not easy to measure** statistically (eg user-friendliness). Indirect measurements such as the number of calls to the help-desk per month can be use as an indication of overall quality/performance.

Metrics should be carefully thought out, objective and stated **clearly**. They must measure **significant aspects** of the system, be used consistently and **agreed with users.**

5 Computer-based monitoring

FAST FORWARD

Systems evaluation may use **computer-based monitoring**. Methods include the use of hardware monitors, software monitors and systems logs.

Computers themselves can be used in systems evaluation. Three methods used are hardware monitors, software monitors and systems logs.

5.1 Hardware monitors

Hardware monitors are devices which measure the presence or absence of electrical signals in selected circuits in the computer hardware.

They might measure **idle time** or **levels of activity** in the CPU, or peripheral activity. Data is sent from the sensors to counters, which periodically write it to disk or tape.

A program will then **analyse** the data and produce an analysis of findings as output. It might identify for example **inefficient co-ordination** of processors and peripherals, or **excessive delays** in writing data to backing storage.

5.2 Software monitors

Software monitors are computer programs which **interrupt the application in use** and record data about it. They might identify, for example, **excessive waiting** time during program execution. Unlike hardware monitors, they may slow down the operation of the program being monitored.

5.3 System logs

Many computer systems provide automatic log details, for example **job start and finish** times or which employee has used which program and for how long. The systems log can therefore provide useful data for analysis.

(a) Unexplained **variations in job running** times might be recorded.
(b) Excessive machine **down-time** is sometimes a problem.
(c) **Mixed workloads** of large and small jobs might be scheduled inefficiently.

6 System performance

6.1 Performance measurement

It is not possible to identify and isolate every consequence of a project and the impact of each on organisational effectiveness. To achieve some approximation to a complete evaluation, therefore, certain **indirect measures** must be used.

(a) **Significant task relevance** attempts to observe the results of system use.

For example, document turnround times might have improved following the acquisition of a document image processing system, or minutes of meetings might be made available and distributed faster following the addition of a company secretarial function to a local area network.

(b) The **willingness** of users **to pay** might give an indication of value.

Charge-out mechanisms may provide an indication of how much users would be prepared to pay in order to gain the benefit of a certain upgrade, for example the availability of a particular report.

(c) **Systems logs** may give an indication of the value of the system if it is a 'voluntary use' system, such as an external database.

(d) **User information satisfaction** is a concept which attempts to find out, by asking users, how they rate their satisfaction with a system. They may be asked for their views on timeliness, quality of output, response times, processing and their overall confidence in the system.

(e) The adequacy of system **documentation** may be measurable in terms of how often manuals are actually used and the number of errors found or amendments made. However, low usage of a user manual, for instance, may mean either that the manual is unclear or that the system is easy to operate.

Question

Evaluating the use of information

Operational evaluation should consider, among other issues, whether input data is properly provided and output is useful. Output documents are often produced simply because 'we always print it'.

How might you identify whether a report is being used?

Answer

You could simply ask recipients if they would object to the report being withdrawn.

A questionnaire could be circulated asking what each recipient of the report does with it and assess its importance.

A charge-out system could be implemented – this would be a strong incentive to cancel requests for unnecessary output.

6.1.1 Performance reviews

FAST FORWARD

Performance reviews can be carried out to look at a wide range of systems functions and characteristics. Technological change often gives scope to **improve** the quality of outputs or reduce the cost of inputs.

Performance reviews will vary in content from organisation to organisation, but the matters which will probably be looked at are as follows.

(a) The **growth** rates in file sizes and the number of transactions processed by the system. Trends should be analysed and projected to assess whether there are likely to be problems with lengthy processing time or an inefficient file structure due to the volume of processing.

(b) The clerical **manpower** needs for the system, and deciding whether they are more or less than estimated.

(c) The identification of any **delays** in processing and an assessment of the consequences of any such delays.

(d) An assessment of the efficiency of **security** procedures, in terms of number of breaches, number of viruses encountered.

(e) A check of the **error rates** for input data. High error rates may indicate inefficient preparation of input documents, an inappropriate method of data capture or poor design of input media.

(f) An examination of whether **output** from the computer is being used to good purpose. (Is it used? Is it timely? Does it go to the right people?)

(g) Operational **running costs**, examined to discover any inefficient programs or processes. This examination may reveal excessive costs for certain items although in total, costs may be acceptable.

6.2 Improving performance

Computer systems efficiency audits are concerned with improving **outputs** from the system and their use and/or reducing the costs of system **inputs**. With falling costs of computer hardware and software, and continual technological advances, there should often be **scope for improvements** in computer systems.

6.2.1 Outputs from a computer system

With regard to outputs, the efficiency of a computer system would be enhanced in any of the following ways.

(a) **More outputs** of some value could be produced by the **same input** resources.

For example:

(i) If the system could process **more transactions** per minute.

(ii) If the system could produce **better quality management information** (eg sensitivity analysis).

(iii) If the system could make information **available to more people**.

(b) **Outputs of little value** could be **eliminated** from the system, thus making savings in the cost of inputs, processing and handling.

For example:

(i) If reports are produced **too frequently**, should they be produced less often?
(ii) If reports are **distributed too widely**, should the distribution list be shortened?
(iii) If reports are **too bulky**, can they be reduced in size?

(c) The **timing** of outputs could be better.

Information should be available in good time for the information-user to be able to make good use of it. Reports that are issued late might lose their value. Computer systems could give managers **immediate** access to the information they require, by means of file enquiry or special software (such as databases or spreadsheet modelling packages).

(d) It might be found that outputs are not as satisfactory as they should be, perhaps because:

(i) **Access** to information from the system is limited, and could be improved by the use of a **database** and a **network** system.

(ii) Available outputs are **restricted** because of the **method of data processing** used (eg batch processing instead of real-time processing) or the **type of equipment** used (eg stand-alone PCs compared with client/server systems).

Question **System capabilities**

What elements of hardware and software might restrict the capabilities of a system?

Answer

A system's capabilities might be limited by the following restrictions.

(a) The size of the computer's memory.
(b) The power of the processor.
(c) The capacity of the computer's backing storage.
(d) The number of printers available.
(e) The number of terminals.
(f) The software's capabilities.

6.2.2 Inputs to a computer system

The efficiency of a computer system could be improved if the same volume (and frequency) of output could be achieved with **fewer input** resources, and at **less cost**. Here's how.

(a) **Multi-user or network systems might be more efficient than stand-alone systems.** Multi-user systems allow several input operators to work on the same files at the same time, so that if one person has a heavy workload and another is currently short of work, the person who has some free time can help his or her busy colleague – thus improving operator efficiency.

(b) **Real-time** systems might be more efficient than batch processing.

(c) Using computers and external storage media with **bigger storage** capacity. A frequent complaint is that **'waiting time'** for the operator can be very long and tedious. Computer systems with better backing storage facilities can reduce this operator waiting time, and so be more efficient.

(d) Using more **up-to-date software**.

Management might also wish to consider whether time spent **checking and correcting** input data can be eliminated. An **alternative method of input** might be chosen. For example bar codes and scanners should eliminate the need to check for input errors.

Chapter Roundup

- A **post-implementation review** is carried out to see whether the targeted performance criteria have been met, and to review of costs and benefits. The review should culminate in the production of a **report**.
- There are three types of systems maintenance. **Corrective** maintenance is carried out following a systems failure, **perfective** maintenance aims to make enhancements and **adaptive** maintenance takes account of anticipated changes in the processing environment.
- **User groups** enable personnel who come into contact with a particular system to meet and share their views.
- A system can be **evaluated** by reference to technical, operational, social and economic factors.
- **Efficiency** is a measure of how well **resources** have been utilised irrespective of the purpose for which they are employed. **Effectiveness** is a measure of whether the organisation has achieved its **objectives**.
- Systems evaluation may use **computer-based monitoring**. Methods include the use of hardware monitors, software monitors and systems logs.
- **Performance reviews** can be carried out to look at a wide range of systems functions and characteristics. Technological change often gives scope to **improve** the quality of outputs or reduce the cost of inputs.

Quick Quiz

1. What should the post-implementation review establish?
2. Adaptive maintenance is carried out to fix 'bugs'. TRUE or FALSE?
3. What is the purpose of regression testing?
4. Define 'end-user development'.
5. What is an information centre?
6. How does a cost-benefit review differ from a cost-benefit analysis?
7. What are metrics used for?
8. What does a systems efficiency audit measure?

Answers to Quick Quiz

1 Whether the system objectives and targeted performance criteria have been met.

2 FALSE. See section 2.1.

3 To ensure a change to a program has not resulted in unforeseen changes elsewhere in the system.

4 The direct, hands-on development of computer systems without the involvement of systems professionals.

5 A unit of staff with good awareness of computer systems who provide support to users.

6 The review uses actual data. The analysis relies on estimates.

7 To measure system quality.

8 The efficiency of the system. The audit focuses on inputs and outputs.

Now try the questions below from the Exam Question Bank

Number	Level	Marks	Time
Q12	Examination	20	36 mins
Q15	Examination	20	36 mins

Exam question bank

Questions 14 – 19 of this Exam question bank are from the **Pilot Paper**.

Questions 18 and 19 include **detailed guidance** within the question and answer.

Read the **Scenario guidance** at the front of this question bank before attempting any questions.

Tackling Scenario questions

Tackling the 60 mark scenario

Section A of the Paper 2.1 examination comprises a written scenario with three compulsory questions, each worth 20 marks.

A scenario is simply a history or description of an organisation facing a particular set of circumstances. There is usually some discussion of how the organisation's current situation developed, and there is often one or more central characters charged with the task of resolving the problem, or exploiting the opportunity.

The essential function of this type of question is to test a candidate's ability to tackle relatively complex, unstructured problems. There **may be several feasible solutions** and candidates should not necessarily expect there to be a single definitive answer. The solution will involve the use of techniques which have been learned, but usually also requires the exercise of judgement and (possibly) creative thinking. Preparation to answer case/scenario-based questions cannot rely on reading alone, but must be heavily supplemented **by question practice under examination conditions**.

It is important to realise that with scenario-based questions, marks are earned through a combination of the subject matter contained in the answer and the quality of the reasoning and exposition displayed. Recommendations may be required. Acceptable recommendations may vary, but must be sensible and fully justified. Drawing on your own practical experience is often useful.

Candidates' chances of success will be significantly enhanced if they are **familiar with the current business environment**. An easy way to achieve this is to read selectively from the *Financial Times* and other business publications and websites.

Key points to remember when tackling scenario questions

- Answer the question asked – tailor what you know to fit the question requirements
- Plan your answer – this will help clarify your thoughts
- Structure your answer eg introduction, body of answer, conclusion
- Justify your recommendations

1 Characteristics of information — 14 mins

Required

Describe the characteristics that should apply to information supplied to a Finance Director to ensure that the information is easy to understand. (8 marks)

Questions 2 – 4 are based on the following scenario

The Accounting Academy (AA) is a specialist ACCA training company offering Study Schools in Foundation, Certificate and Professional Stage examination papers. It was formed eight years ago by the charismatic lecturer and author Jon Lowe. The courses are essentially pre-revision courses intended to concentrate students' minds for the final revision phase. The company currently organises 15 courses in 7 different countries for each examination sitting. These courses are residential and are held in universities or conference centres. The Foundation Stage is covered in a five day course and the Certificate and Professional Stages combined in a nine day course. The average attendance is 30 on a Foundation course, 25 on a Certificate and 50 at the Professional level.

Jon Lowe is currently Course Director of the Accounting Academy and the only full-time lecturer. All other lecturers are freelance. Courses are advertised in accounting publications throughout the world. The Study Schools achieve pass rates well above the national average.

The company's headquarters are in London where three administrative assistants handle enquiries, take course bookings, send out joining instructions, photocopy lecture notes and book conference facilities and lecturers. A further administrative assistant maintains the accounting records on a single user personal computer (PC). The office suite occupied by AA is divided into the Admin. Office, a small Accounts Office, a meeting room and Jon Lowe's office. The total space occupied is about 1200 sq. feet.

A year ago Jon Lowe decided to seek new investment in the company. Initial meetings with an investment group were successful and the investors commissioned a business review to identify the company's strengths and weaknesses. The review summarised these as follows:

Strengths

Consistent achievement of high pass rates
International reputation of Jon Lowe
High quality residential conference centre provision
Focus on ACCA examinations
Pre-payment for courses leads to strong cashflow position

Weaknesses

Strong seasonal variation in cash flow
Over-reliance on the lecturing of Jon Lowe
Time-consuming administrative procedures
Inadequate and untimely financial information
Inconsistency in the quality of course material produced by individual freelance lecturers

As a result of their review, the new investors have suggested that the company should begin to employ full-time lecturers and offer an all-year-round course programme covering full-time courses, Study Schools and Revision Courses. Their plan also suggests that ways should be found to exploit related markets. The plan has been accepted by Jon Lowe and the company's bankers.

However, it is envisaged that there will be a six-fold increase in student numbers in the next three years and hence a thorough review of the company's administrative procedures has been recommended because it is recognised that these are unlikely to be adequate to meet the requirements of the newly expanded company. A preliminary interview has been held with administrative staff. The summarised results of this meeting follow:

Administrative arrangements

The three staff in the Admin. Office all undertake the following tasks:

They take telephone and written enquiries from students about the Study Schools. Each enquiry is logged on a standard form giving the enquirer's name, address, details of the enquiry itself, action taken and the source of the enquiry. The last piece of information is particularly important as it allows the Academy to target its advertising more carefully. Consequently, the assistant must look at a standard Source List while processing the enquiry and code it accordingly. Typical codes are:

0001 The Accounting Professional
0002 Accountants Training Update
0003 Accountancy Today... etc
0020 Personal recommendation

The enquiry forms are stored in order of receipt until the end of the week. On the following Monday one of the administrative assistants goes through each enquiry form to create an Enquiry Summary List which is sent to Jon Lowe. This is a list of each source code, the source description and the number of enquiries logged the previous week for each source. This information is taken into consideration by Jon Lowe when he is reviewing his advertising strategy.

Completed application forms from students are also handled in this office. The application form is checked against the Course list to make sure that valid dates and courses have been booked. The application form must be accompanied with a cheque or bankers draft for the full Study School fee. If a payment is not enclosed or invalid dates or courses have been booked then the application form is returned to the student with an explanatory note. However, if the course details are correct and a payment has been enclosed then the application form is copied and the copy sent with the payment to Edith Donaldson who handles accounting and financial matters. She will also deal with any over or under-payment of the course fee. The original copy of the application form is filed in the appropriate section of a ring binder and a booking confirmation letter is sent to the student. This is produced on an electronic typewriter.

Four weeks before the course, joining instructions are sent to each student due to attend. These are currently prepared on an electronic typewriter. The assistant checks the venue (from the Course List) and calls in a set of standard paragraphs concerning administrative and travel arrangements for that venue. The student's name and address is found on the application form in the binder and is individually typed in. A Delegate List is also typed up and sent to the Lecturer showing delegate name, company and any special dietary requirements. A copy of this is also sent to the conference centre where the course is being held.

Once the course is completed the lecturer collects post-course questionnaires from the students and sends them to the Admin. Office. These are stored until time allows one of the assistants to type up a one-page summary report to send to Jon Lowe. This report is essentially a statistical summary of the questionnaires together with positive and negative comments entered by the delegate. Particularly adverse statements will be followed up by Jon Lowe.

2 The Accounting Academy: Feasibility study — 36 mins

The company intends to undertake a feasibility study to identify the costs and benefits of computerisation.

Required

(a) Identify and briefly describe four areas of the current or proposed business that you recommend should be included within the scope of such a study. (10 marks)

(b) Justify your selection of the business areas by discussing the business benefits that should result from their computerisation. (10 marks)

3 The accounting academy: 'Off-the-shelf' v bespoke software; security issues — 36 mins

The head of the investment group is keen for the rapid computerisation of the company. He has indicated that he wishes to fulfil system requirements using 'off-the-shelf' application software packages rather than commissioning a bespoke software solution.

Required

(a) Discuss four potential disadvantages or problems of adopting this approach at the Accounting Academy. (10 marks)

(b) It is likely that the system will be implemented with a PC network linked to a central file server. What are the security and audit issues raised by this type of implementation and what steps and precautions might be taken to address these? (10 marks)

4 The Accounting Academy: Process model (DFD) 36 mins

Required

(a) Draw a Process Model (Data Flow Diagram) of the administrative arrangements described in the notes summarising the preliminary meeting with staff of the Accounting Academy. **(15 marks)**

(b) Provide an explanatory key to this model. **(5 marks)**

5 Cost-benefit analysis; critical path 36 mins

You are the project manager responsible for a proposed new computer-based application for a medium sized retail chain.

Required

(a) Identify and briefly describe four investment appraisal techniques you could use to demonstrate the costs and benefits of the proposed new system. **(10 marks)**

You have drawn up an outline timetable for the introduction of the new system. The first draft of this is shown below.

Task	*Description*	*Planned duration (weeks)*	*Preceding activities*
A	Communication – inform staff at each shop of the proposal and indicate how it will affect them	1	-
B	Carry out systems audit at each shop	2	A
C	Agree detailed implementation plan with board of directors	1	B
D	Order and receive hardware requirements	4	C
E	Install hardware at all shops	4	D
F	Install software at all shops	2	D
G	Arrange training	3	D
H	Test systems at all shops	4	E and F
I	Implement changeover at all shops	10	G and H

(b) Produce a critical path analysis of the draft implementation plan. (This should identify the critical path and the total elapsed time.) **(10 marks)**

Questions 6 – 8 are based on the following scenario

Bay Town Health Centre is a non-profit-making medical practice serving a small town. It employs four doctors, one nurse, one receptionist and a clerk. All managerial decisions are taken by the four doctors.

There are approximately seven thousand patients registered with the practice. The state pays a fee to the practice for each registered patient. The income from the state is sufficient to fund the operating costs of the practice and the salaries of the doctors and support staff. The doctors can supplement their income by treating a small number of private patients and by performing minor operations. In such cases the doctor will pay a charge to the practice to cover the use of the facilities in the medical centre.

Approximately seven years ago the doctors purchased a computerised database to record patient details, medical history and treatment given. All accounting functions are paper-based. Recent changes in legislation require the practice to submit monthly reports that provide accurate figures for:

- The number of registered patients
- The number of patients treated in the preceding month
- The cost of the treatment
- The administrative costs for the preceding month
- Any income received from private patients

The doctors believe that there is no alternative other than to replace the existing information system with a new, integrated system if they are to meet the demands of the new legislation. In addition, the doctors would like the new system to provide electronic diaries for work-scheduling and making appointments for patients, on-line searching of medical literature and the automatic generation of repeat prescriptions for patients who have long-term treatment.

6 Bay Town Health Centre: Costs and benefits 36 mins

Required

Identify, with your reasons, the costs and benefits of purchasing a new information system for the practice. **(20 marks)**

7 Bay Town Health Centre: Decision making 36 mins

Required

'A new information system always aids decision making'. **Discuss the validity of this statement both in general terms and with respect to the practice.** **(20 marks)**

8 Bay Town Health Centre: Ensuring accuracy 36 mins

Required

Outline the steps that you would take to ensure that information held on the new system would be secure, accurate and coherent. **(20 marks)**

9 Gantt chart 36 mins

The Drugs Advisory Service is a charitable organisation which provides advice and counselling to clients from three offices in residential areas approximately twenty miles apart. The service was established three years ago and funded by the government. New funding arrangements have recently been agreed with the Health Authority under a contract which obliges the service to measure all aspects of its performance and provide information which indicates that it is giving 'value for money'. Many of the counsellors feel that completing statistical records is inappropriate to the work they do, especially in dealing with very distressed clients.

Required

Prepare a Gantt chart to show the principal project management stages in preparing to meet the new information requirements of the funders. **(20 marks)**

Questions 10 – 12 are based on the following scenario

SWM Ltd is a manufacturing company with three divisions, all of which operate from the same site. The company's main finished goods warehouse is located about one mile away. The main manufacturing site is the location for all other functions, including the IT department.

The company runs a corporate database on a mainframe computer with networked terminals. The terminals do not at present have any independent processing capacity. Departmental managers have become concerned at the speed of processing when several applications or users require computer time at the same time. The chief executive has also expressed concern about the high cost of software maintenance.

The warehouse stock records are maintained on a minicomputer in the warehouse. Each morning, details of the previous day's sales orders taken are sent by courier to the warehouse. The data, which is stored on a floppy disk, is downloaded to the warehouse system, which generates despatch documentation, including invoices, and picking lists. The warehouse's 'free' and 'allocated' stock records are updated.

At the end of each day, details of stock movements are sent to the main site and the mainframe's stock records are updated. These are referred to by sales order processing staff to ensure goods are in stock when booking orders. Copy invoices are also sent to the accounts department for posting to customer ledgers.

A recent review of software maintenance costs by the chief accountant has revealed the following.

(a) The mainframe has limited reporting capabilities. Recent requests for the provision of reports of sales by region and by product group have resulted in substantial reprogramming effort in order to add the required fields and routines.

(b) It is not possible to produce reports containing summary level information at the same time as routine reports are generated. This has meant that senior managers either content themselves with working with the long transactions listings used by operational staff in the relevant department or ask subordinates to prepare summaries 'manually', which the latter usually do with spreadsheet packages.

10 SWM Ltd: System deficiencies — 36 mins

Required

Write a report to Departmental Managers identifying any information deficiencies in the current system and recommending ways in which the processing of data could be speeded up. **(20 marks)**

11 SWM Ltd: System controls — 36 mins

Required

What controls should be adopted to retain the integrity and the security of the data in the system. **(20 marks)**

12 SWM Ltd: Software maintenance — 36 mins

Required

Draft a report to the chief executive describing the types of software maintenance encountered in computer systems. **(20 marks)**

13 New system implementation — 36 mins

A new company is to be formed by the merger of two existing organisations to set up a national chain of cash and carry retail shops for cut-price furniture and kitchen units. A characteristic of the company policy is to be centralised stock control, with small local stocks and twice-weekly deliveries to each store. As management accountant you have been nominated as a member of a feasibility study team being formed to evaluate the proposals from different manufacturers for the supply of computer hardware and software to implement the required information system.

Required

State who you would expect to see as the other members of a feasibility study team of five. (2 marks)

(b) **Identify the major information requirements of the system. (4 marks)**

(c) **Describe the principal stages involved in the implementation of the proposed system in the 100 shops already open for business which, at present, operate rather different systems. (10 marks)**

(d) **Explain the criteria used to evaluate the choice of system. (4 marks)**

14 User requirements — 36 mins

A business analyst is preparing to interview a user about how insurance claims are handled by the business.

Required

(a) **Briefly describe four specific activities the business analyst should undertake in preparation for the meeting. (8 marks)**

During the meeting, the user specifies the following requirements.

Insurance claims are received into the department. On receipt they are defined as Pending Claims. A Claims Inspector reviews the claims. The result of the review is either an Accepted Claim or a Rejected Claim. Accepted Claims are then paid. After six months all Paid Claims are archived.

(b) **Construct a flowchart model for this business requirement. (8 marks)**

(c) **Provide an explanatory key to this model so that the user can understand it. (4 marks)**

15 Post-implementation and change issues — 36 mins

Required

(a) **Describe the meaning and purpose of a post-implementation review. (5 marks)**

The Human Resources Directors of a large company wants to measure the success of the application software he has commissioned and implemented for a personnel system.

(b) **Briefly describe three measures he could use to quantify the success of the application software and state what each of these three measures is attempting to assess. (8 marks)**

It is expected that the user will define new requirements (and change old ones) throughout the life of the system.

(c) **List the components of a procedure for recording, prioritising and implementing these changes. (7 marks)**

Questions 16 – 18 are based on the following scenario

CAET Insurance offers motor, home, property and personal insurance. It has recently developed a holiday insurance product that it provides to the public. A potential customer is able to telephone a specially trained adviser who asks a number of pertinent questions. The answers to these questions are entered directly into a computer system that calculates and displays the premium. The adviser communicates the premium to the potential customer who may either accept or reject it. Accepted quotations are paid for by credit card and printed off and sent to the customer, along with the payment details.

The software to support the on-line holiday insurance quotation was developed in-house by the Information Systems (IS) department. It was developed in a GUI-based programming language and was the first system to be produced by the Information Systems department using this language. The project was delivered late and it exceeded its budget. The software has suffered many problems since it was installed. Some of these have been solved. However, there are still significant problems in the actual function that the advisers use to record the details of potential customers and produce the quotation.

In a recent meeting with the IS department, the advisers identified four main problems.

Illogical data entry

The advisers claim that the sequence is illogical. The questions jump from personal details, to holiday location, to travel details, back to personal details, to holiday location etc. There seems to have been little thought about logically grouping the questions and as a result potential customers become 'confused'.

Unclear field entry

Some of the information we ask for is mandatory and some is optional. Furthermore, the relevance of some questions depends on the answer to a previous question. For example, travel method is only relevant if the potential customer is travelling abroad. Unfortunately, the system does not show if a field is mandatory or optional and it shows all fields, whether they are relevant or not to a particular quotation.

Inconsistent cursor control

The information has to be entered very quickly. Many fields are filled completely during data entry. On some screens, the cursor jumps to the next field immediately after filing the previous field. In other screens, the cursor only moves after pressing the TAB key even when the field is filled. This inconsistency is very irritating, we often find ourselves over-typing completed fields and it is particular confusing for new advisers who are not used to the software.

Performance problems

One of the primary requirements of the system was the ability to process enquiries on-line and to produce instant quotations. However, at peak times the system is too slow to produce the quotation. Consequently, we have to promise to telephone the potential customer back and this destroys the immediate impact of the system. Hence the system is not fulfilling one of its primary requirements.

CAET Insurance has brought in a consultant to review the on-line holiday insurance system. The consultant has made a number of observations regarding the project and the developed software. Two summary paragraphs are repeated below.

Extract from the management summary

Project

The IS department failed to recognise that this was a very risky project. Three issues made it particularly risky.

- The users of the system had no experience in the holiday insurance industry hence they found it difficult to specify their requirements in advance.
- The decision to use a programming language that the department had not used before.

- The system had exacting performance requirements.

All projects at CAET Insurance are supposed to undergo a risk assessment as part of producing the Project Quality Plan (PQP). This risk assessment was omitted from this project for reasons that are still unclear. This was a serious omission.

The software

There is considerable evidence that the product is unstable and suffers from significant performance problems. My recommendation is that the bespoke system is abandoned and a suitable application software package is selected and installed. My research suggests that there are a number of possible solutions in the marketplace and these packages offer 'tried, tested, and error-free solutions'. It will be more cost-effective, in the long run, to adopt one of these packages rather than maintain the bespoke in-house software.

16 CAET Insurance: Project management — 36 mins

The consultant has pointed out that the project did not undergo the required risk assessment. This risk assessment would have required the project team to identify ways to avoid or reduce the chance of each risk occurring.

Required

(a) In retrospect what could have been suggested at the start of the project to avoid or reduce each of the following three risks identified in the consultant's report?

(i) The users of the system had no experience in the holiday insurance industry hence they found it difficult to specify their requirements in advance.

(ii) The decision to use a programming language that the department had not used before.

(iii) The system had exacting performance requirements. **(12 marks)**

(b) The risk assessment is an important part of the Project Quality Plan (PQP). Two other terms used in the CAET Insurance PQP are:

(i) Project Sponsor.
(ii) Project Plan.

Explain the meaning and significance of each of these items. **(8 marks)**

Further questions relating to CAET Insurance follow.

17 CAET Insurance: Software design — 36 mins

One of the key requirements of the holiday insurance system was the need to speedily process requests for an insurance quotation over the telephone. The users have identified four specific problems with the on-line insurance quotation function.

(i) Illogical data entry.
(ii) Unclear field entry.
(iii) Inconsistent cursor control.
(iv) Performance problems.

The IS department still believes that these four problems can be solved and that there is no need to abandon the development of the bespoke system and use an application package solution.

Required

(a) Suggest how each of the following four problems could be solved, now that the system is live, and comment on the difficulty of implementing your solutions.

(i) Illogical data entry. **(2 marks)**
(ii) Unclear field entry. **(2 marks)**
(iii) Inconsistent cursor control. **(3 marks)**
(iv) Performance problems. **(4 marks)**

(b) Suggest how each of the following four problems could have been prevented or detected before the system went live.

(i) Illogical data entry. **(2 marks)**
(ii) Unclear field entry. **(2 marks)**
(iii) Inconsistent cursor control. **(2 marks)**
(iv) Performance problems. **(3 marks)**

Questions 18 and 19 also refer to CAET and include detailed guidance – see the following pages.

18 CAET Insurance: Quality assurance and testing 36 Mins

The consultant has suggested that one of the main advantages of the application software package approach is that the software is tried and tested.

Required

(a) **Bespoke application systems developed in the IS department has to pass through the following three stages**

(i) **Requirements analysis.**
(ii) **Systems design.**
(iii) **Programming.**

Describe the quality assurance and testing associated with each of these three stages of the IS development process. (12 marks)

(b) **Explain where quality assurance and testing should still be applied by the IS department when using an application software package approach and hence comment on the consultant's assertion that the software is 'tried, tested and error-free'. (8 marks)**

Approaching the answer

You should read through the requirement, and then re-read and annotate relevant material from the scenario, highlighting points to include in your answer. An example is shown below.

Could customers enquire/ purchase via a website?

CAET Insurance offers motor, home, property and personal insurance. It has recently developed a holiday insurance product that it provides to the public. A potential

Could customers enter details direct via a website?

customer is able to telephone a specially trained adviser who asks a number of pertinent questions. The answers to these questions are entered directly into a computer system that calculates and displays the premium. The adviser communicates the premium to the potential customer who may either accept or reject it. Accepted quotations are paid for by credit card and printed off and sent to the customer, along with the payment details.

Could existing insurance quotation software have been purchased and adapted?

Did staff possess the required development expertise?

Probably a 4GL

The software to support the on-line holiday insurance quotation was developed in-house by the Information Systems (IS) department. It was developed in a GUI-based programming language and was the first system to be produced by the Information

Was this wise? Training provided to developers?

Systems department using this language. The project was delivered late and it exceeded its budget. The software has suffered many problems since it was

Poor project management and system development procedures?

Problems with an essential feature.

installed. Some of these have been solved. However, there are still significant problems in the actual function that the advisers use to record the details of potential customers and produce the quotation.

In a recent meeting with the IS department, the advisers identified four main problems.

Illogical data entry.

> Were the advisers consulted during development?

The advisers claim that the sequence is illogical. The questions jump from personal details, to holiday location, to travel details, back to personal details, to holiday location etc. There seems to have been little thought about logically grouping the questions and as a result potential customers become 'confused'.

Unclear field entry

Some of the information we ask for is mandatory and some is optional. Furthermore, the relevance of some questions depends on the answer to a previous question. For example, travel method is only relevant if the potential customer is travelling abroad. Unfortunately, the system does not show if a field is mandatory or optional and it shows all fields, whether they are relevant or not to a particular quotation.

> This is a basic requirement, shows a lack of user consultation in development process

Inconsistent cursor control

The information has to be entered very quickly. Many fields are filled completely during data entry. On some screens, the cursor jumps to the next field immediately after filing the previous field. In other screens, the cursor only moves after pressing the TAB key even when the field is filled. This inconsistency is very irritating, we often find ourselves over-typing completed fields and it is particular confusing for new advisers who are not used to the software.

> Was user-acceptance testing carried out?

Performance problems

One of the primary requirements of the system was the ability to process enquiries on-line and to produce instant quotations. However, at peak times the system is too slow to produce the quotation. Consequently, we have to promise to telephone the potential customer back and this destroys the immediate impact of the system. Hence the system is not fulfilling one of its primary requirements.

> This will cause potential customers to go elsewhere

> How was system developed and released with such a major flaw?

CAET Insurance has brought in a consultant to review the on-line holiday insurance system. The consultant has made a number of observations regarding the project and the developed software. Two summary paragraphs are repeated below.

> Understanding of business and system?

Extract from the management summary

Project

The IS department failed to recognise that this was a very risky project. Three issues made it particularly risky.

> Risk management

- The users of the system had no experience in the holiday insurance industry hence they found it difficult to specify their requirements in advance.
- The decision to use a programming language that the department had not used before.
- The system had exacting performance requirements.

> Research similar systems? Allow flexibility in the development process

> If this language was most suitable, the project could have been outsourced

> Essential these were met – they haven't been eg system response time

All projects at CAET Insurance are supposed to undergo a risk assessment as part of producing the Project Quality Plan (PQP). This risk assessment was omitted from this project for reasons that are still unclear. This was a serious omission.

Post-project review?

Indeed! Poor project management

The software

There is considerable evidence that the product is unstable and suffers from significant performance problems. My recommendation is that the bespoke system is abandoned and a suitable application software package is selected and installed. My research suggests that there are a number of possible solutions in the marketplace and these packages offer 'tried, tested, and error-free solutions'. It will be more cost-effective, in the long run, to adopt one of these packages rather than maintain the bespoke in-house software.

Availability? Modifications required?

Very unlikely

What about software quality?

Required

Six elements to include – QA and testing for each of the three stages.

'V' model links QA and testing

(a) Bespoke application systems developed in the IS department has to pass through the following three stages

(i) Requirements analysis.

(ii) Systems design.

(iii) Programming.

Describe the quality assurance and testing associated with each of these three stages of the IS development process. (12 marks)

QA and testing still vital even when purchasing a package rather than developing in-house

(b) Explain where quality assurance and testing should still be applied by the IS department when using an application software package approach and hence comment on the consultant's assertion that the software is 'tried, tested and error-free'. (8 marks)

In what environment? Different situation and users. Very unlikely that software will be completely error-free.

Answer plan

Organise the relevant points you have noted into a coherent answer plan. Not all the points you have noticed will have to go into your answer – you should spend a few minutes thinking them through and prioritising them.

(a) Quality assurance and testing at three stages of systems development

Intro

- Briefly link 'V' model to scenario

Requirements analysis

- Input, processing and output documentation
- Check against system

Systems design

- Based on business requirements
- Formal walkthroughs
- Testing – system, user acceptance

Programming

- Individual modules
- Unit test

(b) Quality assurance and testing related to application package

Intro

- Program design not required

Quality assurance

- Requirements specification still required

Testing

- User acceptance

Other points

- Software yet to be tested in this organisation
- Unlikely to be error free

You should flesh out the points contained in your plan and link them to form a coherent answer. Structured answers, with short paragraphs, should help ensure your answer remains focussed.

19 Outsourcing, legacy systems and PM software 36 mins

Managing information systems

A recently appointed financial director has reviewed how information systems are developed in a public sector authority. She has suggested that the information systems (IS) staff should concentrate on developing new systems, rather than maintaining the existing ones. She suggests that 'the maintenance of legacy systems should be outsourced to an external software house'.

Required

(a) Briefly explain what is meant by the term 'outsourced'. **(3 marks)**

(b) Briefly explain what is meant by the term 'legacy systems'. **(3 marks)**

(c) Describe two likely benefits of the financial director's recommendation to outsource the maintenance of legacy systems. **(4 marks)**

She has also suggested that all systems development projects should use a project management software package to help plan, control, monitor and report progress in the proposed new development projects.

(d) Explain what is meant by a project management software package. **(4 marks)**

(e) Briefly describe two advantages of using a project management software package. **(6 marks)**

Approaching the answer

You should read through the requirement, and then re-read and annotate relevant material from the scenario, highlighting points to include in your answer. An example is shown below.

Managing information systems.

Availability of funds likely to be centrally controlled

A recently appointed financial director has reviewed how information systems are developed in a public sector authority. She has suggested that the information systems (IS) staff should concentrate on developing new systems, rather than maintaining the existing ones. She suggests that 'the maintenance of legacy systems should be outsourced to an external software house'.

Procedures may be bureaucratic

Define. Consider likelihood of outsiders having the expertise to maintain

Required

(a) Briefly explain what is meant by the term 'outsourced'. **(3 marks)**

Mark allocations give a clue as to the length/detail required

(b) Briefly explain what is meant by the term 'legacy systems'. **(3 marks)**

(c) Describe two likely benefits of the financial director's recommendation to outsource the maintenance of legacy systems. **(4 marks)**

She has also suggested that all systems development projects should use a project management software package to help plan, control, monitor and report progress in the proposed new development projects.

These requirements are very clear. Ensure your answer does exactly what you were asked to do!

(d) Explain what is meant by a project management software package. **(4 marks)**

(e) Briefly describe two advantages of using a project management software package. **(6 marks)**

Answer plan

For shorter questions such as this, you may decide an answer plan is not required. The marked-up question could in effect be used as an answer plan. If you prefer to prepare a plan, do not take too long. For example, if part of a question is worth 3 marks, you should spend less than 5 minutes on that part of the question (this includes reading, planning and writing time).

Always read the question carefully - to ensure your answer does exactly what the question required.

(a) Define outsourced, link to scenario.

(b) Explain legacy systems, link to scenario.

(c) Benefits outsourcing legacy systems.

- Cost savings
- Access to expertise

(d) Explain PM software, 4 marks so include examples and uses.

(e) Benefits PM software.

- Resource allocation/planning
- Changes easier to make – documentation updated

You should flesh out the points contained in your plan and link them to form a coherent answer. Structured answers, with short paragraphs, should help ensure your answer remains focussed.

Exam answer bank

1 Characteristics of information

The Finance Director has a strategic decision-making role within the organisation. Strategic decision-making requires information with the following characteristics:

The information should be **summarised**. An overview of how a given situation could affect the organisation as a whole will be of more use to the accountant than the detail. Detail may be available in the form of appendices should this be required.

Information should be **presented appropriately**. The method of presentation should help understanding. It may be appropriate to present information in an electronic document, which can be amended quickly, rather than in a paper-based report. If information is presented in the form of a lengthy report, a table of contents and **summary** of the report's findings should be provided at the beginning.

If the information is provided in a report, this should have appropriate paragraphs and **headings** and use **clear language**. If appropriate the information may be posted on the company's intranet (ie the contents are not confidential and the intranet is used efficiently by those who need to view the information).

The information needs to be **complete**. All the information that can affect a decision should be received and reviewed.

The information must be **timely**. In many situations, circumstances may change quickly, meaning information goes out of date rapidly.

The information should be **relevant**. Information should be filtered so that only the recipient only receives information that suits his or her requirements. If the source data is detailed, it may be appropriate to summarise this information before communicating it.

2 The Accounting Academy: Feasibility study

Tutorial note. Part (a) provides a good example of how important it is to read and interpret questions correctly. The question does not require students to describe how a feasibility study is conducted. The question requires you to select relevant areas of the business described in the scenario for inclusion in a feasibility study – your knowledge of feasibility studies should help you do this, but avoid the temptation spend most of your answer explaining the feasibility study process.

Part (b) requires you to take the information you provided in part (a) a step further. It pays to read all parts of the question before starting your answer – for example by reading the requirement for part (b) before answering part (a), you can ensure you choose business areas that suit both parts of the question.

(a) The areas of the business recommended for inclusion within the scope of the feasibility study are as follows.

   (i) *Production of course material.* Inconsistencies in quality have been identified. Greater control is required over individual freelance lecturers. A 'house style' could be imposed and a central databank of material maintained to enable use of material in appropriate modules.

   (ii) *Finance.* Since there are strong seasonal variations in cashflow, a cashflow forecasting model should be a key part of this. The opportunity should also be taken to review accountancy procedures, including invoicing and cash handling. 'Inadequate and untimely financial information' is a key area to address.

   (iii) *Marketing.* There is potentially useful data available in the organisation in the form of the source data about the origin of student enquiries. This data is not really being used to its full potential. The Academy should also consider mailshots, an obvious target for computerisation.

(iv) *Administration.* Administrative arrangements are fairly complex. A review of this area of the business would be extremely useful. WP in particular is needed, as various pieces of mail are sent to each student.

(b) Areas where business benefits could be identified are as follows.

(i) *Increased income (and profitability).* If marketing activities are improved to make them more focused, attendances could rise further than anticipated. The six-fold increase referred to is presumably 'across-the-board'. Good marketing could help attract students who might otherwise select rival courses.

(ii) *Cost savings.* An area often identified as being justification for computerisation of business activities is cost-cutting. There is certainly scope for this here. The small size of personnel in administrative operation makes redundancies unlikely, but it is likely that the same staff, once trained, will be able to take on *more* work, so that when student numbers increase, fewer new staff will be required than would be the case under the current system.

(iii) *Improved control of financial position.* Computerisation will overcome the problem of inadequate and untimely financial information, allowing better planning in the light of available and forecast cash resources. Reliance on such factors as short-term overdrafts may be eliminated if these are a feature.

(iv) *Improved quality.* Improvements in the quality of material (as identified in (a) above) may help to enhance the image of the Academy, as will word processed (as opposed to typewritten) documents/letters.

3 The Accounting Academy: 'Off-the-shelf' v bespoke software; security issues

Tutorial note. The advantages and disadvantages of off-the-shelf and bespoke software are likely to be examined frequently. Learn the general principles, then when faced with an exam question select and explain those you consider most relevant to the specific question/situation.

In part (a), it is important that you relate your knowledge of potential disadvantages of off-the-shelf applications to the situation at The Accounting Academy conducted.

In part (b), remember 'non-technical' security issues, such as physical threats, and the 'typical' threats to networks such as viruses.

(a) Disadvantages of off-the-shelf packages are as follows.

(i) The *requirements* of the Accounting Academy are extremely *varied.* It may be difficult to identify suitable packages for all these requirements. WP is probably the least problematic as modern packages will provide facilities such as mailmerge and address labelling. A spreadsheet *could* be used for cashflow forecasting, but a dedicated package would probably be preferable. As for finance, given the status of the Academy and the nature of its operation it might be difficult to identify a suitable package. Some tailoring of packages might be necessary; alternatively some amendments to the company's operations could be necessitated if the package solution is inadequate.

(ii) Given that one package will not satisfy all the Academy's requirements, the issue of *compatibility* arises. The company will have to consider whether different packages might produce incompatible data. A further problem, whether or not data is compatible is the issue of interface. If data needs to be transferred between packages, they will need to be able to recognise each other's file formats. The requirement for different packages might result in *duplication* of data, for example student and lecturer names and addresses might be held in more than one package. This would make file maintenance difficult.

(iii) Use of a package (or packages) involves reliance on the supplier of the package. Not all suppliers have the reputation and stability of, say, Microsoft, Lotus or Borland. Suppliers can go out of business or change their strategic direction (eg from products into services) and this can leave a package without support. This results in it not being upgraded while rival packages improve and possibly in the loss of technical support. If an organisation buys a bespoke package, the organisation becomes the 'owner' and, provided that the package is of a certain standard, the owner can commission upgrades and enhancements. In addition, some packages are supplied with poor *documentation* and without tutorial facilities. These, while not affecting the package's functionality, can impede users wishing to use the package effectively.

(iv) The decision to purchase a package can be made without adequate *recognition* of the organisation's *requirements*. The Academy is going through a period of change and it might be difficult to identify the organisation's requirements clearly (let alone meet them, as described in (i)). If the requirements analysis is poor or non-existent, the package might be purchased for the wrong reasons, for example, it is a good offer or it has a 'nice' interface! This could lead to a package which is inappropriate for actual business requirements being acquired.

(b) Physical security comprises two sorts of controls, protection against natural and man-made disasters, such as fire, flood and sabotage, and protection against intruders gaining physical access to the system. These threats can be grouped alternatively as accidental and deliberate. The physical environment has a major effect on information system security, and so planning it properly is an important precondition of an adequate security plan.

Fire is the most serious hazard to computer systems. Destruction of data can be even more costly than the destruction of hardware. A proper fire safety plan is an essential feature of security procedures, in order to prevent fire, detect fire and put out the fire.

The other main area of physical security is *access control*, to prevent intruders getting anywhere near the computer equipment or storage media. Methods of controlling human access include:

(i) Personnel (security guards).

(ii) Mechanical devices (eg keys, whose issue is recorded).

(iii) Electronic identification devices (eg card-swipe systems, where a card is passed through a reader).

Theft is also a problem, particularly where so much computer equipment is easily portable. A PC need not be larger than a briefcase and even a laser printer can be carried by one person. To some extent this can be guarded against by means similar to those described above, but with much equipment located in ordinary offices and no longer kept in a single secure location other measures must be taken. Regular 'stock controls' or physical inspections may be necessary, and a strictly imposed form of bookings used when staff take PCs off-site, either to customers or home.

Hacking has received newspaper coverage in recent years. The use of telecommunications links across, and between, large organisations, whether multinational companies or national defence departments, makes them vulnerable to determined hackers. Again the risk varies from 'nuisance value' to potential loss of material either through destruction or to competitors. Certain companies in London now advertise a service by which, for a fee, they can obtain bank account details and financial information about any named individual for customers: this kind of illegal activity is made easier by the use of IT.

Another risk is from *viruses*. These may be carried on games software or pirated software; they can be also spread on computer networks and via e-mail. At best, they are a nuisance; at worst tremendously harmful to data to the extent of wiping hard disks clean. All disks coming into an organisation and, periodically, all computers, should be checked using proprietary anti-virus software.

In smaller companies the security officer is normally responsible for the whole computer function and is often the finance manager or equivalent. System security may be less formal especially where the officer knows all the users personally. Nevertheless it is advisable that at least a basic password structure is applied to the system.

Data integrity can be corrupted by system faults and user error as well as unauthorised access. The regular back up of data should be a disciplined procedure for all computer systems. This may happen daily and the copies are often kept off premises. Security copies of the system programs may be kept at a bank or with solicitors (possibly at the request of insurers). Proper shut-down procedures should also be carried out only by authorised personnel and the network should not be left on and unattended.

Data integrity will also be maintained by keeping information on the system to a realistic minimum. This will involve deleting or archiving redundant data. This has the additional benefits of improving response times and reducing the time taken for back-up procedures. Random checks and reconciliations of data from audit trails or system enquiry will also highlight, by exception, problems which have occurred.

4 The Accounting Academy: Process model (DFD)

Tutorial note. In the examination, the ACCA should use the terminology relating to models specified in the syllabus. So, you may be asked to produce a process model, which would imply that the question is best suited to either a DFD or a flowchart. Ensure you are familiar with the modelling terminology used by the ACCA. This terminology is shown below:

ACCA term	Model included in this book
Process model	Data Flow Diagram; Flowchart.
Static structure model	Entity Relationship Model.
Events models	Entity Life History.

(a)

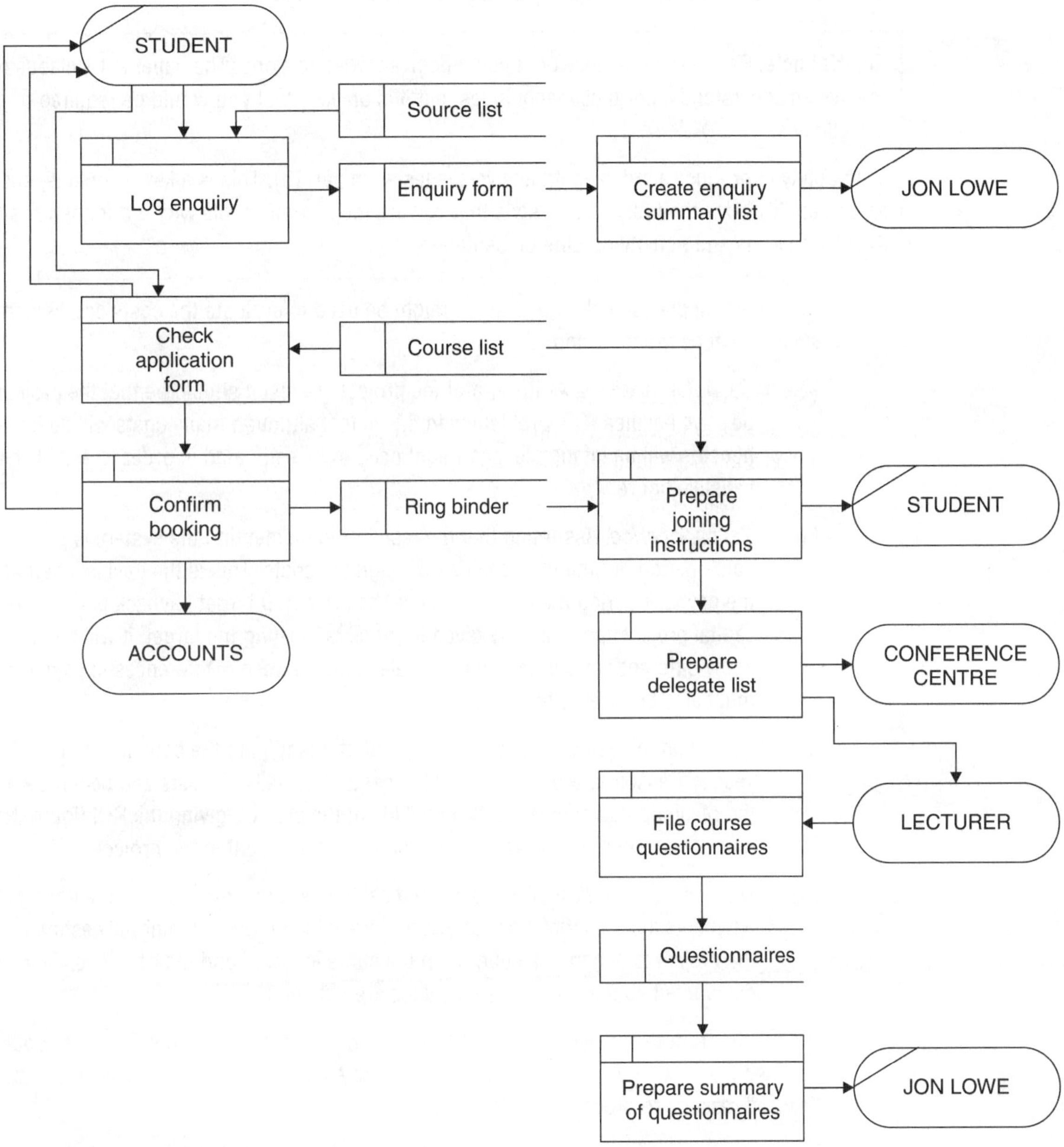

(b) Explanatory Key.

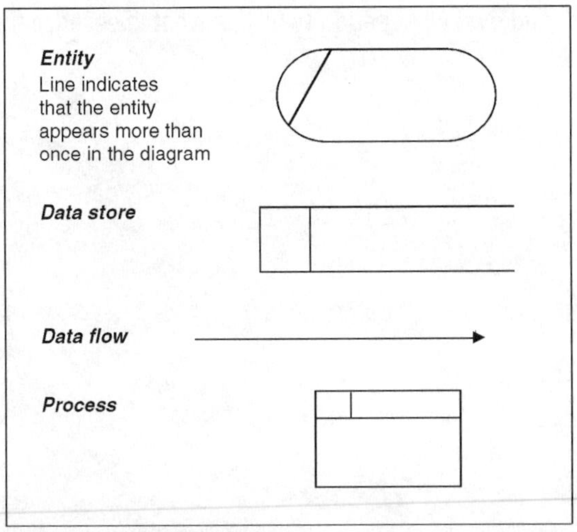

5 Cost-benefit analysis; critical path

Tutorial note. Part (a) can be answered using book knowledge alone. The paper 2.1 syllabus requires you to have an understanding of these techniques, but it is unlikely that you would be required to perform the calculations.

Your ability to produce a critical path analysis is tested in part (b). This is a key technique, ensure you are able to apply it. Use the presentation style that you are most comfortable with – our answer shows both Activity on Node and Activity on Line presentations.

(a) Investment appraisal techniques which might be used to evaluate the costs and benefits of a new system include the following.

(i) *Cash flow analysis.* At the end of the project the result should be that the project produces a positive balance. The problem with this is that although many costs will be tangible, many benefits will be intangible, and might need to be estimated in order to establish any kind of sensible figure.

(ii) *Payback period.* Assuming that the result of implementing the system is positive then after some period of time the benefits outweigh the costs. This is the payback period. The shorter the payback period the more attractive the project. If target payback periods are set and capital project approval only given to projects meeting the target, it will be necessary to apply different periods to different scales of investment. Differences in payback patterns must also be taken into account.

(iii) *Return on investment.* This is the method of quantifying the benefit in terms of the rate per year expressed as a percentage of the costs. Normally all costs and benefits are totalled and the result spread over the anticipated life of the project, giving the ROI figure. No attempt is made to account for the value of holding the investment in the project.

(iv) *Discounted cash flow.* The discounted cash flow takes into account the timing of both payments and benefits, and returns a figure which more meaningfully estimates the value of the project taking into account both the sums involved and their timings. Flows are discounted so that their present values are obtained.

The results from the analysis methods above might be compared to results which could be obtained from using the same funds elsewhere, to establish whether there were compelling financial reasons to proceed with the project.

Each of the sets of figures from the accounting mechanisms listed above could be perhaps better presented graphically rather than in tabular form. This would visually emphasise that the project was going to make a 'profit', and over what period (which is what in essence the figures illustrate).

Critical path analysis *[One of the following]*

Activity on line notation

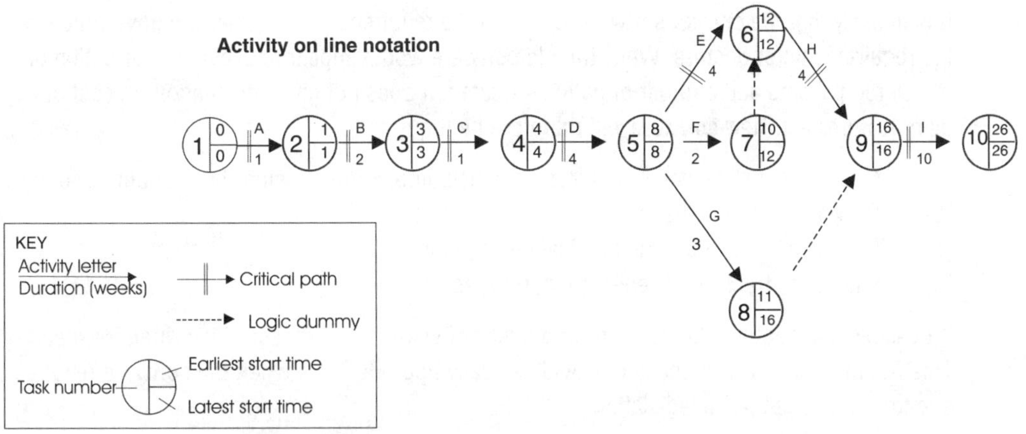

Activity on node notation

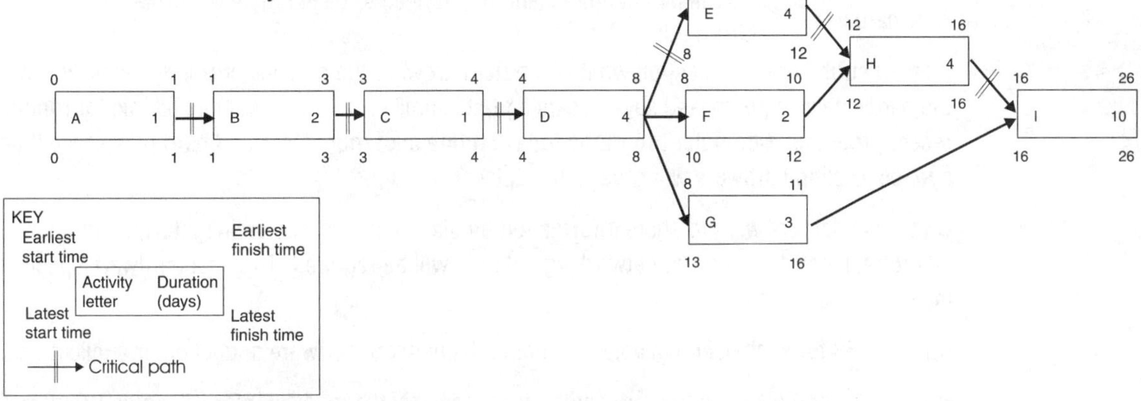

The critical path is A, B, C, D, E, H, I. The total elapsed time is 26 weeks.

6 Bay Town Health Centre: Costs and benefits

Tutorial note. When faced with a single requirement worth 20 marks, it is easy to sometimes lose focus and produce a rambling answer that doesn't make a great deal of sense, doesn't cover the required range of points – and therefore doesn't score well.

Before you start your answer, you should produce an answer plan that identifies the points you wish to make (we demonstrate one approach to this process in the final two questions of this question-bank). Your answer should then be structured into a series of short paragraphs (with headings). This should ensure a wide-range of points are made, and make it easy for the marker to identify these points – and give you credit for them.

The costs and benefits included in our answer are not the only valid points – there are a large number of points that could be included.

Costs

Most of the costs of the new information system are tangible, that is they can be quantified and relate to specific items of computer hardware or software. There may be an intangible cost to the practice in that if an upgrade is not carried out, then patient service, as compared to other practices, may decline. In the medium- to long-term, the practice may lose income as patients switch to other practices providing better information and service.

New software

It is unlikely that the current software will meet the requirements of either the government legislation, or the requirements of doctors. While the old software would appear to provide information on number of registered patients and number of patients treated, it does not give information on cost of treatments or diary features etc. New software will therefore be required to:

(a) Meet the new legislation requirements including computerising the accounting function
(b) Provide electronic diaries
(c) Provide access to on-line medical information
(d) Enable the tracking of repeat prescriptions

If possible, the doctors should try to purchase software that is specifically written for medical practices. This will make it easier to use and provide an easy upgrade route when the software requires amendment due to further changes in legislation.

Cost of software must include an appropriate number of user licences; effectively one for each computer.

New hardware

It is not clear from the question what computer hardware the practice currently owns. However, given that the hardware was purchased seven years ago, it is unlikely that this will be suitable for running more recent programs. Computer programs today require a lot more RAM and hard disk space than seven years ago, so existing hardware will have to be replaced.

Given that doctors want to share information on diaries and access online information on medical literature, then some form of networking solution will be required. The final hardware specification will include the following.

(a) A PC for each user, capable of running the network software and all other applications required.

(b) A central file store to store central files, possibly the medical information on CD, e-mail, and diary software

(c) A backup solution (such as a tape backup system)

(d) Printers

(e) Either a CD-ROM drive on the central file server or a secure server for Internet access, depending on whether the medical database is available on CD or from the Internet

Data conversion

Some of the data on the existing system, particularly the medical history files, will be needed on the new database. The doctors will need to ensure that the data files from the old software can be transferred onto the new software. Depending on the compatibility of the systems, there will be cost involved in transferring the data. Quotes will be necessary from the software house supplying the new system to determine the cost of conversion.

Internet access

Internet access may be necessary either for the medical database information or to allow for e-mail (possibly for advising patients of appointments in the future). Future use of e-mail will confirm the requirement for a secure server.

Benefits

Many of the benefits will be intangible and therefore difficult to quantify.

Meet government legislation

The main benefit of the new system is that the medical practice will meet the requirements of the new government legislation.

Better information for doctors

The doctors have indicated that they require additional information to run the practice. The hardware and software specification above will help to provide this information. Having access to this information will be a motivational factor for the doctors, as well as helping them to provide more accurate diagnosis because they will have on-line access to appropriate medical information and patients' medical histories.

Better information for administration staff

The administration person will also have access to improved information; in particular the patient booking systems and databases will provide a better and more accurate information on patients.

Better information for patients

Patients will receive a better service from the medical practice, both in terms of booking appointments and service from doctors.

Repeat prescriptions

The repeat prescription part of the software will also enable the practice to provide a better service as well as saving some time for the administrator.

Competitive advantage for practice

Finally, by providing a better service to patients (that is the customers), the practice may obtain some competitive advantage over similar practices. It is therefore possible that the practice income will increase as more patients are attracted to the practice.

7 Bay Town Health Centre: Decision making

Tutorial note. You should be wary of any statement that includes the word 'always'! It should be clear to you, particularly after studying for this paper, that a poor quality information system is unlikely to lead to better decision making.

This question allows you to make general points on their own, and also requires you to refer specifically to The Bay Town Health Centre. You could have structured your answer using two main headings – 'General' and 'Bay Town' – and used sub-headings for each point you made.

A wide variety of points could have been made – the solution provided below is only one possible answer.

Introduction

The statement 'a new information system always aids decision-making' is incorrect. A new information system that is poorly planned, designed and/or implemented is likely to be worse than the 'old system', and therefore result in poorer decision-making.

Possible problems with new information systems

Accuracy of systems specification

To provide accurate information to the users, any new system will need to be based on an accurate systems specification. This means that user requirements will be collected during the planning phase of the systems change, and these requirements incorporated into the systems specification and final systems design. If user requirements are omitted from the specification, or the final design is not based on the specification, then user requirements will not be met.

In the case of the Bay Town Health Centre, the doctors have suggested some requirements for a new system, such as the electronic diaries. However, it is not clear whether these requirements have been included in any specification. Similarly, the requirements from the doctors appear to be quite vague which may result in the delivered system not meeting the expectations of the doctors. Prior to the purchase of any system, detailed user requirements will be needed to ensure that the system does meet doctors' needs.

Type of system used

The type of system that is being used will limit provision of information by computer systems. Many systems, which are written to provide current or historical information, are unlikely to be able to give indications concerning future trends or events. Care is therefore required in implementing a system that is appropriate for the tasks being undertaken.

In the case of the medical practice, all the systems being implemented appear to produce historical or similar factual information. However, implementing some form of Expert System may provide additional information for doctors, either during diagnosis or by identifying future illness from past data.

Provision of information

Information provided by the system may not aid decision making because it does not comply with the characteristics of good information.

Timeliness of information

The timing of provision of information from a system will have a major effect on its usefulness. Information that is provided late may not be particularly useful.

If doctors at the Bay Town Medical Centre only received electronic diary updates every day, rather than in real-time, they may not know which patient they are seeing next. Incorrect medical histories will be accessed possibly resulting in inaccurate or poor decisions.

Accessibility to information system

To aid decision making, information from the system must be accessible. There is little point in information being available if it cannot be used.

It is not clear from the information about the Bay Town Medical Centre, whether on-line terminals will be available for each doctor. These will be needed to access the medical databases and patient treatment information.

Accuracy of information

If information is not accurate, then incorrect decisions may be taken. Provision of inaccurate information may not be a fault of the information system, but rather an error caused by the human operator.

If medical history information is updated incorrectly, either the wrong patient files are amended or incorrect illness details are entered into the correct patient file, then the medical information will be inaccurate and incorrect decisions may be made. Appropriate training will be required for the administrator at the Centre, although this will not guard against the occasional human error.

Other factors preventing the information system from aiding decision-making

Lack of training

Many new information systems are implemented into organisations where the staff are very busy. This means that sufficient time will not always be made available for training and familiarisation with the system. Although the system provides the information needed for decision making, lack of knowledge of that system by users precludes them from using that information and therefore making accurate decisions.

Staff at the Bay Town Health Centre appear to be very busy, and this may impact on the amount of training time. In particular, doctors must provide an appropriate service to their patients; if they are conscientious then they may be unwilling to take time away from patient consultation for training. However, given the diverse nature of the new systems being implemented, sufficient time must be found for training. If this is not done then customer service will suffer in the medium-term because doctors will not be able to find the information to carry out their jobs correctly.

Hardware specification causing delays

The hardware being used by the information system may be inadequate. This may result in delays in processing and displaying information on-screen, or even loss of information where processing memory or hard disk space is inadequate.

There does not appear to be a formal systems specification for the medical centre. It is important to produce this to ensure that the software will run without any degradation in performance caused by the issues noted above.

Conclusion

In conclusion, the statement should read 'a properly planned and implemented information system will always be able to aid decision-making'. As explained above, problems with the development process or other factors outside the control of the system mean there are limits to the effectiveness of information systems.

8 Bay Town Health Centre: Ensuring accuracy

Tutorial note. Structure your answer around the three items mentioned in the requirement; secure; accurate and coherent. A very brief definition of each of these factors should follow each heading – these definitions may earn you an easy mark and could help you decide what points should be made under each heading.

Related issues such as Data Protection legislation may be referred to, but this question does not require you to provide detailed analysis of such legislation.

Again, this question could have been answered using a wide variety of points – our solution is only one possible answer.

Security

Security generally means protected from unauthorised access and change. Information on the medical centre's computer system must be kept secure. Under the Data Protection Act, access to medical information must be restricted to authorised individuals, and access by data subjects is also restricted. Therefore, additional security will be required to ensure that data subjects cannot review their records.

It is recommended that the main steps taken to ensure the security of data include the following:

(a) Restricting PC access to authorised users by implementing the following measures.

  (i) Locking rooms where the PCs are located when not in use.

  (ii) Having screen-savers with passwords which are activated after a few minutes idle time.

(b) The following steps should be taken to restrict access to sensitive data held on the system.

  (i) Keeping the data on a server that is not attached to the Internet. This will remove the threat of hacking from outside the medical centre.

  (ii) Password protecting the individual data files so that they cannot be opened without the appropriate password being used.

  (iii) If necessary, encrypting the data files so if they are stolen they cannot be read without the decryption software and key.

  (iv) The system backup should be maintained in a secure location.

Accuracy

Accuracy means factually correct. Data on the PCs needs to be accurate partly as a result of the Data Protection Act requirements, but also because inaccurate data may either breach the new government reporting requirements or even cause an incorrect diagnosis to be made.

The method of ensuring accuracy of data depends on the data being discussed.

Medical history files

Accuracy of personal information can normally be checked by printing out that information and asking the data subject to verify that the information is correct. This approach cannot be taken with medical information due to the restrictions of the Data Protection Act, as already noted. There is the additional complication that errors may have occurred in transferring the information from the old to the new system. Steps that can be taken to ensure accuracy will include the following.

(a) Performing a manual comparison (by medical centre staff) of data from the old and new systems with any differences being corrected.

(b) Doctors checking information on-screen during consultations with patients.

(c) A review of patient's medical history by doctors with an investigation into any unusual entries.

(d) Having input controls built into the software to try and detect inaccurate information. This control will be effectively limited to factual information such as names and addresses, due to the diverse nature of the medical information being input.

Accounting information and statistics on patients

Verifying the accuracy of this information is likely to be easier because there are fewer security issues regarding the Data Protection Act.

(a) Any items of expenditure can be agreed to supporting purchase invoices.

(b) Individual patients can be matched to the electoral roll to ensure that they exist (frauds have been uncovered in some medical practices where patients have remained on the records of a medical practice, even though they have either moved to a new location or died).

(c) A list of all patients can be obtained and signed as correct by one or more of the doctors.

(d) The new computer program can be reviewed to ensure that there are appropriate controls over the input of data, such as range and completeness checks on names, addresses and telephone numbers.

Coherent

Coherent normally means consistent and orderly. This answer assumes that the examiner requires comment on whether the information is consistent and essentially easy to access and use (orderly).

Medical history files

These files will need to present information in the same manner on-screen so doctors are not confused by different screen layouts and possibly miss important information. The main method of checking this objective will be to review the software prior to implementation to ensure that it meets the needs of the doctors and that the screen designs are understandable and logical. In particular, information on the screen should follow the order that it is required by the doctor, such as name, address, details of last visit etc.

The software program itself will also need reviewing to ensure that information is filed appropriately, with access being quick and effective. The doctor and patient will not want to have to wait for more than say 10 seconds for the required medical information to be displayed on-screen.

Accounting information and statistics on patients

Checking that the information is in a common format and easy to access will again be a function of the software itself. A review of any new software will need to be undertaken to ensure that these objectives are met.

9 Gantt chart

Tutorial note. This question is unusual in that no specific information relating to the implementation was given in the question. Because of this, a wide range of activities and times would have been acceptable. An examination question would more likely provide specific activities and timescales.

A Gantt chart showing the principal management stages for this project is shown below.

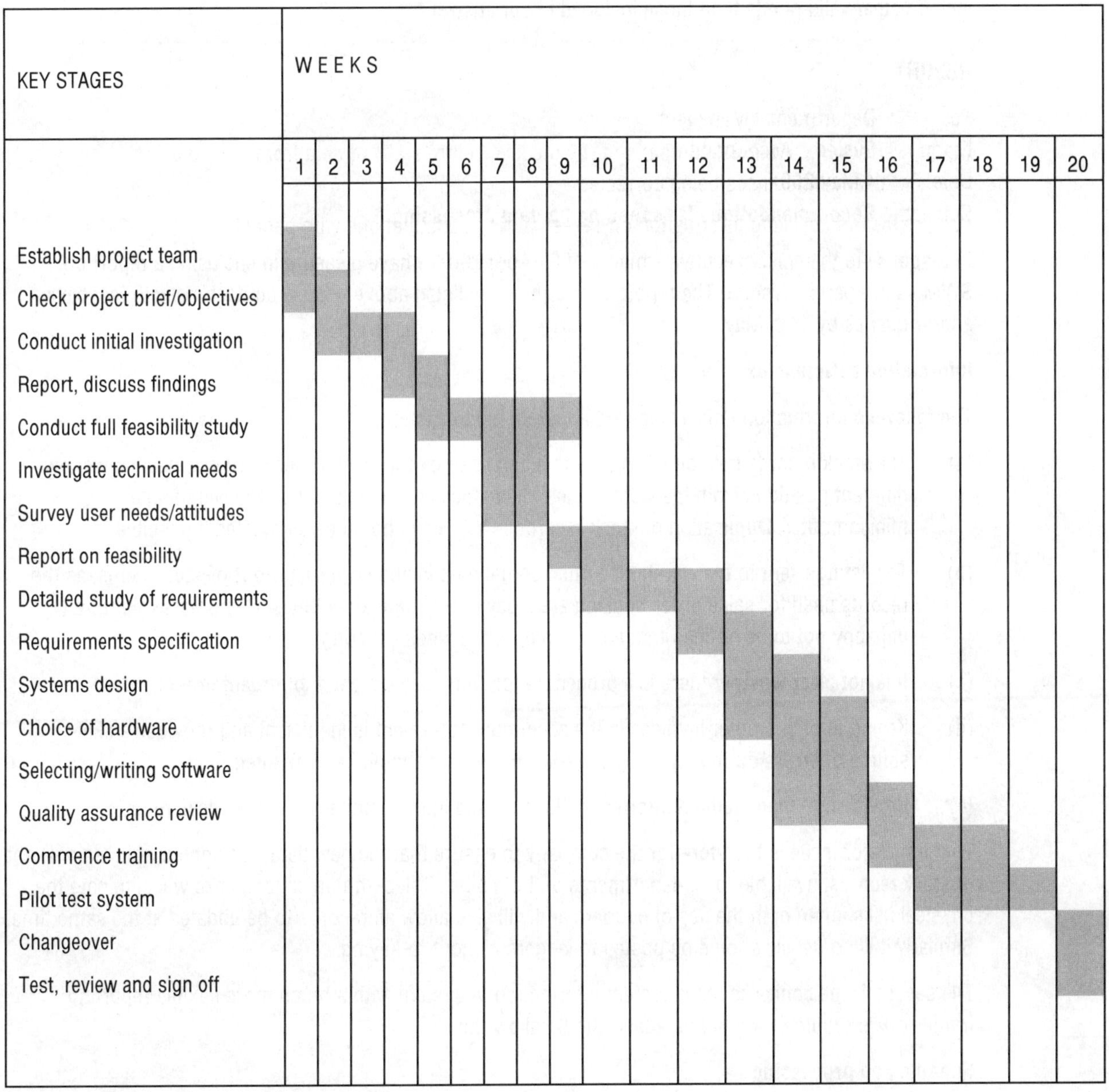

Note

Preparation for a number of the stages may begin earlier, the time must be regarded as the 'core time' during which intensive attention will be given.

10 SWM Ltd: System deficiencies

Tutorial note. Whenever you are required to write a report ensure you pick up the couple of easy marks on offer for the format of the report. Head-up your answer with 'REPORT', show where the report is to and from, include the date and subject.

This question has two main parts – identifying information deficiencies and recommending ways of speeding up processing. Include these parts as section headings within your report. Your answer could include other valid points than those included in our answer.

REPORT

To: Departmental Managers
From: Systems Accountant
Date: 4 May 200X
Subject: **Recommendations for speeding up data processing**

In response to the chief executive's memo of 21 April 200X, I have pleasure in enclosing a report on SWM's information system. The report covers the topic listed above. Please contact me with feedback and/or queries by 11th May.

Information deficiencies

The following information deficiencies are apparent in the system.

(a) The stock records held on the mainframe and used by the sales order team will inevitably show different positions from the warehouse's own stock control system on the warehouse minicomputer. Duplication of stock records in this way should be eliminated if possible.

(b) The listings sent to the warehouse must sometimes include orders for out-of-stock items, as the records used for sales order booking are a day out-of-date at all times. Customers might be unhappy not to be notified that there is a problem when ordering.

(c) It is not clear whether there is a procedure for same day despatch of urgent orders.

(d) Keying in of customer invoices in the accounts department is inefficient and provides a likely source of errors during input. Such re-keying of data should be eliminated.

(e) Provision of management information is, as noted in the company's own review, poor.

The first major issue is therefore for the company to ensure that the new database should hold a single set of stock records, available to all departments on both sites. Telecommunications links will eliminate the physical risks inherent in the use of couriers and will also allow all records to be updated at the same time. Similarly, billing details should be posted to ledgers without re-keying.

The second issue concerns management information. A system with a much more flexible reporting framework is required. A good database should allow this.

Speeding up processing

The comments above will enable all departments to have access to up-to-date data. Other suggestions for speeding up processing are as follows.

(a) An upgrade to the existing processor may be necessary. If the number of users or volume of transactions processed is higher than was ever envisaged when the existing system was purchased, it may be necessary to install a more powerful, and faster, processor.

(b) An increase in available RAM (random access memory) would allow more relevant program files and data files to be stored in RAM during processing. This would reduce the number of transfers between RAM and hard disks during processing.

(c) The system could be redesigned so that more local processing is performed using PCs and perhaps minicomputers at local sites. The mainframe could then be used for the stock database and for bulk storage and printing applications. Local terminals could be replaced by processors and used for small/medium-sized local requirements.

(d) An analysis could be performed of how time-critical various processing operations are. Batch processing of non-critical operations could be scheduled for overnight/weekend running: this might improve processing speeds for higher priority operations done during working hours.

(e) A new operating system (perhaps an open system) might be appropriate. This would be likely to provide improvements in processing speed. Of course, this might require the mainframe to be replaced too.

(f) A separate processor designed specifically to deal with communications and related issues could be installed 'between' the mainframe and the terminals. This 'front-end processor' would deal with protocols, sending and receiving messages, terminal allocation, security and related technical matters, leaving the mainframe free to continue with processing.

11 SWM Ltd: System controls

Tutorial note. A different approach to the answer shown below would have been to start by defining data integrity (see Chapter 13) and security, and then using Security Controls and Integrity Controls as your main headings. Much of the material in Chapter 13 could have potentially been used to answer this question.

Controls

Information is a vital resource of any organisation, and steps have to be taken to insure its security and integrity as if it were any other valuable asset. Just as there are systems to ensure against theft or destruction of tangible assets, so too are measures taken to protect data and information.

Physical access

It is possible to enumerate any number of threats to the integrity and privacy of data held in any system. There are basic physical dangers such as fire, which need guarding against. Controls to minimise risk include fireproof cabinets where important files are kept. Also, there are basic measures relating to physical access by unauthorised people to an organisation's premises. These physical controls relate both to the equipment and the storage media. In a database system like the one described, this is likely to be a random access storage medium. Both backup copies and backup systems can be maintained in case of disasters.

Particular risks at SWM Ltd relate to the use of couriers and floppy disks to transfer data between sites. Even assuming back-ups are available, it is still possible that loss or corruption of disks could retard processing by 24 hours.

In a new multi-user database system, the database file will be held centrally, and the problem of physical access to the medium on which the data is stored will not be multiplied over several sites. Also, it will be easier to keep backup copies of one set of files than of several.

Logical access

The database contains data relating to a number of different applications, some of which might be for restricted viewing only. Access to the entire database should be restricted also, for the same reasons. The type of control that will serve both functions is a password system, in which each user is given a unique code. The password can determine entry to the database, and also restrict users to specific views of it.

A further measure would be to restrict an individual user to one terminal, so that the password keyed in from that terminal could be checked to see that it corresponds in some way to the terminal itself.

For this system to work, passwords must be kept strictly confidential between users, and also as far as outsiders are concerned. Passwords should be changed regularly.

Communications

If data is transferred over a telecommunications link (as proposed earlier in this solution), controls should be made as far as possible to minimise the risks of hacking. Data sent over the link can be subjected to encryption and authentication procedures. Dial-back procedures can be used: they request callers to hang up and they then telephone the caller ensuring that the number is taken from a pre-set database.

Errors

The integrity of data can also be threatened by error. Human error can occur both in systems design and programming. Controls in the design stage, to avoid bugs, include adherence to programming standards, testing and so forth, before the database system is implemented. The same can be said for controls over system maintenance and updating. Proper documentation, testing and authorisation should minimise the risk of further design error.

Other forms of error can occur in the operational stage. There can be programmed controls over data input. These include check digits, range checks, format checks and so forth. The user interface can be so designed to make input of data strictly guided.

Personnel

Controls over personnel relate to a separation of functions as far as possible between programming staff and operational staff, so that operational staff do not have the opportunity to amend programs fraudulently, and so that programming staff do not get the opportunity to interfere with live data for fraudulent ends. For sensitive positions strict recruitment procedures should be followed.

With end-user computing, some of these controls are hard to maintain. In the situation outlined in this case, however, control over the database is maintained centrally so this is not so much of a problem.

12 SWM Ltd: Software maintenance

Tutorial note.

You should have found this question straightforward if you have studied Chapter 14 of this text.

The answer below would have accumulated marks as follows:

Report format and clear layout	2
Maintenance explanation	2
Corrective maintenance	6
Adaptive maintenance	6
Perfective maintenance	4
	20

REPORT

To: Chief Executive
From: Systems Accountant
Date: 10 May 200X
Subject: **Report on software maintenance**

This report will explain the types of software maintenance necessary to ensure software remains efficient.

Software maintenance is carried out for three possible reasons.

- To correct errors or 'bugs' (Corrective maintenance)
- To meet changes in internal operating procedures or external regulations (Adaptive maintenance)
- To keep up with new technical developments (Perfective maintenance)

We will look at each type of maintenance in turn.

Corrective maintenance

Testing procedures should identify most potential faults prior to installation. However, faults may not become apparent until certain combinations of conditions occur. Correction of these more obscure faults may be time-consuming and expensive.

Faults may also become apparent when consistently higher than expected volumes of data are processed. Volume limits are a key part of any transaction processing software and it is important that these are reviewed regularly to maintain efficiency. Increases in volume may require software and hardware upgrades (such as additional RAM).

Hardware failures can require changes to the operating system software. Additional warnings or error messages may be introduced. Procedures to back up files automatically when a system fails may be written into the software.

Some 'bugs' may only become apparent under certain hardware environments.

Adaptive maintenance

Software houses may regularly upgrade standard applications or general-purpose packages to provide additional features or make them user-friendlier. Customers need to decide whether to accept the upgrade, which is rarely supplied free of charge and will involve staff commitment to the new software. Non-acceptance of upgrades may lead to less effective support from the software supplier whose expertise is focused on the latest version of the package.

The operating procedures and needs of the user may change. This is very common with outputs such as reports and screen layouts, which are often changed to suit user requirements. Data processing operations are less often changed because they are more likely to reflect standard procedures whereas computer outputs evolve to meet the needs of the business. Many applications packages now allow users to customise the software (to a certain extent) themselves. For example, one person's 'standard' Excel spreadsheet screen may look different to another's – toolbars, the number of sheets, gridlines, the formula bar are all subject to user settings. Customised user generated reports are a common feature of accounting packages.

Hardware upgrades are common in larger systems and this often results in operating software being changed or entirely rewritten. Hardware changes range from a simple memory upgrade to changing from multi-user to networked systems.

External regulation often leads to mandatory changes in software, which can be quite extensive. A typical example is the change to various tax rates after the annual budget statement in the UK. These are normally straightforward and are often planned for in financial applications packages. However, the consequences of, for example, introducing multiple VAT rates would generally be complex and expensive for most businesses.

Perfective maintenance

Users may request enhancements to software which is not producing errors, but which could be made more user-friendly or improved in some other way. This may involve, for example, redesigning menu screens or switching to graphical user interfaces.

It may be possible to rewrite sections of programs to improve efficiency and response times. As noted above, output may be redesigned to provide better quality information. Off-the-shelf software products may undertake perfective maintenance in response to advances made in a competitor's product.

13 New system implementation

Tutorial note. When faced with a question that has a number of small parts, use the individual mark allocations as a guide to how much detail is required in your answer. In this question, your answer to part (c) should have taken half the time you spent on the whole question.

(a) The other members of the feasibility study team must bring their own particular knowledge and expertise to the study. There must be **operational expertise**, and this might be provided by three managers:

(i) The central stores manager.
(ii) The distribution manager.
(iii) The manager of a store or group of stores in the chain.

The management accountant should have an understanding of the costs and financial aspects, and some IS knowledge too, but it would also be sensible to include the IS manager in the team (assuming of course that the organisation has an IS manager).

(b) Major **information requirements** of the system are as follows.

(i) Current amounts of stock held centrally and locally, for each item, in physical quantities and value.

(ii) Stock-outs in the central stores, and locally, and their duration.

(iii) Periodic sales for each item, analysed by store and in total.

(iv) Stock delivery requirements (each half-week) for each store – ie stock orders for each store and in total.

(v) Delivery loads and schedules for each vehicle – ie delivery schedules.

(c) The **principal stages in the implementation of the proposed** system are as follows.

(i) **Select the hardware and software** required, as a result of the feasibility study. Order the hardware and software, with agreed delivery dates. Arrangements for back-up and maintenance should be made.

(ii) **Install the equipment** centrally and in the shops. If there is to be a staged implementation of the new system, equipment might only be installed in a few selected shops at first.

(iii) There must be **staff training**, ideally provided by the supplier or dealer. If training is made to coincide with the delivery of the hardware and software, the staff can carry on training by practising on the company's own equipment after the training course has ended.

One or two 'experts' in the system should be appointed. These would deal with queries from other operators of the system, and act as the link with the supplier's back up and maintenance service.

(iv) **Testing**. Ideally, the new system should first of all be tested on 'dummy' data. The testing process could be used both to iron out operational snags with the new system and to continue the process of staff training.

(v) **File creation**. Files for the new system must be created before the system can be operational. This can be a long and tedious process.

(vi) **Changeover to the new system**. The changeover to the new system should be planned carefully. To start with, a few stores and head office could begin to operate the new system in a pilot run. Lessons could be learned from the pilot run and applied to the subsequent introduction of all the other stores to the system. (The option of parallel running would probably not be practicable for retailing operations, where stores staff might only have time to record sales once, using whatever point-of-sale hardware is introduced for the new system.)

(vii) **Review and evaluation**. The new system should be reviewed and evaluated, once it has settled down, to determine whether or not it is achieving its intended objectives.

(d) **Criteria to evaluate the choice of system**

(i) **Reliability**. The reliability of the software and hardware should be checked, eg by following up references from other users of similar systems.

(ii) **Costs and benefits**. The benefits of the system should outweigh the costs. The costs would include software and hardware purchase costs and running costs such as maintenance and the rental of any data communication links that might be used etc.

The benefits might be difficult to evaluate but include:

(1) Lower stockholding costs

(2) Fewer stockouts and so more sales and profits

(3) Possibly, fewer staff costs

The **expected operational life** of the system would also be relevant to the comparison of costs and benefits.

(iii) **Better management information**. The quality of the management information will be a factor in the choice of system, although the benefits of a better MIS (apart from those listed above) would be virtually impossible to evaluate in financial terms.

(iv) The **flexibility of the system**. Will it allow the user to expand and modify the use of the system as operational requirements change over time?

14 User requirements

Tutorial note: In part (b) you were required to produce a flowchart model. The ACCA have stated that in the examination questions will be able to be answered using a range of techniques. Ensure you are familiar with the modelling terminology used by the ACCA. This terminology is shown below:

ACCA term	Model included in this book
Process model	Data Flow Diagram; Flowchart.
Static structure model	Entity Relationship Model.
Events models	Entity Life History.

Models should include a 'key' or 'legend' that would enable an outsider to understand the conventions used in the model.

(a) To prepare for the meeting with the user, the analyst will need to carry out the activities below.

Confirm the time and location of the meeting. All attendees will need to know where the meeting is held, and the analyst may need to ensure sufficient chairs tables etc. are available and book refreshments.

Confirm the objectives of the meeting. The user will need to know why the meeting is being held; a list of objectives should be circulated to all attendees prior to the meeting.

Prepare for the meeting – background information. The analyst will need to research the history of the company, check current procedure manuals and clarify any technical terms that may be used. This will help the analyst identify the situation of the user and 'talk the user's language'.

Prepare for the meeting – questions to ask. The analyst will need to plan and write out the questions to be asked during the meeting. A checklist of points to be covered may also be required to ensure that all the information required is actually obtained.

(b) **Flowchart model for Insurance claim**

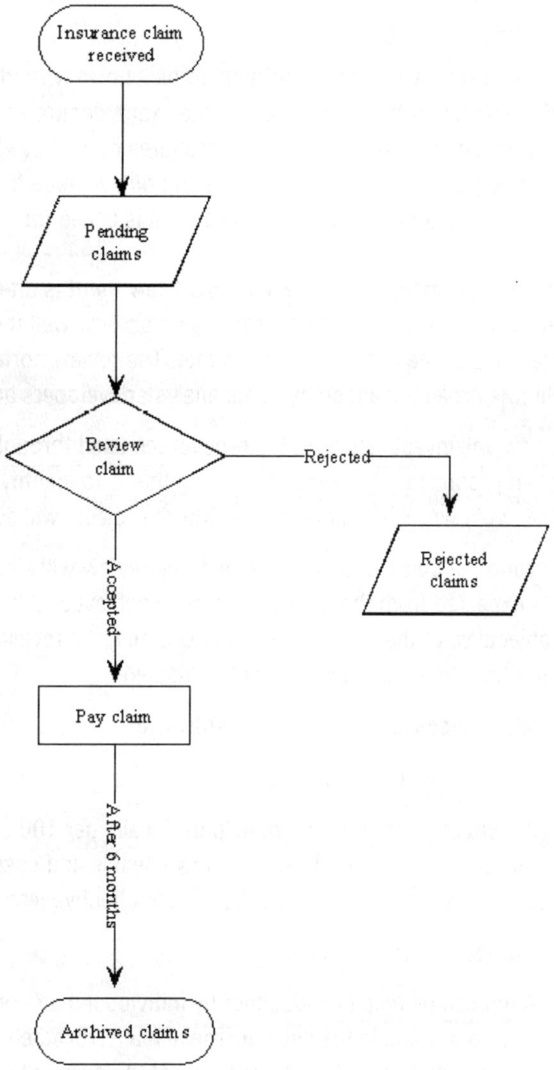

Key for flowchart model

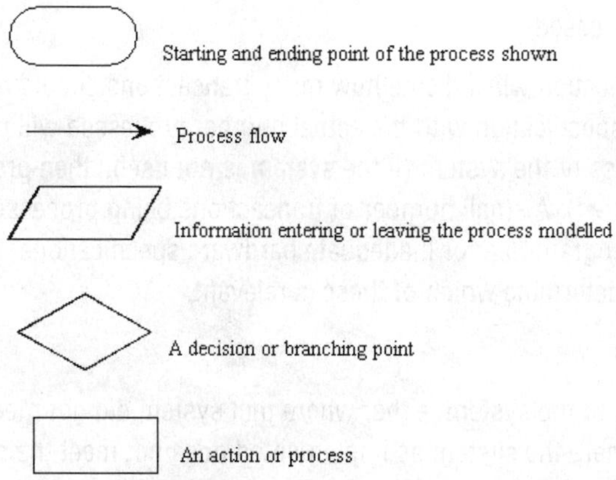

Note: A range of different answers could have effectively shown the process described in this question and scored well. If your model follows the narrative provided in the question, **don't worry if it does not match the model shown here**.

15 Post-implementation and change issues

> **Tutorial note**. Part (a) provides an opportunity to pick up easy marks for simply reproducing 'book knowledge'. If questions of this type appear in the exam, ensure you explain yourself sufficiently to pick up all the of the marks on offer. A wide range of measures could have been used in part (b). We provide four measures for study purposes – your answer should only include three. Part (c) is unusual in that it requires you to produce a list – always produce what is asked for.

(a) A post-implementation review takes place a few months after system implementation is complete. The review is to receive feedback from users on how well the system is working and to check that the objectives of the project have been met. The review normally takes the form of a meeting between the project sponsor, systems analyst, developers and users.

The review will investigate both the procedures used throughout the project and the systems that have been produced. The purpose of doing this is to identify what features of the project went well, and what went wrong or badly, so that future projects will avoid these problems.

In reviewing the objectives of the project, the review will also check whether or not the business benefits expected from the project have been achieved. Where benefits have not been achieved, or other objectives of the project have not been met, the review may also recommend remedial action to ensure that the required benefits are obtained.

(b) **Measures of success for application software**

(i) Number of calls to the help desk

Ascertaining the number of help desk calls per 100 employees (or some other useful number) will help to determine how useable and user-friendly the system is. The number of calls may also give an indication of the effectiveness of the training provided.

(ii) Number of errors reported

A log can be maintained, either by individual users or the help desk, of the number and type of errors found in the system. The actual error rate provides an indication of the quality of programming and the effectiveness of the different stages of testing (user acceptance, system and module).

(iii) Number of transactions processed

The original software specification will indicate how many transactions should be processed. Comparing the specification with the actual number processed will provide information on the usefulness of the system (if the system is not useful then presumably it will be used less than expected). A small number of transactions being processed could also be indicative of poor programming or inadequate hardware specifications, so further analysis may be needed to determine which of these is relevant.

(iv) Number of change requests

Users may request changes to the system, either where that system did not meet their original requirements, or where the system as implemented does not meet their expectations in some way. Changes requested due to initial specifications not being met provides some measure on the quality of the design and testing processes. Changes requested because the software is not meeting expectations may indicate weaknesses in this method of obtaining data for the initial specification.

(c) A procedure for recording, prioritising and implementing change requested for a live system are outlined below.

- A means for the user to record and request a change to the system
- A method of collating these change requests
- A means of providing an impact analysis and business case for each change
- A process for reviewing each request with agreed criteria for accepting or rejecting a request
- A method of prioritising requests that have been accepted
- Provision of appropriate documentation to record each change request with analysis and design implications for the existing system
- A method of allocating amendments to programmers
- A process for reviewing the work of programmers and ensuring that the change meets the initial specification
- A process for testing the change within the whole program suite
- Procedures for informing users date and nature of the change
- Procedures for updating system and user documentation prior to the release of the change
- A process for releasing that change into the live software

16 CAET Insurance: Project management

Tutorial note. For part (a) your answer should use the elements described in (i), (ii) and (iii) as headings. Our answer includes sub-headings within each of these, relating to avoiding risk and reducing risk. This is not necessary, but does help ensure a wide range of points are included.

If you have studied Chapters 5 and 6 of this text you should have found part (b) straightforward.

(a) (i) **Risk: Lack of user experience in the holiday industry**

Avoiding risk

Experience in the holiday industry could be obtained by either recruiting new staff with the appropriate experience, or by helping existing staff obtain that experience, through their work and possibly by attendance on some appropriate training courses. However, using the latter option will almost certainly have delayed the systems project.

Reducing risk

Involving users throughout the design process could reduce the risk of implementing an incorrect or partly functional system. Specifically, system prototypes and pilot testing could be carried out to check the appropriateness of any system design.

Reviewing similar systems that may already be available on the market or at third parties may also reduce risk. The latter will be difficult to achieve where third parties do not want to share their knowledge although a review of propriety software will at least indicate the functionality that can be included in any new system.

(ii) **Decision to use a programming language with no experience of that language in-house**

Avoiding risk

This risk can be avoided, either gaining the appropriate experience in-house, or by using a different programming language that in-house already have experience in. The choice will depend on how important it is to use the functionality in the chosen language.

Reducing risk

If the unfamiliar language has to be used, then risk of failure can be reduced firstly, by allowing more time in the project plan for training or hiring of staff. Another alternative is to put back the project delivery time to recognise that problems may occur in writing and testing the software. These alternatives may be more appropriate than implementing software that fails or causes errors shortly after implementation.

(iii) **Exacting performance problems**

Avoiding risk

Performance problems can be avoided by decreasing the use of the computer system at busy times. This may mean storing customer telephone calls in a queue and only taking the number of calls that the system will process or promising to call customers back at a less busy time. As a last resort, CAET could stop giving quotes on-line, although this may not be an acceptable option, given CAET's commitment to using the system.

Reducing risk

Checking that high specification hardware is installed to provide adequate processing power can reduce the risk of poor performance. Faster hardware will decrease the waiting time for response from the system.

Alternatively, prototypes can be produced during the design and build phase to test the system response times. If performance cannot be improved, then at least expectations of users and customers regarding performance can be managed.

(b) (i) **Project sponsor**

The project sponsor is the customer for the system. This person is not necessarily the finance director, but the manager of the business unit or department where the new system will be implemented. The sponsor will have made the business case for any new or revised system, and will seek to ensure that those benefits are delivered in the final system.

As the project sponsor is responsible for delivering the benefits of the project, that person will also be promoting the project prior to implementation. Promotion in this case will mean ensuring that appropriate resources are allocated to the project as well as ensuring potential users are aware of the project and are briefed on the benefits of that project. Lack of a project sponsor will increase the risk of project failure, due to lack of co-ordination of the activities of the project and possible lack of priority for the project within the organisation.

(ii) **Project plan**

The project plan provides an overall picture of the project showing the activities to be carried out, the time of those activities and how the different activities are related to each other. Most project plans are presented as some form of chart (eg GANTT chart) or network so that interconnections between the activities can be seen clearly.

The project plan is used to estimate the total time to complete the project and identify those activities, which must be completed on time to avoid the whole project being finished late. The effect on total project duration from changes in activities can also be estimated by entering revised times for activities into the plan. If no plan is produced, then the overall project time and critical activities will be difficult to predict. There will also be an increased risk of late completion due to overall lack of control.

17 CAET Insurance: Software design

Tutorial note. Look at our answer below – note how the lengths of different parts of the answer differ. For example, Part (a) (iv) includes the most material. This is because this part of the question is worth 4 marks, while many of the other parts are worth 2 marks. Of course, to earn marks what you write must be relevant to the question asked – but with short questions often the key is not to write too much, and to gauge the length of your answer by the marks on offer.

(a) (i) **Illogical data entry**

The logical order to input data into the system needs to be ascertained from the users of the system. This error could have been identified in a prototype and the screen design amended at this time. However, given that the correct fields appear to be available, rather than some fields actually missing, the screen should be fairly easy to amend. Within the GUI interface, each field will have its own placeholder (similar to those in Microsoft Access), so these can be dragged to a new location and the order of using the fields amended to reflect the user requirement.

(ii) **Unclear field entry**

Mandatory fields should be easy to identify, possibly by using a different colour to shade the field or providing a darker boarder around the input box. Similarly, displaying some fields should be made dependent on entries actually made in previous fields. Again, using the GUI interface tools, amendments to field properties should be fairly easy to accomplish.

(iii) **Inconsistent cursor control**

Inconsistent cursor control is difficult for the user as the action of the cursor is difficult to predict, as the case study shows. A survey of users will help to identify which action on the completion of each field is actually appropriate. Pressing the tab key may be the easiest option because the software may not always identify when a field is complete (eg when does an address end?). However, as long as the action is consistent and logical, then the actual alternative chosen is irrelevant.

The change should again be easy to implement by ensuring that the properties for completion of input in each field are the same.

(iv) **Performance problems**

Performance problems are more difficult to remedy as they may require amendments to hardware or software, which are simply not possible post-implementation. However, it may be possible to:

Add additional disk space, RAM memory or upgrade network cards to a higher specification or install a more recent processor to try and improve overall system performance. All of these alternatives should help to reduce the response time.

Alternatively, the actual use of system resources in terms of which programs are being run at specific times can also be reviewed. If resource-intensive programs, such as file re-organisation, are being run during the day, then these can be deferred to a less busy time. This will free up system resources for more important programs such as the on-line insurance system.

(b) (i) **Illogical data entry**

Ensuring that the screen correctly reflects the method of work would normally be checked during the design stage of a system, specifically by using a prototype of the screen layout. At this time, amendments to the screen design could be made prior to the final system being built, avoiding these errors at the user acceptance test. However, given that this is a new system, even a prototype may have been of limited use because users could still have been uncertain about how they wanted to input data.

(ii) **Unclear field entry**

The issue of some fields being optional could again have been detected at the build stage using a prototype to check which fields actually needed to be completed for each data record. Alternatively, data collection during the building of a logical model during system design may also have detected that some fields were optional.

However, in the current situation, some design standard is required to distinguish optional from mandatory fields. This will ensure that optional fields will only be shown when they are required.

(iii) **Inconsistent cursor control**

The lack of consist use of the cursor again implies a lack of standards during the design phase of the software. Stating the action to take on completion of a field in a style manual would help to ensure this error did not occur, or if it did, the manual would show which style should be applied.

Design errors would be detected during systems testing, as this is now a systems standard.

(iv) **Performance problems**

The performance of the system should be checked during system testing; specifically checking system response time when processing increasingly large amounts of data. It is possible that this load testing was not carried out, or that the system was inadequately tested at this time, with only a small number of transactions being processed. If the problem had been detected during testing, then the software could have been amended to try and enhance performance prior to going live.

It is also possible that performance problems were not detected before the system went live because system testing was carried-out in an environment that did not match the live environment. For example, testing may have been performed on hardware with different specifications.

18 CAET Insurance: Quality assurance and testing

Tutorial note. Compare this answer to the marked-up question and the Answer plan we provided in the question bank – this should show the thinking process used to produce this answer.

You could have drawn a simple 'V' model to explain your answer to parts (i) – (iii). If you did, you should still break the explanation part of your answer up into the separate parts of the question.

Structuring your answer exactly as the question was structured means it is less likely you will omit to answer all areas of the question – and makes it easier to mark (and therefore easier fro the marker to give you marks).

In part (b), ensure your answer covers all areas. The requirement may be broken down into three areas; software packages and testing, software packages and quality assurance; and the consultant's statement.

Brief introduction including mention of the 'V' model

(a) The three areas of application development mentioned in the question relate to the three stages of testing outlined in the 'V' model of system development. In this model, analysis and testing are linked at three specific points:

(i) Requirements analysis and user acceptance testing

(ii) Systems design and systems testing

(iii) Program design and unit or module testing.

(i) **Requirements analysis**

Structure your answer around the question requirements

In the requirements analysis stage, documentation is produced to show what the system is required to do in terms of input, output and processing. The documentation will be produced in text or graphical form, and then checked to ensure that it is complete and adheres to appropriate design standards.

In user acceptance testing, the requirements analysis is re-visited and checked against the new system. The new system should fulfil the requirements previously defined in the requirements analysis; if it does not, then further amendments may be required before the users sign-off the system.

(ii) **Systems design**

During system design, the architectural software design is produced from the business requirements and technical specification for the software. Documentation is produced to specific design standards so it can be checked using formal walkthroughs.

For each of the three stages, include points relating to quality assurance and testing

In systems testing, all of the individual programs are tested together as one integrated suite of software. The integrated software is compared back to the original design specification to check that the programs work as outlined in this design. If the design is not met then the systems testing fails and amendments to the overall design of the software may still be required. When the systems testing is complete, the integrated software is forwarded for user acceptance testing.

(iii) **Programming**

At this stage, the individual programs or modules of the software are designed. The actual designs will again be produced in accordance with specific design standards and tested prior to the program itself being written.

After the program is written, it is checked back to the program specification to ensure that this has been met. This testing is normally called unit testing. Any errors in the program modules are corrected or debugged before the individual programs are sent for systems testing.

Start with a brief explanation of the application software package approach

(b) Using an application software package approach means that software is purchased from a third party supplier ready for use within the organisation. This means that systems design and program design and their associated testing phases are not required because the software house will have already performed this testing.

Emphasise the fact that steps must be taken to ensure the packaged software is suitable, and must be tested

However, a specification of requirements will still be required, and therefore user acceptance testing will also be required. The specification of requirements is necessary because the software must still meet the business needs of the organisation. The requirements must therefore be listed and compared to the specification for the program. It will be very difficult to amend the application software after it has been implemented, so checking requirements is essential.

User acceptance testing is also necessary to ensure that the requirement specification is met, and that the software adequately supports the business needs of the users as well as the volume of transactions.

It is unlikely that any large software package is completely error-free, it is important that there are no major errors

The comment concerning 'tried, tested and error free' may be incorrect.

Firstly, the software has not been tested in the organisation, so it may not meet the specific requirements of users. The testing to date has been against the requirements of designers in the software house, not the organisation where the software is being implemented.

Secondly, the software is unlikely to be 100% error free. The software house may not have been able to test all combinations of the different software modules or with the specific transactions that will be used in the organisation in a live situation. Errors may still occur.

19 Outsourcing, legacy systems and PM software

Tutorial note. Parts (a) and (b) are worth 3 marks each – so some explanation is required to score full marks.

You may well have come up with different valid advantages than the ones we included for part (c). This question asks for likely advantages, so you are able to include advantages that may not be definite - for example, we state that outsourcing may give access to COBOL programming expertise, it may not, but that doesn't prevent us scoring marks, as it is likely.

For part (d), it would not be sufficient to simply name a popular project management package such as Microsoft Project. To earn the four marks on offer, your answer should refer to the types of tasks and functions the software can perform.

A range of advantages could have been provided for part (e). You should name the advantage and then provide detail to collect the two marks on offer per advantage.

Ensure you explain the term in the context of information systems

(a) 'Outsourced' means transferring responsibility to an outside agency. In the context of IS/IT, outsourcing means that part or all of the IT systems within an organisation are provided or maintained by a third party supplier. In the situation described in the scenario, it is the legacy systems that are to be outsourced.

The terms of the outsourcing contract will include number of years and cost of the service, as well as precise details of the service such as changes to be made to the systems or any new reports that will be generated.

Parts (a) and (b) provide an opportunity to pick-up 'easy' marks. Ensure you provide enough detail to earn all of the marks on offer

(b) The term legacy systems in an organisation relates to the old systems, implemented some time ago, which are no longer updated. Legacy systems are likely to have been written in older languages such as COBOL or FORTRAN, which are now rarely used. So it is possible that the software cannot communicate with more recent systems, and the data is only accessible from within the legacy system.

However, legacy systems are generally reliable, and the users see very little need to amend or upgrade. Similarly, it may be difficult to present a business case to replace the systems.

(c) Outsourcing of the legacy systems may provide the following benefits to the organisation.

(i) Access to programming expertise

Most new software systems are written in more modern computer languages, so it is not necessary to maintain expertise in relatively old languages in-house. It may even be difficult to find programmers with appropriate experience to maintain the programmes, as the computer language is old.

However, an outsourcing company may still employ COBOL programmers, because the costs can be shared across a wider client base. The company can continue to obtain access to this expertise as required.

> Your answer could have included other benefits of outsourcing
>
> Only two benefits are required – we have provided three for study purposes

(ii) Cost savings

Outsourcing may provide a cheaper alternative to employing staff to maintain the legacy systems. Very few changes are likely to be required to the systems, so it is unlikely that in-house staff would be fully employed maintaining them. Purchasing the expertise as and when required is likely to be a cheaper option.

Cost may also be saved because all changes to the legacy systems will need a business case to justify the expenditure. As this is now an external cost, very good business cases will be required to justify the amendments.

(iii) Morale

If a third party provides maintenance of the legacy systems, then programming staff can concentrate on new in-house projects. This is likely to enhance employee morale, as producing new systems is normally more enjoyable than maintaining old systems.

> Part (d) is another opportunity to pick-up marks for simply reproducing 'book knowledge'
>
> Provide sufficient information to earn the 4 marks available

(d) Project management software is a specific program which is design to help plan and control a project. Popular examples include Microsoft Project and Project Manager Workbench.

These packages allow managers to plan projects by constructing network diagrams or GANTT charts along with budgets when costs are allocated to individual activities within each project. Network diagrams will also allow the critical path of the project to be highlighted. The cost effect of amendments to a project may also be determined.

Inputting completed activities can help monitor the progress of a project, and a variety of reports are normally available to help monitor the progress of the project.

(e) Advantages of using project management software

> You may have come up with other valid advantages – although most advantages of PM software relate to the ability to produce and amend complex documents and diagrams very quickly

(i) Allocation of resources across projects

Project management software will identify the critical path for a project. This will help to ensure that appropriate resources are allocated to the activities on the critical path to ensure that they are not delayed. The software can also be used to allocate resources over several projects running at the same time. Updating several manual project plans and keeping these concurrent with each other will be quite difficult; however, this activity will be relatively simple using project management software.

(ii) Changes to projects

Amendments to projects can be input into project management software to quickly identify the effects on the timescale and resources needed for the project. The effect of making different amendments could also be compared so that amendments causing the smallest change to the project can be selected. The effect of amending resource allocation over all projects can easily be seen by reviewing outputs from the software.

Index

Review Form & Free Prize Draw – Paper 2.1 Information Systems (6/05)

All original review forms from the entire BPP range, completed with genuine comments, will be entered into one of two draws on 31 January 2006 and 31 July 2006. The names on the first four forms picked out on each occasion will be sent a cheque for £50.

Name: ____________________ **Address:** ____________________

How have you used this Interactive Text?
(Tick one box only)

☐ Home study (book only)
☐ On a course: college ____________
☐ With 'correspondence' package
☐ Other ____________

Why did you decide to purchase this Interactive Text? *(Tick one box only)*

☐ Have used BPP Texts in the past
☐ Recommendation by friend/colleague
☐ Recommendation by a lecturer at college
☐ Saw advertising
☐ Saw information on BPP website
☐ Other ____________

During the past six months do you recall seeing/receiving any of the following?
(Tick as many boxes as are relevant)

☐ Our advertisement in *ACCA Student Accountant*
☐ Our advertisement in *Pass*
☐ Our advertisement in *PQ*
☐ Our brochure with a letter through the post
☐ Our website www.bpp.com

Which (if any) aspects of our advertising do you find useful?
(Tick as many boxes as are relevant)

☐ Prices and publication dates of new editions
☐ Information on Text content
☐ Facility to order books off-the-page
☐ None of the above

Which BPP products have you used?

Text	☑	*Success CD*	☐	*Learn Online*	☐
Kit	☐	*i-Learn*	☐	*Home Study Package*	☐
Passcard	☐	*i-Pass*	☐	*Home Study PLUS*	☐

Your ratings, comments and suggestions would be appreciated on the following areas.

	Very useful	*Useful*	*Not useful*
Introductory section (Key study steps, personal study)	☐	☐	☐
Chapter introductions	☐	☐	☐
Key terms	☐	☐	☐
Quality of explanations	☐	☐	☐
Case studies and other examples	☐	☐	☐
Exam focus points	☐	☐	☐
Questions and answers in each chapter	☐	☐	☐
Fast forwards and chapter roundups	☐	☐	☐
Quick quizzes	☐	☐	☐
Question Bank	☐	☐	☐
Answer Bank	☐	☐	☐
Index	☐	☐	☐
Icons	☐	☐	☐

Overall opinion of this Study Text *Excellent* ☐ *Good* ☐ *Adequate* ☐ *Poor* ☐

Do you intend to continue using BPP products? *Yes* ☐ *No* ☐

On the reverse of this page are noted particular areas of the text about which we would welcome your feedback.
The BPP author of this edition can be e-mailed at: barrywalsh@bpp.com

Please return this form to: Nick Weller, ACCA Publishing Manager, BPP Professional Education, FREEPOST, London, W12 8BR

Review Form & Free Prize Draw (continued)

TELL US WHAT YOU THINK

Please note any further comments and suggestions/errors below

Free Prize Draw Rules

1. Closing date for 31 January 2006 draw is 31 December 2005. Closing date for 31 July 2006 draw is 30 June 2006.
2. Restricted to entries with UK and Eire addresses only. BPP employees, their families and business associates are excluded.
3. No purchase necessary. Entry forms are available upon request from BPP Professional Education. No more than one entry per title, per person. Draw restricted to persons aged 16 and over.
4. Winners will be notified by post and receive their cheques not later than 6 weeks after the relevant draw date.
5. The decision of the promoter in all matters is final and binding. No correspondence will be entered into.

ACCA Order

To BPP Professional Education, Aldine Place, London W12 8AW

Tel: 020 8740 2211 Fax: 020 8740 1184

email: publishing@bpp.com website: www.bpp.com

Order online www.bpp.com/mybpp

Mr/Mrs/Ms (Full name)

Daytime delivery address

Postcode

Daytime Tel Date of exam (month/year) Scots law variant Y / N

Occasionally we may wish to email you relevant offers and information about courses and products. Please tick to opt into this service. ☐

	6/05 Texts	1/05 Kits	1/05 Passcards	Success CDs	7/05 i-Learn	7/05 i-Pass	Learn Online
PART 1							
1.1 Preparing Financial Statements (UK)	£26.00 ☐	£12.95 ☐	£9.95 ☐	£14.95 ☐	£40.00 ☐	£30.00 ☐	£100 ☐
1.2 Financial Information for Management	£26.00 ☐	£12.95 ☐	£9.95 ☐	£14.95 ☐	£40.00 ☐	£30.00 ☐	£100 ☐
1.3 Managing People	£26.00 ☐	£12.95 ☐	£9.95 ☐	£14.95 ☐	£40.00 ☐	£30.00 ☐	£100 ☐
PART 2							
2.1 Information Systems	£26.00 ☐	£12.95 ☐	£9.95 ☐	£14.95 ☐	£40.00 ☐	£30.00 ☐	£100 ☐
2.2 Corporate and Business Law (UK)**	£26.00 ☐	£12.95 ☐	£9.95 ☐	£14.95 ☐	£40.00 ☐	£30.00 ☐	£100 ☐
2.3 Business Taxation FA2004 (12/05 exams)	£24.95 ☐ (8/04)	£12.95 ☐	£9.95 ☐	£14.95 ☐	£34.95 ☐ (8/04)	£24.95 ☐ (8/04)	£100 ☐
2.3 Business Taxation FA2005	£26.00 ☐†	£12.95 ☐	£9.95 ☐	£14.95 ☐	£40.00 ☐ (9/05)	£30.00 ☐ (9/05)	£100 ☐
2.4 Financial Management and Control	£26.00 ☐	£12.95 ☐	£9.95 ☐	£14.95 ☐	£40.00 ☐	£30.00 ☐	£100 ☐
2.5 Financial Reporting (UK)	£26.00 ☐ (7/05)	£12.95 ☐	£9.95 ☐	£14.95 ☐	£40.00 ☐	£30.00 ☐	£100 ☐
2.6 Audit and Internal Review (UK)	£26.00 ☐	£12.95 ☐	£9.95 ☐	£14.95 ☐	£40.00 ☐	£30.00 ☐	£100 ☐
PART 3						8/04	
3.1 Audit and Assurance Services (UK)	£26.00 ☐	£12.95 ☐	£9.95 ☐	£14.95 ☐		£30.00 ☐ (4/05)	£60 ☐
3.2 Advanced Taxation FA2004 (12/05 exams)	£24.95 ☐	£12.95 ☐	£9.95 ☐	£14.95 ☐		£24.95 ☐	£60 ☐
3.2 Advanced Taxation FA2005	£26.00 ☐†	£12.95 ☐	£9.95 ☐	£14.95 ☐		£30.00 ☐ (9/05)	£60 ☐
3.3 Performance Management	£26.00 ☐	£12.95 ☐	£9.95 ☐	£14.95 ☐		£24.95 ☐	£60 ☐
3.4 Business Information Management	£26.00 ☐	£12.95 ☐	£9.95 ☐	£14.95 ☐		£24.95 ☐	£60 ☐
3.5 Strategic Business Planning and Devt	£26.00 ☐	£12.95 ☐	£9.95 ☐	£14.95 ☐		£24.95 ☐	£60 ☐
3.6 Advanced Corporate Reporting (UK)	£26.00 ☐ (7/05)	£12.95 ☐	£9.95 ☐	£14.95 ☐		£24.95 ☐	£60 ☐
3.7 Strategic Financial Management	£26.00 ☐	£12.95 ☐	£9.95 ☐	£14.95 ☐		£24.95 ☐	£60 ☐
INTERNATIONAL STREAM						7/05	
1.1 Preparing Financial Statements (Int'l)	£26.00 ☐	£12.95 ☐	£9.95 ☐		£40.00 ☐	£30.00 ☐	£100 ☐
2.2 Corporate and Business Law (Global)	£26.00 ☐	£12.95 ☐	£9.95 ☐				
2.5 Financial Reporting (Int'l)	£26.00 ☐	£12.95 ☐	£9.95 ☐		£40.00 ☐	£30.00 ☐	£100 ☐
2.6 Audit and Internal Review (Int'l)	£26.00 ☐	£12.95 ☐	£9.95 ☐		£40.00 ☐	£30.00 ☐	£100 ☐
3.1 Audit and Assurance Services (Int'l)	£26.00 ☐	£12.95 ☐	£9.95 ☐			£30.00 ☐	£60 ☐
3.6 Advanced Corporate Reporting (Int'l)	£26.00 ☐	£12.95 ☐	£9.95 ☐		£40.00 ☐ (12/05)	£30.00 ☐	£60 ☐
Success in Your Research and Analysis Project - Tutorial Text (10/05)	£26.00 ☐						
Learning to Learn Accountancy (7/02)	£9.95 ☐						
Business Maths and English (6/04)	£9.95 ☐						

SUBTOTAL £

†(**8/05** for 6/06 & 12/06 exams. New edition Kit, Passcard, i-Learn and i-Pass available in 2006)

POSTAGE & PACKING

Study Texts/Kits

	First	*Each extra*	*Online*	
UK	£5.00	£2.00	£2.00	£
EU*	£6.00	£4.00	£4.00	£
Non EU	£20.00	£10.00	£10.00	£

Passcards/Success CDs/i-Learn/i-Pass

	First	*Each extra*	*Online*	
UK	£2.00	£1.00	£1.00	£
EU*	£3.00	£2.00	£2.00	£
Non EU	£8.00	£8.00	£8.00	£

Learning to Learn Accountancy/Business Maths and English

	Each	*Online*	
UK	£3.00	£2.00	£
EU*	£6.00	£4.00	£
Non EU	£20.00	£10.00	£

Grand Total (incl. Postage)

I enclose a cheque for £
(Cheques to *BPP Professional Education*)

Or charge to Visa/Mastercard/Switch

Card Number

Expiry date Start Date

Issue Number (Switch Only)

Signature

We aim to deliver to all UK addresses inside 5 working days; a signature will be required. Orders to all EU addresses should be delivered within 6 working days. All other orders to overseas addresses should be delivered within 8 working days. *EU includes the Republic of Ireland and the Channel Islands. **For Scots law variant students, a free **Scots Law Supplement** is available with the 2.2 Text. Please indicate in the name and address section if this applies to you.

Mr/Mrs/Ms (Full name)

Daytime delivery address

Postcode

Daytime Tel — Date of exam (month/year) — Scots law variant Y / N

	Home Study Package*	Home Study PLUS*	Success CDs	7/05 i-Learn	Learn Online
PART 1					
1.1 Preparing Financial Statements UK	£115.00 ☐	£180.00 ☐	£14.95 ☐	£40.00 ☐	£100.00 ☐
1.2 Financial Information for Management	£115.00 ☐	£180.00 ☐	£14.95 ☐	£40.00 ☐	£100.00 ☐
1.3 Managing People	£115.00 ☐	£180.00 ☐	£14.95 ☐	£40.00 ☐	£100.00 ☐
PART 2					
2.1 Information Systems	£115.00 ☐	£180.00 ☐	£14.95 ☐	£40.00 ☐	£100.00 ☐
2.2 Corporate and Business Law UK***	£115.00 ☐	£180.00 ☐	£14.95 ☐	£40.00 ☐	£100.00 ☐
2.3 Business Taxation FA2004 (12/05 exams)	£115.00 ☐	£180.00 ☐	£14.95 ☐	£34.95 ☐ (8/04)	£100.00 ☐
2.3 Business Taxation FA2005 (2006 exams)	£115.00 ☐	£180.00 ☐	£14.95 ☐	£40.00 ☐ (9/05)	£100.00 ☐
2.4 Financial Management and Control	£115.00 ☐	£180.00 ☐	£14.95 ☐	£40.00 ☐	£100.00 ☐
2.5 Financial Reporting UK	£115.00 ☐	£180.00 ☐	£14.95 ☐	£40.00 ☐	£100.00 ☐
2.6 Audit and Internal Review UK	£115.00 ☐	£180.00 ☐	£14.95 ☐	£40.00 ☐	£100.00 ☐
PART 3					
3.1 Audit and Assurance Services UK	£115.00 ☐	£150.00 ☐	£14.95 ☐		£60.00 ☐
3.2 Advanced Taxation FA2004 (12/05 exams)	£115.00 ☐	£150.00 ☐	£14.95 ☐		£60.00 ☐
3.2 Advanced Taxation FA2005 (2006 exams)	£115.00 ☐	£150.00 ☐	£14.95 ☐		£60.00 ☐
3.3 Performance Management	£115.00 ☐	£150.00 ☐	£14.95 ☐		£60.00 ☐
3.4 Business Information Management	£115.00 ☐	£150.00 ☐	£14.95 ☐		£60.00 ☐
3.5 Strategic Business Planning and Development	£115.00 ☐	£150.00 ☐	£14.95 ☐		£60.00 ☐
3.6 Advanced Corporate Reporting UK	£115.00 ☐	£150.00 ☐	£14.95 ☐		£60.00 ☐
3.7 Strategic Financial Management	£115.00 ☐	£150.00 ☐	£14.95 ☐		£60.00 ☐
INTERNATIONAL STREAM					
1.1 Preparing Financial Statements (Int'l)	£115.00 ☐	£180.00 ☐		£40.00 ☐	£100.00 ☐
2.2 Corporate and Business Law (Global)	£115.00 ☐				
2.5 Financial Reporting (Int'l)	£115.00 ☐	£180.00 ☐		£40.00 ☐	£100.00 ☐
2.6 Audit and Internal Review (Int'l)	£115.00 ☐	£180.00 ☐		£40.00 ☐	£100.00 ☐
3.1 Audit and Assurance Services (Int'l)	£115.00 ☐	£150.00 ☐			£60.00 ☐
3.6 Advanced Corporate Reporting (Int'l)	£115.00 ☐	£150.00 ☐		£40.00 ☐ (12/05)	£60.00 ☐
Success in Your Research and Analysis Project - Tutorial Text (10/05)	£26.00 ☐				
Learning to Learn Accountancy (7/02)	Free/£9.95 ☐				
Business Maths and English (6/04)	Free/£9.95 ☐				

SUBTOTAL £

ACCA Order

To BPP Professional Education, Aldine Place, London W12 8AW

Tel: 020 8740 2211 Fax: 020 8740 1184

email: publishing@bpp.com website: www.bpp.com

Order online www.bpp.com/mybpp

Occasionally we may wish to email you relevant offers and information about courses and products. Please tick to opt into this service. ☐

POSTAGE & PACKING

Home Study Packages

	First	Each extra	Each	
UK	£6.00	£6.00	-	£
EU**	-	-	£15.00	£
Non EU	-	-	£50.00	£

Success CDs/i-Learn

	First	Each extra	Online	
UK	£2.00	£1.00	£1.00	£
EU**	£3.00	£2.00	£2.00	£
Non EU	£8.00	£8.00	£8.00	£

Learning to Learn Accountancy/Business Maths and English/Success in Your Research and Analysis Project

	Each	Online	
UK	£3.00†	£2.00	£
EU**	£6.00	£4.00	£
Non EU	£20.00	£10.00	£

(†£5.00 Success in Your Research and Analysis Project)

Postage and packing not charged on free copy ordered with Home Study Course.

Grand Total (incl. Postage)

I enclose a cheque for £
(Cheques to *BPP Professional Education*)

Or charge to Visa/Mastercard/Switch

Card Number

Expiry date Start Date

Issue Number (Switch Only)

Signature

We aim to deliver to all UK addresses inside 5 working days; a signature will be required. Orders to all EU addresses should be delivered within 6 working days. All other orders should be delivered within 8 working days. *Home Study Courses include Texts, Kits, Passcards and i-Pass (i-Pass not available for 2.2 Global and 3.1 International). You can also order one free copy of either Learning to Learn Accountancy or Business Maths and English per Home Study course, to a maximum of one of each per person. **EU includes the Republic of Ireland and the Channel Islands. ***For Scots law variant students, a free **Scots Law Supplement** is available with the 2.2 Text.